# Research Topics

in

# Functional Programming

# Research Topics

in

# Functional Programming

EDITED BY

## David A. Turner

University of Kent

Addison-Wesley Publishing Company

Reading, Massachusetts • Menlo Park, California • New York
Don Mills, Ontario • Wokingham, England • Amsterdam • Bonn
Sydney • Singapore • Tokyo • Madrid • San Juan

This book is in the University of Texas at Austin Year of Programming Series.

**Library of Congress Cataloging-in-Publication Data**

Research topics in functional programming / edited by David A. Turner
      p.  cm. — (University of Texas at Austin year of programming series)
      Papers from a meeting held at The University of Texas at Austin, Aug. 1987.
      Includes bibliographical references.
      ISBN 0-201-17236-4
      1. Functional programming (Computer science) I. Turner, D. A. II. Series: UT year of programming series.
QA76.62.R47 1990
005.1'1—dc20                                 89-28793
                                               CIP

Reproduced by Addison-Wesley from camera-ready copy supplied by the U.T. Year of Programming office.

ABCDEFGHIJ–MA–943210

# The UT Year of Programming Series

The design for the books was commissioned by the publisher, Addison-Wesley. The designer was Jean Hammond, and the design was transformed into a LaTeX style specification by William H. Miner Jr. of TeX*niques* in Austin, Texas. The book was composed in LaTeX, primarily by the UT Year of Programming staff —Suzanne Kain Rhoads, Ana M. Hernandez, and Hamilton Richards Jr.— using Macintosh[1] SE personal computers, but also by several authors who supplied their manuscripts as TeX[2] or LaTeX source files. The Macintosh implementation of TeX —TeXTURES— is a product of Blue Sky Research of Portland, Oregon. Illustrations were redrawn for the book using Cricket Draw.[3] Draft versions of the manuscript were printed on an Apple[4] LaserWriter II NTX printer, and the final copy was produced on a Linotronic 100[5] by Publishing Experts of Austin.

The typeface in which the book is set is Lucida,[6] a product of Adobe Systems Incorporated, whose permission to use a beta version of the Lucida Math fonts is gratefully acknowledged; a few additional POSTSCRIPT characters were created using Fontographer.[7] Lucida was installed in LaTeX and TeXTURES by Buff Miner and by David Mallis of Publishing Experts; the value of their dedication and expertise is beyond calculation.

The publisher's vital assistance and patient encouragement were personified by Peter S. Gordon (Publishing Partner for Computer Science), Helen M. Goldstein (Assistant Editor), Helen M. Wythe (Production Supervisor), Mona Zeftel (Electronic Production Consultant), and Lorraine Ferrier (Copy Editor).

1. Macintosh is a trademark of Apple Computer, Inc.
2. TeX is a trademark of the American Mathematical Society.
3. Cricket Draw is a trademark of Cricket Software, Inc.
4. Apple and LaserWriter are registered trademarks of Apple Computer, Inc.
5. Linotronic 100 is a trademark of Allied Corporation.
6. Lucida is a registered trademark of Bigelow & Holmes.
7. Fontographer is a registered trademark of Altsys Corporation.

# The UT Year of Programming Series

*Series editor:* HAMILTON RICHARDS JR. The University of Texas at Austin

*Developments in Concurrency and Communication*
  *Editor:* C. A. R. HOARE Oxford University

*Logical Foundations of Functional Programming*
  *Editor:* GERARD HUET INRIA Rocquencourt

*Research Topics in Functional Programming*
  *Editor:* DAVID TURNER University of Kent

*Formal Development of Programs and Proofs*
  *Editor:* EDSGER W. DIJKSTRA The University of Texas at Austin

# Contents

# Foreword

*T*his volume is a product of the 1987 University of Texas Year of Programming ("YoP"), an initiative of UT-Austin's Department of Computer Sciences underwritten by grants from Lockheed/Austin, an anonymous donor, and—principally—the U. S. Office of Naval Research[8]. The Year of Programming's general objectives were

> to advance the art and science of programming by bringing together leading computing scientists for discussions and collaboration, and
>
> to disseminate among leading practitioners the best of what is known— and being discovered—about the theory and practice of programming.

These objectives grew out of the original proposal's statement of purpose:

> Programming includes all aspects of creating an executable representation of a problem [solution]... from mathematical formulation to rep-

---

8. under Contract N00014-86-K-0763

resentation of an algorithm [for a] specific architecture.... The Year of Programming will...address...the conversion of programming into a mathematical...discipline.

Almost from the outset, it was agreed that the Year of Programming would make its greatest contribution by steering away from topics and formats already well addressed by industrial concerns, government agencies, and the technical societies. Hence it was decided to leave such topics as programming psychology, sociology, and management to entities better qualified to deal with them, and to concentrate on those aspects of programming most amenable to scientific treatment.

As planning progressed, the YoP developed mainly into a series of Programming Institutes. Although each institute focused on a different sector of computing's scientific frontier, all proceeded from a conviction that good programming is the art and science of keeping things simple, and that the conversion of programming from a craft into a mathematical discipline requires an unorthodox type of mathematics in which the traditional distinction between "pure" and "applied" need not appear.

Each institute was organized by a scientific director recruited for his contributions to the art and science of programming or to the mathematics that it requires. Each director in turn enlisted a few colleagues—between four and a dozen or so—to assist him in discussing, refining, and presenting their school of thought. Over a period of one or two weeks, each institute team presented tutorials, research papers, and public lectures, and engaged in panel discussions and workshops. The institutes' audiences numbered from 30 to over 100, and converged on Austin from many parts of North America and Europe.

The selection criterion was wide enough to admit a broad variety of approaches, and many institute topics were considered. From a welter of conflicting schedules and commitments finally emerged six Programming Institutes, whose scientific directors and topics were as follows:

1. C. A. R. Hoare, Oxford University (visiting UT Austin for the academic year 1986–87). *Concurrent Programming*, 23 February–6 March.

2. David Gries, Cornell University. *Encapsulation, Modularization, and Reusability*, 1–10 April.

3. Gérard Huet, INRIA. *Logical Foundations of Functional Programming*, 8–12 June.

4. Michael J. C. Gordon, Cambridge University, and Warren A. Hunt Jr., University of Texas, Austin (co-directors). *Formal Specification and Verification of Hardware*, 8–17 July.

**5.** David A. Turner, University of Kent, Canterbury, UK. *Declarative Programming*, 24–29 August.

**6.** Edsger W. Dijkstra, University of Texas, Austin. *Formal Development of Programs and Proofs*, 26–30 October.

The volume you hold in your hands is a product of the fifth Programming Institute. It is not a proceedings in the usual sense, for it is not a mere collection of materials brought to the Institute by its participants. Instead, it attempts to capture the essence of the institute as seen after the fact—and after some reflection—by its principal participants. Some of the articles do indeed closely resemble their authors' presentations in Austin; others were not presented at all, but are included here as indispensable background material. Still others represent work that was carried out either at the institute or as a result of it.

Whatever success YoP has achieved reflects primarily the caliber and dedication to excellence of the many computing scientists who contributed as scientific directors, lecturers, workshop participants, and authors. Enlisting such dedicated colleagues to serve as scientific directors was mainly the achievement of the YoP executive subcommittee's three leaders —James C. Browne, Edsger W. Dijkstra, and C. A. R. Hoare. Their task was greatly eased by the resources put at YoP's disposal by its sponsors, which made it possible for YoP to attract the very best scientific talent in the field; personifying the sponsors' support and encouragement were Charles Holland and Andre van Tilborg at the Office of Naval Research, and Stephen Sherman at Lockheed. Finally, the YoP Management Committee deserves great credit for its guidance, and for much sage advice and wise counsel, from YoP's earliest days.

Hamilton Richards Jr.

# *Preface*

$T$his volume is, essentially, the proceedings of a meeting which took place at The University of Texas at Austin in August 1987. The meeting was entitled "The Institute of Declarative Programming" and was one of six such institutes hosted by UT as part of their highly successful "Year of Programming".

The main part of the meeting was devoted to the presentation of research papers in the area of functional programming, and it these (or subsequently revised versions of them) that form most of the following chapters.

For the convenience of the reader we have included two additional chapters of a more tutorial nature (the first two). The first of these, which is reprinted from SIGPLAN Notices, is an overview of the strongly typed lazy functional language Miranda.[1] The Miranda language is coming to be quite widely used (in fact several of the other papers use Miranda notation) and may be regarded as representative of one of the major schools of modern functional programming.

---

1. Miranda is a trademark of Research Software Ltd.

The other tutorial paper, by John Hughes, is an exposition from first principles of "why functional programming matters". Specifically, by a series of well chosen examples, he shows how two of the central features of many functional languages — lazy evaluation (or more precisely infinite data structures) and higher-order functions permit important modes of program decomposition not available to the user of a conventional language such as PASCAL or C.

The remaining papers in the volume follow fairly closely the presentations given by their authors at the Institute of Declarative Programming. As such they form an interesting and representative collection of papers on a variety of important research topics in the field of functional programming. The ordering of topics is somewhat arbitrary; in the hope of assisting the reader to find his way around the volume here are a few words of explanation of the contents of the various chapters.

The paper by Hans Boehm and Robert Cartwright (which was presented at the Austin meeting by Cartwright) deals with the intiguing problem of performing exact real arithmetic on a computer. We have grown used to the idea that in computer science a "real number" is one represented to limited precision, e.g. by one of the usual floating-point formats. The mathematician's definition of the reals, however, is as (equivalence classes of) converging sequences of rationals. Within a functional language the possibility arises of representing such objects directly, and of performing *exact* arithmetic on them — in fact it turns out there are two ways of doing this, one using infinite (i.e. 'lazy') lists, and the other using higher-order functions. Performing exact real arithmetic *efficiently* is an extremely challenging research problem. The Boehm/Cartwright paper provides an excellent overview of some the subtleties which arise in this area, and of the current state of knowledge.

The lambda calculus is the prototypical functional language, and has been analysed extensively. Samson Abramsky's paper develops a new semantic model for the lambda calculus, starting from the observation that the 'classical' model, based on head normal forms, Bohm trees etc, forces us to equate terms that in a practical implementation may be distinguishable, because we normally work with weak head normal forms. In Abramsky's model, for example, we distinguish $\bot$ from $(\lambda x.\bot)$, whereas in the 'classical' account they are identified. He develops an elegant and rather pleasing theory based on this non-standard model.

The claim that this is the appropriate model for *strongly typed* lazy functional languages such as Miranda seems open to challenge, however. A point that was made in discussion is that for a language like Miranda, no experiment can be performed which would succeed in distinguishing $\bot$ from $(\lambda x.\bot)$, because all the programs which attempt to make this distinction turn out to be ill-typed. The Miranda implementor is therefore free to reduce either to head normal form, or to weak head normal form, without the user being able to find out (except perhaps in performance terms) which of these two implementation strategies is being used. For Miranda, the appropriate function domain is therefore the standard one, in which $\bot$ and $(\lambda x.\bot)$ are identified [2].

For *typeless* lazy functional languages, such as SASL, however, it seems that Abramsky's non-standard lambda calculus model is indeed a good fit.

John Hughes's paper deals with the important topic of static analysis of programs, an area which has been the focus of much activity recently and in which there are many interesting open problems. He describes a new technique, which he calls "Backward Analysis", which is dual to the more usual methods of abstract interpretation, and which he argues is inherently more efficient. There is a difficulty with applying the new method to higher-order programs, and Hughes shows how this can be overcome by a synthesis of the "forward" and "backward" techniques.

Peter Buneman's paper deals with the relationship between functional programming and database programming languages. As he remarks, we have the curious state of affairs that researchers in programming languages and researchers in databases have been working almost entirely independently of one another, despite a great number of shared issues. In particular it seems an entirely reasonable research goal to find an account of *data type* that is adequate for both purposes. Buneman is one of the very few people who are working on the interface between these two communities, and his paper is strongly recommended as an exploration of some of the main issues in this area.

Keshav Pingali's paper deals with an interesting variety of what we might call quasi-functional programming, in which an otherwise functional language is extended by the addition of updatable data objects called *I-structures*. These I-structures are somewhat like arrays, but there is a strong restriction on the way they can be updated. It is best to think of them as coming into being with the value $\bot$ stored at each element; it is then permitted to update the value of an element from $\bot$ to 1, say, but not to subsequently update the 1 to 2. I-structures were originally proposed by Arvind (of MIT), and have been the subject of considerable discussion in the dataflow community. Pingali here describes some novel and illuminating applications of I-structures which arise in the *implementation* of lazy functional languages.

The papers by Thompson and by Turner both deal, in different ways, with some of the problems that arise in describing interactive processes in a pure functional language. Turner's paper discusses the approaches that have been

---

2. See S. J. Thompson, "A Logic for Miranda", *Formal Aspects of Computing 1*, 4 (Oct.–Dec. 1989).

proposed by various authors for programming a system of communicating processes in a functional manner, and a set of design decisions which were made in a project undertaken at the University of Kent to write a whole operating system in Miranda.

Simon Thompson's paper develops a systematic approach to the important problem of controlling the interleaving of input and output events in interactive programs written in a pure functional language. He shows that a small set of higher-order functions can provide an adequate set of combining forms for controlling interactive input-output behaviour in an elegant and transparent way. He further shows that a purely denotational account of the semantics of these combining forms (in terms of partial histories) adequately accounts for their having the desired operational behaviour. This latter point may be regarded as worth stressing, for there seems to be a widespread (and quite unjustified) belief that the relative ordering of input-output events cannot be fully controlled or specified within a purely functional notation.

Much of the current interest in functional programming, especially in the USA, is a result of John Backus's pioneering work in the field. The paper by Backus, Williams and Wimmers (presented at the meeting by Backus) describes the design of the new language FL, which is a successor to Backus's well known language FP. The design decisions of FL provide an extremely interesting contrast to those of Miranda. The type structure of FL is dynamic rather than static, the semantics of function application is strict, and FL programs have an implicitly controlled history component which is used to deal with input-output and persistent storage (i.e. file access). The hallmark of the design, as with the earlier language FP, is a concern both to be able write highly efficient programs and at the same time to have a rich set of algebraic laws that can be used as the basis of a theory of program transformation.

The work of Richard Bird is also very much concerned with algebraic laws for the manipulation of programs. During the last few years he has developed a powerful and remarkably compressed "calculus of functions", within which he is able to derive many interesting algorithms by a systematic process of calculation starting from their specifications. The paper illustrates this algebraic approach to program synthesis by posing and solving a non-trivial problem about coding sequences.

Joseph Goguen's paper presents and argues the case for a programming style, based on his *logical programming language* OBJ, which is quite different from that of higher-order languages such as Miranda and ML. Interestingly, and in sharp contrast to these other languages, OBJ is first order, but achieves through the use of *parameterised modules* much of what is more conventionally done using higher-order functions. Needless to say, the claim that higher order functions are not in fact necessary provoked a lively discussion at the Austin meeting. I will not attempt to reproduce that discussion here, but refer the reader to Goguen's well written paper. One interesting issue that arose in the discussion, and which the reader is invited to ponder, is whether either of the representations of exact real numbers (see the Cartwright chapter) could be carried through in the OBJ style. [I don't know the answer to this question — it is a challenge for the reader! —DT].

One of the most challenging areas of current research in programming languages, and the subject of David MacQueen's paper, is the attempt to find fully adequate type systems. (One aspect of this, to which we have already referred in connection with Peter Buneman's paper, is the need to unify the concept of type found in programming languages with that found in database systems.) Polymorphic type systems are now well understood and seem very satisfactory for small scale programming. A more powerful theory is required to provide an adequate type discipline for large scale programming, where the need arises to handle hybrid objects ("modules", say) containing both types and data objects. David MacQueen's excellent paper shows how these latter problems may be resolved within the framework of a *second order type system*, taking the design of the module system for Standard ML as the basis for the discussion. MacQueen is, of course, the main designer of the Standard ML module system, and is here reviewing the rationale for its design.

I am conscious that the above collection of very brief summaries in no way does justice to the papers in this volume. The remedy to this lies in the hands of the reader. I hope that he (or she) will be stimulated into tackling some of the many still unsolved research problems of functional programming.

I would like to take this opportunity to thank The University of Texas, on behalf of myself and the other participants in the Institute of Declarative Programming, for hosting such an enjoyable and stimulating meeting, and the sponsors of the Year of Programming for making it possible. Last but not least, many thanks are due to Hamilton Richards of The University of Texas, the coordinator of the Year of Programming committee, and his assistant Suzanne Rhoads; without their support and assistance neither the Institute of Declarative Programming nor this volume of proceedings would have come into being.

David Turner

# Research Topics

in

# Functional Programming

# An Overview of Miranda[1]

# 1

## David Turner
University of Kent

Miranda is an advanced functional programming system that runs under the UNIX operating system.[2] The aim of the Miranda system is to provide a modern functional programming language, embedded in an "industrial quality" programming environment. It is now being used at a growing number of sites for teaching functional programming and as a vehicle for the rapid prototyping of software. The purpose of this short article is to give a brief overview of the main features of Miranda. The topics we shall discuss, in order, are:

basic ideas,

the Miranda programming environment,

---

1. This chapter first appeared in *SIGPLAN Notices*, December 1986. It has been revised to remove some small technical errors in the original, and to bring it up to date for inclusion in this volume.
2. UNIX is a trademark of AT&T Bell Laboratories. Miranda is a trademark of Research Software Ltd.

guarded equations and block structure,

pattern matching,

currying and higher order functions,

list comprehensions,

lazy evaluation and infinite lists,

polymorphic strong typing,

user-defined types,

type synonyms,

abstract data types,

separate compilation and linking, and

current implementation status.

## 1  *Basic Ideas*

The Miranda programming language is purely functional — there are no side effects or imperative features of any kind. A program (actually we don't call it a program, we call it a "script") is a collection of equations defining various functions and data structures that we are interested in computing. The order in which the equations are given is not in general significant. There is, for example, no obligation for the definition of an entity to precede its first use. Here is a very simple example of a Miranda script:

$$z = sq\ x/sq\ y$$
$$sq\ n = n * n$$
$$x = a + b$$
$$y = a - b$$
$$a = 10$$
$$b = 5$$

Notice the absence of syntactic baggage — Miranda is, by design, rather terse. There are no mandatory type declarations, although the language is strongly typed (see Section 8). There are no semicolons at the end of definitions — the parsing algorithm makes intelligent use of layout. Note that the notation for function application is simply juxtaposition, as in *sq x*. In the definition of the *sq* function, *n* is a formal parameter — its scope is limited to the equation in which it occurs (whereas the other names introduced above have the whole script for their scope).

The most commonly used data structure is the list, which in Miranda is written with square brackets and commas, e.g.:

> *week_days* = ["Mon","Tue","Wed","Thur","Fri"]
>
> *days* = *week_days* ++ ["Sat","Sun"]

Lists can be concatenated by the '++' operator. Other useful operations on lists include infix ':', which *cons*es an element to the front of a list, '#', which takes the length of a list, and infix '!', which does subscripting. So for example $0 : [1, 2, 3]$ has the value $[0, 1, 2, 3]$, #*days* is 7, and *days*!0 is "Mon".

There is also an operator '−−', which does list subtraction. For example,

> $[1, 2, 3, 4, 5] -- [2, 4]$  is  $[1, 3, 5]$

There is a shorthand notation, using '..', for lists whose elements form an arithmetic series. Here, for example, are definitions of the factorial function and of a number *result*, which is the sum of the odd numbers between 1 and 100 (*sum* and *product* are library functions):

> *fac n* = *product* [1..*n*]
>
> *result* = *sum* [1, 3..100]

The elements of a list must all be of the same type. A sequence of elements of mixed type is called a tuple, and it is written using parentheses instead of square brackets. An example is:

> *employee* = ("Jones", *True, False*, 39)

Tuples are analogous to records in Pascal (whereas lists are analogous to arrays). Tuples cannot be subscripted — their elements are extracted by pattern matching (see Section 4).

## 2 *The Programming Environment*

The Miranda system is interactive and runs under UNIX as a self-contained subsystem. The basic action is to evaluate expressions, supplied by the user at the terminal, in the environment established by the current script. For example evaluating *z* in the context of the first script given above would produce the result 9.

The Miranda compiler works in conjunction with a screen editor (normally this is "vi" but it can be set to any editor of the user's choice). Scripts are automatically recompiled after edits, and any syntax or type errors are signalled immediately. The polymorphic type system permits a very high proportion of logical errors to be detected at compile time.

There is quite a large library of standard functions. There is an online reference manual documenting all aspects of the system. There is also a good interface to UNIX, permitting Miranda functions to take data from, and send results to, arbitrary UNIX files, and it is also possible to invoke Miranda functions directly from the UNIX shell and to combine them, via UNIX pipes, with processes written in other languages.

### 3 *Guarded Equations and Block Structure*

In a Miranda script an equation can have several alternative right-hand sides distinguished by "guards" (the guard is written on the right following a comma[3]). So, for example, the greatest-common-divisor function can be written as follows:

$$
\begin{aligned}
gcd\ a\ b\ &=\ gcd\ (a - b)\ b, &&\textbf{if } a > b \\
&=\ gcd\ a\ (b - a), &&\textbf{if } a < b \\
&=\ a, &&\textbf{if } a = b
\end{aligned}
$$

The last guard in such a series of alternatives can be written "**otherwise**" to indicate a default case.

It is also permitted to introduce local definitions on the right-hand side of a definition, by means of a "**where**" clause. Consider, for example, the following definition of a function for solving quadratic equations (it either fails or returns a list of one or two real roots):

$$
\begin{aligned}
quadsolve\ a\ b\ c\ &=\ error\ \text{"complex roots"}, &&\textbf{if } delta < 0 \\
&=\ [-b/(2 * a)], &&\textbf{if } delta = 0 \\
&=\ [-b/(2 * a) + radix/(2 * a), \\
&\quad\ -b/(2 * a) - radix/(2 * a)], &&\textbf{if } delta > 0 \\
&\textbf{where} \\
&delta = b * b - 4 * a * c \\
&radix = sqrt\ delta
\end{aligned}
$$

---

3. For compatibility with earlier versions of Miranda the use of **if** in guards is optional.

**Where** clauses may be nested to arbitrary depth, allowing Miranda programs to be organized with a nested block structure. Indentation of inner blocks is compulsory, as layout information is used by the parser.

## 4 *Pattern Matching*

It is permitted to define a function by giving several separate equations, distinguished by the use of different patterns in the formal parameters. This provides another method of case analysis that is often more elegant than the use of guards. We now give some simple examples of pattern matching on natural numbers, lists, and tuples. Here is another definition of the factorial function, and a definition of Ackerman's function:

$$fac\ 0 = 1$$
$$fac\ (n+1) = (n+1) * fac\ n$$

$$ack\ 0\ n = n+1$$
$$ack\ (m+1)\ 0 = ack\ m\ 1$$
$$ack\ (m+1)\ (n+1) = ack\ m\ (ack\ (m+1)\ n)$$

Here is a (naive) definition of a function for computing the $n$th Fibonacci number:

$$fib\ 0 = 0$$
$$fib\ 1 = 1$$
$$fib\ (n+2) = fib\ (n+1) + fib\ n$$

Here are some simple examples of functions defined by pattern matching on lists:

$$sum\ [\ ] = 0$$
$$sum\ (a : x) = a + sum\ x$$

$$product\ [\ ] = 1$$
$$product\ (a : x) = a * product\ x$$

$$reverse\ [\ ] = [\ ]$$
$$reverse\ (a : x) = reverse\ x ++ [a]$$

Accessing the elements of a tuple is also done by pattern matching. For example the selection functions on 2-tuples can be defined thus:

$fst\,(a, b) = a$

$snd\,(a, b) = b$

As final examples we give the definitions of two Miranda library functions, *take* and *drop*, which return the first *n* members of a list, and the rest of the list without the first *n* members, respectively:

*take* $0\,x = [\,]$

*take* $(n+1)\,[\,] = [\,]$

*take* $(n+1)\,(a : x) = a :$ *take* $n\,x$


*drop* $0\,x = x$

*drop* $(n+1)\,[\,] = [\,]$

*drop* $(n+1)\,(a : x) =$ *drop* $n\,x$

Notice that the two functions are defined in such a way that the identity *take* $n\,x$ ++ *drop* $n\,x = x$ always holds, even in the pathological case that the length of *x* is less than *n*.

## 5 *Currying and Higher-Order Functions*

Miranda is a fully higher-order language— functions are first-class citizens and can be both passed as parameters and returned as results. Function application is left-associative, so when we write *f x y* it is parsed as $(f x)\,y$, meaning that the result of applying *f* to *x* is a function, which is then applied to *y*. The reader may test his or her understanding of higher-order functions by working out the value of *answer* in the following script:

*answer* = *twice twice twice suc* 0

*twice* $f x = f(f x)$

*suc* $x = x + 1$

Note that in Miranda every function of two or more arguments is actually a higher-order function. This is very useful as it permits partial parameterization. For example *member* is a library function such that *member x a* tests whether the list *x* contains the element *a* (returning *True* or *False* as appropriate). By partially parameterizing *member* we can derive many useful predicates, such as

$$vowel \quad = \quad member \quad ['a','e','i','o','u']$$

$$digit \quad = \quad member \quad ['0','1','2','3','4','5','6','7','8','9']$$

$$month \quad = \quad member \quad ["Jan","Feb","Mar","Apr","Jun","Jul",$$
$$"Aug","Sep","Oct","Nov","Dec"]$$

As another example of higher-order programming consider the function *foldr*, defined by

$$foldr\ op\ k\ [\ ] = k$$

$$foldr\ op\ k\ (a : x) = op\ a\ (foldr\ op\ k\ x)$$

All the standard list-processing functions can be obtained by partially parameterizing *foldr*. Some examples are

$$sum \qquad = \quad foldr\ (+)\ 0$$

$$product \quad = \quad foldr\ (*)\ 1$$

$$reverse \quad = \quad foldr\ postfix\ [\ ]$$
$$\textbf{where}$$
$$postfix\ a\ x = x ++ [a]$$

## 6 *List Comprehensions*

List comprehensions give a concise syntax for a rather general class of iterations over lists. The notation is adapted from Zermelo-Frankel set theory. A simple example of a list comprehension is

$$[n * n \mid n \leftarrow [1..100]\,]$$

This is a list containing (in order) the squares of all the numbers from 1 to 100. The above expression would be read aloud as "list of all $n * n$ such that $n$ is drawn from the list 1 to 100". Note that $n$ is a local variable of the above expression. The variable-binding construct to the right of the bar is called a "generator"; the '$\leftarrow$' sign denotes that the variable introduced on its left ranges over all the elements of the list on its right. The general form of a list comprehension in Miranda is

$$[body \mid qualifiers]$$

where each qualifier is either a generator, of the form *var ← exp*, or else a filter, which is a boolean expression used to restrict the ranges of the variables introduced by the generators. When two or more qualifiers are present they are separated by semicolons. An example of a list comprehension with two generators is given by the following definition of a function for returning a list of all the permutations of a given list:

> *perms* [ ] = [[ ]]
>
> *perms x* = [ *a* : *y* | *a* ← *x*; *y* ← *perms* (*x* −−[*a*]) ]

The use of a filter is shown by the following definition of a function that takes a number and returns a list of all its factors,

> *factors n* = [ *i* | *i* ← [ 1 .. *n* **div** 2 ]; *n* **mod** *i* = 0 ]

List comprehensions often allow remarkable conciseness of expression. We give two examples. Here is a Miranda statement of Hoare's "Quicksort" algorithm, as a method of sorting a list:

> *sort* [ ] = [ ]
>
> *sort* (*a* : *x*)  = *sort* [ *b* | *b* ← *x*; *b* ≤ *a* ]
>
>                    ++ [*a*] ++
>
>                    *sort* [ *b* | *b* ← *x*; *b* > *a* ]

Next is a Miranda solution to the eight-queens problem. We have to place eight queens on chess board so that no queen gives check to any other. Since any solution must have exactly one queen in each column, a suitable representation for a board is a list of integers giving the row number of the queen in each successive column. In the following script the function *queens n* returns all safe ways to place queens on the first *n* columns. A list of all solutions to the eight-queens problem is therefore obtained by printing the value of (*queens* 8).

> *queens* 0  = [[ ]]
>
> *queens* (*n*+1)  = [ *q* : *b* | *b* ← *queens n*; *q* ← [0..7]; *safe q b* ]
>
> *safe q b*  = *and* [ ~ *checks q b i* | *i* ← [0 .. #*b*−1 ]]
>
> *checks q b i*  = *q* = *b* ! *i* ∨ *abs* (*q* − *b* ! *i*) = *i*+1

## 7  *Lazy Evaluation and Infinite Lists*

Miranda's evaluation mechanism is "lazy", in the sense that no subexpression is evaluated until its value is known to be required. One consequence of this is that it is possible to define functions that are nonstrict (meaning that they are capable of returning an answer even if one of their arguments is undefined). For example we can define a conditional function as follows:

> *cond True x y = x*
>
> *cond False x y = y*

and then use it in such situations as *cond* $(x=0)$ 0 $(1/x)$.

The other main consequence of lazy evaluation is that it makes it possible to write down definitions of infinite data structures. Here are some examples of Miranda definitions of infinite lists (note that there is a modified form of the ".." notation for endless arithmetic progressions):

> | *ones* | = | 1 : *ones* |
> | *repeat a* | = | *x* **where** *x = a : x* |
> | *nats* | = | [0..] |
> | *odds* | = | [1, 3..] |
> | *squares* | = | [ *n * n* \| *n* ← [0..] ] |
> | *perfects* | = | [ *n* \| *n* ← [1..]; *sum (factors n) = n* ] |
> | *primes* | = | *sieve* [2..] |
> | | | **where** |
> | | | *sieve (p : x) = p : sieve* [ *n* \| *n* ← *x*; *n* **mod** *p* > 0 ] |

One interesting application of infinite lists is to act as lookup tables for caching the values of a function. For example our earlier naive definition of *fib* can be improved from exponential to linear complexity by changing the recursion to use a lookup table, thus:

> *fib* 0 = 1
>
> *fib* 1 = 1
>
> | *fib (n+2)* | = | *flist* ! (*n*+1) + *flist* ! *n* |
> | | | **where** |
> | | | *flist* = [ *fib n* \| *n* ← [0..] ] |

Another important use of infinite lists is that they enable us to write functional programs representing networks of communicating processes. Consider, for example, the Hamming-numbers problem: to print in ascending order all numbers of the form $2^a * 3^b * 5^c$, for $a, b, c \geq 0$. There is a nice solution to this problem in terms of communicating processes, which can be expressed in Miranda as follows:

$$hamming \ = \ 1 : merge \ (f \ 2) \ (merge \ (f \ 3) \ (f \ 5))$$

**where**

$$f \ a \ = \ [ \ n * a \mid n \leftarrow hamming \ ]$$

$$merge \ (a : x) \ (b : y) \ \ = \ \ a : merge \ x \ (b : y), \quad \textbf{if} \ a < b$$
$$= \ \ b : merge \ (a : x) \ y, \quad \textbf{if} \ a > b$$
$$= \ \ a : merge \ x \ y, \qquad \quad \textbf{otherwise}$$

## 8 *Polymorphic Strong Typing*

Miranda is strongly typed. That is, every expression and every subexpression has a type, which can be deduced at compile time, and any inconsistency in the type structure of a script results in a compile-time error message. We here briefly summarize Miranda's notation for its types.

There are three primitive types, called *num*, *bool*, and *char*. The type *num* comprises integer and floating-point numbers (the distinction between integers and floating-point numbers is handled at run time and is not regarded as being a type distinction). There are two values of type *bool*, called *True* and *False*. The type *char* comprises the ASCII character set — character constants are written in single quotes, using *C* escape conventions, e.g., 'a', '$', '\n', etc.

If *T* is a type, then [*T*] is the type of lists whose elements are of type *T*. For example [[1, 2], [2, 3], [4, 5]] is of type [[*num*]]; that is, it is a list of lists of numbers. String constants are of type [*char*]; in fact a string such as "hello" is simply a shorthand way of writing ['h','e','l','l','o'].

If *T1* to *Tn* are types, then (*T1*, ..., *Tn*) is the type of tuples with objects of these types as components. For example, the type of (*True*, "hello", 36) is (*bool*, [*char*], *num*).

If *T1* and *T2* are types, then *T1* $\rightarrow$ *T2* is the type of a function with arguments in *T1* and results in *T2*. For example the function *sum* is of type [*num*] $\rightarrow$ *num*. The function *quadsolve*, given earlier, is of type *num* $\rightarrow$ *num* $\rightarrow$ *num* $\rightarrow$ [*num*]. Note that '$\rightarrow$' is right associative.

Miranda scripts can include type declarations. These are written using '::' to mean "is of type", for example:

$$sq :: num \rightarrow num$$

$$sq \ n = n * n$$

The type declaration is not necessary, however. The compiler is always able to deduce the type of an identifier from its defining equation. Miranda scripts often contain type declarations, as these are useful for documentation (and they provide an extra check, since the typechecker will complain if the declared type is inconsistent with the inferred one).

Types can be polymorphic, in the sense of Milner [1]. This is indicated by using the symbols *, **, * * *, etc., as an alphabet of generic type variables. For example, the identity function, defined in the Miranda library as

>   *id x = x*

has the following type:

>   *id* :: * → *

This means that the identity function has many types, namely, all those that can be obtained by substituting an arbitrary type for the generic type variable, e.g., *num* → *num*, *bool* → *bool*, (* → **) → (* → **), and so on.

We illustrate the Miranda type system by giving types for some of the functions so far defined in this chapter:

>   *fac* :: *num* → *num*
>
>   *ack* :: *num* → *num* → *num*
>
>   *sum* :: [*num*] → *num*
>
>   *month* :: [*char*] → *bool*
>
>   *reverse* :: [*] → [*]
>
>   *fst* :: (*, **) → *
>
>   *snd* :: (*, **) → **
>
>   *foldr* :: (* → ** → **) → ** → [*] → **
>
>   *perms* :: [*] → [[*]]

## 9 *User-Defined Types*

The user may introduce new types. This is done by an equation in '::='. For example a type of labeled binary trees (with numeric labels) would be introduced as follows:

>   *tree* ::= *Nilt* | *Node num tree tree*

This introduces three new identifiers — *tree*, which is the name of the type, and *Nilt* and *Node*, which are the constructors for trees. *Nilt* is an atomic constructor, while *Node* takes three arguments, of the types shown. Here is an example of a tree built using these constructors:

$t1 = Node\ 7\ (Node\ 3\ Nilt\ Nilt)\ (Node\ 4\ Nilt\ Nilt)$

To analyze an object of user-defined type, we use pattern matching. For example here is a definition of a function for taking the mirror image of a tree:

*mirror Nilt = Nilt*

*mirror (Node a x y) = Node a (mirror y) (mirror x)*

User-defined types can be polymorphic; this is shown by introducing one or more generic type variables as parameters of the '::=' equation. For example we can generalize the definition of tree to allow arbitrary labels, thus

*tree ∗ ::= Nilt | Node ∗ (tree ∗) (tree ∗)*

This introduces a family of *tree* types, including *tree num*, *tree bool*, *tree* (*char → char*), etc.

The types introduced by '::=' definitions are called "algebraic types". Algebraic types are a very general idea. They include scalar enumeration types, e.g.,

*color ::= Red | Orange | Yellow | Green | Blue | Indigo | Violet*

and also give us a way to define union types such as

*bool_or_num ::= Left bool | Right num*

It is interesting to note that all the basic data types of Miranda could be defined from first principles, using '::=' equations. For example, here are type definitions for *bool*, (natural) numbers, and lists:

*bool ::= True | False*

*nat ::= Zero | Suc nat*

*list ∗ ::= Nil | Cons ∗ (list ∗)*

Having types such as *num* built in is done for reasons of efficiency— it isn't logically necessary.

It is also possible to associate "laws" with the constructors of an algebraic type, which are applied whenever an object of the type is built. For example we can associate laws with the *Node* constructor of the *tree* type above, so that trees are always balanced. We omit discussion of this feature of Miranda here for lack of space; interested readers will find more details in the references [2, 3].

## 10 *Type Synonyms*

The Miranda programmer can introduce a new name for an already existing type. We use '==' for these definitions, to distinguish them from ordinary value definitions. Two examples are

> *string* == [*char*]
>
> *matrix* == [[*num*]]

Type synonyms are entirely transparent to the typechecker — it is best to think of them as macros.

It is also possible to introduce synonyms for families of types. This is done by using generic type symbols as formal parameters, as in

> *array* * == [[*]]

so now, for example, *array num* is the same type as *matrix*.

## 11 *Abstract Data Types*

In addition to concrete types, introduced by '::=' or '==' equations, Miranda permits the definition of abstract types, whose implementation is "hidden" from the rest of the program. To show how this works we give the standard example of defining *stack* as an abstract data type (here based on lists):

> **abstype** *stack* *
>
> **with**   *empty* :: *stack* *
>
>       *isempty* :: *stack* * $\rightarrow$ *bool*
>
>       *push* :: * $\rightarrow$ *stack* * $\rightarrow$ *stack* *
>
>       *pop* :: *stack* * $\rightarrow$ *stack* *
>
>       *top* :: *stack* * $\rightarrow$ *
>
> *stack* * == [*]
>
> *empty* = [ ]
>
> *isempty x* = (*x* = [ ])
>
> *push a x* = (*a* : *x*)
>
> *pop* (*a* : *x*) = *x*
>
> *top* (*a* : *x*) = *a*

We see that the definition of an abstract data type consists of two parts. The first is a declaration of the form "**abstype** ...  **with** ...", where the names following the "**with**" are called the "signature" of the abstract data type. These names are the interface between the abstract data type and the rest of the program. The second part is a set of equations giving bindings for the names introduced in the abstype declaration. These are called the implementation equations.

The type abstraction is enforced by the typechecker. The mechanism works as follows. When checking the implementation equations, the typechecker treats the abstract type and its representation as being the same type. In the whole of the rest of the script, the abstract type and its representation are treated as two separate and completely unrelated types. This is somewhat different from the usual mechanism for implementing abstract data types, but it has a number of advantages. It is discussed at somewhat greater length in [3].

## 12 *Separate Compilation and Linking*

The basic mechanisms for separate compilation and linking are extremely simple. Any Miranda script can contain one or more directives of the form

   *%include "pathname"*

where *pathname* is the name of another Miranda script file — which might it-self contain *%include* directives, and so on recursively (the *%include* structure may not, however, be cyclic). The visibility of names to an including script is controlled by a directive in the included script, of the form

   *%export names*

It is permitted to export types as well as values. It is not permitted to export a value to a place where its type is unknown, so if an object of a locally defined type is exported, the typename must be exported also. Exporting the name of a '::=' type automatically exports all its constructors. If a script does not contain an *%export* directive, then the default is that all the names (and typenames) it defines will be exported (but not those which it acquired by an *%include* statement).

It is also permitted to write a parameterized script, in which certain names and/or typenames are declared as "free". For example, we might wish to write a package for doing matrix algebra without knowing what the type of the matrix elements are going to be. A header for such a package could look like this:

> *%free {element :: type*
>
> > *zero, unit :: element*
> >
> > *mult, add, subtract, divide :: element → element → element*
> >
> > *}*

> *%export matmult determinant eigenvalues eigenvectors . . .*
>
> || here would follow definitions of *matmult*, *determinant*,
>
> || *eigenvalues*, etc. in terms of the free identifiers *zero*,
>
> || *unit*, *mult*, *add*, *subtract*, and *divide*.

In the using script, the corresponding *%include* statement must give a set of bindings for the free variables of the included script. For example here is an instantiation of the matrix package sketched above, with real numbers as the chosen element type:

> *%include "matrix_pack"*
>
> > *{element == num; zero = 0; unit = 1*
> >
> > *mult = \*; add = +; subtract = −; divide = /*
> >
> > *}*

The three directives *%include*, *%export*, and *%free* provide the Miranda programmer with a flexible and type-secure mechanism for structuring larger pieces of software from libraries of smaller components.

Separate compilation is administered without user intervention. Each file containing a Miranda script is shadowed by an object-code file created by the system, and object-code files are automatically recreated and relinked if they become out of date with respect to any relevant source. (This behavior is strongly analogous to that achieved by the UNIX program *make*, except that here the user is not required to write a *make* file — the necessary dependency information is inferred from the *%include* directives in the Miranda source.)

## 13 *Current Implementation Status*

An implementation of Miranda is available for ORION, VAX, SUN, GOULD, Apollo and several other machines running Berkeley UNIX, and also for the HP 9000 series under System V. This is an interpretive implementation that works by compiling Miranda scripts to an intermediate code based on combinators. It is currently running at 300 sites (as of August 1989). Licensing information can be obtained from the net address

INTERNET: `mira-request%ukc@nsfnet-relay.ac.uk`

UUCP: `mcvax!ukc!mira-request`

JANET: `mira-request@ukc.ac.uk`

or by real mail from:

Research Software Ltd
23 St Augustines Road
Canterbury
Kent CT1 1XP
England

Ports to some other UNIX machines are planned in the near future. Also under study (to appear on a somewhat longer timescale) is the possibility of native-code compilers for Miranda on a number of machines, to provide a much faster implementation.

## References

[1] Milner, R. "A theory of type polymorphism in programming". *Journal of Computer and System Sciences 17* (December 1978), pp. 348–375.

[2] Thompson, S. J. "Laws in Miranda". *Proceedings of the 4th ACM International Conference on LISP and Functional Programming* (Boston, August). ACM, New York, 1986.

[3] Turner, D. A. "Miranda: A non-strict functional language with polymorphic types". *Proceedings IFIP International Conference on Functional Programming Languages and Computer Architecture* (Nancy, France, September). Lecture Notes in Computer Science, vol. 201. Springer-Verlag, Berlin, 1985.

# *Why Functional Programming Matters*[1]

# 2

## John Hughes
The University, Glasgow

## *Abstract*

$A$s software becomes more and more complex, it is more and more important to structure it well. Well-structured software is easy to write and to debug, and provides a collection of modules that can be reused to reduce future programming costs. In this paper we show that two features of functional languages in particular, higher-order functions and lazy evaluation, can contribute significantly to modularity. As examples, we manipulate lists and trees, program several numerical algorithms, and implement the alpha-beta heuristic (an algorithm from Artificial Intelligence used in game-playing programs). We conclude that since modularity is the key to successful programming, functional programming offers important advantages for software

---

1. This chapter appeared in the April 1989 issue of *The Computer Journal*; copyright belongs to The British Computer Society.

development.

---

## 1 *Introduction*

This paper is an attempt to demonstrate to the larger community of (non-functional) programmers the significance of functional programming, and also to help functional programmers exploit its advantages to the full by making it clear what those advantages are.

Functional programming is so called because its fundamental operation is the application of functions to arguments. A main program itself is written as a function that receives the program's input as its argument and delivers the program's output as its result. Typically the main function is defined in terms of other functions, which in turn are defined in terms of still more functions, until at the bottom level the functions are language primitives. All of these functions are much like ordinary mathematical functions, and in this paper they will be defined by ordinary equations. We are following Turner's language Miranda [4] here, but the notation should be readable without specific knowledge of this.

The special characteristics and advantages of functional programming are often summed up more or less as follows. Functional programs contain no assignment statements, so variables, once given a value, never change. More generally, functional programs contain no side-effects at all. A function call can have no effect other than to compute its result. This eliminates a major source of bugs, and also makes the order of execution irrelevant — since no side-effect can change an expression's value, it can be evaluated at any time. This relieves the programmer of the burden of prescribing the flow of control. Since expressions can be evaluated at any time, one can freely replace variables by their values and vice versa — that is, programs are "referentially transparent". This freedom helps make functional programs more tractable mathematically than their conventional counterparts.

Such a catalogue of "advantages" is all very well, but one must not be surprised if outsiders don't take it too seriously. It says a lot about what functional programming isn't (it has no assignment, no side effects, no flow of control) but not much about what it is. The functional programmer sounds rather like a mediæval monk, denying himself the pleasures of life in the hope that it will make him virtuous. To those more interested in material benefits, these "advantages" are totally unconvincing.

Functional programmers argue that there *are* great material benefits — that a functional programmer is an order of magnitude more productive than his or her conventional counterpart, because functional programs are an order of magnitude shorter. Yet why should this be? The only faintly plausible reason one can suggest on the basis of these "advantages" is that conventional programs consist of 90% assignment statements, and in functional programs these can be omitted! This is plainly ridiculous. If omitting assignment statements brought such enormous benefits then FORTRAN programmers would have been doing it for twenty years. It is a logical impossibility to make a language more powerful by omitting features, no matter how bad they may be.

Even a functional programmer should be dissatisfied with these so-called advantages, because they give no help in exploiting the power of functional languages. One cannot write a program that is particularly lacking in assignment statements, or particularly referentially transparent. There is no yardstick of program quality here, and therefore no ideal to aim at.

Clearly this characterization of functional programming is inadequate. We must find something to put in its place — something that not only explains the power of functional programming but also gives a clear indication of what the functional programmer should strive towards.

## 2 *An Analogy with Structured Programming*

It's helpful to draw an analogy between functional and structured programming. In the past, the characteristics and advantages of structured programming have been summed up more or less as follows. Structured programs contain no *goto* statements. Blocks in a structured program do not have multiple entries or exits. Structured programs are more tractable mathematically than their unstructured counterparts. These "advantages" of structured programming are very similar in spirit to the "advantages" of functional programming we discussed earlier. They are essentially negative statements, and have led to much fruitless argument about "essential *goto*s" and so on.

With the benefit of hindsight, it's clear that these properties of structured programs, although helpful, do not go to the heart of the matter. The most important difference between structured and unstructured programs is that structured programs are designed in a modular way. Modular design brings with it great productivity improvements. First of all, small modules can be coded quickly and easily. Second, general-purpose modules can be reused, leading to faster development of subsequent programs. Third, the modules of a program can be tested independently, helping to reduce the time spent debugging.

The absence of *goto*s, and so on, has very little to do with this. It helps with "programming in the small", whereas modular design helps with "programming in the large". Thus one can enjoy the benefits of structured programming in FORTRAN or assembly language, even if it is a little more work.

It is now generally accepted that modular design is the key to success-ful programming, and recent languages such as MODULA-II [6] and Ada [5] include features specifically designed to help improve modularity. However, there is a very important point that is often missed. When writing a modular program to solve a problem, one first divides the problem into subproblems, then solves the subproblems, and finally combines the solutions. The ways in which one can divide up the original problem depend directly on the ways in which one can glue solutions together. Therefore, to increase one's ability to modularize a problem conceptually, one must provide new kinds of glue in the programming language. Complicated scope rules and provision for sepa-rate compilation help only with clerical details — they can never make a great contribution to modularization.

We shall argue in the remainder of this paper that functional languages provide two new, very important kinds of glue. We shall give some examples of programs that can be modularized in new ways and can thereby be simpli-fied. This is the key to functional programming's power — it allows improved modularization. It is also the goal for which functional programmers must strive — smaller and simpler and more general modules, glued together with the new glues we shall describe.

## 3  *Gluing Functions Together*

The first of the two new kinds of glue enables simple functions to be glued together to make more complex ones. It can be illustrated with a simple list-processing problem — adding the elements of a list. We can define lists[2] by

$$listof * ::= Nil \mid Cons * (listof *)$$

which means that a list of *s (whatever * is) is either *Nil*, representing a list with no elements, or a *Cons* of a * and another list of *s. A *Cons* represents a list whose first element is the * and whose second and subsequent elements are the elements of the other list of *s. Here * may stand for any type — for example, if * is "integer" then the definition says that a list of integers is either empty or a *Cons* of an integer and another list of integers. Following normal practice, we will write down lists simply by enclosing their elements in square brackets, rather than by writing *Cons*es and *Nil*s explicitly. This is

---

2. In Miranda, lists can also be defined using the built-in constructor (:), but the notation used here is equally valid.

simply a shorthand for notational convenience. For example,

| []        | means | *Nil*                          |
|-----------|-------|--------------------------------|
| [1]       | means | *Cons* 1 *Nil*                 |
| [1, 2, 3] | means | *Cons* 1 (*Cons* 2 (*Cons* 3 *Nil*)) |

The elements of a list can be added by a recursive function *sum*. The function *sum* must be defined for two kinds of argument: an empty list (*Nil*), and a *Cons*. Since the sum of no numbers is zero, we define

$$sum\ Nil = 0$$

and since the sum of a *Cons* can be calculated by adding the first element of the list to the sum of the others, we can define

$$sum\ (Cons\ n\ list) =\ num + sum\ list\ .$$

Examining this definition, we see that only the boxed parts below are specific to computing a sum.

$$sum\ Nil\ =\ \boxed{0}$$
$$sum\ (Cons\ n\ list) = n\ \boxed{+}\ sum\ list\ .$$

This means that the computation of a sum can be modularized by gluing together a general recursive pattern and the boxed parts. This recursive pattern is conventionally called *foldr* and so *sum* can be expressed as

$$sum\ =\ foldr\ (+)\ 0\ .$$

The definition of *foldr* can be derived just by parameterizing the definition of *sum*, giving

$$(foldr\ f\ x)\ Nil\ = x$$
$$(foldr\ f\ x)\ (Cons\ a\ l) = f\ a\ ((foldr\ f\ x)\ l)$$

Here we have written brackets around (*foldr f x*) to make it clear that it replaces *sum*. Conventionally the brackets are omitted, and so ((*foldr f x*) *l*) is written as (*foldr f x l*). A function of three arguments such as *foldr*, applied to only two, is taken to be a function of the one remaining argument, and in general, a function of $n$ arguments applied to only $m$ of them ($m < n$) is taken to be a function of the $n - m$ remaining ones. We will follow this convention in future.

Having modularized *sum* in this way, we can reap benefits by reusing the parts. The most interesting part is *foldr*, which can be used to write down a function for multiplying together the elements of a list with no further programming:

> *product* = *foldr* (∗) 1 .

It can also be used to test whether any of a list of booleans is true

> *anytrue* = *foldr* (∨) *False*

or whether they are all true

> *alltrue* = *foldr* (∧) *True* .

One way to understand (*foldr f a*) is as a function that replaces all occurrences of *Cons* in a list by *f*, and all occurrences of *Nil* by *a*. Taking the list [1, 2, 3] as an example, since this means

> *Cons* 1 (*Cons* 2 (*Cons* 3 *Nil*))

then (*foldr* (+) 0) converts it into

> (+) 1 ((+) 2 ((+) 3 0)) = 6

and (*foldr* (∗) 1) converts it into

> (∗) 1 ((∗) 2 ((∗) 3 1)) = 6 .

Now it's obvious that (*foldr Cons Nil*) just copies a list. Since one list can be appended to another by *Cons*ing its elements onto the front, we find

> *append a b* = *foldr Cons b a* .

As an example,

> *append* [1, 2] [3, 4] = *foldr Cons* [3, 4] [1, 2]
>
> > = *foldr Cons* [3, 4] (*Cons* 1 (*Cons* 2 *Nil*))
> >
> > = *Cons* 1 (*Cons* 2 [3, 4]))
> >
> > > (replacing *Cons* by *Cons* and *Nil* by [3, 4])
> >
> > = [1, 2, 3, 4] .

We can count the number of elements in a list using the function *length*, defined by

> *length* = *foldr count* 0
>
> *count a n* = *n* + 1

because *count* increments 0 as many times as there are *Cons*es.   A function that doubles all the elements of a list could be written as

$$doubleall \ = \ foldr \ doubleandcons \ Nil$$

where

$$doubleandcons \ n \ list \ = \ Cons \ (2 * n) \ list \ .$$

The function *doubleandcons* can be modularized even further, first into

$$doubleandcons \ = \ fandcons \ double$$

where

$$double \ n = 2 * n$$
$$fandcons \ f \ el \ list \ = \ Cons \ (f \ el) \ list$$

and then by

$$fandcons \ f = \ Cons \ . \ f$$

where "." (function composition, a standard operator) is defined by

$$(f \ . \ g) \ h = f \ (g \ h) \ .$$

We can see that the new definition of *fandcons* is correct by applying it to some arguments:

$$fandcons \ f \ el \ \ = \ (Cons \ . \ f) \ el$$
$$= \ Cons \ (f \ el)$$

so

$$fandcons \ f \ el \ list = \ Cons \ (f \ el) \ list \ .$$

The final version is

$$doubleall \ = foldr \ (Cons \ . \ double) \ Nil \ .$$

With one further modularization we arrive at

$$doubleall \ = map \ double$$
$$map \ f = foldr \ (Cons \ . \ f) \ Nil$$

where *map* — another generally useful function — applies any function *f* to all the elements of a list.

We can even write a function to add all the elements of a matrix, represented as a list of lists. It is

$$summatrix \ = \ sum \ . \ map \ sum \ .$$

The function *map sum* uses *sum* to add up all the rows, and then the leftmost *sum* adds up the row totals to get the sum of the whole matrix.

These examples should be enough to convince the reader that a little modularization can go a long way. By modularizing a simple function (*sum*) as a combination of a "higher-order function" and some simple arguments, we have arrived at a part (*foldr*) that can be used to write many other functions on lists with no more programming effort.

We do not need to stop with functions on lists. As another example, consider the datatype of ordered labeled trees, defined by

$$treeof * ::= Node * (listof (treeof *)).$$

This definition says that a tree of *s is a node, with a label which is a *, and a list of subtrees which are also trees of *s. For example, the tree

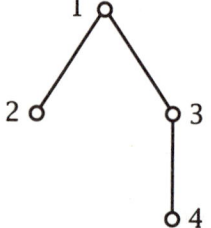

would be represented by

> *Node* 1
>     (*Cons* (*Node* 2 *Nil*)
>         (*Cons* (*Node* 3
>                 (*Cons* (*Node* 4 *Nil*) *Nil*))
>             *Nil*)) .

Instead of considering an example and abstracting a higher-order function from it, we will go straight to a function *foldtree* analogous to *foldr*. Recall that *foldr* took two arguments: something to replace *Cons* with and something to replace *Nil* with. Since trees are built using *Node*, *Cons*, and *Nil*, *foldtree* must take three arguments— something to replace each of these with. Therefore we define

> *foldtree f g a* (*Node label subtrees*) =
>     *f label* (*foldtree f g a subtrees*)
> *foldtree f g a* (*Cons subtree rest*) =
>     *g* (*foldtree f g a subtree*) (*foldtree f g a rest*)
> *foldtree f g a Nil*  = *a* .

Many interesting functions can be defined by gluing *foldtree* and other functions together. For example, all the labels in a tree of numbers can be added together using

   *sumtree* = *foldtree* (+) (+) 0 .

Taking the tree we wrote down earlier as an example, *sumtree* gives

   (+)    1
         ((+) ((+) 2 0)
              ((+) ((+)  3
                        ((+) ((+) 4 0) 0))
         0))
   = 10 .

A list of all the labels in a tree can be computed using

   *labels* = *foldtree Cons append Nil* .

The same example gives

   *Cons* 1
         (*append* (*Cons* 2   *Nil*)
              (*append* (*Cons* 3
                        (*append* (*Cons* 4 *Nil*) *Nil*))
              *Nil*))
   = [1, 2, 3, 4] .

Finally, one can define a function analogous to *map* which applies a function *f* to all the labels in a tree:

   *maptree f* = *foldtree* (*Node* . *f*) *Cons Nil* .

All this can be achieved because functional languages allow functions that are indivisible in conventional programming languages to be expressed as a combinations of parts — a general higher-order function and some particular specializing functions. Once defined, such higher-order functions allow many operations to be programmed very easily. Whenever a new datatype is defined, higher-order functions should be written for processing it. This makes manipulating the datatype easy, and it also localizes knowledge about the details of its representation. The best analogy with conventional programming is with extensible languages — in effect, the programming language can be extended with new control structures whenever desired.

## 4 *Gluing Programs Together*

The other new kind of glue that functional languages provide enables whole programs to be glued together. Recall that a complete functional program is just a function from its input to its output. If *f* and *g* are such programs, then (*g* . *f*) is a program that, when applied to its input, computes

$$g \, (f \, input) \, .$$

The program *f* computes its output, which is used as the input to program *g*. This might be implemented conventionally by storing the output from *f* in a temporary file. The problem with this is that the temporary file might occupy so much memory that it is impractical to glue the programs together in this way. Functional languages provide a solution to this problem. The two programs *f* and *g* are run together in strict synchronization. Program *f* is started only when *g* tries to read some input, and runs only for long enough to deliver the output *g* is trying to read. Then *f* is suspended and *g* is run until it tries to read another input. As an added bonus, if *g* terminates without reading all of *f*'s output, then *f* is aborted. Program *f* can even be a nonterminating program, producing an infinite amount of output, since it will be terminated forcibly as soon as *g* is finished. This allows termination conditions to be separated from loop bodies — a powerful modularization.

Since this method of evaluation runs *f* as little as possible, it is called "lazy evaluation". It makes it practical to modularize a program as a generator that constructs a large number of possible answers, and a selector that chooses the appropriate one. While some other systems allow programs to be run together in this manner, only functional languages (and not even all of them) use lazy evaluation uniformly for every function call, allowing any part of a program to be modularized in this way. Lazy evaluation is perhaps the most powerful tool for modularization in the functional programmer's repertoire.

We have described lazy evaluation in the context of functional languages, but surely so useful a feature should be added to nonfunctional languages — or should it? Can lazy evaluation and side-effects coexist? Unfortunately, they cannot: Adding lazy evaluation to an imperative notation is not actually impossible, but the combination would make the programmer's life harder, rather than easier. Because lazy evaluation's power depends on the programmer giving up any direct control over the order in which the parts of a program are executed, it would make programming with side effects rather difficult, because predicting in what order —or even whether— they might take place would require knowing a lot about the context in which they are embedded. Such global interdependence would defeat the very modularity that —in functional languages— lazy evaluation is designed to enhance.

### 4.1 *Newton-Raphson Square Roots*

We will illustrate the power of lazy evaluation by programming some numerical algorithms. First of all, consider the Newton-Raphson algorithm for finding square roots. This algorithm computes the square root of a number $n$ by starting from an initial approximation $a0$ and computing better and better ones using the rule

$$a_{i+1} = (a_i + n/a_i)/2 .$$

If the approximations converge to some limit $a$, then

$$a = (a + n/a)/2$$

so

$$
\begin{aligned}
2a &= a + n/a \\
a &= n/a \\
a * a &= n \\
a &= \sqrt{n} .
\end{aligned}
$$

In fact the approximations converge rapidly to a limit. Square root programs take a tolerance (*eps*) and stop when two successive approximations differ by less than *eps*.

The algorithm is usually programmed more or less as follows:

```
C    N IS CALLED ZN HERE SO THAT IT HAS THE RIGHT TYPE
     X = A0
     Y = A0 + 2. * EPS
C    Y'S VALUE DOES NOT MATTER SO LONG AS ABS(X-Y).GT.EPS
100     IF ABS(X-Y).LE.EPS GOTO 200
     Y = X
     X = (X + ZN/X) / 2.
     GOTO 100
200     CONTINUE
C    THE SQUARE ROOT OF ZN IS NOW IN X.
```

This program is indivisible in conventional languages. We will express it in a more modular form using lazy evaluation and then show some other uses to which the parts may be put.

Since the Newton-Raphson algorithm computes a sequence of approximations it is natural to represent this explicitly in the program by a list of approximations. Each approximation is derived from the previous one by the function

$$next\ n\ x = (x + n/x)/2$$

so (*next n*) is the function mapping one approximation onto the next. Calling this function *f*, the sequence of approximations is

$$[a0,\ f\,a0,\ f(f\,a0),\ f(f(f\,a0)),\ \dots\,].$$

We can define a function to compute this:

$$repeat\ f\ a = Cons\ a\ (repeat\ f\ (f\ a))$$

so that the list of approximations can be computed by

$$repeat\ (next\ n)\ a0\,.$$

The function *repeat* is an example of a function with an "infinite" output — but it doesn't matter, because no more approximations will actually be computed than the rest of the program requires. The infinity is only potential: All it means is that any number of approximations can be computed if required; *repeat* itself places no limit.

The remainder of a square root finder is a function *within*, which takes a tolerance and a list of approximations and looks down the list for two successive approximations that differ by no more than the given tolerance. It can be defined by

*within eps* (*Cons a* (*Cons b rest*))

$$= b, \qquad\qquad\qquad \textbf{if}\ abs\ (a - b) \le eps$$

$$= within\ eps\ (Cons\ b\ rest), \quad \textbf{otherwise}\,.$$

Putting the parts together, we have

$$sqrt\ a0\ eps\ n = within\ eps\ (repeat\ (next\ n)\ a0)\,.$$

Now that we have the parts of a square root finder, we can try combining them in different ways. One modification we might wish to make is to wait for the ratio between successive approximations to approach 1, rather than for the difference to approach 0. This is more appropriate for very small numbers (when the difference between successive approximations is small to start with) and for very large ones (when rounding error could be much larger than the tolerance). It is only necessary to define a replacement for *within*:

*relative eps* (*Cons a* (*Cons b rest*))

$$= b, \qquad\qquad\qquad \textbf{if}\ abs\ (a/b - 1) \le eps$$

$$= relative\ eps\ (Cons\ b\ rest), \quad \textbf{otherwise}\,.$$

Now a new version of *sqrt* can be defined by

*relativesqrt a0 eps n = relative eps (repeat (next n) a0).*

It is not necessary to rewrite the part that generates approximations.

### 4.2 *Numerical Differentiation*

We have reused the sequence of approximations to a square root. Of course, it is also possible to reuse *within* and *relative* with any numerical algorithm that generates a sequence of approximations. We will do so in a numerical differentiation algorithm.

The result of differentiating a function at a point is the slope of the function's graph at that point. It can be estimated quite easily by evaluating the function at the given point and at another point nearby and computing the slope of a straight line between the two points. This assumes that if the two points are close enough together, then the graph of the function will not curve much in between. This gives the definition

*easydiff f x h = (f(x + h) − f x)/h .*

In order to get a good approximation the value of $h$ should be very small. Unfortunately, if $h$ is too small then the two values $f(x + h)$ and $f(x)$ are very close together, and so the rounding error in the subtraction may swamp the result. How can the right value of $h$ be chosen? One solution to this dilemma is to compute a sequence of approximations with smaller and smaller values of $h$, starting with a reasonably large one. Such a sequence should converge to the value of the derivative, but will become hopelessly inaccurate eventually due to rounding error. If (*within eps*) is used to select the first approximation that is accurate enough, then the risk of rounding error affecting the result can be much reduced. We need a function to compute the sequence:

*differentiate h0 f x =  map (easydiff f x) (repeat halve h0)*

*halve x = x/2 .*

Here *h0* is the initial value of $h$, and successive values are obtained by repeated halving. Given this function, the derivative at any point can be computed by

*within eps (differentiate h0 f x) .*

Even this solution is not very satisfactory because the sequence of approximations converges fairly slowly. A little simple mathematics can help here.

The elements of the sequence can be expressed as

> the right answer + an error term involving $h$,

and it can be shown theoretically that the error term is roughly proportional to a power of $h$, so that it gets smaller as $h$ gets smaller. Let the right answer be $A$, and let the error term be $B \times h^n$. Since each approximation is computed using a value of $h$ twice that used for the next one, any two successive approximations can be expressed as

$$a_i = A + B \times 2^n \times h^n$$

and

$$a_{i+1} = A + B \times h^n.$$

Now the error term can be eliminated. We conclude

$$A = \frac{a_{n+1} \times 2^n - a_n}{2^n - 1}.$$

Of course, since the error term is only roughly a power of $h$ this conclusion is also approximate, but it is a much better approximation. This improvement can be applied to all successive pairs of approximations using the function

> *elimerror n (Cons a (Cons b rest))*
>
> = *Cons ((b * (2^n) − a)/(2^n − 1)) (elimerror n (Cons b rest)).*

Eliminating error terms from a sequence of approximations yields another sequence, which converges much more rapidly.

One problem remains before we can use *elimerror* — we have to know the right value of $n$. This is difficult to predict in general but is easy to measure. It's not difficult to show that the following function estimates it correctly, but we won't include the proof here:

> *order (Cons a (Cons b (Cons c rest)))*
>
> = *round (log2 ((a − c)/(b − c) − 1))*
>
> *round x = x* rounded to the nearest integer
>
> *log2 x =* the logarithm of $x$ to the base 2 .

Now a general function to improve a sequence of approximations can be defined:

> *improve s = elimerror (order s) s.*

The derivative of a function $f$ can be computed more efficiently using *improve*, as follows:

> *within eps (improve (differentiate h0 f x)).*

The function *improve* works only on sequences of approximations that are computed using a parameter *h*, which is halved for each successive approximation. However, if it is applied to such a sequence its result is also such a sequence! This means that a sequence of approximations can be improved more than once. A different error term is eliminated each time, and the resulting sequences converge faster and faster. Hence one could compute a derivative very efficiently using

> *within eps (improve (improve (improve (differentiate h0 f x)))) .*

In numerical analysts' terms, this is likely to be a fourth-order method, and it gives an accurate result very quickly. One could even define

> *super s = map second (repeat improve s)*
>
> *second (Cons a (Cons b rest)) = b ,*

which uses *repeat improve* to get a sequence of more and more improved sequences of approximations and constructs a new sequence of approximations by taking the second approximation from each of the improved sequences (it turns out that the second one is the best one to take — it is more accurate than the first and doesn't require any extra work to compute). This algorithm is really very sophisticated — it uses a better and better numerical method as more and more approximations are computed. One could compute derivatives very efficiently indeed with the program:

> *within eps (super (differentiate h0 f x)) .*

This is probably a case of using a sledgehammer to crack a nut, but the point is that even an algorithm as sophisticated as *super* is easily expressed when modularized using lazy evaluation.

### 4.3 *Numerical Integration*

The last example we will discuss in this section is numerical integration. The problem may be stated very simply: Given a real-valued function *f* of one real argument, and two points *a* and *b*, estimate the area under the curve that *f* describes between the points. The easiest way to estimate the area is to assume that *f* is nearly a straight line, in which case the area would be

> *easyintegrate f a b = (f a + f b) \* (b − a)/2 .*

Unfortunately this estimate is likely to be very inaccurate unless *a* and *b* are close together. A better estimate can be made by dividing the interval from *a* to *b* in two, estimating the area on each half, and adding the results. We can define a sequence of better and better approximations to the value of the integral by using the formula above for the first approximation, and then adding together better and better approximations to the integrals on each half to calculate the others. This sequence is computed by the function

$$integrate\ f\ a\ b\ = Cons\ (easyintegrate\ f\ a\ b)$$
$$(map\ addpair\ (zip2\ (integrate\ f\ a\ mid\ )$$
$$(integrate\ f\ mid\ b)))$$
$$\textbf{where}\ mid\ = (a + b)/2\ .$$

The function *zip2* is another standard list-processing function. It takes two lists and returns a list of pairs, each pair consisting of corresponding elements of the two lists. Thus the first pair consists of the first element of the first list and the first element of the second, and so on. We can define *zip2* by

$$zip2\ (Cons\ a\ s)\ (Cons\ b\ t) = \ Cons\ (a, b)\ (zip2\ s\ t)\ .$$

In *integrate*, *zip2* computes a list of pairs of corresponding approximations to the integrals on the two subintervals, and *map addpair* adds the elements of the pairs together to give a list of approximations to the original integral.

Actually, this version of *integrate* is rather inefficient because it continually recomputes values of *f*. As written, *easyintegrate* evaluates *f* at *a* and at *b*, and then the recursive calls of *integrate* re-evaluate each of these. Also, (*f mid*) is evaluated in each recursive call. It is therefore preferable to use the following version, which never recomputes a value of *f*:

$$integrate\ f\ a\ b = \ integ\ f\ a\ b\ (f\ a)\ (f\ b)$$
$$integ\ f\ a\ b\ fa\ fb\ = \quad Cons\quad ((fa + fb) * (b - a)/2)$$
$$map\ addpair(zip2\ (integ\ f\ a\ m\ fa\ fm)$$
$$(integ\ f\ m\ b\ fm\ fb)))$$
$$\textbf{where}\quad m = (a + b)/2$$
$$fm = f\ m\ .$$

The function *integrate* computes an infinite list of better and better approximations to the integral, just as *differentiate* did in the section above. One can therefore just write down integration routines that integrate to any required accuracy, as in

$$within\ eps\ (integrate\ f\ a\ b)$$
$$relative\ eps\ (integrate\ f\ a\ b)\ .$$

This integration algorithm suffers from the same disadvantage as the first differentiation algorithm in the preceding subsection — it converges rather slowly. Once again, it can be improved. The first approximation in the sequence is computed (by *easyintegrate*) using only two points, with a separation of $b - a$. The second approximation also uses the midpoint, so that the separation between neighboring points is only $(b - a)/2$. The third approximation uses this method on each half-interval, so the separation between neighboring points is only $(b - a)/4$. Clearly the separation between neighboring points is halved between each approximation and the next. Taking this separation as $h$, the sequence is a candidate for improvement using the function *improve* defined in the preceding section. Therefore we can now write down quickly converging sequences of approximations to integrals, for example,

> *super* (*integrate sin* 0 4)

and

> *improve* (*integrate f* 0 1)
>
> **where** $f x = 1/(1 + x * x)$ .

(This latter sequence is an eighth-order method for computing $\pi/4$. The second approximation, which requires only five evaluations of $f$ to compute, is correct to five decimal places.)

In this section we have taken a number of numerical algorithms and programmed them functionally, using lazy evaluation as glue to stick their parts together. Thanks to this, we have been able to modularize them in new ways, into generally useful functions such as *within*, *relative*, and *improve*. By combining these parts in various ways we have programmed some quite good numerical algorithms very simply and easily.

## 5 *An Example from Artificial Intelligence*

We have argued that functional languages are powerful primarily because they provide two new kinds of glue: higher-order functions and lazy evaluation. In this section we take a larger example from Artificial Intelligence and show how it can be programmed quite simply using these two kinds of glue.

The example we choose is the alpha-beta "heuristic", an algorithm for estimating how good a position a game-player is in. The algorithm works by looking ahead to see how the game might develop, but it avoids pursuing unprofitable lines.

Let game positions be represented by objects of the type *position*. This type will vary from game to game, and we assume nothing about it. There must be some way of knowing what moves can be made from a position: Assume that there is a function,

> *moves* :: *position* → *listof position* ,

that takes a game-position as its argument and returns the list of all positions that can be reached from it in one move. As an example, Fig. 1 shows *moves* for a couple of positions in tic-tac-toe (noughts and crosses). This assumes that it is always possible to tell which player's turn it is from a position. In tic-tac-toe this can be done by counting the xs and Os; in a game like chess one would have to include the information explicitly in the type *position*.

Given the function *moves*, the first step is to build a game tree. This is a tree in which the nodes are labeled by positions, so that the children of a node are labeled with the positions that can be reached in one move from that node. That is, if a node is labeled with position *p*, then its children are labeled with the positions in (*moves p*). Game trees are not all finite: If it's possible for a game to go on forever with neither side winning, its game tree is infinite. Game trees are exactly like the trees we discussed in Section 2 — each node has a label (the position it represents) and a list of subnodes. We can therefore use the same datatype to represent them.

A game tree is built by repeated applications of *moves*. Starting from the root position, *moves* is used to generate the labels for the subtrees of the root. It is then used again to generate the subtrees of the subtrees and so on. This pattern of recursion can be expressed as a higher-order function,

> *reptree f a = Node a (map (reptree f) (f a))* .

Using this function another can be defined which constructs a game tree from a particular position:

> *gametree p = reptree moves p* .

---

**Figure 1.**   *moves* for two positions in tic-tac-toe.

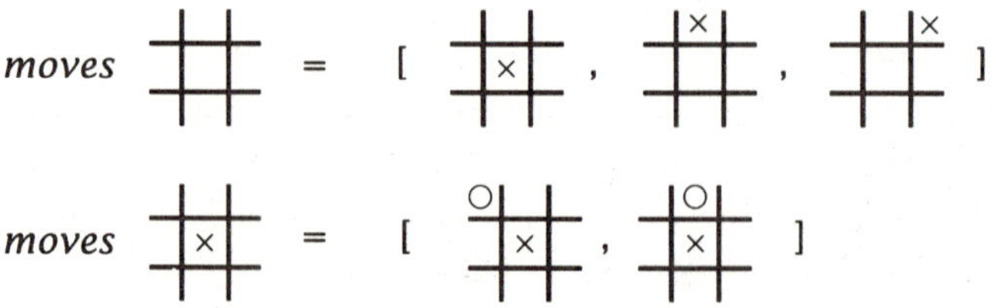

As an example, consider Fig. 2. The higher-order function used here (*reptree*) is analogous to the function *repeat* used to construct infinite lists in the preceding section.

The alpha-beta algorithm looks ahead from a given position to see whether the game will develop favorably or unfavorably, but in order to do so it must be able to make a rough estimate of the value of a position without looking ahead. This "static evaluation" must be used at the limit of the look-ahead, and may be used to guide the algorithm earlier. The result of the static evaluation is a measure of the promise of a position from the computer's point of view (assuming that the computer is playing the game against a human opponent). The larger the result, the better the position for the computer. The smaller the result, the worse the position. The simplest such function would return (say) 1 for positions where the computer has already won, −1 for positions where the computer has already lost, and 0 otherwise. In reality, the static evaluation function measures various things that make a position "look good", for example material advantage and control of the center in chess. Assume that we have such a function,

$$static :: position \rightarrow number.$$

Since a game tree is a (*treeof position*), it can be converted into a (*treeof number*) by the function (*maptree static*), which statically evaluates all the

**Figure 2.**    Part of a game tree for tic-tac-toe.

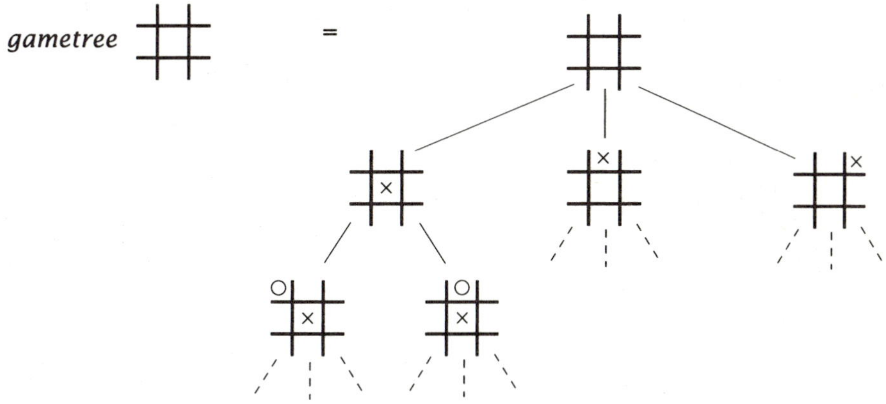

positions in the tree (which may be infinitely many). This uses the function *maptree* defined in Section 2.

Given such a tree of static evaluations, what is the true value of the positions in it? In particular, what value should be ascribed to the root position? Not its static value, since this is only a rough guess. The value ascribed to a node must be determined from the true values of its subnodes. This can be done by assuming that each player makes the best moves possible. Remembering that a high value means a good position for the computer, it is clear that when it is the computer's move from any position, it will choose the move leading to the subnode with the maximum true value. Similarly, the opponent will choose the move leading to the subnode with the minimum true value. Assuming that the computer and its opponent alternate turns, the true value of a node is computed by the function *maximize* if it is the computer's turn and *minimize* if it is not:

> *maximize (Node n sub) = max (map minimize sub)*
>
> *minimize (Node n sub) = min (map maximize sub).*

Here *max* and *min* are functions on lists of numbers that return the maximum and minimum of the list respectively. These definitions are not complete because they recurse forever — there is no base case. We must define the value of a node with no successors, and we take it to be the static evaluation of the node (its label). Therefore the static evaluation is used when either player has already won, or at the limit of look-ahead. The complete definitions of *maximize* and *minimize* are

> *maximize (Node n Nil) = n*
>
> *maximize (Node n sub) = max (map minimize sub)*
>
> *minimize (Node n Nil) = n*
>
> *minimize (Node n sub) = max (map maximize sub).*

One could almost write a function at this stage that would take a position and return its true value. This would be:

> *evaluate = maximize . maptree static . gametree .*

There are two problems with this definition. First of all, it doesn't work for infinite trees, because *maximize* keeps on recursing until it finds a node with no subtrees — an end to the tree. If there is no end then *maximize* will return no result. The second problem is related — even finite game trees (like the one for tic-tac-toe) can be very large indeed. It is unrealistic to try to evaluate the whole of the game tree — the search must be limited to the next few moves. This can be done by pruning the tree to a fixed depth,

$$prune\ 0\ (Node\ a\ x) \qquad = Node\ a\ Nil$$
$$prune\ (n+1)\ (Node\ a\ x)\ = Node\ a\ (map\ (prune\ n)\ x)\ .$$

The function (*prune n*) takes a tree and "cuts off" all nodes further than *n* from the root. If a game tree is pruned it forces *maximize* to use the static evaluation for nodes at depth *n*, instead of recursing further. The function *evaluate* can therefore be defined by

$$evaluate\ =\ maximize\ .\ maptree\ static\ .\ prune\ 5\ .\ gametree\ ,$$

which looks (say) five moves ahead.

Already in this development we have used higher-order functions and lazy evaluation. Higher-order functions *reptree* and *maptree* allow us to construct and manipulate game trees with ease. More importantly, lazy evaluation permits us to modularize *evaluate* in this way. Since *gametree* has a potentially infinite result, this program would never terminate without lazy evaluation. Instead of writing

$$prune\ 5\ .\ gametree\ ,$$

we would have to fold these two functions together into one that constructed only the first five levels of the tree. Worse, even the first five levels may be too large to be held in memory at one time. In the program we have written, the function

$$maptree\ static\ .\ prune\ 5\ .\ gametree$$

constructs parts of the tree only as *maximize* requires them. Since each part can be thrown away (reclaimed by the garbage collector) as soon as *maximize* has finished with it, the whole tree is never resident in memory. Only a small part of the tree is stored at a time. The lazy program is therefore efficient. This efficiency depends on an interaction between *maximize* (the last function in the chain of compositions) and *gametree* (the first); without lazy evaluation, therefore, it could be achieved only by folding all the functions in the chain together into one big one. This would be a drastic reduction in modularity, but it is what is usually done. We can make improvements to this evaluation algorithm by tinkering with each part; this is relatively easy. A conventional programmer must modify the entire program as a unit, which is much harder.

So far we have described only simple minimaxing. The heart of the alpha-beta algorithm is the observation that one can often compute the value returned by *maximize* or *minimize* without looking at the whole tree. Consider the tree:

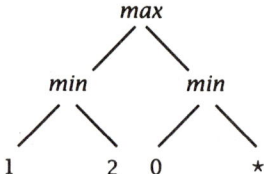

Strangely enough, it is unnecessary to know the value of the asterisk in order to evaluate the tree. The left minimum evaluates to 1, but the right minimum clearly evaluates to something at most 0. Therefore the maximum of the two minima must be 1. This observation can be generalized and built into *maximize* and *minimize*.

The first step is to separate *maximize* into an application of *max* to a list of numbers; that is, we decompose *maximize* as

$$maximize = max \,.\, maximize' \,.$$

(We decompose *minimize* in a similar way. Since *minimize* and *maximize* are entirely symmetrical we shall discuss *maximize* and assume that *minimize* is treated similarly.) Once decomposed in this way, *maximize* can use *minimize'*, rather than *minimize* itself, to discover which numbers *minimize* would take the minimum of. It may then be able to discard some of the numbers without looking at them. Thanks to lazy evaluation, if *maximize* doesn't look at all of the list of numbers, some of them will not be computed, with a potential saving in computer time.

It's easy to "factor out" *max* from the definition of *maximize*, giving

$$
\begin{aligned}
maximize' \; (Node \; n \; Nil) \quad &= \quad Cons \; n \; Nil \\
maximize' \; (Node \; n \; l) \quad &= \quad map \; minimize \; l \\
&= \quad map \; (min \,.\, minimize') \; l \\
&= \quad map \; min \; (map \; minimize' \; l) \\
&= \quad mapmin \; (map \; minimize' \; l) \\
&\hspace{1.2em} \textbf{where} \; mapmin = map \; min \,.
\end{aligned}
$$

Since *minimize'* returns a list of numbers, the minimum of which is the result of *minimize*, (*map minimize' l*) returns a list of lists of numbers, and *maximize'* should return a list of those lists' minima. Only the maximum of this list matters, however. We shall define a new version of *mapmin* that omits the minima of lists whose minimum doesn't matter.

> *mapmin (Cons nums rest)*
>
> = *Cons (min nums) (omit (min nums) rest)* .

The function *omit* is passed a "potential maximum" — the largest minimum seen so far — and omits any minima that are less than this:

> *omit pot Nil = Nil*
>
> *omit pot (Cons nums rest)*
>
> = *omit pot rest,*                              **if** *minleq nums pot*
>
> = *Cons (min nums) (omit (min nums) rest),*  **otherwise** .

The function *minleq* takes a list of numbers and a potential maximum, and it returns *True* if the minimum of the list of numbers does not exceed the potential maximum. To do this, it does not need to look at the entire list! If there is any element in the list less than or equal to the potential maximum, then the minimum of the list is sure to be. All elements after this particular one are irrelevant — they are like the question mark in the example above. Therefore *minleq* can be defined by

> *minleq Nil pot = False*
>
> *minleq (Cons n rest) pot =* *True,*           **if** $n \leq pot$
>
> = *minleq rest pot,*   **otherwise** .

Having defined *maximize'* and *minimize'* in this way it is simple to write a new evaluator:

> *evaluate = max . maximize' . maptree static . prune 8 . gametree* .

Thanks to lazy evaluation, the fact that *maximize'* looks at less of the tree means that the whole program runs more efficiently, just as the fact that *prune* looks at only part of an infinite tree enables the program to terminate. The optimizations in *maximize'*, although fairly simple, can have a dramatic effect on the speed of evaluation and so can allow the evaluator to look further ahead.

Other optimizations can be made to the evaluator. For example, the alpha-beta algorithm just described works best if the best moves are considered first, since if one has found a very good move then there is no need to consider worse moves, other than to demonstrate that the opponent has at least one good reply to them. One might therefore wish to sort the subtrees at each node, putting those with the highest values first when it is the computer's move and those with the lowest values first when it is not. This can be done with the function

> *highfirst (Node n sub) = Node n (sort higher (map lowfirst sub))*
>
> *lowfirst (Node n sub) = Node n (sort (not . higher) (map highfirst sub))*
>
> *higher (Node n1 sub1) (Node n2 sub2) = n1 > n2 ,*

where *sort* is a general-purpose sorting function. The evaluator would now be defined by

> *evaluate*
>
> *= max . maximize' . highfirst . maptree static . prune 8 . gametree .*

One might regard it as sufficient to consider only the three best moves for the computer or the opponent, in order to restrict the search. To program this, it is necessary only to replace *highfirst* with (*taketree 3 . highfirst*), where

> *taketree n =  foldtree (nodett n) Cons Nil*
>
> *nodett n label sub = Node label (take n sub) .*

The function *taketree* replaces all the nodes in a tree with nodes that have at most *n* subnodes, using the function (*take n*), which returns the first *n* elements of a list (or fewer if the list is shorter than *n*).

Another improvement is to refine the pruning. The program above looks ahead a fixed depth even if the position is very dynamic — it may decide to look no further than a position in which the queen is threated in chess, for example. It's usual to define certain "dynamic" positions and not to allow look-ahead to stop in one of these. Assuming a function *dynamic* that recognizes such positions, we need only add one equation to *prune* to do this:

> *prune 0 (Node pos sub)*
>
> *= Node pos (map (prune 0) sub),*  **if** *dynamic pos .*

Making such changes is easy in a program as modular as this one. As we re-marked above, since the program depends crucially for its efficiency on an interaction between *maximize*, the last function in the chain, and *gametree*, the first, in the absence of lazy evaluation it could be written only as a mono-lithic program. Such a programs are hard to write, hard to modify, and very hard to understand.

## 6 *Conclusion*

In this paper, we've argued that modularity is the key to successful pro-gramming. Languages that aim to improve productivity must support modular programming well. But new scope rules and mechanisms for separate compilation are not enough — modularity means more than modules. Our ability to decompose a problem into parts depends directly on our ability to glue solutions together. To support modular programming, a language must provide good glue. Functional programming languages provide two new kinds of glue — higher-order functions and lazy evaluation. Using these glues one can modularize programs in new and useful ways, and we've shown several examples of this. Smaller and more general modules can be reused more widely, easing subsequent programming. This explains why functional programs are so much smaller and easier to write than conventional ones. It also provides a target for functional programmers to aim at. If any part of a program is messy or complicated, the programmer should attempt to modularize it and to generalize the parts. He or she should expect to use higher-order functions and lazy evaluation as the tools for doing this.

Of course, we are not the first to point out the power and elegance of higher-order functions and lazy evaluation. For example, Turner shows how both can be used to great advantage in a program for generating chemical structures [3]. Abelson and Sussman stress that streams (lazy lists) are a powerful tool for structuring programs [1]. Henderson has used streams to structure functional operating systems [2]. But perhaps we place more stress on functional programs' modularity than previous authors.

This paper is also relevant to the present controversy over lazy evaluation. Some believe that functional languages should be lazy; others believe they should not. Some compromise and provide only lazy lists, with a special syntax for constructing them (as, for example, in SCHEME [1]). This paper provides further evidence that lazy evaluation is too important to be relegated to second-class citizenship. It is perhaps the most powerful glue functional programmers possess. One should not obstruct access to such a vital tool.

## *Acknowledgments*

This paper owes much to many conversations with Phil Wadler and Richard Bird in the Programming Research Group at Oxford. Magnus Bondesson at Chalmers University, Göteborg, pointed out a serious error in an earlier version of one of the numerical algorithms, and thereby prompted development of many of the others. Ham Richards and David Turner did a superb editorial job, including converting the notation to Miranda. This work was carried out with the support of a Research Fellowship from the U.K. Science and Engineering Research Council.

## *References*

[1] Abelson, H. and Sussman, G. J. *The Structure and Interpretation of Computer Programs.* MIT Press, Cambridge, Mass., 1984.

[2] Henderson, P. "Purely functional operating systems". In *Functional Programming and its Applications.* Cambridge University Press, Cambridge, 1982.

[3] Turner, D. A. "The semantic elegance of applicative languages". In *ACM Symposium on Functional Languages and Computer Architecture* (Wentworth, N.H.). ACM, New York, 1981.

[4] Turner, D. A. "An overview of Miranda". *SIGPLAN Notices,* December 1986 (reproduced in this volume).

[5] United States Department of Defense. *The Programming Language Ada Reference Manual.* Springer-Verlag, Berlin, 1980.

[6] Wirth, N. *Programming in Modula–II.* Springer-Verlag, Berlin, 1982.

# Exact Real Arithmetic

## Formulating Real Numbers as Functions

## 3

**Hans Boehm**
**Robert Cartwright**
Rice University

## Abstract

*T*his paper describes our recent experience with several different approaches to performing exact real arithmetic on a computer. The implementation of exact real arithmetic is a challenging research problem because the computational properties of higher-order data objects like the constructive real numbers are counterintuitive. Contrary to our expectations, lazy implementations of the constructive real numbers (based on positional radix notation) perform very poorly. In hindsight, we discovered a simple explanation for this behavior: The granularity in precision imposed by radix notation (in the context of a large base) forces unnecessary computation. On the other hand, implementations based on the explicit functional representation favored by constructive mathematicians perform surprisingly well—despite the fact that this strategy appears poorly suited to incremental evaluation.

Our best functional implementation is fast enough to solve interesting numerical problems, such as finding the solution to a linear system of equations. As machines become faster and more explicitly parallel, we expect exact real arithmetic to become an attractive alternative to limited precision arithmetic for applications where execution efficiency is not critical.

An intriguing property of the constructive real numbers is the fact that they cannot be formulated as an *abstract* data type extending a sequential[1] programming language. We prove that a *universal* set of primitive operations over the constructive reals must include either a representation-dependent operation or a nonsequential operation (such as parallel-or).

---

## 1 *Introduction*

Scientists and engineers typically solve computational problems involving real numbers by performing approximate calculations with limited precision arithmetic. To cope with errors introduced by inexact arithmetic, numerical analysts have devised a wide variety of methods for computing approximate solutions that are relatively insensitive to rounding errors. As a result, contemporary programming languages and systems ignore the possibility of performing exact real arithmetic.

We first became interested in exact real arithmetic because we had an immediate practical need for it. As part of the $\mathbb{R}^n$ project to support scientific program development [12], we are building a program validation system that tests programs against executable formal specifications. The $\mathbb{R}^n$ program validation system is a pragmatic alternative to a formal program verification system. Instead of trying to prove that a program satisfies its formal specifications, it evaluates both the program and its specifications on a representative collection of test data. In essence, the validation system tests the the verification conditions for the program rather than proving them. We call this process *formal program testing*.

Most scientific programs rely on floating-point arithmetic to compute approximate answers to mathematical problems that in principle have exact answers. Numerical analysts have developed two complementary methods for specifying the accuracy of the approximate answers computed by floating-point programs [27]. The most obvious method, called *forward specification*, stipulates a bound on the distance between the exact solution to the input problem and the solution computed by the program (using floating-point arithmetic). The other method, called *backward specification*, stipulates a bound on the distance between the input problem and the nearest problem

---

1. For a precise definition of this term, see Section 5.

that the computed solution solves *exactly*.

These two specification methods are best explained by considering a simple example. Assume that we want to write a floating-point program $P$ to solve the linear system

$$A\mathbf{x} = \mathbf{b}$$

for the vector $\mathbf{x}$ given a nonsingular square matrix $A$ and vector $\mathbf{b}$. A forward specification for $P$ has the form

$$\|A\mathbf{x}' - \mathbf{b}\| < \epsilon[A, \mathbf{b}]$$

where $\mathbf{x}'$ denotes the approximate solution computed by the program, $\|\ \|$ is a suitable matrix norm, and $\epsilon[A, \mathbf{b}]$ is an expression[2] stipulating the error bound that the program is supposed to satisfy. A backward specification for the same program has the form

$$\|A - \alpha[A, \mathbf{b}, \mathbf{x}']\| < \delta[A, \mathbf{b}] \,,$$

where $\mathbf{x}'$ denotes the approximate solution computed by the program, $\alpha[A, \mathbf{b}, \mathbf{x}']$ is an expression defining the nearest matrix[3] $A'$ to $A$ such that

$$A'\mathbf{x}' = \mathbf{b} \,,$$

and $\delta[A, \mathbf{b}]$ is an expression stipulating a bound on the distance between $A$ and $A'$. Since the expression $\alpha[A, \mathbf{b}, \mathbf{x}']$ depends on $A$, $\mathbf{b}$, and $\mathbf{x}'$, the backward specification is a simple predicate on $A$, $\mathbf{b}$, and $\mathbf{x}'$. In the Frobenius norm (where $\|A\| = sqrt(\sum_{i,j} a_{i,j})$)

$$\alpha[A, \mathbf{b}, \mathbf{x}'] = A + \frac{(\mathbf{b} - A\mathbf{x}')\mathbf{x}'^T}{\mathbf{x}'^T\mathbf{x}'} \ .$$

Regardless of which form of specification (forward or backward) a programmer uses to document a floating-point program, the evaluation of the program *specification* on actual test data requires exact real arithmetic. Otherwise, the evaluation process will not correctly determine whether or not the program specification is satisfied.

Exact real arithmetic has many other potential applications in scientific programming where very high precision and a more abstract programming model[4] are more important than execution efficiency. With an appropriate set of programming tools, scientists and engineers could use exact real arithmetic to solve computational problems without worrying about the myriad of

---

2. in the variables $A$ and $\mathbf{b}$
3. relative to the norm $\|\ \|$
4. since roundoff error is nonexistent

programming details (e.g., scaling, order of evaluation, and error estimates) inherent in conventional numerical programming.

Although any computation involving the constructive reals—no matter how efficient the underlying implementation—will almost certainly require more computational resources than the corresponding computation using floating-point arithmetic, the plummeting cost of computer resources suggests that exact arithmetic may become an attractive option in some scientific and engineering applications. Moreover, since many of the atomic steps in exact arithmetic operations (e.g., operations on individual digits) can be performed in parallel, exact real arithmetic is potentially more competitive in efficiency with floating-point arithmetic on some parallel architectures than on conventional uniprocessors. In the future, we anticipate that exact real arithmetic will be a standard feature in high-level programming languages intended for program prototyping and effective specification—just as floating-point arithmetic is a standard feature in general purpose languages.

This paper decribes our recent experience with designing and implementing systems to perform exact real arithmetic. Section 2 briefly reviews the mathematical foundations of exact real arithmetic. Section 3 describes implementation schemes based on *lazy evaluation*—an approach that proved both more complex and less efficient than we expected. Section 4 discusses implementation schemes based on representing constructive real numbers as functions over the rational numbers—a strategy that works surprisingly well and forms the basis for our best implementation. Section 5 addresses the problem of formulating the constructive real numbers as an abstract data type. We prove that the constructive reals cannot be defined as an abstract type consisting of a finite set of sequential, extensional (representation-independent) operations. Section 6 briefly reviews previous research on exact real arithmetic and closely related topics. Finally, Section 7 identifies future topics for research in the area of exact real arithmetic.

## 2 *Mathematical Foundations*

Since there are uncountably many real numbers but only countably many possible data representations, we obviously cannot represent every real number in a computer. Fortunately, there is a countable subset of the real numbers, appropriately dubbed the *constructive reals* (cf. [5, 10, 2]), *recursive reals*, or the *representable reals*, that is closed under all the functions that normally arise in analysis. Moreover, all of the basic operations $\{+, -, \times, /\}$[5] are computable on the constructive reals—assuming that the numbers are

---

5. In the context of the basic operations on the constructive real numbers, we will use the − sign to denote unary negation instead of subtraction.

expressed in a suitable representation.

The intuition underlying the definition of the constructive reals is simple: for the representation of a real number $x$ to have computational significance, there must be a procedure for computing finite approximations to $x$ to arbitrary accuracy. More formally, a real number $x$ is *constructive* if and only if there exists a computable function $f_x$ on the rational numbers with the following property: For any given rational tolerance $\delta$, $|f_x(\delta) - x| \leq \delta$. Any such function $f_x$ is called a *functional representation* for $x$. Two functional representations $f$ and $g$ are equivalent (denoted $f \equiv g$) if and only if they represent the same real number.

Although all of the basic arithmetic operations on constructive real numbers are computable, the standard relational operations $\{<, =, \leq\}$ are not. For each relation $R \in \{<, =, \leq\}$, it is easy to prove that $R$ is not decidable by reducing membership in $K = \{i \mid$ Turing machine $M_i$ halts on $i\}$ to the decidability of $R$. In particular, $i \in K$ iff $\mu_i > 0(\mu_i \neq 0)$ $(\neg[\mu_i \leq 0])$ where $\mu_i$ is the functional representation defined by:[6]

$$\mu_i\left(\frac{1}{2^k}\right) = \begin{cases} 1/2^l & \text{if } M_i(i) \text{ halts in exactly } l \text{ steps and } l \leq k \\ 0 & \text{otherwise.} \end{cases}$$

In practice, there are two different strategies for overcoming this problem.

First, we can define a quasi-relational comparison operator $<_\epsilon$ that is accurate to the specified rational tolerance $\epsilon$. Given any rational number $\epsilon$, $<_\epsilon$ has the following definition:

$$x <_\epsilon y = \begin{cases} \textit{true} & \text{if } x < y - \epsilon \\ \textit{false} & \text{if } x \geq y \\ \text{either } \textit{true} \text{ or } \textit{false} & \text{otherwise.} \end{cases}$$

In other words, $x <_\epsilon y$ implies $x < y$, but $\neg(x <_\epsilon y)$ implies $x + \epsilon \geq y$.

Second, we can view the exact real numbers as a Scott-domain [23, 24] including partial elements (functional representations that diverge) and define the arithmetic conditional operation

**if** $x < 0$ **then** $y$ **else** $z$

that returns $y$ if $x < 0$, $z$ if $x > 0$, and $y \sqcap z$ (the largest partial element that approximates both $y$ and $z$) if $x = 0$. Some facility for execution

---

6. The definition, which applies only to inputs of the form $\frac{1}{2^k}$, can be extended trivially to all rational numbers by coercing an arbitrary input $x$ to the largest rational number $x'$ of the form $\frac{m}{2^k}$ such that $x' \leq x$.

interleaving (dovetailing) is necessary to implement this form of the conditional.

An example that llustrates the difference between these two approaches is the definition of the absolute value function $|\ |$. If we use the quasi-relational comparison operator $<_\epsilon$, the definition has the following form:

$$|x| = \lambda \epsilon . \, if \, x <_\epsilon 0 \; then \; -f_x(\epsilon) \; else \; f_x(\epsilon)$$

where $f_x$ is the functional representation for $x$. In contrast, the definition using the dovetailed arithmetic conditional avoids introducing the tolerance parameter $\epsilon$ and revealing the representation of $x$:

$$|x| = if \, x < 0 \; then \; -x \; else \; x.$$

The principal advantage of the quasi-relational comparison operator is that it does not require dovetailed evaluation, making it much easier to implement efficiently. On the other hand, it is less abstract than the arithmetic conditional because its behavior depends on the representations of its arguments (if they are close together). In practice, we have found that the intensional behavior of the quasi-relational comparison operator does not pose a problem. To evaluate an expression $E$ containing a comparison, we can typically determine the comparison tolerance $\delta$ required to compute the value of $E$ to a given tolerance $\epsilon$—*regardless of the result of the comparison*. If no such tolerance $\delta$ exists, then the function defined by the expression must diverge for some inputs.[7]

If we allow relational operators to diverge when their inputs are equal, then the standard relational operators $\{<, =, \leq\}$ are easy to compute. In fact, it is straightforward to define "partial" operators for $\{<, =, \leq\}$ by writing conventional sequential programs (using $<_\epsilon$ as a primitive operation) to compute them. For example, the following recursive definition computes the partial $<$ operation:

$$x < y = less(x, y, 1) \, ;$$

$$less(x, y, tol) = \begin{cases} true & \text{if } x <_{tol} y \\ false & \text{if } y <_{tol} x \\ less\left(x, y, \frac{tol}{2}\right) & \text{otherwise}\,. \end{cases}$$

---

7. It is easy to show that a computable function over the constructive reals defined on the open interval $(x, y)$ is continuous on $(x, y)$.

## 3 *Lazy Implementations*

In the literature on functional programming, lazy evaluation [16, 14, 13] has frequently been suggested as the appropriate strategy for implementing infinite data objects that have natural representations as streams of symbols because it computes only the elements required to produce an answer and it adroitly avoids recalculating elements computed earlier. Consequently, we initially focused our attention on implementing the constructive real numbers as infinite streams of digits.

### 3.1 *Lazy Representation Schemes*

Although this approach is natural and elegant, it is surprisingly difficult to define a satisfactory stream representation for the constructive reals. The classical mathematical literature (see [17, Section 4.5]) describes two fundamentally different systems of notation for the real numbers as potentially infinite streams of digits: the positional radix representation and the continued fraction representation. In naive form, the positional radix model with radix $B$ represents real numbers as triples consisting of a sign, an unbounded integer exponent, and a lazy sequence of digits in the range $[0, B)$ specifying the fraction. The naive form of the continued fraction representation is similar: A real number is represented as a pair consisting of an integer whole part $e_0$ (which is either positive or negative) and a lazy (possibly finite) sequence of positive integers $e_1, e_2, \ldots$ that specify the *entries* in the continued fraction:

$$e_0 + \cfrac{1}{e_1 + \cfrac{1}{e_2 + \ldots}}.$$

If we impose the restriction that the last entry in a finite continued fraction cannot have the value 1, then the continued fraction representation for every real number is unique.

Unfortunately, there is a subtle flaw in both of these naive formulations. The evaluation mechanism underlying lazy sequences is monotonic; once a digit has been computed it never changes. Although this property makes incremental evaluation easy, it also makes the standard arithmetic operations on the constructive reals uncomputable in some cases.[8]

Consider the following example in positional radix notation with radix 10. Let $x$ and $y$ denote the repeating decimal numbers $.44444\ldots$ and $.55555\ldots$, respectively. The sum $x + y$ has the value $.99999\ldots = 1.0$ but the addition operation cannot determine whether the units digit in the fraction should

---

8. After we discovered this problem, we subsequently learned that constructive mathematicians were already aware of it[22, (see especially p. 371)],[19].

be 0 or 1—no matter how many digits of $x$ and $y$ it inspects! The unknown contents of their infinite tails could force the units digit to be either a 0 or 1. If the sum of the unexplored tail of $x$ plus the unexplored tail of $y$ generates a carry then the units digit in the result must be 1. On the other hand, if the sum of the unexplored tails is less than an infinite sequence of 9's, then the units digit must be 0.

The preceding example is not an isolated phenomenon. Exactly the same problem arises in many different contexts in both the radix expansion model and the continued fraction model. For example, the subtraction operation in both models cannot determine the sign of the number $x-x$, regardless of the value of $x$. Rigorous proofs of these results appear in [8].

Fortunately, there are refinements of both representation schemes that overcome this problem. The refinement of the positional radix model consists of two minor but important modifications:[9]

> First, the sign bit can be eliminated by using a "balanced" radix notation [17, Section 4.5] in which digits can be positive as well as negative. Although the best-known balanced system is balanced ternary (with a radix of 3 and digit values of −1, 0, and 1), any odd, positive radix (greater than 1) works equally well.

> Second, the monotonicity problem in the representation of the fraction as a lazy sequence can be overcome by allowing the range of digits to be larger than the radix, making the radix notation highly redundant. An interesting side-effect of allowing redundancy is that balanced radix notation can be extended to even radixes (including, of course, powers of 2). Representational redundancy weakens the connection between the numerical *value* of an initial segment of a fraction and its representation as a lazy sequence. As a result, the numerical values corresponding to initial segments of a lazy sequence are not necessarily monotonic even though the sequence itself is still monotonic. Representational redundancy enables the evaluator to generate carries (up to a bound determined by the degree of redundancy) for a digit that has already been generated and store them in the generating digit position by using redundant digit values.

A similar refinement of the continued fraction representation has recently been developed by Jean Vuillemin [25]. His representation scheme generalizes the continued fraction model by permitting the entries in a continued fraction to be negative. To ensure convergence, he imposes a complex invari-

---

9. A search of the hardware design literature revealed that a similar representation scheme had previously been proposed and studied by [4] for other reasons.

ant on the sequence of entries in the continued fraction. One of the most interesting and potentially useful properties of Vuillemin's continued fraction representation is that it captures the *projective* real numbers instead of the conventional affine real numbers. In other words, his representation scheme includes the number $\infty$ as an element in the domain.[10]

### 3.2  *Experience with Lazy Implementations*

After we realized that we could solve the computability problem by using redundancy, we constructed several lazy implementations of the constructive reals in Scheme and Russell [6]. Since the evaluation of digits must be performed incrementally, we simply adapted and tuned the familiar elementary-school algorithms for the basic arithmetic operations $\{+, -, \times, /\}$ yielding linear algorithms (in the number of digits in the answer) for addition and negation and a quadratic algorithm for multiplication. The incremental nature of the evaluation process prevented us from applying standard tricks to speed up multiplication and division (e.g., Karatsuba's algorithm for multiplication [3, Section 2.6]). The algorithms for addition and multiplication are given in [8].

Despite the simplicity and elegance of this approach, its performance is disappointing. An unoptimized explicitly functional implementation (see Section 4) was two orders of magnitude faster than our best lazy implementation on most benchmarks. Given this information as hindsight, we discovered that our lazy implementation strategy was inherently inefficient. In order to exploit hardware arithmetic on conventional machines and avoid excessive storage management overhead, a radix representation must use a radix comparable in size to the largest machine integer (approximately $2^{31}$ on most machines). Unfortunately, a large radix forces arithmetic operations to evaluate arguments to more accuracy than necessary because *the precision must be a power of the radix*. For example, to compute the $n$th digit of a sum $a+b$ of two operands $a$ and $b$, the addition operation must evaluate the *entire* $(n+1)$th digits of $a$ and $b$, even though the leading bits alone provide enough information to determine the answer.[11] In the evaluation of an expression containing a long chain of addition operations, this "granularity" effect forces the leaves of the expressions to be evaluated to much more precision than is necessary to mathematically determine the answer. This effect can be compounded in recursive algorithms. The running time of the standard incremental division algorithm (based on the manual division algorithm taught in elementary school), for example, is exponential rather than quadratic because the granularity effect forces unnecessary evaluation.

---

10. For any $x \neq 0$, $x/0 = \infty$.
11. The redundant notation ensures that this is enough to detect a possible carry.

These negative conclusions prompted us to focus our attention on the functional representation scheme discussed in the next section.

## 4 Functional Implementations

In a functional implementation, a constructive real number $r$ is represented by a computable function $f_r$ on the rational numbers where $f_r(\delta)$ approximates $r$ to accuracy $\delta$. One of the obvious advantages of the functional scheme is that the algorithms for addition, negation, and multiplication essentially reduce to the corresponding operations on unbounded integers. Hence, it is possible to compute $n$ digits of a product in less than quadratic time (e.g., $O(n^{1.59})$ using Karatsuba's algorithm [3, Section 2.6]). In our implementation, we simplified the algorithms for the arithmetic operations by restricting input tolerances to the form $\frac{1}{4^k}$ and the corresponding output approximations to the form $\frac{m}{4^k}$ where $k$ and $m$ are integers.[12] As a result, we can represent every constructive real number $x$ by a function $f_x$ mapping integers to integers. The function $f_x$ obeys the following inequality:

$$\left| x - \frac{f_x(k)}{4^k} \right| \leq \frac{1}{4^k} .$$

Given this form of functional representation, the algorithm for the addition operation is simply

$$add(f_x, f_y) = \lambda k.(f_x(k+1) + f_y(k+1)) \ \textbf{div} \ 4 ,$$

where **div** denotes the division operator that rounds its result to the nearest integer. The algorithm for negation is even simpler:

$$neg(f_x) = \lambda k. -f_x(k) .$$

The algorithm for multiplication follows the same pattern as the algorithm for addition but it is more complicated because the argument precision required to produce a result of a given precision depends on the arguments.

Although it is clearly possible to implement an analogous algorithm for division, it is much more complex than multiplication. Consequently, our implementation performs division by computing the reciprocal of the divisor (using Newton's method) and multiplying the reciprocal by the dividend. A more detailed description of the multiplication and division algorithms appears in [9].

---

12. Radix 2 may be more efficient, but the use of radix 4 significantly simplifies the addition algorithm.

## 4.1 *Optimizations to Functional Implementations*

There are many optimizations that can improve the performance of a functional implementation. In our experience, three optimizations have proven most important:

> First, we maintain the best computed approximation for a number as part of its representation. This information permits less accurate approximations to be computed trivially and provides an estimate (required by the reciprocal operation for example) as a seed for more accurate approximations.

> Second, we compute floating-point interval bounds [18] as part of the representation of every constructive real number. These bounds eliminate the need to apply the functional representation to the demanded tolerance if the bounded interval is sufficiently small.

> Third, we represent hereditarily rational numbers[13] explicitly as pairs of unbounded integers. In computations that rely exclusively on the basic arithmetic and relational operations, this optimization reduces the implementation of the constructive reals to conventional rational arithmetic.

## 4.2 *Experience with Functional Implementations*

Our functional implementations of the constructive reals are accessible through a desk calculator and a FORTRAN 77 interpreter.[14] These systems perform exactly like their conventional counterparts except that they use exact real arithmetic instead of limited precision arithmetic.

The desk calculator displays answers in truncated positional radix notation but guarantees that the displayed result is accurate to within 1 unit in the least significant digit. *This invariant is true independent of the number of steps needed to compute the result.* The window on the result can be moved to the right to display more digits of the exact answer, forcing the displayed expression to be evaluated to higher precision (depending on the accuracy of the current internal approximation). A similar facility for inspecting the values of variables is provided by the interpreter.

Performance results have been encouraging, particularly in view of the intended applications. Our best implementation is fast enough for routine use

---

13. A number appearing in a program computation is *hereditarily rational* if an only if it is either a rational constant or the result of applying a basic arithmetic operation {+, −, ×, /} to arguments that are hereditarily rational.
14. For a core subset of the language.

in a desk calculator program. Evaluations of trigonometric functions to several hundred digits introduce a perceptible lag, but this is neither surprising nor a serious problem.

The interpreter is clearly more demanding. Currently the solution of an extremely ill-conditioned 8-by-8 system of linear equations using Gaussian elimination takes about 30 seconds on a Sun-3/280 workstation.[15] Nevertheless, the implementation is fast enough to solve problems of modest size, including many of those that arise in program testing. We expect that a combination of hardware advances and improved implementation methods will make exact real arithmetic more competitive with limited precision arithmetic. We are particularly excited by the prospects for efficient parallel implementation of exact real arithmetic, since the primitive arithmetic operations involve many subcomputations that can be performed in parallel.

## 5 *The Constructive Reals as an Abstract Type*

One of the more interesting problems that we encountered in implementing the constructive real numbers was choosing an appropriate set of primitive operations. We originally hoped to formulate the constructive real numbers $\mathbf{R}$ as an abstract data type $\mathbf{T} = \langle R_T, F_T, \alpha_T \rangle$ consisting of a universe of representations $R_T$, a finite set of strict[16] operations $F_T$ over the types $\{R_T, Integer, Boolean\}$, and an abstraction function $\alpha_T$ mapping $R_T$ onto $\mathbf{R}$. To qualify as an *abstract* implementation of the constructive real numbers $\mathbf{R}$, an abstract data type $\mathbf{T}$ must satisfy the following two properties.

1. *Universality.* $\mathbf{T}$ is *universal* if and only if for any computable function $f$ on $\mathbf{R}$, it is possible to write a program for $f$ in a standard procedural language (e.g., C or Pascal) augmented by $F_T$.

2. *Extensionality* (Representation-independence). $\mathbf{T}$ is *extensional* (*representation-independent*) if and only if every operation in $F_T$ is well-defined with respect to the equivalence relation $\equiv$ defined by:

$$x \equiv y \ \leftrightarrow \ \alpha_T(x) = \alpha_T(y).$$

In other words, every operation in $F_T$ must produce results that are independent of the choice of representation in $R_T$.

---

15. This figure does not presume the special representation for rational numbers discussed above, which reduces the running time by an order of magnitude. Well-conditioned problems run a little faster since they do not require as much precision in intermediate calculations.

16. A $k$-ary function $f$ is strict in its $i$th argument if and only if

$$\forall x_1, \ldots, x_{i-1}, x_{i+1}, \ldots, x_k \ \ f(x_1, \ldots, x_{i-1}, \bot, x_{i+1}, \ldots, x_k) = \bot.$$

Unfortunately, there is no natural finite set of operations on the constructive reals that satisfies the preceding two properties. The following mathematical exposition justifies this claim.

## 5.1 *Mathematical Details*

**Definition**    An open subset of $\mathbf{R}^n$ is *effectively open* if there is a procedure to decide whether the open cube of size $\frac{1}{n}(n > 0)$ centered at the *rational* point $p = (\frac{i_1}{j_1}, \ldots, \frac{i_n}{j_n})$ lies within the set.

**Definition**    A computable function is *strongly computable* if the set of points on which it is defined forms an effectively open set.

**Observation**    All functions normally encountered in elementary analysis are either strongly computable or can be extended to functions that are strongly computable.

**Justification**    It is easy to show that every computable total function is strongly computable. Hence, most of the standard functions in elementary analysis including $\{+, -, \times, sin, cos, exp\}$ are strongly computable. Only five notable functions in analysis are not total: / (division), reciprocal *log*, *tan*, and *sqrt*. Fortunately, it is easy to show that each of these operations is either a strongly computable function or a restriction of a strongly computable function.

(i) The division function is defined on pairs $(x, y)$ such that $y \neq 0$, which is an effectively open set. To test whether the cube of size $\frac{1}{n}$ surrounding a rational point $(x, y)$ does not intersect the line $y = 0$, we simply check that $|y| - \frac{1}{n} \geq 0$.

(ii) Since the reciprocal function is a special case of the division function (when the numerator is 1), the reciprocal function is strongly computable by essentially the same argument as in case (i) above.

(iii) The *log* function is defined on all positive reals, which is an effectively open set. To test whether the cube of size $\frac{1}{n}$ surrounding the rational point $x$ contains only positive reals, we check that $x - \frac{1}{n} \geq 0$.

(iv) The *tan* function is defined for all real numbers other than those of the form $k + \frac{\pi}{2}$ where $k$ is an integer. This domain is an effectively open set because we can decide whether the distance between a rational point $x$ and $k + \frac{\pi}{2}$ is less than $\frac{1}{n}$. Comparisons between rational and irrational numbers always terminate.

**(v)** The *sqrt* function is not strongly computable, since it is defined on a closed set. However, $\lambda x.\sqrt{|x|}$ is a computable extension of the *sqrt* function that is total.

**Definition**   A finite collection $F$ of operations (constants and functions) over the constructive reals is *acceptable* if and only if

**(i)** every function in $F$ is strongly computable, and

**(ii)** $F$ includes the constants $\{0, 1\}$ and the functions $\{+, /\}$ over the constructive reals.

**Definition**   Given an acceptable collection $F$ of operations on the constructive reals, we define a *program-expression* over $F$ to be an expression constructed from the operation symbols for $F$, a fixed collection of *variables*, and a distinguished input variable **In**. We define a *program* over $F$ as any string in the language determined by the following context-free grammar with root symbol *program*:

> *program*   $\longrightarrow$   *program statement* | *statement*
>
> *statement*   $\longrightarrow$   *variable* := *program-expression*
>
> | **Out** := *program-expression*
>
> | **while** *program-expression* > 0 **do** *program*

We interpret a program $P$ as a definition of a unary function $f_P$ mapping the initial value of a variable **In** to the final value of the variable **Out**. The formal inductive definition of $f_P$ in terms of $P$ is straightforward and omitted for the sake of brevity. However, it is important to note that **while** loops continue as long as the control expression is positive; they terminate if it becomes negative. If the control expression ever becomes zero, the program diverges.

## Lemma

For every recursive function $g$ on the integers, there is a program $P$ such that for each integer $n$, $g(n) = f_P(n)$. That is $P$, when restricted to the integers, computes $g$.

**Proof**   A **while** loop with an integer test can be simulated by subtracting $\frac{1}{2}$ from the control expression, thus insuring that the test will converge for integer valued expressions. A conditional statement can be simulated by a loop containing a test on a control variable that is initialized to +1 and set to −1 at the end of the loop body. It is well known that these statements together with assignment, addition, 0, and 1 are sufficient to ensure that this language can define all *partial recursive* functions (functions computable by a Turing machine).    □

The preceding lemma demonstrates that our definition of *program* over the constructive reals is expressive. We can simulate arbitrary computations over the integers by performing the corresponding computations over the constructive reals.

## Lemma

For every program $P$ such that $f_P$ is total (on the constructive reals) there is a program $Q$ with $f_P = f_Q$ of the form:

**Out** := *program-expression mentioning no variables other than* **In** .

**Proof**    Consider execution traces of $P$ consisting of assignments and **while** conditions in the order in which they were executed. We claim that such traces must be independent of the input to $P$. Otherwise, there must be a first **while** condition $E > 0$ where two traces differ. Since the value of $E$ is a continuous function of the input **In**, there must be a value of **In** for which $E$ evaluates to zero (*cf.* [2, Thm 7.5, p.63]). This fact contradicts the assumption that $P$ computes a total function.    □

We now formulate the main theorem.

## Theorem

For every acceptable collection of functions $F$, there is a unary total function $g$ on the constructive reals such that there is no program over $F$ that computes $g$.

**Proof**    We will explicitly construct $g$ by diagonalization over all programs over $F$. By the preceding lemma, we know that program-expressions are the only programs that must be considered. The diagonalization is a trivial construction if all functions in $F$ are total. The following argument allows us to restrict the diagonalization to total functions.

Consider a computable function $f$ defined on an effectively open set $S$. Since $S$ is effectively open, there exists an algorithm $A$ that determines whether a $\frac{1}{n}$ cube surrounding a rational point $r$ is contained in $S$.

We define a sequence of *total* approximations $f_1, \ldots, f_n, \ldots$ to $f$ as follows. For the sake of simplicity, we will initially assume that $f$ is unary and later generalize the definition to functions of higher arity.

**1.** We define $f_n$ to be identical to $f$ on every interval $[\frac{i}{n}, \frac{i+1}{n}]$ where $A$ determines that the "cubes" of size $\frac{1}{n}$ centered on the endpoints $\frac{i}{n}$ and $\frac{i+1}{n}$ lie within

*S*. An affirmative answer for both endpoints insures that *f* is total over the interval.

**2.** We define $f_n$ to be identically zero on every interval $[\frac{i}{n}, \frac{i+1}{n}]$ such that *A* answers in the negative for both endpoints.

**3.** If *A* answers negatively for one endpoint, and affirmatively on the other, we define $f_n$ to be zero at the former and identical to *f* at the latter, and interpolate linearly in the interior of the interval.

The definition of the sequence of approximations $f_1, \ldots, f_n, \ldots$ is easily extended to functions of higher arity. In this case we run *A* on grid points corresponding to denominators of *n* for all of the coordinates. We define $f_n$ to be zero at all grid points at which *A* gives a negative answer, and identical to *f* at all grid points at which it gives a positive answer. If all corners of a cube in this grid are in the latter category, we take $f_n$ to be identical to *f* over the entire cube. Otherwise we interpolate suitably.

## Lemma

Any approximation $f_n$ to a function *f* is total.

**Proof**   Straightforward. It is not necessary to decide in which cube the arguments to $f_n$ reside to produce an approximate answer, since $f_n$ is clearly continuous.   □

## Lemma

For any function *f* (defined on an effectively open set) and any constructive real *x* in the domain of *f*, there is an *n* such that $f_n$ is identical to *f* on a $\frac{1}{n}$ (closed) cube surrounding *x*.

**Proof**   Since the domain of *f* is open, there must be an *m* such that *f* is defined on a $\frac{1}{m}$ cube surrounding *x*. Take *n* to be 2*m*. Clearly all the surrounding grid points must be inside a $\frac{1}{m}$ cube on which *f* is defined.   □

## Lemma

Let *F* be an acceptable collection of functions. Let $F_n$ denote the collection of *n*th total approximations of the functions in *F*. Let *E* be a program-expression over *F* mentioning no variables other than **In**. Let $f_E$ be the (unary) function defined by *E*, and let $f_{E,n}$ be the function defined by *E* when reinterpreted as an expression over $F_n$. For any *x* in the domain of $f_E$, there is an *n* such that $f_E$ is identical to $f_{E,n}$ on a $\frac{1}{n}$ cube surrounding *x*.

**Proof**   The proof proceeds by induction on the structure of *E*. If *E* is the variable **In**, the result is trivial. Thus we can assume that $E$ has the form

$$h(E_1, \ldots, E_k).$$

(In the following discussion we will not distinguish between the symbol $h$ in the expression $E$ and the corresponding function in $F$. It should be apparent from context which meaning is intended.) From the preceding lemma, there is an $m$ such that $h$ is identical to $h_n$ on a $\frac{1}{m}$ closed cube surrounding $(f_{E_1}(x), \ldots, f_{E_k}(x))$. By induction hypothesis, for each $i$, there is an $m_i$ such that $f_{E_i, m_i}$ is identical to $f_{E_i}$ on a $\frac{1}{m_i}$ cube surrounding $x$. It follows from the continuity of $f_{E_i}$ that there is an $n_i$ such that for every $y$ in the $\frac{1}{n_i}$ cube surrounding $x$, $f_{E_i}(y)$ lies within the $\frac{1}{m}$ cube surrounding $f_{E_i}(x)$. Take $n$ to be the maximum of all the $n_i$ and $m_i$. The lemma follows.    $\square$

We are now in a position to construct the diagonal function $g$ for the main theorem. Our goal is to ensure that it is not equal to any $f_E$ for any program-expression $E$ mentioning only the input variable **In**. We do this by diagonalizing over all triples $(E, I, n)$, where $E$ is a program-expression, $I$ is an interval with rational endpoints, and $n$ is a number specifying which approximations of $F$ to use in the evaluation of $E$. The diagonalization step corresponding to $(E, I, n)$ will guarantee that $f_{E,n}$ differs from $g$ at a rational point in the interval $I$. Thus the final function $g$ differs from every $f_{E,n}$ on every rational interval. By the preceding lemma, this implies that $g$ differs from every $f_E$.

To make the construction of $g$ slightly more precise, we define a sequence $g_k$ of finite functions on the rationals as follows.

The function $g_0$ is empty. To define $g_k$, we interpret $k$ as the triple $(E, I, n)$. Let $x$ be a rational number in the interval $I$ at which $g_{k-1}$ is not defined. Let $y$ be the value obtained by interpolating $g_{k-1}$ linearly at $x$. (If $g_{k-1}$ contains no defined points on either side of $x$, let $y$ be zero. If there is a defined point on only one side, use that value.) Compute $f_{E,n}(x)$ to a tolerance of $2^{-k-1}$. If the result of the computation is within $2^{-k-1}$ of $y$, define $g_k(x)$ to be $y + 2^{-k}$. Otherwise define $g_k(x)$ to be $y$.

The function $g_k$ is computable as a set of ordered pairs. Define $g_k{}'$ to be $g_k$ extended to all reals by linear interpolation. Define $g$ to be the limit of the $g_k$. Both convergence and computability of $g$ follows from the fact that $g_k{}'$ does not differ from $g_{k-1}{}'$ by more than $2^{-k}$. Thus $g$ can be evaluated to precision $2^{-k}$ by simply evaluating $g_{k+2}{}'$ to precision $2^{-k-2}$. Since $g$ is equal to $g_k$ at those points at which $g_k$ is defined, and $g_k$ was constructed to be different from the corresponding $f_{E,n}(x)$ on the corresponding interval $I$, it follows that $g$ differs from $f_{E,n}(x)$ on every rational interval.    $\square$

### 5.2 *Implications*

The critical property of the constructive reals underlying the preceding "impossibility" theorem is that a computable function is total on an open interval only if it is continuous on that interval. This property implies that *extensional* predicates on the constructive reals must either be trivial or diverge at some point between any two points where the predicate yields opposing answers. As a result, a program constructed from sequential[17] operations cannot use extensional predicates to produce *new* total functions.

To define arbitrary computable functions over the constructive reals in terms of a finite set of extensional computable operations, we need either nonsequential operations (such as the dovetailed conditional discussed in Section 2) or pathological operations that are not strongly computable (permitting us to simulate nonsequential operations). A good example of a function in the latter category is an interpreter *eval* that interprets constructive real numbers as programs over the constructive reals (in a language that permits dovetailing). More precisely *eval*$(P, x)$ applies the program coded by $P$ (a constructive real number) to the input $x$ (a constructive real number) and returns the result of the computation (a constructive real number). If we allow operations of this form, then we can formulate the constructive reals as an abstract type of sequential, extensional operations. But the extensionality in this case is merely a facade, because the operations can use the constructive real numbers as codes for programs!

## 6 *Previous Work*

Although there has been little previous work on the implementation of the constructive reals, three alternatives to limited precision arithmetic have been widely studied. They are interval arithmetic (cf. [18]), rational arithmetic (cf. [17, Section 4.5]), and arithmetic on algebraic numbers (cf. [1]). Interval arithmetic augments limited-precision arithmetic by maintaining explicit error bounds for all computed quantities. Rational arithmetic performs exact calculations over the rational numbers by using unbounded integers to represent the numerator and denominator. Exact arithmetic can be extended to algebraic numbers (roots of polynomials with integer coefficients) by representing each number as an integer polynomial together with the rational

---

17. A $k$-ary function $f(x_1, \ldots, x_k)$ $(k > 0)$ over a data domain $A$ is *sequential* if and only if it is (i) constant, or (ii) strict in some argument $x_i$ such that every projection function $g_a$, $a \in D$ defined by

$$g_a(x_1, \ldots, x_{i-1}, x_{i+1}, \ldots x_k) = f(x_1, \ldots, x_{i-1}, x_{i+1}, \ldots x_k)$$

is *sequential*.

endpoints of an interval identifying a particular root. Unfortunately, none of these three alternatives supports the exact solution of most computational problems of interest to scientists and engineers. Interval arithmetic does not support exact calculation at all; it simply maintains bounds on the errors in conventional limited precision calculations. In contrast, both rational and algebraic arithmetic produce exact answers, but they do not accommodate many of the functions commonly encountered in scientific and engineering applications. Rational arithmetic breaks down on operations that produce irrational answers for rational inputs, e.g., the square root and trigonometric functions. Similarly, algebraic arithmetic fails on operations that produce transcendental results for algebraic inputs, e.g., the natural logarithm and trigonometric functions.

The earliest discussion of exact real arithmetic that we have found in the literature is a remark by Bill Gosper in the MIT Technical Report entitled HAKMEM [15]. Gosper proposed a lazy implementation of the constructive real numbers based on the regular continued fraction representation. He was aware that the algorithms he proposed would not work for all inputs and suggested that approximate arithmetic could be used as a last resort.

More recently, Wiedmer [26], O'Donnell [20], and Pixley [21] independently studied the problem of devising concrete representations for the constructive reals and invented the same redundant radix representation that we developed for our lazy implementations. In addition, both O'Donnell and Pixley devised and implemented essentially the same addition algorithm as we developed for our lazy implementations.

Redundant radix representations were invented by hardware designers over 25 years ago as a mechanism for avoiding carry propagation in hardware arithmetic [4]. One of our previous papers [8] contains a more extensive review of the relevant hardware literature.

The inadequacy of conventional radix notation as a representation for the constructive reals was recognized by constructive mathematicians long before any computer scientists attacked the problem of implementing the constructive real numbers. In the classic reference on recursion theory [22, (see especially p. 371)], Hartley Rogers includes the proof of this fact as an exercise. A more recent discussion of the problem from the perspective of a constructive mathematician appears in [19].

To our knowledge, there is only one other active research project aimed at producing a practical implementation of exact real arithmetic. Jean Vuillemin at INRIA has developed a sophisticated implementation of the constructive reals based on a redundant continued fraction representation. He has devised incremental addition and multiplication algorithms that are *linear* in the size of input streams. However, the output stream may converge more slowly than either of the inputs, which makes the performance of his scheme difficult to compare with our own (where multiplication is quadratic if output digits are computed incrementally).

## 7 Directions for Future Research

Research on the subject of exact real arithmetic is still in its infancy. We are interested in studying the following five problem areas:

Devising more efficient data representations and algorithms for exact real arithmetic on conventional sequential machines (such as engineering workstations).

Developing an optimizing Fortran compiler for numerical programs employing exact real arithmetic.

Exploring parallel implementation methods for exact real arithmetic suitable for the emerging generation of highly parallel scientific computers (such as CM–2 Connection Machine).

Designing potential hardware extensions for conventional uniprocessors to improve the efficiency of exact real arithmetic.

Constructing program development tools that exploit exact real arithmetic.

We believe that a performance level within roughly one order of magnitude of conventional floating-point computation appears within reach either on a parallel processor or on a uniprocessor augmented by special purpose hardware (of moderate complexity) to accelerate arithmetic on large integers.

## References

[1] Abbott, J. A., Bradford, R. J., and Davenport, J. H. "The Bath algebraic number package". In *Proceedings of the 1986 Symposium on Symbolic and Algebraic Computation* (July). ACM, 1986.

[2] Aberth, O. *Computable Analysis.* McGraw-Hill, New York, 1980.

[3] Aho, A., Hopcroft, J., and Ullman, J. *The Design and Analysis of Computer Algorithms.* Addison-Wesley, Reading, Mass., 1974.

[4] Avizienis, A. "Signed-digit number representations for fast parallel arithmetic". *Institute of Radio Engineers Transactions on Electronic Computers*, 1961, p. 389.

[5] Bishop, E. *Foundations of Constructive Analysis.* McGraw-Hill, New York, 1967.

[6] Boehm, H.-J., Demers, A., and Donahue, J. "A programmer's introduction to Rus-

sell". Technical Report 85–16, Department of Computer Science, Rice University, Houston, Texas, 1985.

[7] Boehm, H.-J., and Demers, A. "Implementing Russell". In *Proceedings of the SIGPLAN '86 Symposium on Compiler Construction.* ACM, 1986 (also *SIGPLAN Notices 21,* 7 (July 1986)), pp. 186–195.

[8] Boehm, H.-J., Cartwright, R. S., O'Donnell, M. J., and Riggle, M. "Exact real arithmetic: A case study in higher order programming". In *Proceedings of the 1986 ACM Conference on Lisp and Functional Programming* (Cambridge, Mass., August). ACM, 1986, pp. 162–173.

[9] Boehm, H.-J. "Constructive real interpretation of numerical programs". In *Proceedings of the ACM SIGPLAN '87 Symposium on Interpreters and Interpretive Techniques.* ACM, 1987.

[10] Bridges, D. S. *Constructive Functional Analysis.* Pitman, London, 1979.

[11] Cartwright, R. S. "Formal Program Testing". In *Proceedings of the Eighth Annual Symposium on Principles of Programming Languages,* (January 1981). ACM, 1981, pp. 125–132.

[12] Cartwright, R. S., and Donahue, J. "The semantics of lazy (and industrious) evaluation". In *Conference Record of the 1982 ACM Symposium on LISP and Functional Programming* (Pittsburg, Pa., August). ACM, 1982, pp. 253–265.

[13] Cartwright, R. S. "$\mathbb{R}^n$: An experimental computer network to support numerical computation". Technical Report, Mathematical Sciences Department, Rice University, Houston, Texas, 1982.

[14] Friedman, D. and Wise, D. "CONS should not evaluate its arguments". In *Proceedings of the Third International Colloquium on Automata, Languages and Programming.* Edinburgh University Press, Edinburgh, 1976, pp. 257–284.

[15] Gosper, W. "Continued fraction arithmetic". HAKMEM Item 101B, MIT Artificial Intelligence Memo 239, MIT, Cambridge, Mass., 1972.

[16] Henderson, P. and Morris, J. Jr. "A lazy evaluator". In *Proceedings of the Third Annual Symposium on Principles of Programming Languages.* ACM, 1976, pp. 95–103.

[17] Knuth, D. *The Art of Computer Programming.* Vol. 2, *Seminumerical Algorithms.* Addison-Wesley, Reading, Mass., 1969.

[18] Moore, R. E. "Methods and applications of interval analysis". In *SIAM Studies in Applied Mathematics.* W. F. Ames, ed. SIAM, 1979.

[19] Myhill, J. "What is a real number?" *American Mathematical Monthly 79,* 7 (1972), pp. 748–754.

[20] O'Donnell, M. J. *Equational Logic as a Programming Language.* MIT Press, Cambridge, Mass., 1985.

[21] Pixley, C. "Demand-driven arithmetic". Unpublished draft, Burroughs Austin Re-

search Center, Austin, Texas, 1984.

[22] Rogers, H. Jr. *Theory of Recursive Functions and Effective Computability.* McGraw-Hill, New York, 1967.

[23] Scott, D. "Lectures on a mathematical theory of computation". Technical Monograph PRG-19, Programming Research Group, Oxford University Computing Laboratory, Oxford, U.K., 1981.

[24] Scott, D. "Domains for denotational semantics". Technical Report, Computer Science Department, Carnegie-Mellon University, Pittsburgh, Pa., 1983.

[25] Vuillemin, J. E. "Exact real computer arithmetic with continued fractions". Unpublished report, INRIA, 1987.

[26] Wiedmer, E. "Computing with infinite objects". *Theoretical Computer Science 10* (1980), pp. 133–155.

[27] Wilkinson, J. H. *The Algebraic Eigenvalue Problem.* Academic Press, London, 1965.

# The Lazy Lambda Calculus

# 4

**Samson Abramsky**
Imperial College of Science, Technology and Medicine

## 1 Introduction

The commonly accepted basis for functional programming is the $\lambda$-calculus; and it is folklore that the $\lambda$-calculus *is* the prototypical functional language in purified form. But what is the $\lambda$-calculus? The syntax is simple and classical; variables, abstraction, and application in the pure calculus, with applied calculi obtained by adding constants. The further elaboration of the theory, covering conversion, reduction, theories, and models, is laid out in Barendregt's already classical treatise [5]. It is instructive to recall the following crux, which occurs rather early in that work (p. 39).

### 1.1 Meaning of $\lambda$-Terms: First Attempt

The meaning of a $\lambda$-term is its normal form (if it exists).

All terms without normal forms are identified.

This proposal incorporates such a simple and natural interpretation of the λ-calculus as a programming language, that if it worked there would surely be no doubt that it was the right one. However, it gives rise to an inconsistent theory! (See the above reference.)

### 1.2 *Second Attempt*

The meaning of λ-terms is based on head normal forms via the notion of *Bohm tree*.

All unsolvable terms (no head normal form) are identified.

This second attempt forms the central theme of Barendregt's book, and gives rise to a very beautiful and successful theory (henceforth referred to as the "standard theory"), as that work shows.

This, then, is the commonly accepted foundation for functional programming; more precisely, for the *lazy* functional languages, which represent the mainstream of current functional programming practice. Examples: MIRANDA [31], LML [4], LISPKIT [12], ORWELL [32], PONDER [11], TALE[6]. But do these languages as defined and implemented actually evaluate terms to head normal form? To the best of my knowledge, *not a single one of them does so.* Instead, they evaluate to *weak head normal form*; i.e., they do not evaluate under abstractions.

**Example**   $\lambda x.(\lambda y.y)M$ is in weak head normal form, but not in head normal form, since it contains the head redex $(\lambda y.y)M$.

So we have a mismatch between theory and practice. Since current practice is well motivated by efficiency considerations and is unlikely to be abandoned readily, it makes sense to see if a good modified theory can be developed for it. To see that the theory really does need to be modified, consider the following.

**Example**   Let $\Omega \equiv (\lambda x.xx)(\lambda x.xx)$ be the standard unsolvable term. Then

$$\lambda x.\Omega = \Omega$$

in the standard theory, since $\lambda x.\Omega$ is also unsolvable; but $\lambda x.\Omega$ is in weak head normal form and hence should be distinguished from $\Omega$ in our "lazy" theory.

We now turn to a second point in which the standard theory is not completely satisfactory.

### 1.3 *Is the λ–Calculus a Programming Language?*

In the standard theory, the λ-calculus may be regarded as being characterized by the type equation

$$D = [D \to D]$$

(for justification of this in a general categorical framework, see e.g., [30, 13, 14]).

It is one of the most remarkable features of the various categories of domains used in denotational semantics that they admit nontrivial solutions of this equation. However, there is no *canonical* solution in any of these categories (in particular, the initial solution is trivial—the one-point domain).

I regard this as a symptom of the fact that the pure λ-calculus in the standard theory *is not a programming language*. Of course, this is to some extent a matter of terminology, but I feel that the expression "programming language" should be reserved for a formalism with a definite computational interpretation (an operational semantics). The pure λ-calculus as ordinarily conceived is too schematic to qualify.

A further indication of the same point is that studies such as Plotkin's "LCF Considered as a Programming Language" [26] have not been carried over to the pure λ-calculus, for lack of any convincing way of doing so in the standard theory. This in turn impedes the development of a theory which integrates the λ-calculus with concurrency and other computational notions.

We shall see that by contrast with this situation, the lazy λ-calculus we shall develop does have a canonical model; that Plotkin's ideas can be carried over to it in a very natural way; and that the theory we shall develop will run quite strikingly in parallel with our treatment of concurrency in [1].

The plan of the remainder of the paper is as follows. In the next section, we introduce the intuitions on which our theory is based, in the concrete setting of λ-terms. We then set up the axiomatic framework for our theory, based on the notion of *applicative transition systems*. This forms a bridge both to the standard theory and to concurrency and other computational notions. We then introduce a domain equation for applicative transition systems and use it to derive a *domain logic* in the sense of [3, 2]. We prove duality, characterization, and final algebra theorems; and obtain a strikingly simple proof of a computational adequacy theorem, which asserts that a term converges operationally if and only if it denotes a nonbottom element in our domain.

We then show how the ideas of [26] can be formulated in our setting. Two distinctive features of our approach are:

the axiomatic treatment of concepts and results which are usually presented concretely in work on programming language semantics

the use of our domain logic as a tool in studying the equational theory over our "programs" ($\lambda$-terms).

Our results can also be interpreted as settling a number of questions and conjectures concerning the domain interpretation of Martin-Löf's intuitionistic type theory raised at the 1983 Chalmers University Workshop on Semantics of Programming Languages [10].

Finally, we consider some extensions and variations of the theory.

## 2 *The Lazy Lambda-Calculus*

We begin with the syntax, which is standard.

**Definition 2.1**   We assume a set Var of variables, ranged over by $x, y, z$. The set $\Lambda$ of $\lambda$-terms, ranged over by M, N, P, Q, R is defined by

$$M \ ::= \ x \mid \lambda x.M \mid MN .$$

For standard notions of free and bound variables, etc., we refer to [5]. The reader should also refer to that work for definitions of notation such as: FV(M), $C[\cdot]$, $\Lambda^0$. Our one point of difference concerns substitution; we write $M[N/x]$ rather than $M[x := N]$.

**Definition 2.2**   The relation $M \Downarrow N$ ("M converges to principal weak head normal form N") is defined inductively over $\Lambda^0$ as follows:

- $\lambda x.M \Downarrow \lambda x.M$ ,

- $\dfrac{M \Downarrow \lambda x.P \quad P[N/x] \Downarrow Q}{MN \Downarrow Q}$ .

## Notation

$$M \Downarrow \ \equiv \ \exists N.M \Downarrow N \qquad (\text{"M converges"}) ,$$

$$M \Uparrow \ \equiv \ \neg(M \Downarrow) \qquad\quad (\text{"M diverges"}) .$$

It is clear that $\Downarrow$ is a partial function; i.e., evaluation is deterministic.

We now have an (unlabeled) transition system $(\Lambda^0, \Downarrow)$. The relation $\Downarrow$ by itself is too "shallow" to yield information about the behavior of a term under all experiments. However, just as in the study of concurrency, we shall use it as a building block for a deeper relation, which we shall call *applicative bisimulation*. To motivate this relation, let us spell out the observational scenario we have in mind.

Given a closed term $M$, the only experiment of depth 1 we can do is to evaluate $M$ and see if it converges to some abstraction (weak head normal form) $\lambda x.M_1$. If it does so, we can continue the experiment to depth 2 by supplying a term $N_1$ as input to $M_1$, and so on. Note that what the experimenter can observe at each stage is only the *fact* of convergence, not which term lies under the abstraction. We can picture matters thus:

Stage 1 of experiment:　$M \Downarrow \lambda x.M_1$; environment "consumes" $\lambda$,
produces $N_1$ as input.

Stage 2 of experiment:　$M_1[N_1/x] \Downarrow \dots$ .

$$\vdots$$

## Definition 2.3 (Applicative Bisimulation)

We define a sequence of relations $\{\lesssim_k\}_{k\in\omega}$ on $\Lambda^0$:

$$M \lesssim_0 N \ \equiv \text{true},$$
$$M \lesssim_{k+1} N \equiv M \Downarrow \lambda x.M_1 \ \Rightarrow \ \exists N_1.[N \Downarrow \lambda y.N_1 \ \& \ \forall P \in \Lambda^0. M_1[P/x] \lesssim_k N_1[P/y]],$$
$$M \sqsubseteq^B N \ \equiv \forall k \in \omega. M \lesssim_k N.$$

Clearly each $\lesssim_k$ and $\sqsubseteq^B$ is a preorder. We extend $\sqsubseteq^B$ to $\Lambda$ by:

$$M \sqsubseteq^B N \ \equiv \ \forall \sigma : \text{Var} \to \Lambda^0. M\sigma \sqsubseteq^B N\sigma$$

(where, e.g., $M\sigma$ means the result of substituting $\sigma x$ for each $x \in FV(M)$ in $M$). Finally,

$$M \sim^B N \ \equiv \ M \sqsubseteq^B N \ \& \ N \sqsubseteq^B M.$$

Using standard techniques [24, 18], $\sim^B$ can be shown to be the maximal fixpoint of a certain function and hence to satisfy

$$M \sqsubseteq^B N$$

$$\Longleftrightarrow$$

$$M \Downarrow \lambda x.M_1 \ \Rightarrow \ \exists N_1.[N \Downarrow \lambda y.N_1 \ \& \ \forall P \in \Lambda^0. M_1[P/x] \sqsubseteq^B N_1[P/y]].$$

Further details are given in the next section.

The applicative bisimulation relation can be described in a more traditional way (from the point of view of $\lambda$-calculus) as a "Morris-style contextual congruence" [23, 26, 19, 5].

**Definition 2.4**  The relation $\sqsubseteq^C$ on $\Lambda^0$ is defined by

$$M \sqsubseteq^C N \equiv \forall C[\cdot] \in \Lambda^0. C[M] \Downarrow \Rightarrow C[N] \Downarrow .$$

This is extended to $\Lambda$ in the same way as $\sqsubseteq^B$.

**Proposition 2.1**

$$\sqsubseteq^B = \sqsubseteq^C.$$

This is a special case of a result we will prove later. Our proof will make essential use of domain logic, despite the fact that the *statement* of the result does not mention domains at all. A direct proof can also be given, along the lines of the "Context Lemma", for the typed $\lambda$-calculus [19, 9].

We now list some basic properties of the relation $\sqsubseteq^B$ (superscript omitted).

**Proposition 2.2**
For all $M, N, P \in \Lambda$:

  (i)   $M \sqsubseteq M$,

  (ii)  $M \sqsubseteq N \,\&\, N \sqsubseteq P \;\Rightarrow\; M \sqsubseteq P$,

  (iii) $M \sqsubseteq N \;\Rightarrow\; M[P/x] \sqsubseteq N[P/x]$,

  (iv)  $M \sqsubseteq N \;\Rightarrow\; P[M/x] \sqsubseteq P[N/x]$,

  (v)   $\lambda x.M \sim \lambda y.M[y/x]$,

  (vi)  $M \sqsubseteq N \;\Rightarrow\; \lambda x.M \sqsubseteq \lambda x.N$,

  (vii) $M_i \sqsubseteq N_i \,(i = 1, 2) \;\Rightarrow\; M_1 M_2 \sqsubseteq N_1 N_2$.

**Proof**   (i)–(iii) and (v)–(vi) are trivial; (vii) follows from (ii) and (iv), since taking $C_1 \equiv [\cdot]M_2$, $M_1 M_2 \sqsubseteq N_1 M_2$, and taking $C_2 \equiv N_1[\cdot]$, $N_1 M_2 \sqsubseteq N_1 N_2$, whence $M_1 M_2 \sqsubseteq N_1 N_2$. It remains to prove (iv), which by Proposition 2.1 is equivalent to

$$M \sqsubseteq^C N \;\Rightarrow\; P[M/x] \sqsubseteq^C P[N/x].$$

We rename all bound variables in $P$ to avoid clashes with $M$ and $N$, and we replace $x$ by $[\cdot]$ to obtain a context $P[\cdot]$ such that

$$P[M/x] = P[M], \quad P[N/x] = P[N].$$

Now let $C[\cdot] \in \Lambda^0$ and $\sigma \in \text{Var} \to \Lambda^0$ be given. Let $C_1[\cdot] \equiv C[P[\cdot]\sigma]$. $M \sqsubseteq^C N$ implies

$$C_1[M\sigma] \Downarrow \;\Rightarrow\; C_1[N\sigma] \Downarrow,$$

which, since $(P[M/x])\sigma = (P[\cdot]\sigma)[M\sigma]$, yields

$$C[(P[M/x])\sigma] \Downarrow \;\Rightarrow\; C[(P[N/x])\sigma] \Downarrow,$$

as required.    □

This proposition can be summarized as saying that $\sqsubseteq^B$ is a *precongruence*. We thus have an (in)equational theory $\lambda\ell = (\Lambda, \sqsubseteq, =)$, where

$$\lambda\ell \vdash M \sqsubseteq N \;\equiv\; M \sqsubseteq^B N,$$
$$\lambda\ell \vdash M = N \;\equiv\; M \sim^B N.$$

What does this theory look like?

## Proposition 2.3

**(i)** The theory $\lambda$ [5] is included in $\lambda\ell$; in particular,

$$\lambda\ell \;\vdash\; (\lambda x.M)N = M[N/x] \quad (\beta).$$

**(ii)** $\Omega \equiv (\lambda x.xx)(\lambda x.xx)$ is a least element for $\sqsubseteq$; i.e.,

$$\lambda\ell \;\vdash\; \Omega \sqsubseteq x.$$

**(iii)** $(\eta)$ is not valid in $\lambda\ell$, e.g.,

$$\lambda\ell \;\nvdash\; \lambda x.\Omega x = \Omega,$$

but we do have the following conditional version of $\eta$:

$$(\Downarrow \eta)\; \lambda\ell \;\vdash\; \lambda x.Mx = M \quad (M \Downarrow, x \notin FV(M))$$

$$(M \Downarrow \;\equiv\; \forall \sigma \in \text{Var} \to \Lambda^0.(M\sigma) \Downarrow).$$

**(iv)** **YK** is a greatest element for $\sqsubseteq$; i.e.,

$$\lambda\ell \;\vdash\; x \sqsubseteq \mathbf{YK}.$$

## Proof

**(i)** This is an easy consequence of Proposition 2.2.

**(ii)** $\Omega \Uparrow$, hence $\Omega \sqsubseteq^B M$ for all $M \in \Lambda^0$.

**(iii)** $\lambda x.\Omega x \not\sqsubseteq_1 \Omega$, since $(\lambda x.\Omega x) \Downarrow$. Now suppose $M \Downarrow$, and let $\sigma : \text{Var} \to \Lambda^0$ be given. Then $(M\sigma) \Downarrow \lambda y.N$. For any $P \in \Lambda^0$,

$$(M\sigma)P \Downarrow Q \quad \Leftrightarrow \quad ((M\sigma)x)[P/x] \Downarrow Q \quad \text{since } x \notin FV(M),$$
$$\Leftrightarrow \quad ((\lambda x.Mx)\sigma)P \Downarrow Q,$$

and so $M \sim^B \lambda x.Mx$, as required.

**(iv)** Note that $\mathbf{YK} \Downarrow \lambda y.N$, where $N \equiv (\lambda x.\mathbf{K}(xx))(\lambda x.\mathbf{K}(xx))$, and that for all $P$,

$$N[P/y] \Downarrow \lambda y.N.$$

Hence for all $P_1, \ldots, P_n$ $(n \geq 0)$,

$$\mathbf{YK}P_1 \ldots P_n \Downarrow,$$

and so $M \sqsubseteq^B \mathbf{YK}$ for all $M \in \Lambda^0$.   $\square$

To understand (iv), we can think of $\mathbf{YK}$ as the infinite process

$$\overset{\lambda}{\underset{\circlearrowleft}{}}$$

solving the equation

$$\xi = \lambda x.\xi.$$

This is a top element in our applicative bisimulation ordering because it converges under all finite stages of evaluation for all arguments—the experimenter can always observe convergence (or "consume an infinite $\lambda$-stream").

We can make some connections between the theory $\lambda\ell$ and [17], as pointed out to me by Chih-Hao Ong. First, 2.3(ii) can be generalized to:

> The set of terms in $\Lambda^0$ which are least in $\lambda\ell$ are exactly the $PO_0$ terms in the terminology of [17].

Moreover, $\mathbf{YK}$ is an $O_\infty$ term in the terminology of [17], although it is *not* a greatest element in the ordering proposed there.

## 3 Applicative Transition Systems

The theory $\lambda\ell$ defined in the previous section was derived from a particular operational model, the transition system $(\Lambda^0, \Downarrow)$. What is the general concept of which this is an example?

**Definition 3.1**   A *quasi-applicative transition system* is a structure $(A, ev)$ where

$$ev : A \to (A \to A).$$

## Notations

**(i)** $a \Downarrow f \equiv a \in \text{dom } ev \,\&\, ev(a) = f$,

**(ii)** $a \Downarrow \equiv a \in \text{dom } ev$,

**(iii)** $a \Uparrow \equiv a \notin \text{dom } ev$.

### Definition 3.2 (Applicative Bisimulation)

Let $(A, ev)$ be a quasi-ats. We define

$$F : Rel(A) \rightarrow Rel(A)$$

by

$$F(R) = \{(a, b) : a \Downarrow f \implies b \Downarrow g \,\&\, \forall c \in A.\, f(c)Rg(c)\}.$$

Then $R \in Rel(A)$ is an *applicative bisimulation* iff $R \subseteq F(R)$; and $\precsim^B \in Rel(A)$ is defined by

$$a \precsim^B b \equiv aRb \text{ for some applicative bisimulation } R.$$

Thus $\precsim^B = \bigcup\{R \in Rel(A) : R \subseteq F(R)\}$ and hence is the maximal fixpoint of the monotone function $F$. Since the relation $\Downarrow$ is a partial function, it is easily shown that the closure ordinal of $F$ is $\leq \omega$, and we can thus describe $\precsim^B$ more explicitly as follows:

- $a \precsim^B b \quad\equiv\quad \forall k \in \omega.\, a \precsim_k b$,
- $a \precsim_0 b \quad\equiv\quad \text{true}$,
- $a \precsim_{k+1} b \quad\equiv\quad a \Downarrow f \implies b \Downarrow g \,\&\, \forall c \in A.\, f(c) \precsim_k g(c)$,
- $a \sim^B b \quad\equiv\quad a \precsim^B b \,\&\, b \precsim^B a$.

It is easily seen that $\precsim^B$, and also each $\precsim_k$, is a preorder; $\sim^B$ is therefore an equivalence.

We now come to our main definition.

### Definition 3.3

An *applicative transition system* (ats) is a quasi-ats $(A, ev)$ satisfying

$$\forall a, b, c \in A.\, a \Downarrow f \,\&\, b \precsim^B c \implies f(b) \precsim^B f(c).$$

An ats has a well-defined quotient $(A/\sim^B, ev/\sim^B)$, where

$$ev/\sim^B([a]) = \begin{cases} [b] \mapsto [f(b)], & a \Downarrow f \\ \text{undefined}, & \text{otherwise}. \end{cases}$$

The reader should now refresh his or her memory of such notions as *applicative structure, combinatory algebra*, and *lambda model* from [5, Chapter 5].

**Definition 3.4**   A *quasi-applicative structure with divergence* is a structure $(A, \cdot, \Uparrow)$ such that $(A, \cdot)$ is an applicative structure, and $\Uparrow \subseteq A$ is a divergence predicate satisfying

$$x \Uparrow \implies (x \cdot y) \Uparrow .$$

Given $(A, \cdot, \Uparrow)$, we can define

$$a \mathrel{\underset{\sim}{\sqsubseteq}}^A b \equiv a \Downarrow \implies b \Downarrow \;\&\; \forall c \in A . a \cdot c \mathrel{\underset{\sim}{\sqsubseteq}}^A b \cdot c$$

as the maximal fixpoint of a monotone function along identical lines to Definition 3.2.

Applicative transition systems and applicative structures with divergence are not quite equivalent, but they are sufficiently so for our purposes:

**Proposition  3.1**

Given an ats $\mathcal{B} = (A, ev)$, we define $\mathcal{A} = (A, \cdot, \Uparrow)$ by

$$a \cdot b \equiv \begin{cases} a, & a \Uparrow \\ f(b), & a \Downarrow f . \end{cases}$$

Then

$$a \mathrel{\underset{\sim}{\sqsubseteq}}^A b \iff a \mathrel{\underset{\sim}{\sqsubseteq}}^B b ,$$

and moreover we can recover $\mathcal{B}$ from $\mathcal{A}$ by

$$ev(a) = \begin{cases} b \mapsto a \cdot b , & a \Downarrow \\ \text{undefined}, & \text{otherwise} . \end{cases}$$

Furthermore, $\cdot$ is compatible with $\mathrel{\underset{\sim}{\sqsubseteq}}^B$; i.e.,

$$a_i \mathrel{\underset{\sim}{\sqsubseteq}}^B b_i \;(i = 1, 2) \implies a_1 \cdot a_2 \mathrel{\underset{\sim}{\sqsubseteq}}^B b_1 \cdot b_2 .$$

We now turn to a language for talking about these structures.

**Definition 3.5**   We assume a fixed set of variables Var. Given an applicative structure $\mathcal{A} = (A, \cdot)$, we define $CL(\mathcal{A})$, the *combinatory terms over* $\mathcal{A}$, by

- $\text{Var} \subseteq CL(\mathcal{A})$,
- $\{c_a : a \in A\} \subseteq CL(\mathcal{A})$,
- $M, N \in CL(\mathcal{A}) \implies MN \in CL(\mathcal{A})$.

Let $Env(\mathcal{A}) \equiv \mathrm{Var} \to A$. Then the *interpretation function*

$$[\![\,\cdot\,]\!]^{\mathcal{A}} : CL(\mathcal{A}) \to Env(\mathcal{A}) \to A$$

is defined by

$$[\![x]\!]^{\mathcal{A}}_{\rho} \quad = \quad \rho x \,,$$
$$[\![c_a]\!]^{\mathcal{A}}_{\rho} \quad = \quad a \,,$$
$$[\![MN]\!]^{\mathcal{A}}_{\rho} \quad = \quad ([\![M]\!]^{\mathcal{A}}_{\rho}) \cdot ([\![N]\!]^{\mathcal{A}}_{\rho}) \,.$$

Given an ats $\mathcal{A} = (A, ev)$, with derived applicative structure $(A, \cdot\,)$, the satisfaction relation between $\mathcal{A}$ and atomic formulae over $CL(\mathcal{A})$, of the forms

$$M \sqsubseteq N, \ M = N, \ M \Downarrow \ M \Uparrow$$

is defined by

$$\mathcal{A}, \rho \models M \sqsubseteq N \quad \equiv \quad [\![M]\!]^{\mathcal{A}}_{\rho} \sqsubseteq^{B} [\![N]\!]^{\mathcal{A}}_{\rho} \,,$$
$$\mathcal{A}, \rho \models M = N \quad \equiv \quad [\![M]\!]^{\mathcal{A}}_{\rho} \sim^{B} [\![N]\!]^{\mathcal{A}}_{\rho} \,,$$
$$\mathcal{A}, \rho \models M \Downarrow \quad \equiv \quad [\![M]\!]^{\mathcal{A}}_{\rho} \Downarrow \,,$$
$$\mathcal{A}, \rho \models M \Uparrow \quad \equiv \quad [\![M]\!]^{\mathcal{A}}_{\rho} \Uparrow \,,$$

while

$$\mathcal{A} \models \phi \equiv \forall \rho \in Env(\mathcal{A}). \ \mathcal{A}, \rho \models \phi \,.$$

This is extended to first-order formulae in the usual way.

Note that equality in $CL(\mathcal{A})$ is being interpreted by bisimulation in $\mathcal{A}$. We could have retained the standard notion of interpretation as in [5] by working in the quotient structure $(A/\sim^{B}, \cdot /\sim^{B})$. This is equivalent, in the sense that the same sentences are satisfied.

**Definition 3.6**   A *lambda transition system* (lts) is a structure $(A, ev, k, s)$, where

$(A, ev)$ is an ats ,

$k, s \in A$, and $A$ satisfies the following axioms (writing **K, S** for $c_k, c_s$):

- **K** $\Downarrow$, **K**$x \Downarrow$
- **K**$xy = x$
- **S** $\Downarrow$, **S**$x \Downarrow$, **S**$xy \Downarrow$
- **S**$xyz = (xz)(yz)$

We now check that these definitions do indeed capture our original example.

**Example**   We define $\ell = (\Lambda^0, ev)$, where

$$ev(M) = \begin{cases} P \mapsto N[P/x], & M \Downarrow \lambda x.N \\ \text{undefined}, & \text{otherwise}. \end{cases}$$

$\ell$ is indeed an ats by 2.6(iv). Moreover, it is an lts via the definitions

$$k \equiv \lambda x.\lambda y.x,$$
$$s \equiv \lambda x.\lambda y.\lambda z.(xz)(yz).$$

We now see how to interpret $\lambda$-terms in any lts.

**Definition 3.7**   Given an lts $\mathcal{A}$, we define $\Lambda(\mathcal{A})$, the $\lambda$-terms over $\mathcal{A}$, by the same clauses as for $CL(\mathcal{A})$, plus the additional one:

- $x \in \text{Var}, M \in \Lambda(\mathcal{A}) \Rightarrow \lambda x.M \in \Lambda(\mathcal{A})$.

We define a translation

$$(\cdot)_{CL} : \Lambda(\mathcal{A}) \to CL(\mathcal{A})$$

by

$$(x)_{CL} \equiv x,$$
$$(c_a)_{CL} \equiv c_a,$$
$$(MN)_{CL} \equiv (M)_{CL}(N)_{CL},$$
$$(\lambda x.M)_{CL} \equiv \lambda^* x.(M)_{CL},$$

where

$$\lambda^* x.x \equiv \mathbf{I} \, (\equiv \mathbf{SKK}),$$
$$\lambda^* x.M \equiv \mathbf{K}M \, (x \notin FV(M)),$$
$$\lambda^* x.MN \equiv \mathbf{S}(\lambda^* x.M)(\lambda^* x.N).$$

We now extend $[\![ \cdot ]\!]$ to $\Lambda(\mathcal{A})$ by

$$[\![ M ]\!]^{\mathcal{A}}_\rho \equiv [\![ (M)_{CL} ]\!]^{\mathcal{A}}_\rho.$$

**Definition 3.8**   We define two sets of formulae over $\Lambda$:

*Atomic formulae:*

$$AF \equiv \{M \sqsubseteq N, \, M = N, \, M \Downarrow, \, N \Uparrow : M, N \in \Lambda\}.$$

*Conditional formulae:*

$$CF \equiv \{\bigwedge_{i \in I} M_i \Downarrow \wedge \bigwedge_{j \in J} N_j \Uparrow \Rightarrow F : F \in AF, M_i, N_i \in \Lambda, I, J \text{ finite}\}.$$

Note that, taking $I = J = \varnothing$, $AF \subseteq CF$. Now given an lts $\mathcal{A}, \mathfrak{I}(\mathcal{A})$, the *theory* of $\mathcal{A}$, is defined by

$$\mathfrak{I}(\mathcal{A}) \equiv \{C \in CF : \mathcal{A} \models C\}.$$

We also write $\mathfrak{I}^0(\mathcal{A})$ for the restriction of $\mathfrak{I}(\mathcal{A})$ to closed formulae; and given a set Con of constants and an interpretation Con $\rightarrow A$, we write $\mathfrak{I}(\mathcal{A}, \text{Con})$ for the theory of conditional formulae built from terms in $\Lambda(\text{Con})$.

## Example (continued)

We set $\lambda\ell = \mathfrak{I}(\ell)$. This is consistent with our usage in the previous section. We saw there that $\lambda\ell$ satisfied much stronger properties than the simple combinatory algebra axioms in our definition of lts. It might be expected that these would fail for general lts; but this is to overlook the powerful extensionality principle built into our definition of the theory of an ats through the applicative bisimulation relation.

## Proposition 3.2

Let $\mathcal{A}$ be an ats. The axiom scheme of *conditional extensionality* over $CL(\mathcal{A})$:

$$(\Downarrow \text{ext}) \quad M \Downarrow \& N \Downarrow \Rightarrow ([\forall x. Mx = Nx] \Rightarrow M = N) \quad (x \notin FV(M) \cup FV(N))$$

is valid in $\mathcal{A}$.

## Proof    Let $\rho \in Env(\mathcal{A})$.

-      $\mathcal{A}, \rho \models M \Downarrow \& N \Downarrow \& \forall x. Mx = Nx$
- $\Rightarrow$    $[\![M]\!]_\rho^{\mathcal{A}} \Downarrow \& [\![N]\!]_\rho^{\mathcal{A}} \Downarrow \& \forall a \in A. [\![M]\!]_\rho^{\mathcal{A}} \cdot a = [\![N]\!]_\rho^{\mathcal{A}} \cdot a$,

  since $x \notin FV(M) \cup FV(N)$,
- $\Rightarrow$    $[\![M]\!]_\rho^{\mathcal{A}} \sim^A [\![N]\!]_\rho^{\mathcal{A}}$
- $\Rightarrow$    $[\![M]\!]_\rho^{\mathcal{A}} \sim^B [\![N]\!]_\rho^{\mathcal{A}}$
- $\Rightarrow$    $\mathcal{A}, \rho \models M = N$.    $\square$

Using this proposition, we can now generalize most of Proposition 2.3 to an arbitrary lts.

## Theorem 3.1

Let $\mathcal{A} = (A, ev, k, s)$ be an lts. Then

**(i)** $(A, ., k, s)$ is a lambda model, and hence $\lambda \subseteq \mathfrak{I}(\mathcal{A})$.

**(ii)** $\mathcal{A}$ satisfies the conditional $\eta$ axiom scheme:

$$(\Downarrow \eta)\ M \Downarrow \Rightarrow \lambda x.Mx = M \quad (x \notin FV(M)).$$

**(iii)** For all $M \in \Lambda^0$:

$$\lambda \ell \vdash M \Downarrow \Rightarrow \mathcal{A} \models M \Downarrow.$$

**(iv)** $\mathcal{A} \models x \sqsubseteq \mathbf{YK}$.

**(v)** $\sqsubseteq$ is a precongruence in $\mathfrak{I}(\mathcal{A})$.

## Proof

**(i)** First, by the very definition of lts, $\mathcal{A}$ is a combinatory algebra. We now use the following result due to Meyer and Scott, cited from [5, Theorem 5.6.3, p. 117]:

Let $\mathcal{M}$ be a combinatory algebra. Define

$$\mathbf{1} \equiv \mathbf{1}_1 \equiv \mathbf{S(KI)}, \quad \mathbf{1}_{k+1} \equiv \mathbf{S(K1}_k).$$

Then $\mathcal{M}$ is a lambda model iff it satisfies

$$\text{(I)} \quad \forall x.\, ax = bx \Rightarrow \mathbf{1}a = \mathbf{1}b,$$

$$\text{(II)} \quad \mathbf{1}_2 \mathbf{K} = \mathbf{K},$$

$$\text{(III)} \quad \mathbf{1}_3 \mathbf{S} = \mathbf{S}.$$

Thus it is sufficient to check that $\mathcal{A}$ satisfies (I)–(III). For (I), note first that $\mathcal{A} \models \mathbf{1}a \Downarrow \& \mathbf{1}b \Downarrow$ by the convergence axioms for an lts. Hence we can apply Proposition 3.2 to obtain

$$\mathcal{A} \models [\forall x.\, \mathbf{1}ax = \mathbf{1}bx] \Rightarrow \mathbf{1}a = \mathbf{1}b.$$

We now assume $\forall x.\, ax = bx$ and prove $\forall x.\, \mathbf{1}ax = \mathbf{1}bx$:

$$
\begin{aligned}
\mathbf{1}ax &= \mathbf{S(KI)}ax \\
&= \mathbf{(KI)}x(ax) \\
&= \mathbf{(KI)}x(bx) \\
&= \mathbf{S(KI)}bx \\
&= \mathbf{1}bx.
\end{aligned}
$$

Conditions (II) and (III) are proved similarly.

**(ii)** Let $\rho \in Env(\mathcal{A})$, and assume $\mathcal{A}, \rho \models M \Downarrow$. We must prove that

$$\mathcal{A}, \rho \models \lambda x.Mx = M.$$

First, note that for any abstraction $\lambda z.P$,

$$\mathcal{A} \models \lambda z.P \Downarrow,$$

by the definition of $\lambda^* z.P$ and the convergence axioms for an lts. Thus since $x \notin FV(M)$, we can apply ($\Downarrow$ ext) to obtain

$$\mathcal{A}, \rho \models [\forall x. (\lambda x.Mx)x = Mx] \rightarrow \lambda x.Mx = M.$$

It is thus sufficient to show

$$\mathcal{A} \models (\lambda x.Mx)x = Mx.$$

But this is just an instance of $(\beta)$, which $\mathcal{A}$ satisfies by (i).

**(iii)** We calculate:

$$
\begin{aligned}
\lambda \ell \vdash M \Downarrow &\Rightarrow M \Downarrow \lambda x.N \\
&\Rightarrow \lambda \vdash M = \lambda x.N \\
&\Rightarrow \mathcal{A} \models M = \lambda x.N \\
&\Rightarrow \mathcal{A} \models M \Downarrow,
\end{aligned}
$$

since $\mathcal{A} \models \lambda x.N \Downarrow$, as noted in (ii).

**(iv)** By (i) and (iii),

$$\mathcal{A} \models \mathbf{YK} \Downarrow \ \& \ \forall x. (\mathbf{YK})x = \mathbf{YK}.$$

Hence we can use the same argument as in Proposition 2.3(iv) to prove that

$$\mathcal{A} \models x \sqsubseteq \mathbf{YK}.$$

**(v)** This assertion amounts to the same list of properties as Proposition 2.2, but with respect to $\mathfrak{I}(\mathcal{A})$. The only difference in the proof is that 2.2(vii) follows immediately from Proposition 3.1 and the fact that $\mathcal{A}$ is an ats, and can then be used to prove 2.2(iv) by induction on $P$. $\qquad \square$

Part (iii) of the theorem tells us that all the closed terms that we expect to converge must do so in any lts. What of the converse? For example, do we have

$$\mathcal{A} \models \Omega \Uparrow$$

in every lts? This is evidently not the case, since we have not imposed any axioms that require *anything* to be divergent.

**Observation 3.1**   Let $\mathcal{A} = (A, ev)$ be an ats in which $ev$ is *total*, i.e., dom $ev = A$. Then $\mathfrak{I}(\mathcal{A})$ is *inconsistent*, in the sense that

$$\mathcal{A} \models x = y.$$

This is of course because the distinctions made by applicative bisimulation are based on divergence.

In the light of this observation and of Theorem 3.1, it is natural to make the following definition in analogy with that in [5].

**Definition 3.9**   An lts $\mathcal{A}$ is *sensible* if the converse to Theorem 3.1(iii) holds; i.e., for all $M \in \Lambda^0$:

$$\mathcal{A} \models M \Downarrow \iff \lambda\ell \vdash M \Downarrow \iff \exists x, N. \ \lambda \vdash M = \lambda x.N.$$

(The second equivalence is justified by an appeal to the standardization theorem [5].)

## 4 A Domain Equation for Applicative Bisimulation

We now embark on the same program as in [1]: to obtain a domain-theoretic analysis of our computational notions, based on a suitable domain equation. What this should be is readily elicited from the definition of ats. The structure map

$$ev : A \rightharpoonup (A \to A)$$

is *partial*; the standard approach to partial maps in domain theory (*pace* Plotkin's recent work on predomains [27]) is to make them into total ones by sending undefined arguments to a "bottom" element, i.e., by changing the type of $ev$ to

$$A \to (A \to A)_\perp .$$

This suggests the domain equation

$$D = (D \to D)_\perp ,$$

i.e., the denotation of the type expression $\operatorname{rec} t.(t \to t)_\perp$. This equation is composed from the function space and lifting constructions. Since **SDom** is closed under these constructions, $D$ is a Scott domain. Indeed, by the same reasoning it is an algebraic lattice. The crucial point is that this equation has a *nontrivial initial solution*, and thus there is a good candidate for a canonical model. To see this, consider the "approximants" $D_k$, with $D_0 \equiv \mathbf{1}$, $D_{k+1} \equiv (D_k \to D_k)_\perp$. Then

$$D_1 \;=\; (\mathbf{1} \to \mathbf{1})_\perp \cong (\mathbf{1})_\perp \cong \mathbb{O} \,,$$
$$D_2 \;\cong\; (\mathbb{O} \to \mathbb{O})_\perp, \quad \text{with four elements}\,,$$
$$\vdots$$

We now unpack the structure of $D$. Our treatment will be rather cursory, as it proceeds along similar lines to our work in [1]. First, there is an isomorphism pair,

$$\text{unfold} : D \to (D \to D)_\perp, \quad \text{fold} : (D \to D)_\perp \to D \,.$$

Next, we recall the categorical description of lifting, as the left adjoint to the forgetful functor

$$U, : \mathbf{Dom}_\perp \to \mathbf{Dom} \,,$$

where $\mathbf{Dom}_\perp$ is the subcategory of strict functions. Thus we have:

A natural transformation $\text{up} : I_{\mathbf{Dom}} \to U \circ (\cdot)_\perp$.

For each continuous map $f : D \to UE$ its unique strict extension

$$\text{lift}(f) : (D)_\perp \to_\perp E \,.$$

Concretely, we can take

$$
\begin{aligned}
(D)_\perp &\equiv \{\perp\} \cup \{<0, d> \mid d \in D\}, \\
x \sqsubseteq y &\equiv x = \perp \,, \\
&\quad \text{or } x = <0, d> \,\&\, y = <0, d'> \,\&\, d \sqsubseteq_D d' \,, \\
\text{up}_D(d) &\equiv <0, d> \,, \\
\text{lift}(f)(\perp) &\equiv \perp_E \,, \\
\text{lift}(f)<0, d> &\equiv f(d) \,.
\end{aligned}
$$

We can now define

$$ev : D \to (D \to D)$$

by

$$ev(d) = \begin{cases} f, & \text{unfold}(d) = <0, f> \\ \text{undefined}, & \text{unfold}(d) = \bot. \end{cases}$$

Thus $(D, ev)$ is a quasi-ats, and we write $d \Downarrow f$, $d \Uparrow$, etc. Note that we can recover $d$ from $ev(d)$ by

$$d = \begin{cases} \text{fold}(<0, f>), & d \Downarrow f \\ \bot_D, & d \Uparrow. \end{cases}$$

The final ingredient in the definition of $D$ is initiality. The only direct consequence of this that we will use is contained in the following theorem.

## Theorem 4.1

$D$ is internally fully abstract, i.e.,

$$\forall d, d' \in D. d \sqsubseteq d' \iff d \precsim^B d'.$$

**Proof**   Unpacking the definitions, we see that for all $d, d' \in D$:

$$d \sqsubseteq d' \iff d \Downarrow f \Rightarrow d' \Downarrow g \& \forall d'' \in D. f(d'') \sqsubseteq g(d'').$$

Thus the domain ordering is an applicative bisimulation and so is included in $\sqsubseteq^B$. For the converse, we need some additional notions. We define $d_k$, $f_k$ for $d \in D$, $f \in [D \to D]$, $k \in \omega$ by

- $d_0 \Uparrow$,
- $d \Uparrow \Rightarrow d_k \Uparrow$,
- $d \Downarrow f \Rightarrow d_{k+1} \Downarrow f_k$,
- $f_k : d \mapsto (fd)_k$.

We can use standard techniques to prove, from the initiality of $D$,

- $\forall d \in D. d = \bigsqcup_{k \in \omega} d_k$.

The proof is completed with a routine induction to show that

$$\forall k \in \omega. d \precsim_k d' \Rightarrow d_k \sqsubseteq d'_k. \quad \square$$

As an immediate corollary of this result, we see that $D$ is an ats. We thus have an interpretation function,

$$[\![ \cdot ]\!]^D : CL(D) \to Env(D) \longrightarrow D.$$

We extend this to $\Lambda(D)$ by

$$[\![\lambda x.M]\!]_\rho^D = \text{fold}(\text{up}(\lambda d \in D.[\![M]\!]_{\rho[x \mapsto d]}^D)) \,.$$

Note that the application induced from $(D, ev)$ can be described by

$$d \cdot d' = \text{lift}(Ap)\,\text{unfold}(d)\,d' \,,$$

where

$$Ap : [D \to D] \to D \to D$$

is the standard application function and is therefore continuous. This together with standard arguments about environment semantics guarantees that our extension of $[\![\,]\!]^D$ is well defined. Note also that $[\![\lambda x.M]\!]_\rho^D \neq \perp_D$, as expected.

We can now define

$$k \quad \equiv \quad [\![\lambda x.\lambda y.x]\!]_\rho^D \,,$$

$$s \quad \equiv \quad [\![\lambda x.\lambda y.\lambda z.(xz)(yz)]\!]_\rho^D$$

for $D$. It is straightforward to verify the following proposition.

## Proposition 4.1
$D$ is an lts.

Thus far, we have merely used our domain equation to construct a particular lts $D$. However, its "categorical" or "absolute" nature should lead us to suspect that we can use $D$ to study the whole class of lts. The medium we will use for this purpose is a suitable *domain logic* in the sense of [2].

## 5 *A Domain Logic for Applicative Transition Systems*

**Definition 5.1**    The syntax of our domain logic $\mathcal{L}$ is defined by

$$\phi \;::=\; \mathbf{t} \mid \phi \wedge \psi \mid (\phi \to \psi)_\perp \,.$$

**Definition 5.2** (Semantics of $\mathcal{L}$)
Given a quasi-ats $\mathcal{A}$, we define the satisfaction relation $\models_\mathcal{A} \subseteq \mathcal{A} \times \mathcal{L}$:

$$a \models_\mathcal{A} \mathbf{t} \qquad\qquad \equiv \qquad \text{true}\,,$$

$$a \models_\mathcal{A} \phi \wedge \psi \qquad \equiv \qquad a \models_\mathcal{A} \phi \,\&\, a \models_\mathcal{A} \psi\,,$$

$$a \models_\mathcal{A} (\phi \to \psi)_\perp \quad \equiv \quad a \Downarrow f \,\&\, \forall b \in A.\, b \models_\mathcal{A} \phi \;\Rightarrow\; f(b) \models_\mathcal{A} \psi\,.$$

## Notation

$$\mathcal{L}(a) \quad\equiv\quad \{\phi \in \mathcal{L} : a \vDash_{\mathcal{A}} \phi\},$$

$$\mathcal{A} \vDash \phi \leq \psi \quad\equiv\quad \forall a \in A. a \vDash_{\mathcal{A}} \phi \implies a \vDash_{\mathcal{A}} \psi,$$

$$\mathcal{A} \vDash \phi = \psi \quad\equiv\quad \forall a \in A. a \vDash_{\mathcal{A}} \phi \iff a \vDash_{\mathcal{A}} \psi,$$

$$\vDash \phi \leq \psi \quad\equiv\quad \forall \mathcal{A}. \mathcal{A} \vDash \phi \leq \psi,$$

$$\lambda \quad\equiv\quad (\mathbf{t} \to \mathbf{t})_{\perp},$$

$$a \sqsubseteq^{\mathcal{L}} b \quad\equiv\quad \mathcal{L}(a) \subseteq \mathcal{L}(b).$$

Note that $\forall a \in A. a \Downarrow \iff a \vDash_{\mathcal{A}} \lambda$.

## Lemma 5.1
Let $\mathcal{A}$ be a quasi-ats. Then

$$\forall a, b \in A. a \precsim^{B} b \implies a \sqsubseteq^{\mathcal{L}} b.$$

**Proof**   We assume $a \precsim^{B} b$ and prove $\forall \phi \in \mathcal{L}. a \vDash_{\mathcal{A}} \phi \implies b \vDash_{\mathcal{A}} \phi$ by induction on $\phi$. The nontrivial case is $(\phi \to \psi)_{\perp}$.

- $a \vDash_{\mathcal{A}} (\phi \to \psi)_{\perp}$,
- $\implies a \Downarrow f$,
- $\implies b \Downarrow g \,\&\, \forall c. f(c) \precsim^{B} g(c)$,
- $\implies \forall c. c \vDash_{\mathcal{A}} \phi \implies f(c) \precsim^{B} g(c) \,\&\, f(c) \vDash_{\mathcal{A}} \psi$,
- $\implies \forall c. c \vDash_{\mathcal{A}} \phi \implies g(c) \vDash_{\mathcal{A}} \psi$,                 ind. hyp.
- $\implies b \vDash_{\mathcal{A}} (\phi \to \psi)_{\perp}$. $\quad\square$

To get a converse to this result, we need a condition on $\mathcal{A}$.

**Definition 5.3**   A quasi-ats A is *approximable* iff

$$\forall a, b_1, \ldots, b_n \in A. ab_1 \ldots b_n \Downarrow \implies \exists \phi_1, \cdots, \phi_n.$$

$$a \vDash_{\mathcal{A}} (\phi_1 \to \cdots (\phi_n \to \lambda)_{\perp} \cdots)_{\perp} \,\&\, b_i \vDash_{\mathcal{A}} \phi_i, \ 1 \leq i \leq n.$$

This is a natural condition, which says that convergence of a function application is caused by some finite amount of information (observable properties) of its arguments.

As expected, we have the following theorem.

## Theorem 5.1 (Characterization Theorem)
Let $\mathcal{A}$ be an approximable quasi-ats. Then

$$\precsim^{B} = \precsim^{\mathcal{L}}.$$

**Proof**   By Lemma 5.1, $\sqsubseteq^B \subseteq \sqsubseteq^L$. For the converse, suppose $a \not\sqsubseteq^B b$. Then for some $k$, $a \not\sqsubseteq^B_k b$, and so for some $c_1, \ldots, c_k \in A$:

$$ac_1 \cdots c_k \Downarrow \ \& \ bc_1 \cdots c_k \Uparrow .$$

By approximability, for some $\phi_1, \ldots, \phi_k \in L$,

$$a \models_A (\phi_1 \to \cdots (\phi_k \to \lambda)_\perp \cdots)_\perp \ \& \ c_i \models_A \phi_i, \ 1 \le i \le k .$$

Clearly $b \not\models_A (\phi_1 \to \cdots (\phi_k \to \lambda)_\perp \cdots)_\perp$, and so $a \not\sqsubseteq^L b$.   $\square$

As a further consequence of approximability, we have the following proposition.

## Proposition 5.1

An approximable quasi-ats is an ats.

**Proof**   Suppose $a \Downarrow f$ and $b \sqsubseteq^B c$. We must show $f(b) \sqsubseteq^B f(c)$. It is sufficient to show that for all $k \in \omega$, $d_1, \ldots, d_k \in A$:

$$f(b)d_1 \ldots d_k \Downarrow \ \Rightarrow \ f(c)d_1 \ldots d_k \Downarrow .$$

Now $f(b)d_1 \ldots d_k \Downarrow$ implies $abd_1 \ldots d_k \Downarrow$; hence by approximability, for some $\phi, \phi_1, \ldots, \phi_k \in L$:

$$a \models_A (\phi \to (\phi_1 \to \cdots (\phi_k \to \lambda)_\perp \cdots)_\perp$$

and

$$b \models_A \phi, \ b_i \models_A \phi_i, \ 1 \le i \le k .$$

By Theorem 5.1, $c \models_A \phi$, and so $abd_1 \ldots d_k \models_A \lambda$, and $f(c)d_1 \ldots d_k \Downarrow$ as required.   $\square$

We now introduce a proof system for assertions of the form $\phi \le \psi$, $\phi = \psi$ ($\phi, \psi \in L$).

### 5.1 *Proof System for $L$*

(REF)  $\phi \le \phi$        (TRANS)  $\dfrac{\phi \le \psi \ \ \psi \le \xi}{\phi \le \xi}$

$(= -I)$  $\dfrac{\phi \le \psi \ \ \psi \le \phi}{\phi = \psi}$        $(= -E)$  $\dfrac{\phi = \psi}{\phi \le \psi \ \ \psi \le \phi}$

$(\mathbf{t} - I)$  $\phi \le \mathbf{t}$

$(\wedge - I)$  $\dfrac{\phi \le \phi_1 \ \ \phi \le \psi_2}{\phi \le \phi_1 \wedge \phi_2}$        $(\wedge - E)$  $\phi \wedge \psi \le \phi \ \ \ \phi \wedge \psi \le \psi$

$$((\rightarrow)_\perp - \leq) \quad \frac{\phi_2 \leq \phi_1 \quad \psi_1 \leq \psi_2}{(\phi_1 \rightarrow \psi_1)_\perp \leq (\phi_2 \rightarrow \psi_2)_\perp}$$

$$((\rightarrow)_\perp - \wedge) \quad (\phi \rightarrow \psi_1 \wedge \psi_2)_\perp = (\phi \rightarrow \psi_1)_\perp \wedge (\phi \rightarrow \psi_2)_\perp$$

$$((\rightarrow)_\perp - \mathbf{t}) \quad (\phi \rightarrow \mathbf{t})_\perp \leq (\mathbf{t} \rightarrow \mathbf{t})_\perp .$$

We write $\mathcal{L} \vdash A$ or just $\vdash A$ to indicate that an assertion $A$ is derivable from these axioms and rules. Note that the converse of $((\rightarrow)_\perp - \mathbf{t})$ is derivable from $(\mathbf{t}-I)$ and $((\rightarrow)_\perp - \leq)$; by abuse of notation we refer to the corresponding equation by the same name.

## Theorem 5.2 (Soundness Theorem)

$$\vdash \phi \leq \psi \implies \vDash \phi \leq \psi .$$

**Proof**   By a routine induction on the length of proofs.   □

So far, our logic has been presented in a syntax-free fashion as far as the elements of the ats are concerned. Now suppose we have an lts $\mathcal{A}$. $\lambda$-terms can be interpreted in $\mathcal{A}$, and for $M \in \Lambda^0$, $\rho \in Env(\mathcal{A})$, we can define

$$M, \rho \vDash_{\mathcal{A}} \phi \equiv [\![M]\!]^{\mathcal{A}}_\rho \vDash_{\mathcal{A}} \phi .$$

We can extend this to arbitrary terms $M \in \Lambda$ in the presence of *assumptions* $\Gamma : \text{Var} \rightarrow \mathcal{L}$ on the variables:

$$M, \Gamma \vDash_{\mathcal{A}} \phi \equiv \forall \rho \in Env(\mathcal{A}). \rho \vDash_{\mathcal{A}} \Gamma \implies [\![M]\!]^{\mathcal{A}}_\rho \vDash_{\mathcal{A}} \phi ,$$

where

$$\rho \vDash_{\mathcal{A}} \Gamma \equiv \forall x \in \text{Var}. \rho x \vDash_{\mathcal{A}} \Gamma x .$$

We write

$$M, \Gamma \vDash \phi \equiv \forall \mathcal{A}. M, \Gamma \vDash_{\mathcal{A}} \phi .$$

We now introduce a proof system for assertions of the form $M, \Gamma \vdash \phi$.

## Notation   $\Gamma \leq \Delta \equiv \forall x \in \text{Var}. \Gamma x \leq \Delta x.$

### 5.2 *Proof System for Program Logic*

$$M, \Gamma \vdash \mathbf{t}$$

$$\frac{M, \Gamma \vdash \phi \quad M, \Gamma \vdash \psi}{M, \Gamma \vdash \phi \wedge \psi}$$

$$\frac{\Gamma \leq \Delta \ \ M, \Delta \vdash \phi \ \ \phi \leq \psi}{M, \Gamma \vdash \psi}$$

$$x, \Gamma[x \mapsto \phi] \vdash \phi$$

$$\frac{M, \Gamma[x \mapsto \phi] \vdash \psi}{\lambda x.M, \Gamma \vdash (\phi \rightarrow \psi)_\perp}$$

$$\frac{M, \Gamma \vdash (\phi \rightarrow \psi)_\perp \ \ N, \Gamma \vdash \phi}{MN, \Gamma \vdash \psi} .$$

## Theorem 5.3 (Soundness of Program Logic)

For all $M$, $\Gamma$, $\phi$:

$$M, \Gamma \vdash \phi \ \Longrightarrow \ M, \Gamma \models \phi .$$

The proof is again routine. Note the striking similarity of our program logic with type inference, in particular with the intersection type discipline and extended applicative type structures of [8]. The crucial *difference* lies in the entailment relation $\leq$, and in particular in the fact that their axiom (in our notation),

$$\mathbf{t} \leq (\mathbf{t} \rightarrow \mathbf{t})_\perp ,$$

is *not* a theorem in our logic; instead, we have the weaker $((\rightarrow)_\perp)$. This reflects a different notion of "function space"; we discuss this further in Section 7.

We now come to the expected connection between the domain logic $\mathcal{L}$ and the domain $D$. The connecting link is the domain equation that is used to define $D$ and from which $\mathcal{L}$ is derived. Since this equation corresponds to the type expression $\sigma \equiv rec\,t.(t \rightarrow t)_\perp$, it falls within the scope of the general theory developed in [2]. The logic $\mathcal{L}$ presented in this section is a streamlined version of $\mathcal{L}(\sigma)$ as defined in [2]. Once we have shown that $\mathcal{L}$ is equivalent to $\mathcal{L}(\sigma)$, we can apply the results of [2] to obtain the desired relationships between $\mathcal{L} \simeq \mathcal{L}(\sigma)$ and $D \simeq D(\sigma)$.[1]

Note that $\mathcal{L}$ as presented contains no disjunctive structure, while the constructs $\rightarrow$, $(\cdot)_\perp$ appearing in $\sigma$ generate no inconsistencies according to the definition of C in [2]. Thus (the Lindenbaum algebra of) $\mathcal{L}_\wedge(\sigma)$, the purely conjunctive part of $\mathcal{L}(\sigma)$, is a meet-semilattice, and applying [2, Theorem 2.3.4], we obtain

$$\mathrm{Spec}\ (\mathcal{L}(\sigma)/{=}_\sigma, \leq_\sigma/{=}_\sigma) \ \cong \ \mathrm{Filt}(\mathcal{L}_\wedge(\sigma)/{=}_\sigma, \leq_\sigma/{=}_\sigma) .$$

---

1. The reader unfamiliar with [2] who is prepared to take Theorems 5.4 and 5.5 on trust is advised to skip the details till after 5.5.

It remains to show that $\mathcal{L}$ is pre-isomorphic to $\mathcal{L}_\wedge(\sigma)$. We can describe the syntax of $\mathcal{L}_\wedge(\sigma)$ as follows:

$L_\wedge(\sigma)$:

$$\phi \;::=\; \mathbf{t} \mid \phi \wedge \psi \mid (\phi)_\perp \quad (\phi \in L(\sigma \to \sigma)).$$

$L_\wedge(\sigma \to \sigma)$:

$$\phi \;::=\; \mathbf{t} \mid \phi \wedge \psi \mid (\phi \to \psi) \quad (\phi, \psi \in L(\sigma)).$$

Using $(()_\perp - \wedge)$ and $(\to -\mathbf{t})$ (i.e., the nullary instances of $(\to -\wedge)$) from [2]), we obtain the following normal forms for $L_\wedge(\sigma)$:

$$\phi \;::=\; \mathbf{t} \mid \phi \wedge \psi \mid (\phi \to \psi)_\perp .$$

In this way we see that $L \subseteq L_\wedge(\sigma)$, and that each $\phi \in L_\wedge(\sigma)$ is equivalent to one in $L$. Moreover, the axioms and rules of $\mathcal{L}$ are easily seen to be derivable in $\mathcal{L}_\wedge(\sigma)$. For example, $((\to)_\perp - \mathbf{t})$ is derivable, since

$$\mathcal{L}_\wedge(\sigma) \vdash (\phi \to \psi)_\perp = (\mathbf{t})_\perp = (\mathbf{t} \to \mathbf{t})_\perp .$$

It remains to show the converse, i.e., that for $\phi, \psi \in \mathcal{L}$:

$$\mathcal{L}_\wedge(\sigma) \vdash \phi \le \psi \;\implies\; \mathcal{L} \vdash \phi \le \psi.$$

For this purpose, we use $((\to)_\perp - \wedge)$ and $((\to)_\perp - \mathbf{t})$ to get normal forms for $\mathcal{L}$.

## Lemma  5.2  (Normal Forms)
Every formula in $\mathcal{L}$ is equivalent to one in $N\mathcal{L}$, where:

$$N\mathcal{L} = \{\textstyle\bigwedge_{i \in I} \phi_i : I \text{ finite}, \; \phi_i \in SN\mathcal{L}, \; i \in I\},$$
$$SN\mathcal{L} = \{(\phi_1 \to \cdots (\phi_k \to \lambda)_\perp \cdots)_\perp : k \ge 0, \phi_i \in N\mathcal{L}, \; 1 \le i \le k\}.$$

Now by [2, Propositions 3.4.5 and 3.4.6], we have

## Lemma  5.3
For $\phi, \psi$ with

$$\phi \equiv \bigwedge_{i \in I}(\phi_i \to \phi_i')_\perp, \qquad \psi \equiv \bigwedge_{j \in J}(\psi_j \to \psi_j')_\perp :$$

$$\mathcal{L}(\sigma) \vdash \phi \le \psi \iff \forall j \in J.\, \mathcal{L}(\sigma) \vdash \bigwedge\{\phi_i' : \mathcal{L}(\sigma) \vdash \psi_j \le \phi_i\} \le \psi_j'.$$

## Proposition  5.2
For $\phi, \psi \in N\mathcal{L}$, if $\mathcal{L}(\sigma) \vdash \phi \le \psi$ then there is a proof of $\phi \le \psi$ using only the meet-semilattice laws and the derived rule $((\to)_\perp)$.

**Proof**   By induction on the complexity of $\phi$ and $\psi$, and the preceding lemma.   □

We have thus shown that

$$\mathcal{L}(\sigma) \cong \mathcal{L}_\Lambda(\sigma) \cong \mathcal{L},$$

and we can apply the duality theorem of [2] to obtain the following theorem.

**Theorem 5.4** (Stone Duality)
$\mathcal{L}$ is the Stone dual of $D$:

**(i)** $D \cong \text{Filt } \mathcal{L}$,

**(ii)** $(\mathcal{K}(D))^{op} \cong (L/=, \leq/=)$

(where $\mathcal{K}(D)$ is the sub-poset of finite elements of $D$).

**Corollary 5.1**
$D \models \phi \leq \psi \iff \mathcal{L} \vdash \phi \leq \psi$.

We can now deal with the program logic over $\lambda$-terms in a similar fashion. The denotational semantics for $\Lambda$ in $D$ given in the previous section can be used to define a translation map

$$(\cdot)^* : \Lambda \to \Lambda(\sigma).$$

The logic presented in this section is equivalent to the endogenous logic of [2] in the sense that

$$M, \Gamma \vdash \phi \iff M^*, \Gamma \vdash \phi,$$

where $M \in \Lambda$, $\Gamma : \text{Var} \to L$, $\phi \in L \subseteq L(\sigma)$. We omit the details, which by now should be routine. As a consequence of this result, we can apply the completeness theorem for endogenous logic from [2], to obtain the following theorem.

**Theorem 5.5**
$D$ is $\mathcal{L}$-complete; i.e., for all $M \in \Lambda$, $\Gamma : \text{Var} \to L$, $\phi \in L \subseteq L(\sigma)$:

$$M, \Gamma \vdash \phi \iff M, \Gamma \models_D \phi.$$

In the previous section, we defined an lts over $D$; and we have now shown that $D$ is isomorphic as a domain to Filt $\mathcal{L}$. We can in fact describe the lts structure over Filt $\mathcal{L}$ directly; and this will show how $D$, defined by a domain equation reminiscent of the $D_\infty$ construction, can also be viewed as a graph model or "PSE algebra" in the terminology of [17].

**Notation**    For $X \subseteq L$, $X^\dagger$ is the filter generated by $X$. This can be defined inductively by:

$$X \subseteq X^\dagger ,$$

$$\mathbf{t} \in X^\dagger ,$$

$$\phi, \psi \in X^\dagger \; \Rightarrow \; \phi \wedge \psi \in X^\dagger ,$$

$$\phi \in X^\dagger, \; \mathcal{L} \vdash \phi \le \psi \; \Rightarrow \; \psi \in X^\dagger .$$

**Definition 5.4**    The quasi-applicative structure with divergence

$$(\text{Filt } \mathcal{L}, \cdot , \Uparrow)$$

is defined as follows:

$$x \Uparrow \quad \equiv \quad x = \{\mathbf{t}\} ,$$

$$x \cdot y \quad \equiv \quad \{\psi : \exists \phi. (\phi \to \psi)_\perp \in x \; \& \; \phi \in y\} \cup \{\mathbf{t}\} .$$

It is easily verified that in this structure

$$x \sqsubseteq^B_{\approx} y \iff x \subseteq y ,$$

and hence that application is monotone in each argument, and Filt $\mathcal{L}$ is an ats. Thus we have an interpretation function,

$$[\![ \cdot ]\!]^{\text{Filt } \mathcal{L}} : CL(\text{Filt } \mathcal{L}) \to Env(\text{Filt } \mathcal{L}) \to \text{Filt } \mathcal{L} ,$$

which is extended to $\Lambda(\text{Filt } \mathcal{L})$ by

$$[\![ \lambda x.M ]\!]^{\text{Filt } \mathcal{L}}_\rho = \{(\phi \to \psi)_\perp : \psi \in [\![ M ]\!]^{\text{Filt } \mathcal{L}}_{\rho[x \to \uparrow\phi]}\}^\dagger .$$

We then make the following definition.

**Definition 5.5**

$$s \quad \equiv \quad [\![ \lambda x.\lambda y.\lambda z.(xz)(yz) ]\!]^{\text{Filt } \mathcal{L}} ,$$

$$k \quad \equiv \quad [\![ \lambda x.\lambda y.x ]\!]^{\text{Filt } \mathcal{L}} .$$

**Proposition 5.3**

Filt $\mathcal{L}$ is an lts. Moreover, Filt $\mathcal{L}$ and $D$ are isomorphic as combinatory algebras.

**Proof**    It is sufficient to show that the isomorphism of the duality theorem preserves application, divergence, and the denotation of $\lambda$-terms, since it then preserves $s$ and $k$ and so is a combinatory isomorphism, and Filt $\mathcal{L}$ is an lts, since $D$ is.

First, we show that application is preserved; i.e., for $d_1, d_2 \in D$,

$$\mathcal{L}(d_1 \cdot d_2) = \mathcal{L}(d_1) \cdot \mathcal{L}(d_2). \qquad (\star)$$

The right-to-left inclusion follows by the same argument as the soundness of the rule for application in Theorem 5.2. For the converse, suppose $\psi \in \mathcal{L}(d_1 \cdot d_2)$, $\mathcal{L} \not\vdash \psi = \mathbf{t}$. By the duality theorem, each $\psi$ in $\mathcal{L}$ corresponds to a unique $c \in \mathcal{K}(D)$ with $\mathcal{L}(c) = \uparrow\psi$. Since application is continuous in $D$, $c \sqsubseteq d_1 \cdot d_2$, $c \neq \bot$ implies that for some $b \in \mathcal{K}(D)$, $\text{fold}(<0, [b, c]>) \sqsubseteq d_1$ and $b \sqsubseteq d_2$. (Here $[b, c]$ is the one-step function mapping $d$ to $c$ if $b \sqsubseteq d$, and to $\bot$ otherwise.) Let $\mathcal{L}(b) = \uparrow\phi$; then $(\phi \to \psi)_\bot \in \mathcal{L}(d_1)$ and $\phi \in \mathcal{L}(d_2)$, as required.

Next, we show that denotations of $\lambda$-terms are preserved; i.e., for all $M \in \Lambda$, $\rho \in Env(D)$,

$$\mathcal{L}(\llbracket M \rrbracket_\rho^D) = \llbracket M \rrbracket_{\mathcal{L} \circ \rho}^{\text{Filt}\,\mathcal{L}}. \qquad (\star\star)$$

This is proved by induction on $M$. The case when $M$ is a variable is trivial; the case for application uses $(\star)$. For abstraction, we argue by structural induction over $\mathcal{L}$. We show the nontrivial case. Let $\phi$, $b$ be paired in the isomorphism of the duality theorem. Then

$$\lambda x.M, \rho \models_D (\phi \to \psi)_\bot$$
$$\Longleftrightarrow \quad M, \rho[x \mapsto b] \models_D \psi$$
$$\Longleftrightarrow \quad M, \mathcal{L}() \circ (\rho[x \mapsto b]) \models_{\text{Filt}\,\mathcal{L}} \psi \qquad \text{ind. hyp.}$$
$$\Longleftrightarrow \quad M, (\mathcal{L}() \circ \rho)[x \mapsto \uparrow \phi] \models_{\text{Filt}\,\mathcal{L}} \psi$$
$$\Longleftrightarrow \quad \lambda x.M, \mathcal{L}() \circ \rho \models_{\text{Filt}\,\mathcal{L}} (\phi \to \psi)_\bot .$$

Finally, divergence is trivially preserved, since the only divergent elements in $D$, Filt $\mathcal{L}$ are $\bot$, $\{\mathbf{t}\}$, and these are in bi-unique correspondence under the isomorphism of the duality theorem.   $\square$

## **Theorem  5.6** (Computational Adequacy)
For all $M \in \Lambda$,

$$M \Downarrow \iff \llbracket M \rrbracket_{\rho_\bot}^D \neq \bot,$$

where $\rho_\bot : x \mapsto \bot$.

**Proof**   First, let $\sigma_\Omega : x \mapsto \Omega$. $M \Downarrow \Rightarrow (M\sigma_\Omega) \Downarrow \lambda x.N \Rightarrow \llbracket M \rrbracket_{\rho_\bot}^D = \llbracket \lambda x.N \rrbracket_{\rho_\bot}^D \neq \bot$.

For the converse, let $\Gamma_t : x \mapsto \mathbf{t}$.

$$
\begin{aligned}
[\![M]\!]^D_{\rho_\perp} \neq \bot \quad &\Rightarrow \quad [\![M]\!]^{\mathrm{Filt}\,\mathcal{L}}_{\rho_\perp} \neq \{\mathbf{t}\} \quad \text{by Proposition 5.3} \\
&\Rightarrow \quad M, \Gamma_t \vdash \lambda \\
&\Rightarrow \quad M, \Gamma_t \models \lambda \qquad\qquad \text{by Theorem 5.3} \\
&\Rightarrow \quad M \Downarrow . \qquad\qquad\qquad\qquad \square
\end{aligned}
$$

The triviality of this proof is notable, since analogous results in the literature have required lengthy arguments involving recursively defined inclusive predicates (cf. [27]).

We can now proceed in exact analogy to [1] and use Stone duality to convert the characterization theorem into a final algebra theorem.

**Definition 5.6**    We define a number of categories of transition systems:

**ATS** Objects: applicative transition systems; morphisms $\mathcal{A} \to \mathcal{B}$: maps $f : A \to B$ satisfying

$$
a \models_A \phi \iff f(a) \models_B \phi .
$$

**LTS:** The subcategory of **ATS** of lts and morphisms that preserve application, $s$ and $k$.

**CLTS:** The full subcategory of **LTS** of those $\mathcal{A}$ satisfying *continuity*:

$$
\psi \neq \mathbf{t}, \; ab \models_A \psi \implies \exists \phi. a \models_A (\phi \to \psi)_\perp \,\&\, b \models_A \phi,
$$

and also

$$
\mathcal{L}(s) = [\![s]\!]^{\mathrm{Filt}\,\mathcal{L}}, \quad \mathcal{L}(k) = [\![k]\!]^{\mathrm{Filt}\,\mathcal{L}} .
$$

Note that continuity implies approximability.

**Theorem  5.7** (Final Algebra)

**(i)** $D$ is final in **ATS**.

**(ii)** Let $\mathcal{A}$ be an approximable lts. The map

$$
t_{\mathcal{A}} : \mathcal{A} \to D
$$

from (i) is an **LTS** morphism iff $\mathcal{A}$ is continuous.

**(iii)** $D$ is final in **CLTS**.

## Proof

**(i)** Given $\mathcal{A}$ in **ATS**, define

$$t_{\mathcal{A}} : \mathcal{A} \to D$$

by

$$t_{\mathcal{A}} \;\equiv\; \mathcal{A} \xrightarrow{\mathcal{L}()} \text{Filt } \mathcal{L} \xrightarrow{\eta} D,$$

where $\eta$ is the isomorphism from the Stone duality theorem. For $a \in A$,

$$\mathcal{L}(a) = \mathcal{L} \circ \eta \circ \mathcal{L}(a) = \mathcal{L} \circ t_{\mathcal{A}}(a),$$

and so $t_{\mathcal{A}}$ is an **ATS** morphism; moreover, it is unique, since for $d, d' \in D$,

$$\mathcal{L}(d) = \mathcal{L}(d') \;\Rightarrow\; \mathcal{K}(d) = \mathcal{K}(d') \;\Rightarrow\; d = d'.$$

**(ii)** That $\mathcal{L}()$ is a combinatory morphism iff $\mathcal{A}$ is in **CLTS** is an immediate consequence of the definitions; the result then follows from the fact that $\eta$ is a combinatory isomorphism.

**(iii)** Immediate from (ii).    $\square$

Note that if $\mathcal{A}$ is approximable, we have:

$$a \sqsubseteq^B b \;\Longleftrightarrow\; t_{\mathcal{A}}(a) \sqsubseteq^B t_{\mathcal{A}}(b).$$

Thus we can regard the final algebra theorem as giving a syntax-free fully abstract semantics for approximable ats. However, from the point of view of applications to programming language semantics, this is not very useful. In the next section, we study full abstraction in a syntax-directed framework, using our domain logic as a tool.

## 6 *Lambda Transition Systems Considered as Programming Languages*

The classical discussion of full abstraction in the $\lambda$-calculus [26, 19] is set in the typed $\lambda$-calculus with ground data. As remarked in the Introduction, this material has not to date been transferred successfully to the pure untyped $\lambda$-calculus. To see why this is so, let us recall some basic notions from [26, 19].

There is a natural notion of *program*, namely, closed term of ground type. Programs either diverge or yield ground constants as results. This provides a natural notion of observable behavior for programs and hence an operational order on them. This is extended to arbitrary terms via ground contexts; in other words, the point of view is taken that only program behavior is directly observable, and the meaning of a higher-type term lies in the observable behavior of the programs into which it can be embedded. Thus both the presence of ground data and the fact that terms are typed enter into the basic definitions of the theory.

By contrast, we have a notion of atomic observation for the lazy $\lambda$-calculus in the absence of types or ground data, namely, convergence to weak head normal form. This leads to the applicative bisimulation relation and hence to a natural operational ordering. We can thus develop a theory of full abstraction in the pure untyped $\lambda$-calculus. Our results will correspond recognizably to those in [26], although the technical details contain many differences. One feature of our development is that we work axiomatically with classes of lts under various hypotheses, rather than with particular languages. (Note that operational transition systems and "programming languages" such as $\lambda\ell$ actually *are* lts under our definitions.)

**Definition 6.1**   Let $\mathcal{A}$ be an lts. $D$ is *fully abstract* for $\mathcal{A}$ if $\mathfrak{I}(\mathcal{A}) = \mathfrak{I}(D)$.

This definition is consistent with that in [19, 26], provided we accept the applicative bisimulation ordering on $\mathcal{A}$ as the appropriate operational preorder. The argument for doing so is made highly plausible by Proposition 2.1, which characterizes applicative bisimulation as a contextual preorder analogous to those used in [19, 26]. We shall prove Proposition 2.1 later in this section.

We now turn to the question of conditions under which $D$ is fully abstract for $\mathcal{A}$. As emerges from [26, 19], this is essentially a question of definability.

**Definition 6.2**   An ats $\mathcal{A}$ is $\mathcal{L}$-*expressive* if for all $\phi \in \mathcal{L}$, for some $a \in \mathcal{A}$:

$$\mathcal{L}(a) = \uparrow\phi \equiv \{\psi \in \mathcal{L} : \mathcal{L} \vdash \phi \leq \psi\}.$$

In the light of Stone duality, $\mathcal{L}$-expressiveness can be read as: "all finite elements of $D$ are definable in $\mathcal{A}$."

**Definition 6.3**   Let $\mathcal{A}$ be an ats.

*Convergence testing* is definable in $\mathcal{A}$ if for some $c \in A$, $\mathcal{A}$ satisfies:

$$c \Downarrow,$$
$$x \Uparrow \Rightarrow cx \Uparrow,$$
$$x \Downarrow \Rightarrow cx = \mathbf{I}.$$

In this case, we use C as a constant to denote $c$.

*Parallel convergence* is definable in $\mathcal{A}$ if for some $p \in A$, $\mathcal{A}$ satisfies:

$$p \Downarrow, \ px \Downarrow,$$
$$x \Downarrow \ \Rightarrow \ pxy \Downarrow,$$
$$y \Downarrow \ \Rightarrow \ pxy \Downarrow,$$
$$x \Uparrow \ \& \ y \Uparrow \ \Rightarrow \ pxy \Uparrow .$$

In this case, we use P to denote such a $p$.

Note that if C is definable, it is unique (up to bisimulation); this is not so for P.

The notion of parallel convergence is reminiscent of Plotkin's parallel *or* and it will play a similar role in our theory. (A sharper comparison will be made later in this section.) The notion of convergence testing is less expected. We can think of the combinator C as a sort of "1-strict" version of $\mathbf{F} \equiv \lambda x.\lambda y.y$:

$$Cxy = \mathbf{F}xy = y \quad \text{if } x \Downarrow,$$

$$Cxy \Uparrow \quad \text{if } x \Uparrow .$$

This 1-strictness allows us to test, sequentially, a number of expressions for convergence. Under the hypothesis that C is definable, we can give a very satisfactory picture of the relationship between all these notions.

## Theorem  6.1 (Full Abstraction)
Let $\mathcal{A}$ be a sensible, approximable lts in which C is definable. The following conditions are equivalent:

  **(i)** Parallel convergence is definable in $\mathcal{A}$.

 **(ii)** $\mathcal{A}$ is $\mathcal{L}$-expressive.

**(iii)** $\mathcal{A}$ is $\mathcal{L}$-complete.

**(iv)** $t_{\mathcal{A}}$ is a combinatory embedding with $\mathcal{K}(D) \subseteq \mathbf{Im} \ t_{\mathcal{A}}$.

 **(v)** $D$ is fully abstract for $\mathcal{A}$.

**Proof**   We shall prove a sequence of implications to establish the theorem, indicating in each case which hypotheses on $\mathcal{A}$ are used.

**(i)** $\Rightarrow$ **(ii)**  ($\mathcal{A}$ sensible, C definable)

Since $\mathcal{A}$ is sensible, $\Omega$ diverges in $\mathcal{A}$.

**Notation**   Given a set Con of constants, $\Lambda(\text{Con})$ is the set of $\lambda$-terms over Con.

For each $\phi \in N\mathcal{L}$ we shall define terms $M_\phi, T_\phi \in \Lambda(\{P, C\})$ such that, for all $\psi \in N\mathcal{L}$

- $M_\phi \models_{\mathcal{A}} \psi \iff \mathcal{L} \vdash \phi \leq \psi$,

- $\begin{cases} T_\phi M_\psi \Downarrow & \text{if } M_\psi \models_{\mathcal{A}} \phi \\ T_\phi M_\psi \Uparrow & \text{otherwise}. \end{cases}$

The definition is by induction on the complexity of

$$\phi \equiv \bigwedge_{i \in I} (\phi_{i,1} \to \cdots (\phi_{i,k_i} \to \lambda)_\perp \cdots)_\perp.$$

If $I = \varnothing$, $M_\phi \equiv \Omega$. Otherwise, we define $M_\phi \equiv M(\phi, k)$, where $k = \max\{k_i \mid i \in I\}$:

$$M(\phi, 0) \quad \equiv \quad \mathbf{K}\Omega,$$
$$M(\phi, i+1) \quad \equiv \quad \lambda x_j. CN^j M(\phi, i),$$

where

$$j \qquad \equiv \quad k - i,$$
$$N^j \qquad \equiv \quad \sum\{N_i^j : j \leq k_i\},$$
$$N_i^j \qquad \equiv \quad C(T_{\phi_{i,1}} x_1)(C(T_{\phi_{i,2}} x_2)(\ldots(C(T_{\phi_{i,j}} x_j))\ldots)),$$
$$\sum \varnothing \qquad \equiv \quad \Omega,$$
$$\sum\{N\} \cup \Theta \quad \equiv \quad PN(\textstyle\sum \Theta),$$
$$T_\phi \qquad \equiv \quad \lambda x. \textstyle\prod\{x M_{\phi_{i,1}} \ldots M_{\phi_{i,k_i}} : i \in I\},$$
$$\textstyle\prod \varnothing \qquad \equiv \quad \mathbf{K}\Omega,$$
$$\textstyle\prod\{N\} \cup \Theta \quad \equiv \quad CN(\textstyle\prod \Theta).$$

We must show that these definitions have the required properties. First, we prove for all $\phi \in N\mathcal{L}$:

**1.** $M_\phi \models_{\mathcal{A}} \phi$,

**2.** $a \models_{\mathcal{A}} \phi \implies T_\phi a \Downarrow$,

by induction on $\phi$:

- $\forall i \in I. a_j \models_{\mathcal{A}} \phi_{i,j} \ (1 \leq j \leq k_i)$

$\implies M_\phi a_1 \ldots a_{k_i} \Downarrow$                 by induction hypothesis (2)

$\therefore \quad M_\phi \vdash_{\mathcal{A}} \phi$.

- $a \models_{\mathcal{A}} \phi$

$\implies T_\phi a \Downarrow$                        by induction hypothesis (1).

We complete the argument by proving, for all $\phi, \psi \in N\mathcal{L}$,

**3.** $M_\phi \vDash_\mathcal{A} \psi \;\Rightarrow\; \mathcal{L} \vdash \phi \le \psi$,

**4.** $M_\psi \vDash_\mathcal{A} \phi \;\Rightarrow\; \mathcal{L} \vdash \psi \le \phi$,

**5.** $\quad T_\phi M_\psi \!\Downarrow \;\Rightarrow\; M_\psi \vDash_\mathcal{A} \phi$,

**6.** $\quad T_\psi M_\phi \!\Downarrow \;\Rightarrow\; M_\phi \vDash_\mathcal{A} \psi$.

The proof is by induction on $n+m$, where $n, m$ are the numbers of subformulae of $\phi, \psi$, respectively. Let

$$\phi \;\equiv\; \bigwedge_{i\in I}(\phi_{i,1} \to \cdots (\phi_{i,k_i} \to \lambda)_\perp \cdots)_\perp\,,$$

$$\psi \;\equiv\; \bigwedge_{j\in J}(\psi_{j,1} \to \cdots (\psi_{j,k_j} \to \lambda)_\perp \cdots)_\perp\,.$$

(3): • $M_\phi \vDash_\mathcal{A} \psi$

$\quad\Rightarrow\; \forall j \in J. M_\phi M_{\psi_{j,1}} \ldots M_{\psi_{j,k_j}} \!\Downarrow$ $\hfill$ by (1)

$\quad\Rightarrow\; \forall j \in J. \exists i \in I. k_j \le k_i \,\&\, T_{\phi_{i,l}} M_{\psi_{j,l}} \!\Downarrow,\; 1 \le l \le k_j$

$\quad\Rightarrow\; M_{\psi_{j,l}} \vDash_\mathcal{A} \phi_{i,l},\; 1 \le l \le k_j$ $\hfill$ ind. hyp. (5)

$\quad\Rightarrow\; \mathcal{L} \vdash \psi_{j,l} \le \phi_{i,l},\; 1 \le l \le k_j$ $\hfill$ ind. hyp. (4)

$\quad\Rightarrow\; \mathcal{L} \vdash \phi \le \psi$.

(4): Symmetrical to (3).

(5): • $T_\phi M_\psi \!\Downarrow$

$\quad\Rightarrow\; \forall i \in I. M_\psi M_{\phi_{i,1}} \ldots M_{\phi_{i,k_i}} \!\Downarrow$

$\quad\Rightarrow\; \forall i \in I. \exists j \in J. k_i \le k_j \,\&\, T_{\psi_{j,l}} M_{\phi_{i,l}} \!\Downarrow,\; 1 \le l \le k_i$

$\quad\Rightarrow\; M_{\phi_{i,l}} \vDash_\mathcal{A} \psi_{j,l},\; 1 \le l \le k_i$ $\hfill$ ind. hyp. (6)

$\quad\Rightarrow\; \mathcal{L} \vdash \phi_{i,l} \le \psi_{j,l},\; 1 \le l \le k_i$ $\hfill$ ind. hyp. (3)

$\quad\Rightarrow\; \mathcal{L} \vdash \psi \le \phi$

$\quad\Rightarrow\; M_\psi \vDash_\mathcal{A} \phi$ $\hfill$ by (1).

(6): Symmetrical to (5).

**(ii)** $\Rightarrow$ **(iii)**   ($\mathcal{A}$ approximable)

**Notation**   For each $\phi \in L$, $a_\phi \in A$ is the element representing $\phi$. Given $\Gamma : \text{Var} \to L$, $\rho_\Gamma \in Env(\mathcal{A})$ is defined by

$$\rho_\Gamma x = a_{\Gamma x}\,.$$

Finally, $\Gamma_{\mathbf{t}} : \mathrm{Var} \to \mathcal{L}$ is the constant map $x \mapsto \mathbf{t}$.

We begin with some preliminary results.

**1.** $\mathcal{A} \models \phi \leq \psi \iff \mathcal{L} \vdash \phi \leq \psi$.

One half is the soundness theorem for $\mathcal{L}$. For the converse, note that

$$\mathcal{A} \models \phi \leq \psi \;\Rightarrow\; a_\phi \models_{\mathcal{A}} \psi$$
$$\Rightarrow\; \mathcal{L} \vdash \phi \leq \psi.$$

**2.** $\forall \psi \in N\mathcal{L}. \; \psi \neq \mathbf{t} \,\&\, ab \models_{\mathcal{A}} \psi \;\Rightarrow\; \exists \phi. \, a \models_{\mathcal{A}} (\phi \to \psi)_\perp \,\&\, b \models_{\mathcal{A}} \phi$.

This is shown by induction on $\psi$.

- $ab \models_{\mathcal{A}} \bigwedge_{i \in I} \psi_i \;(I \neq \varnothing)$
$\Rightarrow\; \forall i \in I. \, ab \models_{\mathcal{A}} \psi_i$
$\Rightarrow\; \forall i \in I. \, \exists \phi_i. \, a \models_{\mathcal{A}} (\phi_i \to \psi_i)_\perp \,\&\, b \models_{\mathcal{A}} \phi_i$       by ind. hyp.
$\Rightarrow\; \forall i \in I. \, a \models_{\mathcal{A}} (\bigwedge_{i \in I} \phi_i \to \psi_i)_\perp \,\&\, b \models_{\mathcal{A}} \bigwedge_{i \in I} \phi_i$
$\Rightarrow\; a \models_{\mathcal{A}} (\bigwedge_{i \in I} \phi_i \to \bigwedge_{i \in I} \psi_i)_\perp \,\&\, b \models_{\mathcal{A}} \bigwedge_{i \in I} \phi_i$.

- $ab \models_{\mathcal{A}} (\psi_1 \to \cdots (\psi_k \to \lambda)_\perp \cdots)_\perp$
$\Rightarrow\; aba_{\psi_1} \dots a_{\psi_k} \Downarrow$
$\Rightarrow\; \exists \phi, \phi_1, \dots, \phi_k. \, b \models_{\mathcal{A}} \phi \,\&\, a_{\psi_i} \models_{\mathcal{A}} \phi_i \;(1 \leq i \leq k)$
     $\&\, a \models_{\mathcal{A}} (\phi \to (\phi_1 \to \cdots (\phi_k \to \lambda)_\perp \cdots)_\perp)_\perp$,
     since $\mathcal{A}$ is approximable
$\Rightarrow\; \mathcal{L} \vdash \psi_i \leq \phi_i \;(1 \leq i \leq k)$
$\Rightarrow\; \mathcal{L} \vdash (\phi \to (\phi_1 \to \cdots (\phi_k \to \lambda)_\perp \cdots)_\perp)_\perp$
     $\leq (\phi \to (\psi_1 \to \cdots (\psi_k \to \lambda)_\perp \cdots)_\perp)_\perp$
$\Rightarrow\; a \models_{\mathcal{A}} (\phi \to \psi)_\perp \,\&\, b \models_{\mathcal{A}} \phi$.

**3.** $\forall M \in \Lambda. \, M, \Gamma \models_{\mathcal{A}} \phi \iff M, \rho_\Gamma \models_{\mathcal{A}} \phi$.

The right-to-left implication is clear, since $\rho_\Gamma \models_{\mathcal{A}} \Gamma$. We prove the converse by induction on $M$

$$x, \Gamma \models_{\mathcal{A}} \phi \iff \mathcal{A} \models \Gamma x \leq \phi$$
$$\iff \mathcal{L} \vdash \Gamma x \leq \phi \qquad\qquad \text{by (1)}$$
$$\iff a_{\Gamma x} \models_{\mathcal{A}} \phi$$
$$\iff x, \rho_\Gamma \models_{\mathcal{A}} \phi.$$

The case for $\lambda x.M$ is proved by induction on $\phi$. We show the nontrivial case.

- $\lambda x.M, \rho_\Gamma \models_{\mathcal{A}} (\phi \to \psi)_\perp$

$$\Longrightarrow \quad M, \rho_\Gamma[x \mapsto a_\phi] \models_{\mathcal{A}} \psi$$

$$\Longrightarrow \quad M, \Gamma[x \mapsto \phi] \models_{\mathcal{A}} \psi \qquad \text{by (outer) induction hypothesis}$$

$$\Longrightarrow \quad \lambda x.M, \Gamma \models_{\mathcal{A}} (\phi \to \psi)_\perp .$$

- $MN, \rho_\Gamma \models_{\mathcal{A}} \psi$

$$\Longrightarrow \quad [\![M]\!]^{\mathcal{A}}_{\rho_\Gamma} [\![N]\!]^{\mathcal{A}}_{\rho_\Gamma} \models_{\mathcal{A}} \psi$$

$$\Longrightarrow \quad \exists \phi. \, [\![M]\!]^{\mathcal{A}}_{\rho_\Gamma} \models_{\mathcal{A}} (\phi \to \psi)_\perp \, \& \, [\![N]\!]^{\mathcal{A}}_{\rho_\Gamma} \models_{\mathcal{A}} \phi \qquad \text{by (2)}$$

$$\Longrightarrow \quad M, \Gamma \models_{\mathcal{A}} (\phi \to \psi)_\perp \, \& \, N, \Gamma \models_{\mathcal{A}} \phi \qquad \text{ind. hyp.}$$

$$\Longrightarrow \quad MN, \Gamma \models_{\mathcal{A}} \psi .$$

**4.** **(i)** $\quad x, \Gamma[x \mapsto \phi] \models_{\mathcal{A}} \psi \quad \Longleftrightarrow \quad \mathcal{L} \vdash \phi \leq \psi ,$

   **(ii)** $\quad \lambda x.M, \Gamma \models_{\mathcal{A}} (\phi \to \psi)_\perp \quad \Longleftrightarrow \quad M, \Gamma[x \mapsto \phi] \models_{\mathcal{A}} \psi ,$

   **(iii)** $\quad MN, \Gamma \models_{\mathcal{A}} \psi \quad \Longleftrightarrow \quad \exists \phi. \, M, \Gamma \models_{\mathcal{A}} (\phi \to \psi)_\perp$

$$\& \, N, \Gamma \models_{\mathcal{A}} \phi .$$

4(i) is proved using (1).

4(ii):

- $\lambda x.M, \Gamma \models_{\mathcal{A}} (\phi \to \psi)_\perp$

$$\Rightarrow \quad \forall \rho, a. \, \rho \models_{\mathcal{A}} \Gamma \, \& \, a \models_{\mathcal{A}} \phi \, \Rightarrow \, [\![\lambda x.M]\!]^{\mathcal{A}}_\rho . a \models_{\mathcal{A}} \psi$$

$$\Rightarrow \quad \forall \rho. \, \rho \models_{\mathcal{A}} \Gamma[x \mapsto \phi] \, \Rightarrow \, M, \rho \models_{\mathcal{A}} \psi$$

$$\text{since } [\![\lambda x.M]\!]^{\mathcal{A}}_\rho . a = [\![M]\!]^{\mathcal{A}}_{\rho[x \mapsto a]} ,$$

$$\Rightarrow \quad M, \Gamma[x \mapsto \phi] \models_{\mathcal{A}} \psi .$$

The converse follows from the soundness of $\mathcal{L}$.

4(iii):

$$MN, \Gamma \models_{\mathcal{A}} \psi \quad \Longleftrightarrow \quad MN, \rho_\Gamma \models_{\mathcal{A}} \psi \qquad \text{by (3)}$$

$$\Longleftrightarrow \quad [\![M]\!]^{\mathcal{A}}_{\rho_\Gamma} [\![N]\!]^{\mathcal{A}}_{\rho_\Gamma} \models_{\mathcal{A}} \psi$$

$$\Longleftrightarrow \quad \exists \phi. \, [\![M]\!]^{\mathcal{A}}_{\rho_\Gamma} \models_{\mathcal{A}} (\phi \to \psi)_\perp \, \& \, [\![N]\!]^{\mathcal{A}}_{\rho_\Gamma} \models_{\mathcal{A}} \phi \qquad \text{by (2)}$$

$$\Longleftrightarrow \quad \exists \phi. \, M, \Gamma \models_{\mathcal{A}} (\phi \to \psi)_\perp \, \& \, N, \Gamma \models_{\mathcal{A}} \phi \qquad \text{by (3)}$$

We can now prove

$$M, \Gamma \models_{\mathcal{A}} \phi \, \Rightarrow \, M, \Gamma \vdash \phi$$

by induction on $M$, using (4).

## (iii) $\Longrightarrow$ (i)

Note that (iii) implies

$$\mathcal{A} \models \phi \leq \psi \quad \Longleftrightarrow \quad \mathcal{L} \vdash \phi \leq \psi .$$

One half is the soundness theorem. For the converse, suppose $\mathcal{A} \models \phi \leq \psi$ and $\mathcal{L} \not\vdash \phi \leq \psi$. Then $\mathbf{I} \models_{\mathcal{A}} (\phi \to \psi)_\perp$ but $\mathbf{I} \not\models (\phi \to \psi)_\perp$, and so $\mathcal{A}$ is not $\mathcal{L}$-complete.

Now suppose that P is not definable in $\mathcal{A}$, and consider

$$\phi \equiv (\lambda \to (\mathbf{t} \to \lambda)_\perp)_\perp \wedge (\mathbf{t} \to (\lambda \to \lambda)_\perp)_\perp ,$$

$$\psi \equiv (\mathbf{t} \to (\mathbf{t} \to \lambda)_\perp)_\perp .$$

Clearly, $\mathcal{L} \not\vdash \phi \leq \psi$. However, for $a \in \mathcal{A}$, if $a \models_{\mathcal{A}} \phi$, then $x \Downarrow$ or $y \Downarrow$ implies $axy \Downarrow$; since P is not definable in $\mathcal{A}$, and in particular, $a$ does not define P, we must have $axy \Downarrow$ even if $x \Uparrow$ and $y \Uparrow$, and hence $a \models_{\mathcal{A}} \psi$. Thus $\mathcal{A} \models \phi \leq \psi$, and so by our opening remark, $\mathcal{A}$ is not $\mathcal{L}$-complete.

## (ii) $\Longrightarrow$ (iv)   ($\mathcal{A}$ approximable)

Clearly Im $t_{\mathcal{A}} \supseteq \mathcal{K}(D)$, by Theorem 5.5(ii). Also, since $\mathcal{A}$ is approximable, we can apply the characterization theorem to deduce that $t_{\mathcal{A}}$ is injective (modulo bisimulation). To show that $t_{\mathcal{A}}$ is a combinatory morphism, we argue as in Proposition 5.3. Application is preserved by $t_{\mathcal{A}}$ using (2) from the proof of (ii) $\Rightarrow$ (iii) and Proposition 5.3. The proof is completed by showing that $t_{\mathcal{A}}$ preserves denotations of $\lambda$-terms; i.e.,

$$\forall M \in \Lambda, \rho \in Env(\mathcal{A}). \, t_{\mathcal{A}}([\![M]\!]_\rho^{\mathcal{A}}) = [\![M]\!]_{t_{\mathcal{A}} \circ \rho}^D .$$

The proof is by induction on $M$. Since it is very similar to the corresponding part of the proof of Proposition 5.3, we omit it. The only nontrivial point is that in the case for abstraction we need

$$\forall a \in A. \, a \models_{\mathcal{A}} \phi \implies M, \rho[x \mapsto a] \models_{\mathcal{A}} \psi$$

if and only if

$$M, \rho[x \mapsto a_\phi] \models_{\mathcal{A}} \psi ,$$

which is proved similarly to (3) in (ii) $\Rightarrow$ (iii).

## (iv) $\Longrightarrow$ (v)

Assuming (iv), $\mathcal{A}$ is isomorphic (modulo bisimulation) to a substructure of $D$. Since formulas in HF are (equivalent to) universal ($\Pi_1^0$) sentences, this yields $\mathfrak{I}(D) \subseteq \mathfrak{I}(\mathcal{A})$. Since $\mathcal{K}(D) \subseteq$ Im $t_{\mathcal{A}}$, to prove the converse it is sufficient to show, for $H \in$ HF,

$$D, \rho \not\models H \implies \exists \rho_0 : Var \to \mathcal{K}(D). \, D, \rho_0 \not\models H .$$

Let $H \equiv P \Rightarrow F$, where $P \equiv \bigwedge_{i \in I} M_i \Downarrow \wedge \bigwedge_{j \in J} N_j \Uparrow$. There are four cases, corresponding to the form of $F$.

Case 1: $F \equiv M \sqsubseteq N$. $D, \rho \not\models P \Rightarrow F$ implies $D, \rho \models P$ and $D, \rho \not\models M \sqsubseteq N$. Since $D$ is algebraic, $D, \rho \not\models M \sqsubseteq N$ implies that for some $b \in \mathcal{K}(D)$, $b \sqsubseteq [\![M]\!]_\rho^D$ and $b \not\sqsubseteq [\![N]\!]_\rho^D$. Since the expression $[\![M]\!]_\rho^D$ is continuous in $\rho$, $b \sqsubseteq [\![M]\!]_\rho^D$ implies that for some $\rho_1 : \text{Var} \to \mathcal{K}(D)$, $\rho_1 \sqsubseteq \rho$ and $b \sqsubseteq [\![M]\!]_{\rho_1}^D$. For all $\rho'$ with $\rho_1 \sqsubseteq \rho' \sqsubseteq \rho$, $[\![N]\!]_{\rho'}^D \sqsubseteq [\![N]\!]_\rho^D$, and hence $b \not\sqsubseteq [\![N]\!]_{\rho'}^D$. Again, since $D$ is algebraic,

$$D, \rho \models M_i \Downarrow \implies \exists \rho_i : \text{Var} \to \mathcal{K}(D). \rho_i \sqsubseteq \rho \,\&\, D, \rho_i \models M_i \Downarrow .$$

Now let $\rho_0 \equiv \bigsqcup_{i \in I} \rho_i \sqcup \rho_1$. This is well defined since $D$ is a lattice. Moreover, $\rho_0 \sqsubseteq \rho$, and $\rho_0 : \text{Var} \to \mathcal{K}(D)$. Since $\rho_0 \sqsupseteq \rho_i$ $(i \in I)$, $D, \rho_0 \models M_i \Downarrow$; while since $\rho_0 \sqsubseteq \rho, D, \rho_0 \models N_j \Uparrow$ $(j \in J)$. Since $\rho_1 \sqsubseteq \rho_0 \sqsubseteq \rho$, $b \sqsubseteq [\![M]\!]_{\rho_0}^D$ and $b \not\sqsubseteq [\![N]\!]_{\rho_0}^D$, and so $D, \rho_0 \not\models M \sqsubseteq N$. Thus $D, \rho_0 \not\models P \Rightarrow F$, as required.

The remaining cases are proved similarly.

**(v) $\implies$ (i)**  ($\mathcal{A}$ sensible)

Consider the formula

$$H \equiv x\Omega(\mathbf{K}\Omega) \Downarrow \wedge x(\mathbf{K}\Omega)\Omega \Downarrow \Rightarrow x\Omega\Omega \Downarrow .$$

It is easy to see that $\mathcal{A} \models H$ iff P is not definable in $\mathcal{A}$. Since P is definable in $D$, the result follows.   □

We now turn to the question of when the bisimulation preorder on an lts can be characterized by means of a contextual equivalence, as in [5, 26, 19].

**Definition 6.4**   Let $\mathcal{A}$ be an lts, $X, Y \subseteq A$. Then $X$ *separates* $Y$ if

$$\forall M, N \in \Lambda^0(Y). \mathcal{A} \not\models M \sqsubseteq N \implies$$
$$\exists P_1, \dots, P_k \in \Lambda^0(X). \mathcal{A} \models MP_1 \dots P_k \Downarrow \,\&\, \mathcal{A} \models NP_1 \dots P_k \Uparrow .$$

In particular, if $X$ separates $A$ we say that it is a *separating set*. For example, $A$ is always a separating set.

**Proposition 6.1**

Let $\mathcal{A}$ be an approximable lts, and suppose $X$ separates $Y$. Then

$$\forall M, N \in \Lambda^0(Y). \mathcal{A} \models M \sqsubseteq N \iff$$
$$\forall C[\cdot] \in \Lambda^0(X). \mathcal{A} \models C[M] \Downarrow \Rightarrow \mathcal{A} \models C[N] \Downarrow .$$

**Proof**   Suppose $\mathcal{A} \not\models M \sqsubseteq N$. Then since $X$ separates $Y$, for some $P_1, \dots, P_k \in \Lambda^0(X)$, $\mathcal{A} \models MP_1 \dots P_k \Downarrow$ and $\mathcal{A} \models NP_1 \dots P_k \Uparrow$. Let $C[\cdot] \equiv [\cdot]P_1 \cdots P_k$. For the converse, suppose $\mathcal{A} \models M \sqsubseteq N$ and $\mathcal{A} \models C[M] \Downarrow$. Since $\mathcal{A}$ is approximable and

$\mathcal{A} \models C[M] = (\lambda x.C[x])M$, for some $\phi$ $\lambda x.C[x] \models_{\mathcal{A}} (\phi \to \lambda)_{\perp}$ and $M \models_{\mathcal{A}} \phi$. Since $\mathcal{A} \models M \sqsubseteq N$, by the characterization theorem $N \models_{\mathcal{A}} \phi$, and so $\mathcal{A} \models C[N] \Downarrow$.   $\square$

As a first application of this proposition, we have the following.

## Proposition 6.2
Let $\mathcal{A}$ be a sensible, approximable lts in which C and P are definable. Then $\{C, P\}$ is a separating set.

**Proof**   By the full abstraction theorem, for each $\phi \in \mathcal{L}$ there is $M_{\phi} \in \Lambda^0(\{C, P\})$ such that

$$M_{\phi} \models_{\mathcal{A}} \psi \iff \mathcal{L} \vdash \phi \leq \psi.$$

Now

- $\mathcal{A} \not\models M \sqsubseteq N$
- $\implies \exists \phi. M \models_{\mathcal{A}} \phi \,\&\, N \not\models \phi,$ since A is approximable
- $\implies \exists \phi_1, \ldots, \phi_k. M \models_{\mathcal{A}} (\phi_1 \to \cdots (\phi_k \to \lambda)_{\perp} \cdots)_{\perp}$
  $\&\, N \not\models_{\mathcal{A}} (\phi_1 \to \cdots (\phi_k \to \lambda)_{\perp} \cdots)_{\perp}$
- $\implies M M_{\phi_1} \ldots M_{\phi_k} \Downarrow \,\&\, N M_{\phi_1} \ldots M_{\phi_k} \Uparrow .$   $\square$

The hypothesis of approximability has played a major part in our work. We now give a useful sufficient condition.

**Definition 6.5**   Let $\mathcal{A}$ be an lts, $X \subseteq A$. Then $\mathcal{A}$ is *X-sensible* if

$$\forall M \in \Lambda^0(X). \mathcal{A} \models M \Downarrow \Rightarrow D \models M \Downarrow .$$

Here $[\![M]\!]^D$ is the denotation in $D$ obtained by mapping each $a \in X$ to $t_{\mathcal{A}}(a)$. Note that if we extend our endogenous program logic to terms in $\Lambda^0(X)$, with axioms

$$a, \Gamma \vdash \phi \ (\phi \in \mathcal{L}(a)),$$

then the soundness and completeness theorems for $D$ still hold, by a straightforward extension of the arguments used above.

## Proposition 6.3
Let $\mathcal{A}$ be an $X$-sensible lts. Then $\mathcal{A}$ is $X$-approximable; i.e.,

$$\forall M, N_1, \ldots, N_k \in \Lambda^0(X). \mathcal{A} \models MN_1 \ldots N_k \Downarrow \Rightarrow \exists \phi_1, \ldots, \phi_k ;$$

$$M \models_{\mathcal{A}} (\phi_1 \to \cdots (\phi_k \to \lambda)_{\perp} \cdots)_{\perp} \,\&\, N_i \models_{\mathcal{A}} \phi_i, \ 1 \leq i \leq k.$$

## Proof

- $\mathcal{A} \models MN_1 \ldots N_k \Downarrow$
- $\Rightarrow$ $D \models MN_1 \ldots N_k \Downarrow$
- $\Rightarrow$ $\exists \phi_1, \ldots, \phi_k. M \models_D (\phi_1 \rightarrow \cdots (\phi_k \rightarrow \lambda)_\perp \cdots)_\perp$

  $\& N_i \models_D \phi_i, \ 1 \le i \le k,$ since D is approximable
- $\Rightarrow$ $\exists \phi_1, \ldots, \phi_k. M \vdash (\phi_1 \rightarrow \cdots (\phi_k \rightarrow \lambda)_\perp \cdots)_\perp$

  $\& N_i \vdash \phi_i, \ 1 \le i \le k,$ by extended completeness
- $\Rightarrow$ $\exists \phi_1, \ldots, \phi_k. M \models_{\mathcal{A}} (\phi_1 \rightarrow \cdots (\phi_k \rightarrow \lambda)_\perp \cdots)_\perp$

  $\& N_i \models_{\mathcal{A}} \phi_i, \ 1 \le i \le k,$ by extended soundness . $\qquad \square$

In particular, if $X$ generates $\mathcal{A}$ and $\mathcal{A}$ is $X$-sensible, then $\mathcal{A}$ is approximable. We now turn to a number of applications of these ideas to syntactically presented lts, i.e., "programming languages".

Firstly, we consider the lts $\ell = (\Lambda^0, eval)$ defined in Section 3 (and studied previously in Section 2). Since $\ell$ is $\varnothing$-sensible by Theorem 3.1, and it is generated by $\varnothing$, it is approximable by Proposition 6.3. Since $\varnothing$ is a separating set for $\Lambda^0$, we can apply Proposition 6.1 to obtain Proposition 2.1.

Next, we consider extensions of $\ell$.

## Definition 6.6

**(i)** $\ell_C$ is the extension of $\ell$ defined by

$$\ell_C = (\Lambda(\{C\}), \Downarrow) ,$$

where $\Downarrow$ is the extension of the relation in Definition 2.2 with the following rules:

- $C \Downarrow C ,$

- $\dfrac{M \Downarrow}{CM \Downarrow \mathbf{I}} .$

**(ii)** $\ell_P$ is the extension $(\Lambda(\{C\}), \Downarrow)$ of $\ell$ with the rules

- $P \Downarrow P ,$

- $PM \Downarrow PM ,$

- $\dfrac{M \Downarrow}{PMN \Downarrow \mathbf{I}} ,$

- $\dfrac{N \Downarrow}{PMN \Downarrow \mathbf{I}} .$

It is easy to see that the relation $\Downarrow$ as defined in both $\ell_C$ and $\ell_P$ is a partial function. Moreover, with these definitions the C and P combinators have the properties required by Definition 6.3; while C is definable in $\ell_P$ by

$$CM \equiv PMM .$$

Since $\ell_C$ is generated by $\{C\}$, and $\ell_P$ by $\{P\}$, these are separating sets. Thus to apply Proposition 6.1, we need only check that $\ell_C$ is C-sensible and $\ell_P$ is P-sensible.

To do this for $\ell_C$, we proceed as follows. Define

$$c \equiv \{(\lambda \rightarrow (\phi \rightarrow \phi)_\perp)_\perp \mid \phi \in \mathcal{L}\}^\dagger \in \text{Filt } \mathcal{L} .$$

Then it is easy to see that $c \subseteq t_{\mathcal{A}}(C)$, and by monotonicity and the soundness theorem,

$$[\![ M[c/C] ]\!]^D \subseteq [\![ M ]\!]^D$$

for $M \in \Lambda^0(\{C\})$. Thus

$$D \models M[c/C] \Downarrow \implies D \models M \Downarrow . \tag{$\star$}$$

Now we prove

$$\forall M, N \in \Lambda^0(\{C\}) . \tag{$\star\star$}$$
$$M \Downarrow N \implies [\![ M[c/C] ]\!]^D = [\![ N[c/C] ]\!]^D \,\& D \models N[c/C] \Downarrow ,$$

which by $(\star)$ yields $\ell_C \models M \Downarrow \implies D \models M \Downarrow$, as required. $(\star\star)$ is proved by a straightforward induction on the length of the proof that $M \Downarrow N$.

The argument for $\ell_P$ is similar, using

$$p \equiv \{(\lambda \rightarrow (\mathbf{t} \rightarrow (\phi \rightarrow \phi)_\perp)_\perp)_\perp \wedge (\mathbf{t} \rightarrow (\lambda \rightarrow (\psi \rightarrow \psi)_\perp)_\perp)_\perp : \phi, \psi \in \mathcal{L}\}^\dagger .$$

Altogether, we have shown the following theorem.

## Theorem 6.2 (Contextual Equivalence)

**(i)** $\forall M, N \in \Lambda^0(\{C\})$:

$$\ell_C \models M \sqsubseteq N \iff \forall C[\cdot] \in \Lambda^0(\{C\}). \ell_C \models C[M] \Downarrow \Rightarrow \ell_C \models C[N] \Downarrow .$$

**(ii)** $\forall M, N \in \Lambda^0(\{P\})$:

$$\ell_P \models M \sqsubseteq N \iff \forall C[\cdot] \in \Lambda^0(\{P\}). \ell_P \models C[M] \Downarrow \Rightarrow \ell_P \models C[N] \Downarrow .$$

As a further application of these ideas, we have the following proposition.

## Proposition 6.4 (Soundness of $D$)

If $\mathcal{A}$ is $X$-sensible, and $X$ separates $X$ in $\mathcal{A}$, then

$$\mathfrak{I}^0(D, X) \subseteq \mathfrak{I}^0(\mathcal{A}, X).$$

## Proof

- $D \models M \sqsubseteq N$
- $\implies \forall C[\cdot] \in \Lambda^0(X). D \models C[M] \sqsubseteq C[N]$
- $\implies D \models C[M] \Downarrow \implies D \models C[N] \Downarrow$
- $\implies \mathcal{A} \models C[M] \Downarrow \implies \mathcal{A} \models C[N] \Downarrow$
- $\implies \mathcal{A} \models M \sqsubseteq N.$

The argument for formulae of other forms is similar.    $\square$

As an immediate corollary of this proposition, we have the following.

## Proposition 6.5

The denotational semantics of each of our languages is *sound* with respect to the operational semantics:

**(i)** $\mathfrak{I}^0(D) \subseteq \mathfrak{I}^0(\ell)$,

**(ii)** $\mathfrak{I}^0(D, \{C\}) \subseteq \mathfrak{I}^0(\ell_C, \{C\})$,

**(iii)** $\mathfrak{I}^0(D, \{P\}) \subseteq \mathfrak{I}^0(\ell_P, \{P\})$.

We now turn to the question of full abstraction for these languages. Since, as we have seen, $\ell_P$ is P-sensible and hence sensible and approximable, and C and P are definable, we can apply the full abstraction theorem to obtain the following.

## Proposition 6.6

$D$ is fully abstract for $\ell_P$.

We now use the sequential nature of $\ell$ and $\ell_C$ to obtain negative full abstraction results for these languages. This will require a few preliminary notions.

**Definition 6.7**    The *one-step reduction* relation $>$ over terms in $\Lambda$ is the least satisfying the following axioms and rules:

- $(\lambda x.M)N > M[N/x]$,

- $$\frac{M > M'}{MN > M'N}\ .$$

This is then extended to $\Lambda(\{C\})$ with the additional rules

- $C(\lambda x.M) > \mathbf{I}$,

- $CC > \mathbf{I}$,

- $$\frac{M > M'}{CM > CM'}\ .$$

We then define

- $\gg\ \equiv\ $ the reflexive, transitive closure of $>$,
- $M\!\uparrow\ \equiv\ \exists\{M_n\}.\,M = M_0\ \&\ \forall n.\,M_n > M_{n+1}$,
- $M\!\not\rightarrow\ \equiv\ M \notin \mathrm{dom}{>}$,
- $M{\downarrow}N\ \equiv\ M \gg N\ \&\ N\!\not\rightarrow$ .

It is clear that $>$ is a partial function. Note that these relations are being defined over *all* terms, not just closed ones. For closed terms, these new notions are related to the evaluation predicate $\Downarrow$ as follows.

## Proposition 6.7

For $M, N \in \Lambda^0\ (\Lambda^0(\{C\})$:

**(i)** $M{\Downarrow}N \iff M{\downarrow}N$,

**(ii)** $M{\Uparrow} \implies M{\uparrow}$ .

We omit the straightforward proof. The following proposition is basic; it says that "reduction commutes with substitution".

## Proposition 6.8

$M \gg N \implies M[P/x] \gg N[P/x]$.

**Proof**   Clearly, it is sufficient to show:

$$M > N \implies M[P/x] > N[P/x]\,.$$

This is proved by induction on $M$, and cases on why $M > N$. We give one case for illustration:

$$M \equiv (\lambda y.M_1)M_2 > N \equiv M_1[M_2/y]\,.$$

We assume $x \neq y$; the other subcase is simpler:

$$
\begin{aligned}
M[P/x] \quad &= \quad (\lambda y.M_1[P/x])M_2[P/x] \\
&> \quad M_1[P/x][M_2[P/x]/y] \\
&= \quad M_1[M_2/y][P/x] \qquad \text{by [5, 2.1.16]} \\
&= \quad N[P/x]. \qquad\qquad \square
\end{aligned}
$$

Now we come to the basic sequentiality property of $\ell$ from which various nondefinability results can be deduced.

## Proposition 6.9

For $M \in \Lambda$, exactly one of the following holds:

  **(i)** $M\!\uparrow$,

 **(ii)** $M \gg \lambda x.N$,

**(iii)** $M \gg xN_1 \dots N_k \ (k \geq 0)$.

**Proof**   Since $>$ is a partial function, the computation sequence beginning with $M$ is uniquely determined. Either it is infinite, yielding (i); or it terminates in a term $N$ with $N\!\not>$, which must be in one of the forms (ii) or (iii).   $\square$

As a consequence of this proposition, we obtain the following theorem.

## Theorem 6.3

C is not definable in $\ell$. Moreover, $D$ is not fully abstract for $\ell$.

**Proof**   We shall show that $\ell$ satisfies

$$x = \mathbf{I} \text{ or } [x\Omega \Downarrow \iff x(\mathbf{K}\Omega) \Downarrow]. \qquad\qquad (\star)$$

Indeed, consider any term $M \in \Lambda^0$. Either $M \Uparrow$, in which case $M\Omega \Uparrow$ and $M(\mathbf{K}\Omega) \Uparrow$, or $M \Downarrow$. In the latter case, by $(\Downarrow \eta)$ we have $\lambda \ell \models M = \lambda x.Mx$. Thus without loss of generality we may take $M$ to be of the form $\lambda x.M'$, with $FV(M) \subseteq \{x\}$. Now applying the three previous propositions to $M'$, we see that in case (i) of Proposition 6.9, $(\lambda x.M')\Omega \Uparrow$ and $(\lambda x.M')(\mathbf{K}\Omega) \Uparrow$; in case (ii), $(\lambda x.M')\Omega \Downarrow$ and $(\lambda x.M')(\mathbf{K}\Omega) \Downarrow$; finally in case (iii), if $k = 0$, $\lambda x.M' = \mathbf{I}$; while if $k > 0$, $(\lambda x.M')\Omega \Uparrow$ and $(\lambda x.M')(\mathbf{K}\Omega) \Uparrow$. Since $\mathbf{C} \neq \mathbf{I}$, $\mathbf{C}\Omega \Uparrow$ and $\mathbf{C}(\mathbf{K}\Omega) \Downarrow$, this shows that C is not definable. Moreover, $(\star)$ implies

$$x\Omega \Uparrow \ \& \ x(\mathbf{K}\Omega) \Downarrow \Rightarrow x = \mathbf{I}, \qquad\qquad (\star\star)$$

which is not satisfied by $D$, since C is definable in $D$, and taking $x = \mathbf{C}$ refutes $(\star\star)$; hence $D$ is not fully abstract for $\ell$.   $\square$

Note that since C is not definable in $\ell$, we could not apply the full abstraction theorem. By contrast, to show that $D$ is not fully abstract for $\ell_C$, it suffices to show that P is not definable. For this purpose, we prove a result analogous to Proposition 6.9.

## Proposition 6.10

For $M \in \Lambda(\{C\})$, exactly one of the following conditions holds:

**(i)** $M\uparrow$,

**(ii)** $M \gg \lambda x.N$,

**(iii)** $M \gg C$,

**(iv)** $M \gg \underbrace{C(C\ldots(C}_{n}(xN_1\ldots N_k)\ldots)\ldots)P_1\ldots P_m \quad (n,k,m \geq 0)$.

**Proof**   Similar to Proposition 6.9.   □

## Theorem 6.4

P is not definable in $\ell_C$; hence $D$ is not fully abstract for $\ell_C$.

**Proof**   We show that $\ell_C$ satisfies

$$x(K\Omega)\Omega \Downarrow \ \& \ x\Omega(K\Omega) \Downarrow \ \Rightarrow \ x\Omega\Omega \Downarrow,$$

and hence, as in the proof of the full abstraction theorem, P is not definable in $\ell_C$. As in the proof of Theorem 6.3, without loss of generality we consider closed terms of the form $\lambda y_1.\lambda y_2.M$. Assume $(\lambda y_1.\lambda y_2.M)(K\Omega)\Omega \Downarrow$ and $(\lambda y_1.\lambda y_2.M)\Omega(K\Omega) \Downarrow$. Applying Proposition 6.10, we see that case (i) is impossible; cases (ii) and (iii) imply that $(\lambda y_1.\lambda y_2.M)\Omega\Omega \Downarrow$; while in case (iv), if $x = y_1$, then $(\lambda y_1.\lambda y_2.M)\Omega(K\Omega) \Uparrow$, *contra hypothesis*; and if $x = y_2$, $(\lambda y_1.\lambda y_2.M)(K\Omega)\Omega \Uparrow$, also *contra hypothesis*. Thus case (iv) is impossible, and the proof is complete. □

For our final nondefinability result, we shall consider a different style of extension of $\ell$, to incorporate *ground data*. We shall consider the simplest possible such extension, where a single atom is added. This corresponds to the domain equation

$$D_* = \mathbf{1} + [D_* \to D_*]$$

(where + is separated sum), which is indeed an extension of our original domain, in the sense that $D$ is a retract of $D_*$. $D_*$ is still a Scott domain (indeed, a coherent algebraic cpo), but it is no longer a lattice; we have introduced *inconsistency* via the sum.

This extension is reflected on the syntactic level by two constants, $\star$ and C. We define

$$\ell_\star = (\Lambda^0(\{\star, C\}), \Downarrow)$$

with $\Downarrow$ extending the definition for $\ell$ as follows:

- $\star \Downarrow \star$,

- $C \Downarrow C$,

- $\dfrac{M \Downarrow \lambda x.N}{CM \Downarrow T}$,

- $\dfrac{M \Downarrow C}{CM \Downarrow T}$,

- $\dfrac{M \Downarrow \star}{CM \Downarrow F}$,

where $T \equiv \lambda x.\lambda y.x$, $F \equiv \lambda x.\lambda y.y$. We see that the C combinator introduced here is a natural generalization (not strictly an extension) of the C defined previously in the pure case. Of course, C corresponds to *case selection*, which in the unary case — lifting being unary separated sum — is just convergence testing.

A theory can be developed for $\ell_\star$ which runs parallel to what we have done for the pure lazy $\lambda$-calculus. Some of the technical details are more complicated because of the presence of inconsistency, but the ideas and results are essentially the same. Our reasons for mentioning this extension are twofold:

1. To show how the ideas we have developed can be put in a broader context. In particular, with the extension to $\ell_\star$ the reader should be able to see, at least in outline, how our work can be applied to systems such as Martin-Löf's type theory under its domain interpretation [10], and (the analogues of) our results in this section can be used to settle most of the questions and conjectures raised in [10].

2. To prove an interesting result that clarifies a point about which there seems to be some confusion in the literature; namely, *what is parallel or?*

The *locus classicus* for parallel *or* in the setting of typed $\lambda$-calculus is [26]. But what of untyped $\lambda$-calculus? In [5, p. 375], we find the following definition:

$$FMN = \begin{cases} \mathbf{I}, & \text{if M or N is solvable} \\ \text{unsolvable}, & \text{otherwise}. \end{cases}$$

which (modulo the difference between the standard and lazy theories) corresponds to our parallel convergence combinator P. The point we wish to make is this: in the pure $\lambda$-calculus, where (in domain terms) there are no inconsistent data values (since everything is a function)—i.e., we have a lattice—parallel convergence does indeed play the role of parallel *or*, as the full abstraction theorem shows. However, when we introduce ground data, and hence inconsistency, a distinction reappears between parallel convergence and parallel *or*, and it is definitely *wrong* to conflate them. To substantiate this claim, we shall prove the following result: even if parallel convergence is added to $\ell_*$, parallel *or* is still not definable. This result is also of interest from the point of view of the fine structure of definability; it shows that parallelism is not all or nothing even in the simple, deterministic setting of $\ell_*$.

**Definition 6.8**   $\ell_*P$ is the extension of $\ell_*$ with a constant P and the rules

- $P \Downarrow P$,

- $PM \Downarrow PM$,

- $\dfrac{M \Downarrow}{PMN \Downarrow \mathbf{I}}$ ,

- $\dfrac{N \Downarrow}{PMN \Downarrow \mathbf{I}}$ .

**Definition 6.9**   Let $\ell'$ be an extension of $\ell_*$. We say that *parallel or is definable in $\ell'$* if for some term $M$

**(i)** $M(\mathbf{K}\Omega)\Omega$ and $M\Omega(\mathbf{K}\Omega)$  converge to abstractions,

**(ii)** $M \star \star \Downarrow \star$ .

## Theorem  6.5
Parallel *or* is not definable in $\ell_*P$.

**Proof**   We proceed along similar lines to our previous nondefinability results. First, we extend our definition of $>$ as follows:

- constructor$(M) \equiv M$ is an abstraction, P, C or $\star$ ,

- constructor$(M) \, \& \, M \neq \star \;\Rightarrow\; CM > T$ ,

- $C\star > F$ ,

- $\dfrac{M > M'}{CM > CM'}$ ,

- constructor($M$) or constructor($N$) $\Rightarrow PMN > \mathbf{I}$,

- $\dfrac{M > M' \ N > N'}{PMN > PM'N'}$ .

With these extensions, $>$ is still a partial function, and Propositions 6.8 and 6.9 still hold. For each $M \in \Lambda(\{\star, C, P\})$, one of the following two disjoint conditions must hold:

- $M\uparrow$,

- $M \gg N \,\&\, N \nrightarrow$ .

We now define $\mathcal{T}$ to be the set of all terms $M$ in $\Lambda(\{\star, C, P, \perp\})$, where $\perp$ is a new constant, such that

- $FV(M) \subseteq \{y_1, y_2\}$,

- $M$ contains no $>$-redex.

Note that $\mathcal{T}$ is closed under subterms.    □

## Lemma  A
For all $M \in \mathcal{T}$,

$$M[\mathbf{K}\Omega/y_1, \Omega/y_2]\downarrow a \ \& \ M[\Omega/y_1, \mathbf{K}\Omega/y_2]\downarrow b \ \& \ M[\star/y_1, \star/y_2]\downarrow c$$
$$\Rightarrow a = b = c = \star \text{ or } \star \notin \{a, b, c\}.$$

**Proof**    By induction on $M$. Since terms in $\mathcal{T}$ contain no $>$-redexes, $M$ must have one of the following forms:

   **(i)** $xN_1 \ldots N_k \ \ (x \in \{y_1, y_2\}, k \geq 0)$,

  **(ii)** $\star N_1 \ldots N_k \ \ (k \geq 0)$,

 **(iii)** $\lambda x.N$,

  **(iv)** $C$

   **(v)** $P$

  **(vi)** $PN$,

 **(vii)** $CNN_1 \ldots N_k \ \ (k \geq 0)$,

**(viii)** $PM_1M_2N_1 \ldots N_k \ \ (k \geq 0)$,

  **(ix)** $\perp N_1 \ldots N_k \ \ (k \geq 0)$.

Most of these cases can be disposed of directly; we deal with the two that use the induction hypothesis.

(vii) First, we can apply the induction hypothesis to $N$ to conclude that $N[c_1/y_1, c_2/y_2]$ converges to the same result (i.e., either an abstraction or $\star$) for all three argument combinations $c_1, c_2$; we can then apply the induction hypothesis to either $N_1 N_3 \ldots N_k$ or $N_2 N_3 \ldots N_k$.

(viii) Under the hypothesis of the lemma, we must have

$$(P M_1 M_2)[c_1/y_1, c_2/y_2] \Downarrow \mathbf{I}$$

for all three argument combinations $c_1, c_2$; hence we can apply the induction hypothesis to $N_1 \ldots N_k$. $\square$

## Lemma B

Let $M \in \Lambda\ (\{\star, C, P\})$, with $FV(M) \subseteq \{y_1, y_2\}$. Then for some $M' \in \mathcal{T}$, for all $P, Q \in \Lambda^0(\{\star, C, P\})$:

$$M[P/y_1, Q/y_2] \downarrow \star \iff M'[P/y_1, Q/y_2] \downarrow \star.$$

**Proof**    Given $M$, we obtain $M'$ as follows; working in an inside-out fashion, we replace each subterm $N$ by

$$\begin{cases} N', & \text{if } N \downarrow N' \\ \bot, & \text{if } N \uparrow. \end{cases}$$

Now suppose that we are given a putative term in $\Lambda^0(\{\star, C, P\})$ defining parallel *or*. As in the proof of Theorem 6.4, we may take this term to have the form $\lambda y_1.\lambda y_2.M$. Applying Lemma B, we can obtain $M' \in \mathcal{T}$ from $M$; but then applying Lemma A, we see that $\lambda y_1.\lambda y_2.M'$ cannot define parallel *or*. Applying Lemma B again, we conclude that $\lambda y_1.\lambda y_2.M$ cannot define parallel *or* either. $\square$

## 7 Variations

Throughout this chapter, we have focused on the lazy $\lambda$-calculus. We round off our treatment by briefly considering the varieties of function space.

**1.** The Scott function space $[D \to E]$, the standard function space of all continuous functions from $D$ to $E$. In terms of our domain logic $\mathcal{L}$, we can obtain this construction by adding the axiom

$$\mathbf{t} \leq (\mathbf{t} \to \mathbf{t}). \tag{1}$$

Note that with (1), $\mathcal{L}$ collapses to a single equivalence class (corresponding to the trivial one-point solution of $D = [D \rightarrow D]$). For this reason, Coppo et al. have to introduce atoms in their work on extended applicative type structures [8].

2. The strict function space $[D \rightarrow_\perp E]$, all *strict* continuous functions. This satisfies (1), and also

$$(\mathbf{t} \rightarrow_\perp \phi) \leq \mathbf{f} \ (\phi \neq \mathbf{t}). \tag{2}$$

3. The lazy function space $[D \rightarrow E]_\perp$, which satisfies neither (1) nor (2). This has of course been our object of study in this chapter.

4. The Landin-Plotkin function space $[D \rightarrow_\perp E]_\perp$, the lifted strict function space. This satisfies (2) but not (1). The reason for our nomenclature is that this construction in the category of domains and strict continuous functions corresponds to Plotkin's $[D \rightharpoonup E]$ construction in his (equivalent) category of predomains and partial functions [27]. Moreover, this may be regarded as the formalization of Landin's applicative-order $\lambda$-calculus, with abstraction used to protect expressions from evaluation, as illustrated extensively in [16, 15, 7].

The intriguing point about these four constructions is that (1) and (2) are *mathematically* natural, yielding cartesian closure and monoidal closure in, e.g., **CPO** and **CPO**$_\perp$, respectively (the latter being analogous to partial functions over sets); while (3) and (4) are *computationally* natural, as argued extensively for (3) in this chapter, and as demonstrated convincingly for (4) by Plotkin in his work on predomains [27]. Much current work is aimed at providing good categorical descriptions of generalizations of (4) [29, 28, 20, 22, 21]; a similar program has been carried out for (3) by Chih-Hao Ong.

## 8 *Further Directions*

Our development of the lazy $\lambda$-calculus represents no more than a beginning. An extensive study has been undertaken by Chih-Hao Ong; anyone interested in pursuing the subject further is strongly recommended to read his thesis [25]. His results include a syntactic characterization of the local structure of lazy PSE models, a construction of a fully abstract model for $\ell_C$, and a category-theoretic characterisation of the lazy $\lambda$-calculus.

## *Acknowledgments*

I would like to thank Henk Barendregt, Peter Dybjer, Per Martin-Löf, Chih-Hao Ong, Gordon Plotkin, and Jan Smith for inspiring discussions on these topics. Per Martin-Löf's ideas on the domain interpretation of his type theory have been particularly influential. The first version of this material was developed during and shortly after a most enjoyable visit to the Programming Methodology Group, Chalmers University Göteborg, in March 1984; and presented at the Seminar on Concurrency at CMU in July 1984. The present version crystallized during and between visits to the University of Nijmegen in March–April and August 1986, and was presented in seminars there in August 1986, and at the Institute of Declarative Programming at Austin in August 1987. I would like to thank my hosts on all these occasions for their hospitality, and particularly Bengt Nördstrom, Per Martin-Löf, Raymond Boute, and David Turner. Finally, my thanks to the U.K. Science and Engineering Research Council and the Alvey Programme for financial support.

## References

[1] Abramsky, S. "A domain equation for bisimulation". *Information and Computation*, 1990 (to appear).

[2] Abramsky, S. "Domain theory in logical form". *Annals of Pure and Applied Logic*, 1990 (to appear).

[3] Abramsky, S. "Domain theory in logical form (extended abstract)". *Symposium on Logic In Computer Science*, pp. 47–53. IEEE Computer Society Press, New York, 1987.

[4] Augustsson, L. "A compiler for lazy ML". *ACM Symposium on Lisp and Functional Programming* (Austin, August), pp. 218–227. ACM, New York, 1984.

[5] Barendregt, H. *The Lambda Calculus: Its Syntax and Semantics*. North-Holland, Amsterdam, (revised edition) 1984.

[6] Barendregt, H. and van Leeuwen, M. "Functional programming and the language TALE". Technical Report 412, University of Utrecht, Dept. of Mathematics, 1986.

[7] Burge, W. H. *Recursive Programming Techniques*. Addison-Wesley, Reading, Mass., 1975.

[8] Coppo, M., Dezani-Ciancaglini, M., Honsell,F., and Longo, G. "Extended type structure and filter lambda models". *Logic Colloquium '82*, G. Lolli, G. Longo, and A. Marcja, eds., pp. 241–262. Elsevier Science Publishers B.V. (North-Holland), Amsterdam, 1984.

[9] Curien, P.-L.*Categorical Combinators, Sequential Algorithms and Functional Programming*. Research Notes in Theoretical Computer Science, Pitman, London, 1986.

[10] Dybjer, P., Nordström, B., Petersson, K., and Smith, J., eds. *Workshop on Semantics of Programming Languages*. Programming Methodology Group, Chalmers University of Technology, Göteborg, Sweden, August 1983.

[11] Fairbairn, J. "Design and implementation of a simple typed language based on the lambda calculus". PhD thesis, University of Cambridge, 1985.

[12] Henderson, P. *Functional Programming: Applications and Implementation.* Prentice-Hall, Englewood Cliffs, New Jersey, 1980.

[13] Koymans, C. P. J. "Models of the lambda calculus". *Information and Control 52* (1982), pp. 206–332.

[14] Lambek, J. and Scott, P. J. *Introduction to Higher Order Categorical Logic.* Cambridge Studies in Advanced Mathematics, vol. 7, Cambridge University Press, 1986.

[15] Landin, P. J. "A correspondence between ALGOL 60 and Church's lambda notation". *Communications of the ACM 8* (1965), pp. 89–101,158–165.

[16] Landin, P. J. "The mechanical evaluation of expressions". *Computer Journal 6* (1964), pp. 308–320.

[17] Longo, G. "Set-theoretical models of lambda calculus: Theories, expansions and isomophisms". *Annals of Pure and Applied Logic 24* (1983), pp. 153–188.

[18] Milner, R. "Calculi for synchrony and asynchrony". *Theoretical Computer Science 25* (1983), pp. 267–310.

[19] Milner, R. "Fully abstract models of typed lambda-calculi". *Theoretical Computer Science 4* (1977), pp. 1–22.

[20] Moggi, E. "Categories of partial morphisms and the lambda-calculus". *Category Theory and Computer Programming*, D. Pitt, S. Abramsky, A. Poigné, and D. Rydeheard, eds., pp. 242–251. Lecture Notes in Computer Science, vol. 240. Springer-Verlag, Berlin, 1986.

[21] Moggi, E. "Partial morphisms in categories of effective objects". *Information and Computation 76* (1988), 2/3, pp. 250–277.

[22] Moggi, E. "The partial lambda calculus". PhD thesis, University of Edinburgh, 1988.

[23] Morris, J. H. "Lambda calculus models of programming languages". PhD thesis, Massachusets Institute of Technology, 1968.

[24] Moschovakis, Y. *Elementary Induction on Abstract Structures.* North-Holland, Amsterdam, 1974.

[25] Ong, C.-H. L. "The lazy $\lambda$-calculus: An investigation into the foundations of functional programming". PhD thesis, Imperial College, University of London, 1988.

[26] Plotkin, G. D. "LCF considered as a programming language". *Theoretical Computer Science 5* (1977), p. 223–255.

[27] Plotkin, G. D. "Lectures on predomains and partial functions". Notes for a course given at the Center for the Study of Language and Information, Stanford University, 1985.

[28] Robinson, E. and Rosolini, G. "Categories of partial maps". Computing Laboratory and DPMMS, Cambridge University, 1987.

[29] Rosolini, G. "Continuity and effectiveness in topoi". PhD thesis, Carnegie-Mellon University, 1986.

[30] Scott, D. S. "Relating theories of lambda calculus". *To H. B. Curry: Essays in Combinatory Logic, Lambda Calculus and Formalism*, J. R. Hindley and J. P. Seldin, eds., pp. 403–450. Academic Press, New York, 1980.

[31] Turner, D. A. "Miranda: A non-strict functional language with polymorphic types". *Functional Programming Languages and Computer Architecture*, J.-P. Jouannaud, ed., pp. 1–16. Lecture Notes in Computer Science, vol. 201. Springer-Verlag, Berlin, 1985.

[32] Wadler, P. "Introduction to ORWELL". Technical Report, Programming Research Group, Oxford University, 1985.

# Compile-time Analysis of Functional Programs

## 5

**John Hughes**
University of Glasgow

## 1 Introduction

Good compilers for functional languages increasingly rely on sophisticated compile-time analysis to detect opportunities for optimization. As a result, techniques for performing these analyses are developing very rapidly. In this paper we give an informal introduction to two kinds of analysis technique: forwards and backwards analysis. Forwards analysis, or *abstract interpretation*, essentially consists of running the program with partial information about its inputs, to derive partial information about its result. This technique has been widely used for a number of different analysis problems. Backwards analysis is used to derive contextual information by "running the program backwards": It has an efficiency advantage. We will show how the techniques are applied to first-order functional languages, taking strictness analysis as our principal example, and then we will go on to describe three other applications of backwards analysis. We show how backwards analysis can be extended to analyze data structures. Finally we give some pointers to related work.

## 2 An Informal Introduction to Forwards and Backwards Analysis

Both types of program analysis may be thought of as propagating information around the syntax tree of the analyzed program. A forwards analyzer starts with information about the values of variables occurring in each expression and propagates it upwards through the syntax tree to derive information about the value of the expression as a whole. In contrast, a backwards analyzer starts with information about the context of the entire expression and propagates it downwards through the syntax tree to the leaves to derive information about the contexts in which subexpressions occur. Surprisingly, a problem can often be solved in either way.

For example, consider strictness analysis of the following function:

$$f \, x \, y \;=\; \textbf{if } x = 0 \textbf{ then } 0 \textbf{ else } x * y$$

The syntax tree of the body is shown in Fig. 2.1.

Strictness analysis aims to discover which of the parameters of each function are certain to be used in every call. Such parameters, in which the function is said to be *strict*, may be passed by value even in a lazy language, instead of by need, which is more expensive. Strictness analysis may be per-

**Figure 2.1.**   Syntax tree of $f \, x \, y \;=\; \textbf{if } x = 0 \textbf{ then } 0 \textbf{ else } x * y$.

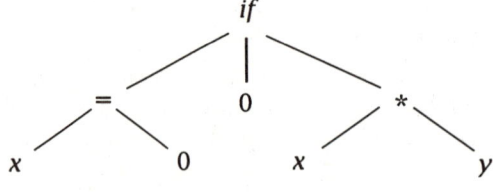

formed forwards by propagating information of the form "certainly uses $x$" and "may not use $x$" up through the tree. The result in this example is illustrated in Fig. 2.2, using the conventional notation that **0** denotes "certainly uses..." and **1** denotes "may not use...". The analysis shows that $f$ is strict in $x$. Figure 2.3 depicts a second analysis, showing that $f$ is not strict in $y$.

The same problem can be solved backwards, by propagating contextual information of the form "is certainly evaluated" and "may not be evaluated". We adopt the notation $S$ (for *strict*) and $L$ (for *lazy*) for these two pieces of information. Now, if $S$ propagates from the root of the syntax tree for $f$ to any occurrence of $x$, then $f$ must be strict in $x$. A backwards analysis of $f$

**Figure 2.2.**   Forwards strictness analysis: $f$ is strict in $x$.

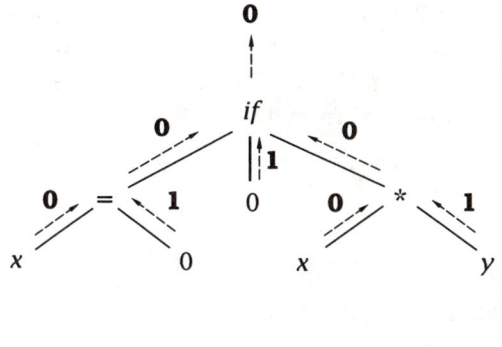

**Figure 2.3.**   Forwards strictness analysis: $f$ is not strict in $y$.

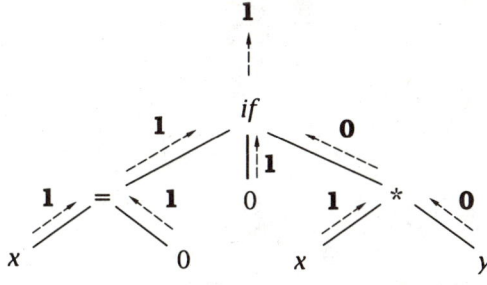

is shown in Fig. 2.4, demonstrating that $f$ is strict in $x$ but not in $y$. (Note the resemblance to attribute evaluation: Forwards analysis uses synthesized attributes while backwards analysis uses inherited ones. A mixed analysis using both can perform backwards analysis of higher-order programs [14]).

A comparison of these examples reveals one of the advantages of backwards over forwards analysis— it can be more efficient. A single backwards propagation suffices to show that $f$ is strict in $x$ and not in $y$; deriving the same result forwards requires twice as much work. This advantage appears to be quite significant in practice. However, the example does not reveal that forwards and backwards analysis are not equally powerful! There are cases where either one may produce better information than the other, so the choice between the two is not clear cut.

This presentation of analysis methods as propagating information around syntax trees, while intuitive, leaves many questions unanswered. For example, how are recursive functions analyzed? A literal implementation could propagate information around a loop for ever. What happens if a function is called in several different contexts? To answer these questions we must describe the analysis methods formally.

## 3 *Formalization of Forwards Analysis*

Forwards analysis is the easier to formalize and the more widely known, so we will consider it first. Many of the same ideas will reappear when we turn to backwards analysis.

**Figure 2.4.** Backwards analysis: $f$ is strict in $x$ but not in $y$.

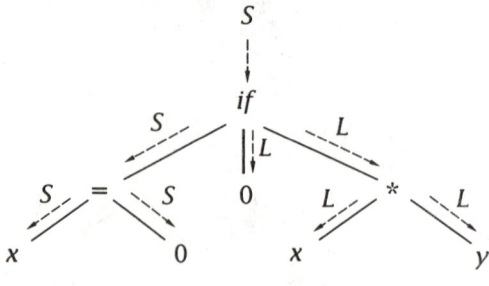

### 3.1 *Representing Information*

We must first decide how to represent the information being propagated. It is usual to use the elements of a domain, called the abstract domain. Its elements are called *abstract values* (since they represent partial information about the *values* of expressions). The use of a domain, rather than a set, guarantees that *recursive equations always have a solution*; this is of great importance when recursive programs are analyzed.

For example, the domain used for strictness analysis is

$$
\begin{array}{c}
\mathbf{1} \\
| \\
\mathbf{0}
\end{array}
$$

with the interpretation

> may or may not use the variable in question
> |
> certainly does use the the variable

Note that the most precise information appears at the bottom of the domain and the least precise at the top. At first sight this seems unintuitive, but it can be explained by giving a more careful interpretation to $\mathbf{0}$ and $\mathbf{1}$. The true interpretation of $\mathbf{0}$ is "certainly evaluates to $\perp$ if the variable in question has the value $\perp$," which is nearly but not quite the same as the looser statement above. The true interpretation of $\mathbf{1}$ is "may evaluate to any result at all". So $\mathbf{0}$ and $\mathbf{1}$ may be thought of as defining sets of possible values, and the domain is ordered by the subset ordering.

We can now give an intuitive meaning to the domain operations. Since $a \sqsubseteq b$ means $a$ is more precise than $b$, the least upper bound $a \sqcup b$ must represent the most precise information that is less precise than both $a$ and $b$— that is, the interpretation of $a \vee$ the interpretation of $b$. Similarly, the greatest lower bound $a \sqcap b$ represents $a \wedge b$. Every abstract domain must have a top element, representing "no information at all". Finally, the least solution of any recursive equation is the *most informative* solution— and therefore the one we want.

### 3.2 *Defining Propagation*

To define propagation we must specify the abstract value that propagates out of an expression in terms of the abstract values propagating in from its subexpressions. We will use a very simple first-order language, in which the only expressions are variables, constants, function applications, and conditionals. Assuming $\rho$ is an environment giving the abstract values of variables, we will define

$$[E]\rho$$

to be the abstract value propagated from the expression $E$.

Clearly

$$[x]\rho \ = \ \rho[x]$$

when $x$ is a variable. The information propagated from a constant is always the same, so with each constant $k$ we associate its abstract value $k^\#$ and define

$$[k]\rho \ = \ k^\#$$

The abstract value of a function call is a function of the abstract values of its arguments, so let us associate an "abstract function" $f^\#$ with each function $f$, and define

$$[f\,E_1\ldots E_n]\rho \ = \ f^\#[E_1]\rho\ldots[E_n]\rho$$

(see Fig. 3.1).

We will return to the question of how abstract functions are defined shortly.

Only the conditional expression remains. In the case of strictness analysis, observe that a conditional expression may evaluate to a non-$\perp$ value if the condition does, and if either the *then* or the *else* branch does. Bearing in mind the associations between *and* and $\sqcap$ and between *or* and $\sqcup$, we can express this as

$$[\textbf{if } E_1 \textbf{ then } E_2 \textbf{ else } E_3]\rho \ = \ [E_1]\rho \sqcap ([E_2]\rho \sqcup [_3]\rho)$$

---

**Figure 3.1.**   Abstract function.

which is, in fact, correct. (For other analysis problems, conditionals might need to be analyzed differently.)

Let us return to our example:

$$f\,x\,y\ =\ \textbf{if}\ x=0\ \textbf{then}\ 0\ \textbf{else}\ x*y$$

Applying these rules, the abstract value of the body is

$$[\textbf{if}\ x=0\ \textbf{then}\ 0\ \textbf{else}\ x*y]\rho$$

$$=\ \ [x=0]\rho\sqcap([0]\rho\sqcup[x*y]\rho)$$

$$=\ \ [x]\rho=^{\#}0^{\#}\sqcap(1^{\#}\sqcup[x]\rho*^{\#}[y]\rho)\,.$$

Constants certainly do not evaluate to $\bot$, so $0^{\#}$ and $1^{\#}$ are both **1**. Moreover, primitive operations can return non-$\bot$ only if both arguments are non-$\bot$, so

$$a=^{\#}b\ \ =\ \ a\sqcap b\,,$$

$$a*^{\#}b\ \ =\ \ a\sqcap b\,.$$

The abstract value of the body is therefore

$$([x]\rho\sqcap\textbf{1})\sqcap(\textbf{1}\sqcup([x]\rho\sqcap[y]\rho))\,,$$

which can be simplified, using $\textbf{1}\sqcap a=a$ and $\textbf{1}\sqcup a=\textbf{1}$, to

$$[x]\rho\,.$$

We still have to define the abstract functions associated with user-defined functions. It's natural to define them in terms of propagation through their bodies; thus if $g$ is defined by

$$g\,x_1\ldots x_n\ =\ E\,,$$

then we define

$$g^{\#}\,v_1\ldots v_n\ =\ \ [E]\{x_1\leftarrow v_1\ \ldots\ x_n\leftarrow v_n\}\,,$$

where $\{x_1\leftarrow v_1\ \ldots\ x_n\leftarrow v_n\}$ denotes an environment in which each $x_i$ is bound to $v_i$. So in our example, we define $f^{\#}$ by

$$f^{\#}\,u\,v=u\,.$$

To determine whether $f$ is strict in its first parameter, we propagate **0** ("certainly uses...") from that parameter, and **1** from all the others. If the result is **0**, then $f$ certainly uses its first argument. Clearly $f^{\#}\,\textbf{0}\,\textbf{1}$ is **0** and $f^{\#}\,\textbf{1}\,\textbf{0}$ is **1**, so $f$ does use its first parameter but may not use its second.

Notice that if we take a set of function definitions and derive their associated abstract functions, we obtain a very similar set of definitions in which
every function and constant has a $^\#$ appended to it. This explains the term
"abstract interpretation" — forwards analysis may be thought of as interpreting the program using alternative definitions of the primitive functions, that
produce and operate on abstract data instead of real values.

### 3.3 *Dealing with Recursion*

Naturally, recursive functions give rise to recursive abstract functions. Consider for example

$$g\,x\,y \;=\; \textbf{if } x{=}0 \textbf{ then } y \textbf{ else } g\,(x-1)\,y\,,$$

whose abstract function is

$$g^\#\,u\,v \;=\; (u \sqcap \mathbf{1}) \sqcap (v \sqcup g^\#\,(u \sqcap \mathbf{1})\,v)$$

$$=\; u \sqcap (v \sqcup g^\#\,u\,v)\,.$$

Is $g$ strict in $y$? To determine this, we have to evaluate $g^\#\,\mathbf{1}\,\mathbf{0}$:

$$g^\#\,\mathbf{1}\,\mathbf{0} = \mathbf{1} \sqcap (\mathbf{0} \sqcup g^\#\,\mathbf{1}\,\mathbf{0})\,.$$

Now we benefit from choosing to represent information by elements of a
domain: every recursive equation has a least solution, which in this case is
$\mathbf{0}$— so $g$ is strict in $y$.

But how can we calculate these least solutions? In general, a set of mutually
recursive functions can be expressed as the fixed point of a higher-order
operator:

$$\langle f_1^\#, \ldots, f_n^\# \rangle = F\langle f_1^\#, \ldots, f_n^\# \rangle$$

for some $F$, so

$$\langle f_1^\#, \ldots, f_n^\# \rangle = \textbf{fix } F\,,$$

and the fixed point is the limit of an ascending chain,

$$\langle f_1^\#, \ldots, f_n^\# \rangle = \bigcup_{i=0}^{\infty} F^i \bot\,.$$

This is of more than theoretical interest: *if the chain is finite then we can use
this limit to calculate the fixed point.* The best way to guarantee finiteness
of the chain is to ensure that it lies in a finite domain. We can do this by
choosing a finite abstract domain $A$ to start with— for then all the function
spaces $A^n \rightarrow A$, in which the abstract functions lie, are also finite.

As an example, let us tabulate successive approximations to $g^{\#}$, using the rules

$$g_0^{\#}\, u\, v\ =\ \mathbf{0}\,,$$

$$g_{n+1}^{\#}\, u\, v\ =\ u \sqcap (v \sqcup g_n^{\#}\, u\, v)\,.$$

Here is the table:

| $u$ | $v$ | $g_0^{\#}$ | $g_1^{\#}$ | $g_2^{\#}$ |
|-----|-----|-----|-----|-----|
| **0** | **0** | **0** | **0** | **0** |
| **0** | **1** | **0** | **0** | **0** |
| **1** | **0** | **0** | **0** | **0** |
| **1** | **1** | **0** | **1** | **1** |

In this example the limit is reached in one step. Tabulation can stop after the next step produces an identical column, demonstrating that the limit has been reached.

In principle, the problem is now solved; recursive abstract functions can be calculated by tabulating successive approximations. In practice the tables required may be too large: $|A|^n$ rows for a function of $n$ arguments, where $|A|$ is the number of elements in the abstract domain. Cleverer representations of functions have been found— nevertheless, comparing successive approximations for equality (to determine if the limit has been reached) is an NP-complete problem, and in the worst case the limit may be reached only after an exponential number of iterations. The potential inefficiency of a forwards analzyer is therefore rather worrying.

## 4 *Formalization of Backwards Analysis*

Backwards analysis can be formalized in a closely analogous way to forwards analysis— in fact, backwards analysis may be regarded as an abstract interpretation in which the abstract values are *functions* on contexts, rather than contexts themselves. However, we believe a formalization from first principles is clearer.

### 4.1 *Representing Contextual Information*

Just as in the forwards case, our first step must be to choose a representation for contextual information. For the same reasons, we choose to use the elements of a domain. We call this the *context domain*, and we call its elements *contexts*. We restrict ourselves to finite context domains so that recursive equations can again be solved by a fixed-point iteration.

As an example, the context domain used for simple strictness analysis is

L
|
S

with the interpretation

may or may not be evaluated
|
certain to be evaluated

Once again, more precise information appears below less precise information in the domain ordering. Contexts cannot be thought of as sets of possible values, but they can be regarded as sets of possible subsequent executions, or continuations. Thus $S$ represents the set of subsequent executions that do use the expression in question, while $L$ represents the set of all subsequent executions; as before, the domain is ordered by set inclusion.

Note that it is possible for two contexts to convey contradictory information — for example, "certain to be evaluated" and "certain not to be evaluated". What interpretation should we place on the greatest lower bound of these two, which is supposed to be "more precise" than both? Intuitively it represents a contradiction, or alternatively the empty set of possible subsequent executions. We understand this by interpreting a context as a set of subsequent *correctly terminating* executions. Thus if control ever reaches an expression standing in a contradictory context, then subsequent execution cannot terminate correctly.

### 4.2 *Formalizing Propagation*

Abstract interpretation defines the propagation of abstract values from the leaves to the root of a syntax tree; we must now formalize the propagation of contexts from the root to the leaves. In particular, we must formalize the propagation of contexts to the free variables of an expression. We do so by defining

$$\alpha \xrightarrow{E} x$$

to be the context propagated to $x$ when $\alpha$ is propagated through $E$. Clearly we have at least that

$$\alpha \xrightarrow{x} x = \alpha$$

What should $\alpha \xrightarrow{y} x$ be, when $y$ is different from $x$? More generally, what is the context of a variable in an expression that does not contain it? In order to give a complete definition of $\xrightarrow{E}$ we must introduce a notional context, which we call *ABSENT*, to play this role. So

$$\alpha \xrightarrow{y} x = ABSENT$$

Introducing *ABSENT* may be compared to the Arab invention of zero— while it seems a strange beast at first, its presence is justified by the resulting simplification of everything else.

Every context domain must contain an element *ABSENT*, but it need not necessarily be distinct from all the other elements. For example, in the $\{S, L\}$ domain for strictness analysis, we may safely take *ABSENT* to be $L$— if an expression does not contain a given variable, we just record that it does not necessarily evaluate that variable.

To define forwards analysis of a function call, we used an abstract function $f^\#$ mapping values propagated from $n$ arguments to the value propagated from the call. To define backwards analysis, we will use $n$ *context functions*, $f_1$ to $f_n$, with $f_i$ mapping the context of the call to the context propagated to the $i$th parameter (see Fig. 4.1).

So, for example, we will have

$$\alpha \xrightarrow{f x y} x = f_1 \alpha,$$
$$\alpha \xrightarrow{f x y} y = f_2 \alpha.$$

But what if $x$ occurs more than once in $E$? In that case different contexts may propagate to each occurrence— for example, in $\alpha \xrightarrow{f x x} x$, the context $f_1 \alpha$ propagates to the first occurrence, while $f_2 \alpha$ propagates to the second. These two contexts must be combined into a *net context*, containing the information in both. We will introduce a new operator, &, to combine the contexts of different occurrences. Now we can define propagation through an arbitrary function call:

$$\alpha \xrightarrow{f E_1 \ldots E_n} x = f_1 \alpha \xrightarrow{E_1} x \ \& \cdots \& \ f_n \alpha \xrightarrow{E_n} x.$$

**Figure 4.1.**   Context-mapping functions.

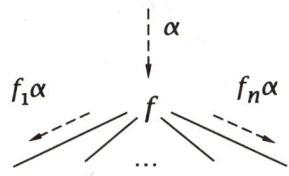

If $x$ occurs in only some of the $E_i$, we would not expect the others to contribute to the overall result, so we require that *ABSENT* be an identity for &.

As an example, in the case of strictness analysis & has the following definition; note that $L$ is indeed an identity.

| & | S | L |
|---|---|---|
| S | S | S |
| L | S | L |

This table captures the idea that if $S$ propagates to *any* occurrence of $x$, then $x$ *is* certain to be evaluated. (Here & is just ⊓, but this is not always so.)

Apart from conditionals, which we will discuss in the next section, this completes the definition of propagation through a tree. We need only show how definitions of context functions are derived. Once again, we define context functions in terms of propagation through the associated function bodies, so if $f$ is defined by

$$f x_1 \ldots x_n = E,$$

then we define

$$f_i \, \alpha = \alpha \xrightarrow{E} x_i$$

for each $i$ in the range 1 to $n$.

As before, recursive functions give rise to recursive context functions, which can be calculated by iteration to a limit. However, the efficiency of this iteration is much less problematic in the case of backwards analysis. Recall that an $n$-ary function, when analyzed forwards, gives rise to an abstract function in the domain $A^n \rightarrow A$. Such a function requires a table of $|A|^n$ entries to represent it, and a fixed-point iteration to calculate it may run for $O(|A|^n)$ steps. In contrast, when analyzed backwards the same function gives rise to $n$ context functions in the domain $C \rightarrow C$ (where $C$ is the context domain). Each function can be represented by a table of $|C|$ entries, and a fixed-point iteration to calculate all of them cannot run for more than $n \times |C|^2$ steps. It follows that in the worst case backwards analysis requires time square in the size of the program, rather than exponential.

### 4.3 *Conditional Expressions*

We have delayed the description of propagation through conditional expressions until now, because it presents a slight problem. Consider the example of strictness analysis: we cannot say that either the *then* or the *else* branch is certain to be evaluated (since it depends on the value of the condition), and so we must propagate the context $L$ to each branch. But then in an example such as

**if** $x=0$ **then** $y$ **else** $y$,

$L$ will be propagated to both occurrences of $y$, and so the net context will be lazy even though the expression clearly evaluates $y$.

To avoid this problem, conditionals must be treated in a rather special way. Consider

$$\alpha \xrightarrow{\textbf{if } E_1 \textbf{ then } E_2 \textbf{ else } E_3} x .$$

We know that one of $E_2$ and $E_3$ will be evaluated in context $\alpha$— we just don't know which. If the *then* branch is chosen, $x$ will be evaluated in context

$$\alpha \xrightarrow{E_2} x ,$$

whereas if the *else* branch is chosen the context of $x$ will be

$$\alpha \xrightarrow{E_3} x .$$

One of these two must occur, and so we can at least say that the context of $x$ is

$$\alpha \xrightarrow{E_2} x \ \sqcup \ \alpha \xrightarrow{E_3} x$$

(recalling the correspondence between $\sqcup$ and $\vee$).

So in the case of strictness analysis, rather than propagating $L$ through the *then* and *else* branches and combining the results with & (which is certain to give $L$), we propagate $S$ through both branches and combine the results with $\sqcup$. If a variable is evaluated in *both* arms of the conditional, then its resulting context will be $S$.

Putting all this together, propagation through conditionals is defined by

$$\alpha \xrightarrow{\textbf{if } E_1 \textbf{ then } E_2 \textbf{ else } E_3} x$$

$$=$$

$$\alpha \xrightarrow{E_1} x \ \& \ (\alpha \xrightarrow{E_2} x \ \sqcup \ \alpha \xrightarrow{E_3} x) .$$

(In more complex analyses than simple strictness, the context propagated to the condition $E_1$ may be not $\alpha$, but some function of $\alpha$ instead.)

## 5　*Examples of Backwards Analysis*

In this section we'll look at several examples of analysis problems that can be solved backwards. Three of them are variants of strictness analysis; the fourth classifies data into long-term and transient.

## 5.1 Strictness Analysis

First of all let's look at an example of simple strictness analysis using the domain

$$
\begin{array}{c}
L \\
| \\
S
\end{array}
$$

that we have already discussed. We will analyze the recursive function

$$g\, x\, y \;=\; \textbf{if } x{=}0 \textbf{ then } y \textbf{ else } g\,(x-1)\,y$$

that we took as our example for forwards strictness analysis in Section 3.3. Applying the rules given above, we find

$$
\begin{aligned}
g_1\,\alpha \;&=\; \alpha \xrightarrow{\textbf{if } x=0 \textbf{ then } y \textbf{ else } g\,(x-1)\,y} x \\
&=\; \alpha \xrightarrow{x=0} x \;\&\; (\alpha \xrightarrow{y} x \;\sqcup\; \alpha \xrightarrow{g\,(x-1)\,y} x) \\
&=\; =_1 \alpha \;\&\; (L \;\sqcup\; g_1\,\alpha \xrightarrow{x-1} x) \\
&=\; =_1 \alpha \;\&\; L \\
&=\; =_1 \alpha \;,
\end{aligned}
$$

$$
\begin{aligned}
g_2\,\alpha \;&=\; \alpha \xrightarrow{\textbf{if } x=0 \textbf{ then } y \textbf{ else } g\,(x-1)\,y} y \\
&=\; \alpha \xrightarrow{x=0} y \;\&\; (\alpha \xrightarrow{y} y \;\sqcup\; \alpha \xrightarrow{g\,(x-1)\,y} y) \\
&=\; L \;\&\; (\alpha \sqcup g_2\,\alpha) \\
&=\; \alpha \sqcup g_2\,\alpha \;.
\end{aligned}
$$

Here $=_1$ and $-_1$ are context functions associated with primitive operators; we have to give their definitions. Since $=$ and $-$ are both strict these are

| $=_i$ | |
|---|---|
| $S$ | $S$ |
| $L$ | $L$ |

| $-_i$ | |
|---|---|
| $S$ | $S$ |
| $L$ | $L$ |

for $i$ equal to 1 or 2. Nonstrict primitives such as lazy *cons* have context functions of the form

| $cons_i$ | |
|---|---|
| $S$ | $L$ |
| $L$ | $L$ |

The function $cons_i$ maps the context of a list into the context of one of its components, and so the result is always lazy.

Now it is clear that $g_1 S = S$, so $g$ is strict in $x$, while we can calculate $g_2$ by a fixed-point iteration:

| | $g_2^0$ | $g_2^1$ | $g_2^2$ |
|---|---|---|---|
| $S$ | $S$ | $S$ | $S$ |
| $L$ | $S$ | $L$ | $L$ |

So $g_2 S = S$, and $g$ is also strict in $y$.

## 5.2 *Strictness-and-Absence Analysis*

A slight extension of strictness analysis distinguishes *ABSENT* from $L$, using the context domain

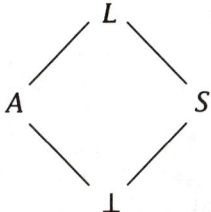

(Here $\perp$ represents contradictory information; recall the discussion in Section 4.1.) This analysis can be used to identify expressions that are certainly never evaluated as well as those that certainly are. A compiler need not generate any code at all for an expression that is never evaluated; it could perhaps optimize function calls by not passing unnecessary parameters, or it could invoke the garbage collector early to recycle data that are known not to be required.

We must extend the definitions of primitive context functions to cover the new cases. Suitable definitions are:

| $=_i$ | |
|---|---|
| $\perp$ | $\perp$ |
| $A$ | $A$ |
| $S$ | $S$ |
| $L$ | $L$ |

| $cons_i$ | |
|---|---|
| $\perp$ | $\perp$ |
| $A$ | $A$ |
| $S$ | $L$ |
| $L$ | $L$ |

Note that contradiction propagates, and that we do know that if a data structure is never evaluated, neither are its components ($cons_i\, A = A$).

Now let's analyze a slight variant of our previous example:

$$h\, x\, y \;=\; \textbf{if } x{=}0 \textbf{ then } x \textbf{ else } h\,(x{-}1)\, y.$$

Here $h$ is evidently strict in $x$, so we will consider only its second context function. Applying the definition gives

$$h_2\, a \;=\; \alpha \xrightarrow{\;\textbf{if } x\text{-}0 \textbf{ then } x \textbf{ else } h\,(x-1)\,y\;} y$$

$$=\; \alpha \xrightarrow{\;x\text{-}0\;} y \;\&\; (\alpha \xrightarrow{\;x\;} y \;\sqcup\; \alpha \xrightarrow{\;h\,(x-1)\,y\;} y)$$

$$=\; A \;\&\; (A \sqcup h_2\, \alpha)$$

$$=\; A \sqcup h_2\, \alpha .$$

Now let's tabulate the approximations to $h_2$:

|   | $h_2^0$ | $h_2^1$ | $h_2^2$ |
|---|---|---|---|
| $\bot$ | $\bot$ | $A$ | $A$ |
| $A$ | $\bot$ | $A$ | $A$ |
| $S$ | $\bot$ | $A$ | $A$ |
| $L$ | $\bot$ | $A$ | $A$ |

The analysis discovers that $y$ can never be used.

### 5.3 *Sharing Analysis*

Strictness-and-absence analysis can be thought of as making a very crude estimate of the number of times a value is used. It distinguishes only between zero uses and nonzero uses. We can usefully make the analysis slightly more refined by distinguishing between zero, one, and many uses. This allows us to identify "unshared" expressions whose values are used at most once. Unshared expressions can be compiled more efficiently— for example, an unshared closure need not be updated when its value is computed, and a simpler storage manager may suffice for unshared objects.

We will use subsets of $\{0, 1, M\}$ as contexts, representing the possible number of uses of an expression— zero times, once, and many times. For example, an expression in the context $\{0, 1\}$ may or may not be used, but it will be used no more than once. An expression in context $\{1, M\}$ will be used at least once, and an expression in context $\{0, M\}$ will be used not at all or many times. The context domain is ordered by set inclusion, so that $\emptyset$ is the least element and $\sqcup$ is set union. The strictness-and-absence contexts correspond to sharing analysis contexts as follows:

$$\bot \;=\; \emptyset \qquad\qquad\qquad S \;=\; \{1, M\}$$

$$A \;=\; \{0\} \qquad\qquad\qquad L \;=\; \{0, 1, M\}$$

We can count the uses of a variable by summing the uses of its occurrences, so we define

$$\alpha \& \beta \;=\; \{a + b \mid a \in \alpha,\ b \in \beta\}$$

(where $1 + 1 = M$, $M + 0 = M$, $M + 1 = M$, and $M + M = M$). The arguments of primitives such as + are used exactly the same number of times as their results, so we define

$$+_i \alpha \ = \ \alpha$$

and so on. All we can say about lazy *cons*, however, is that neither the head nor tail of a *cons* cell can be used more times than the *cons* cell itself:

$$cons_i \, \alpha \ = \ \{b \mid \exists a \in \alpha . \, b \sqsubseteq a\}$$

so

$$cons_i \, \{M\} \ = \ \{0, 1, M\}$$
$$cons_i \, \{1\} \ = \ \{0, 1\}.$$

With these definitions, let's return to our previous example:

$$g \, x \, y \ = \ \textbf{if } x{=}0 \textbf{ then } y \textbf{ else } g \, (x{-}1) \, y \, .$$

This time the context functions are

$$g_1 \, \alpha \ = \ \alpha \xrightarrow{\textbf{if } x{=}0 \textbf{ then } y \textbf{ else } g \, (x{-}1) \, y} x$$
$$= \ \alpha \xrightarrow{x{=}0} x \ \& \ (\alpha \xrightarrow{y} x \sqcup \alpha \xrightarrow{g \, (x{-}1) \, y} x)$$
$$= \ =_1 \alpha \ \& \ (\{0\} \sqcup -_1 (g_1 \, \alpha))$$
$$= \ \alpha \ \& \ (\{0\} \sqcup g_1 \, \alpha)$$

since $=_1 \alpha = \alpha$ and $-_1 \alpha = \alpha$, and

$$g_2 \, \alpha \ = \ \alpha \xrightarrow{\textbf{if } x{=}0 \textbf{ then } y \textbf{ else } g \, (x{-}1) \, y} y$$
$$= \ \alpha \xrightarrow{x{=}0} y \ \& \ (\alpha \xrightarrow{y} y \sqcup \alpha \xrightarrow{g \, (x{-}1) \, y} y)$$
$$= \ \{0\} \ \& \ (\alpha \sqcup g_2 \, \alpha)$$
$$= \ \alpha \sqcup g_2 \, \alpha \, .$$

Rather than tabulate $g_1$ and $g_2$ in their entirety, we will just evaluate $g_1\{1\}$ and $g_2\{1\}$ to analyze an unshared call of $g$. These are the least solutions of

$$g_1 \, \{1\} \ = \ \{1\} \ \& \ (\{0\} \sqcup g_1 \, \{1\}) \, ,$$
$$g_2 \, \{1\} \ = \ \{1\} \sqcup g_2 \, \{1\}.$$

We use a fixed-point iteration to calculate these solutions as usual.

| | 1st | 2nd | 3rd | 4th |
|---|---|---|---|---|
| $g_1$ {1} | ∅ | {1} | {1, M} | {1, M} |
| $g_2$ {1} | ∅ | {1} | {1} | {1} |

So the first argument may be shared, but the second is guaranteed to be unshared.

## 5.4 *Lifetime Analysis*

In this section we show how backwards analysis can be used to distinguish *transient* data (whose lifetime is known to be short) from data that may persist for some time. This information could be used to guide storage allocation. For example, a datum with a lifetime shorter than that of the function call that creates it can be allocated on a stack. When a generational garbage collector is used, transient and long-term data may be allocated different generations [16]. In a persistent programming language (one where data may survive longer than the run that creates them), long-term data must be movable to the disc, but transient data need not be.

We will use a two-point context domain to detect transience:

$$
\begin{array}{c}
P \\
| \\
T
\end{array}
$$

Here $T$ is interpreted as "transient" and $P$ is interpreted as "may persist for a long time". We classify data as transient if it can never be referred to from any persistent data structure. Since a variable is transient only if all its occurrences are in transient contexts, we must define & by

| & | $T$ | $P$ |
|---|---|---|
| $T$ | $T$ | $P$ |
| $P$ | $P$ | $P$ |

As a result, *ABSENT* must be taken to be $T$. Every function that uses and discards its argument propagates a transient context, so primitives such as +, −, etc. have context functions of the form

| $+_i$ | |
|---|---|
| $T$ | $T$ |
| $P$ | $T$ |

On the other hand, primitives that build their arguments into data structures must propagate the same context they receive:

| $cons_i$ | |
|---|---|
| $T$ | $T$ |
| $P$ | $P$ |

Since the boolean in a conditional expression is used and discarded, we must use a different rule for conditionals:

$$\alpha \xrightarrow{\textbf{if } E_1 \textbf{ then } E_2 \textbf{ else } E_3} x$$

$$= T \xrightarrow{E_1} x \;\&\; (\alpha \xrightarrow{E_2} x \sqcup \alpha \xrightarrow{E_3} x)$$

$$= \alpha \xrightarrow{E_2} x \sqcup \alpha \xrightarrow{E_3} x$$

since $T \xrightarrow{E_1} x$ is always $T$.

Now let's apply lifetime analysis to our familiar example:

$$g\,x\,y \;=\; \textbf{if } x{=}0 \textbf{ then } y \textbf{ else } g\,(x-1)\,y\,.$$

We find

$$g_1\,\alpha \;=\; \alpha \xrightarrow{\textbf{if } x{=}0 \textbf{ then } y \textbf{ else } g\,(x-1)\,y} x$$

$$=\; \alpha \xrightarrow{y} x \sqcup \alpha \xrightarrow{g\,(x-1)\,y} x$$

$$=\; T \sqcup -_1(g_1\,a)$$

$$=\; T \sqcup T$$

$$=\; T\,,$$

so $g$'s first argument is always transient. On the other hand,

$$g_2\,\alpha \;=\; \alpha \xrightarrow{\textbf{if } x{=}0 \textbf{ then } y \textbf{ else } g\,(x-1)\,y} y$$

$$=\; \alpha \xrightarrow{y} y \sqcup \alpha \xrightarrow{g\,(x-1)\,y} y$$

$$=\; \alpha \sqcup g_2\,\alpha\,,$$

and fixed-point iteration gives

|   | $g_2^0$ | $g_2^1$ | $g_2^2$ |
|---|---|---|---|
| $T$ | $T$ | $T$ | $T$ |
| $P$ | $T$ | $P$ | $P$ |

so $g$'s second argument may persist if $g$ is called in a persistent context.

**Technical Note** This analysis really works only for strict functional languages, because it doesn't take into account the possibility of a persistent lazy closure for an expression such as $x+1$, which contains a reference to a variable that will be used only transiently, when the closure is evaluated. In such a case $x$ must be regarded as persistent. To extend the analysis to a lazy language would require a combined strictness-and-lifetime analysis, using a

domain such as

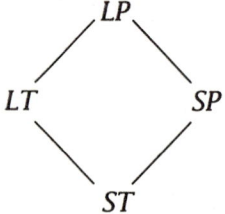

Here *ST* stands for strict-and-transient, and so on. Now even functions that use their arguments transiently would propagate lazy-and-persistent to those arguments if called in such a context— for example, $+_i$ would be defined by

| $+_i$ | |
|-------|------|
| *ST*  | *ST* |
| *LT*  | *LT* |
| *SP*  | *ST* |
| *LP*  | *LP* |

## 6 *Backwards Analysis of Data Structures*

One of the main attractions of backwards analysis is the ease with which it can be extended to analyze data structures. Instead of using a single context domain, we associate a different one with each type. Contexts can then carry additional type-specific information. So that the analyzer can determine which context domain to use, we restrict ourselves to strongly —indeed, monomorphically— typed languages.

In this section we will show how the analyses in the previous section can be extended, first to product types, then to sum types, and finally to recursive data types.

### 6.1 *Product Types*

The contexts we have seen so far can tell us, for example, that a data structure is certain to be evaluated or to be transient, but they cannot give us separate information about the components. Yet the fact that a pair (say) is evaluated does not necessarily imply that both components are. We call the contexts used above *atomic*, since they cannot distinguish the components of a structure, and we use them to construct more complex contexts that can.

***Pair Contexts: A First Attempt*** We will write pair contexts in the form

$$\alpha_{(\beta, \gamma)} ,$$

where $\alpha$ is an atomic context relating to the pair itself, and $\beta$ and $y$ are (possibly nonatomic) contexts relating to the components. For example, $S_{(S,L)}$ denotes a context in which a pair and its first component are evaluated, although the second may not be. Similarly $T_{(P,P)}$ is the context of a transient pair with persistent components.

When such a context propagates to a pair $(E_1, E_2)$, the contexts $\beta$ and $y$ are propagated to the components. We can express this by defining the context functions associated with the pair-construction function, which we denote $(-, -)$:

$$(-, -)\, a\, b = (a, b).$$

These context functions are defined by

$$(-, -)_1 \, \alpha_{(\beta, y)} \;\; = \;\; \beta,$$
$$(-, -)_2 \, \alpha_{(\beta, y)} \;\; = \;\; y.$$

We select the components of pairs by pattern matching, thus:

$$fst(x, y) \;\; = \;\; x,$$
$$snd(x, y) \;\; = \;\; y,$$

so we must define the context functions associated with such functions. We do so by defining the context propagated to a *pattern*, rather than just a variable. Then

$$fst_1 \, \alpha \;\; = \;\; \alpha \xrightarrow{x} (x, y),$$
$$snd_1 \, \alpha \;\; = \;\; \alpha \xrightarrow{y} (x, y),$$

and in general, if $f$ is defined by

$$f\, p_1 \ldots p_n \;\; = \;\; E,$$

where $p_1, \ldots, p_n$ are patterns, then $f_i$ is defined by

$$f_i \, \alpha \;\; = \;\; \alpha \xrightarrow{E} p_i.$$

The context propagated to a pattern is formed from the contexts propagated to the variables in it:

$$\alpha \xrightarrow{E} (x, y) \;\; = \;\; \beta_{(\alpha \xrightarrow{E} x, \, \alpha \xrightarrow{E} y)}$$

for a suitable choice of $\beta$ depending on the particular analysis being performed. For example, since pattern matching is strict, $\beta$ would be the same as $\alpha$ in the case of strictness analysis— strict if $\alpha$ is strict and lazy if it is lazy. Another example: Arguments matched against a pattern are not built into persistent data structures, so in lifetime analysis $\beta$ is $T$. Applying strictness analysis to *fst* therefore yields

$$fst_1\ \alpha\ =\ \alpha \xrightarrow{x} (x, y)$$

$$=\ \alpha_{(\alpha \xrightarrow{x} x,\ \alpha \xrightarrow{x} y)}$$

$$=\ \alpha_{(\alpha, L)}\ .$$

When *fst* is called in a strict context, its argument is in context $S_{(S,L)}$— it and its first component will be evaluated. *Note*: we are abusing notation here slightly. If $\alpha$ is itself a subscripted context then $\beta$ is just the atomic part of $\alpha$, so for example

$$fst_1\ S_{(S,S)}\ =\ S_{(S_{(S,\,\dot{S})},\,L)}\ .$$

Before we can make use of pair contexts we have to extend the operators $\sqcup$ and & to them; this we do by combining the corresponding parts:

$$\alpha_{(\beta,\,\gamma)}\ \&\ \alpha'_{(\beta',\,\gamma')}\ =\ (\alpha\ \&,\ \alpha')_{(\beta\,\&\,\beta',\,\gamma\,\&\,\gamma')}\ ,$$

$$\alpha_{(\beta,\,\gamma)}\ \sqcup\ \alpha'_{(\beta',\,\gamma')}\ =\ (\alpha\ \sqcup\ \alpha')_{(\beta\sqcup\beta',\,\gamma\sqcup\gamma')}\ .$$

Let us strictness-analyze two example functions:

$$add\ p\ =\ fst\ p + snd\ p\ ,$$

$$select\ b\ p\ =\ \textbf{if}\ b\ \textbf{then}\ fst\ p\ \textbf{else}\ snd\ p\ .$$

The context function for *add* is

$$add_1\ \alpha\ =\ fst_1(+_1\ \alpha)\ \&\ snd_1(+_2\ \alpha)$$

$$=\ fst_1\ \alpha\ \&\ snd_1\ \alpha$$

$$=\ \alpha_{(\alpha, L)}\ \&\ \alpha_{(L, \alpha)}$$

$$=\ (\alpha\ \&\ \alpha)_{(\alpha\,\&\,L,\,L\,\&\,\alpha)}$$

$$=\ \alpha_{(\alpha,\,\alpha)}\ ,$$

so if *add* is called in a strict context, then both components of its argument are evaluated. In contrast, *select*'s second context function is

$$select_2\ \alpha\ =\ fst_1\ \alpha\ \sqcup\ snd_1\ \alpha$$

$$=\ \alpha_{(\alpha, L)}\ \sqcup\ \alpha_{(L, \alpha)}$$

$$=\ (\alpha\ \sqcup\ \alpha)_{(\alpha\sqcup L,\,L\sqcup\alpha)}$$

$$=\ \alpha_{(L, L)}\ ,$$

so although *select* is strict in its second argument, neither component is certain to be evaluated.

***Pair Contexts: A Refinement*** If a pair is not certain to be used, then we cannot be certain that its components are. Therefore, in the case of strictness analysis, the only lazy pair context is $L_{(L,L)}$— contexts such as $L_{(S,L)}$ make no sense. Similarly, in the case of sharing analysis, any pair context with 0 at the top level must have 0 in all component contexts— so $\{0, 1\}_{(\{0\}, \{0, M\})}$ is OK, but $\{0, 1\}_{(\{1\}, \{0, M\})}$ is not. In general, any context $\alpha_{(\beta, \gamma)}$ in which $\alpha \sqsupseteq ABSENT$ must also satisfy $\beta \sqsupseteq ABSENT$ and $\gamma \sqsupseteq ABSENT$.

As a result, nested $L$s in a strictness context carry no information. We can remedy this by interpreting nested contexts as the contexts that apply to the components *given that the pair is actually used*. The interpretation of contexts headed by $S$ is unchanged, but $L_{(S,S)}$ is now allowed, with the interpretation that the components of a pair in that context are certain to be evaluated if the pair is. Given such information, a compiler could generate code to construct the pair that would evaluate the components strictly, without building a closure. Since the code is executed only when the pair is actually used, these are the only circumstances under which it has to work! Note that $L_{(L,L)}$ is also allowed, with the meaning that, even given that the pair itself is used, the components may not be. In this case the pair and both of its components must be represented by closures. (This refinement is essential if head-strictness of lists is to be detected.)

Perhaps surprisingly, *ABSENT* is now represented by a pair context with the bottom element of the context domain as subscripts— for example $L_{(S,S)}$ for strictness analysis, or $\{0\}_{(\emptyset, \emptyset)}$ for sharing analysis. Since *ABSENT* represents a context in which the components cannot be used, we are free to give them contradictory contexts which can never apply.

In order to derive these lazy contexts with strict components, we have to alter the way lazy contexts are propagated. To see why, let us strictness-analyze a call *(fst p)* in a lazy context:

$$fst\ (x, y)\ =\ x\ ,$$

$$L \xrightarrow{\ fst\ p\ } p\ =\ fst_1\ L\ ,$$

$$\begin{aligned}
fst_1\ L\ &=\ L \xrightarrow{\ x\ } (x, y) \\
&=\ L_{(L \xrightarrow{x} x,\ L \xrightarrow{x} y)} \\
&=\ L_{(L,L)}\ .
\end{aligned}$$

But of course, we expect $p$ to be in the context $L_{(S,L)}$— if it is ever used, then its first component will certainly also be used. How can we correct this? Notice that if *(fst p)* is actually evaluated, then $p$'s context is effectively $S \xrightarrow{fst\ p} p$, which is $S_{(S,L)}$. It is a lazy version of this context that is the correct result in this case. This suggests that we redefine propagation of a lazy context to propagate the strict version, then make the result lazy afterwards. Formally,

$$\alpha \xrightarrow{E} p$$

$$= \quad ABSENT \sqcup \textbf{strict } \alpha \xrightarrow{E} p \qquad\qquad \text{if } alpha \sqsupseteq ABSENT$$

$$= \quad \dots \text{previous definition} \dots \qquad\qquad \text{otherwise}$$

where **strict** will be defined shortly. In our example, we now find

$$L \xrightarrow{fst\ p} p$$

$$= \quad ABSENT \sqcup S \xrightarrow{fst\ p} p$$

$$= \quad L_{(S,S)} \sqcup S_{(S,L)}$$

$$= \quad L_{(S,L)} \, .$$

Obviously in the case of simple strictness analysis, **strict** $\alpha = S$, but we can define it in general as the least context satisfying

$$\alpha \sqcup ABSENT \quad = \quad \textbf{strict } \alpha \sqcup ABSENT \, .$$

In the case of sharing analysis then

$$\textbf{strict } \alpha \quad = \quad \alpha - \{0\}$$

and in the case of lifetime analysis

$$\textbf{strict } \alpha \quad = \quad \alpha$$

(since $ABSENT = T$, the bottom of the context domain). This change in the definition of propagation also allows us to make the convenient assumption that context functions are always called with a strict context as their argument.

We also have to take account of the new interpretation in the definition of &, which can no longer be defined component-wise. To see this, consider a pair used in the two contexts

$$L_{(S,S)} \, \& \, S_{(L,L)} \quad \neq \quad S_{(S,S)} \, .$$

Here we can definitely say that the pair is evaluated, but since the context $L_{(S,S)}$ may not use the pair at all we can only say that the components may be. If we generalize this slightly to

$$L_{(\alpha,\beta)} \, \& \, S_{(\alpha',\beta')} \, ,$$

then we can say that the first component may be used in the context $\alpha'$ (if the lazy occurrence is not actually used), or in the context $\alpha\&\alpha'$ (if it is). So the net context of the first component is $\alpha' \sqcup (\alpha\&\alpha')$, and the net context of the pair is

$$S_{(\alpha' \sqcup (\alpha\&\alpha'),\ \beta' \sqcup (\beta\&\beta'))} \cdot$$

In general, we define & by

$$\alpha_{(\beta,\gamma)} \ \& \ \alpha'_{(\beta',\gamma')}$$

$$= \ (\alpha \& \alpha')_{(\beta\sqcup\beta'\sqcup(\beta\&\beta'),\ \gamma\sqcup\gamma'\sqcup(\gamma\&\gamma'))} \qquad\qquad \text{if both } \alpha, \alpha' \sqsupseteq ABSENT$$

$$= \ (\alpha \& \alpha')_{(\beta'\sqcup(\beta\&\beta'),\ \gamma'\sqcup(\gamma\&\gamma'))} \qquad\qquad \text{if only } alpha \sqsupseteq ABSENT$$

$$= \ (\alpha \& \alpha')_{(\beta\sqcup(\beta\&\beta'),\ \gamma\sqcup(\gamma\&\gamma'))} \qquad\qquad \text{if only } \alpha' \sqsupseteq ABSENT$$

$$= \ (\alpha \& \alpha')_{(\beta\&\beta',\ \gamma\&\gamma')} \qquad\qquad \text{if neither } \sqsupseteq ABSENT \ .$$

So in the example we began with,

$$L_{(S,S)} \ \& \ S_{(L,L)}$$

$$= \ (L\&S)_{(L\sqcup(S\&L),\ L\sqcup(S\&L))} \qquad\qquad \text{since } L \sqsupseteq ABSENT$$

$$= \ S_{(L,L)} \ ,$$

as expected.

Taking an example from sharing analysis, consider a pair $p$ used in two unshared occurrences *fst p* and *snd p*. The two contexts of $p$ are $\{1\}_{(\{1\},\ \{0\})}$ and $\{1\}_{(\{0\},\ \{1\})}$, and their net context is

$$\{1\}_{(\{1\},\ \{0\})} \ \& \ \{1\}_{(\{0\},\ \{1\})}$$

$$= \ (\{1\} \& \{1\})_{(\{1\}\&\{0\},\ \{0\}\&\{1\})}$$

$$= \ \{M\}_{(\{1\},\ \{1\})} \ .$$

The pair itself is shared, but each component is unshared. Now suppose the first occurrence, *fst p*, may not be evaluated at all. Then the net context of the pair is

$$\{0, 1\}_{(\{1\},\ \{0\})} \ \& \ \{1\}_{(\{0\},\ \{1\})}$$

$$= \ (\{0, 1\} \& \{1\})_{(\{0\}\sqcup(\{1\}\&\{0\}),\ \{1\}\sqcup(\{0\}\&\{1\}))}$$

$$= \ \{1, M\}_{(\{0,1\},\ \{1\})} \ .$$

The pair may be shared, the second component is unshared, and the first is either unshared or not used at all.

As another example, let us perform sharing analysis of two alternative definitions of the function that adds together the two components of a pair:

$$addpair1\ p\ =\ fst\ p + snd\ p\ ,$$

$$addpair2\ (x, y)\ =\ x + y\ .$$

The context functions are

$$addpair1_1\ \alpha$$

$$=\ \alpha \xrightarrow{fst\ p + snd\ p} p$$

$$=\ fst_1(+_1\ \alpha)\ \&\ snd_1(+_2\ \alpha)$$

$$=\ \alpha_{(\alpha,\ \{0\})}\ \&\ \alpha_{(\{0\},\ \alpha)}$$

$$=\ (\alpha\ \&\ \alpha)_{(\alpha,\ \alpha)} \qquad\qquad\qquad\qquad \text{since } \alpha \text{ is strict}$$

and

$$addpair2_1\ \alpha$$

$$=\ \alpha \xrightarrow{x+y} (x, y)$$

$$=\ \alpha_{(\alpha \xrightarrow{x+y} x,\ \alpha \xrightarrow{x+y} y)}$$

$$=\ \alpha_{(\alpha,\ \alpha)}\ .$$

When the functions are called in an unshared context, we find

$$addpair1_1\ \{1\}\ =\ \{M\}_{(\{1\},\ \{1\})}\ ,$$

$$addpair2_1\ \{1\}\ =\ \{1\}_{(\{1\},\ \{1\})}\ ,$$

so the components are unshared in each case, but the pair itself is shared by $addpair_1$.

## 6.2 *Sum Types*

Sum types are those with several variants— for example, the Miranda data type

$$sum\ *\ ::=\ left\ *\ |\ right\ *\ .$$

Functions on sum types are defined by several equations, as in

$$isleft \; (left \; x) \quad = \quad \textbf{true} \, ,$$

$$isleft \; (right \; x) \quad = \quad \textbf{false} \, .$$

We can extend the ideas in the previous section straightforwardly to sum types by using contexts with *multiple* subscripts, one for each variant. For example, contexts of the above type take the form

$$\alpha_{left \; \beta, \; right \; y} \, ,$$

with the interpretation that $\alpha$ applies to the sum object itself, and if this object is of the form $(left \; x)$ then $\beta$ applies to $x$, while if it is of the form $(right \; y)$ then $y$ applies to $y$. So the context functions associated with the type's constructors are

$$left_1 \; \alpha_{left \; \beta, \; right \; y} \quad = \quad \beta \, ,$$

$$right_1 \; \alpha_{left \; \beta, \; right \; y} \quad = \quad y \, .$$

The operators & and ⊔ are extended component-wise to contexts with multiple subscripts: for example

$$S_{left \; S, \; right \; L} \; \& \; S_{left \; L, \; right \; S} \quad = \quad S_{left \; S, \; right \; S} \, .$$

We have to extend the definition of the context propagated to a pattern. Consider for example

$$outleft \; (left \; x) \quad = \quad x \, ,$$

which is undefined for arguments of the form $(right \; y)$. Its context function is

$$outleft_1 \; \alpha \quad = \quad \alpha \xrightarrow{x} left \; x$$

$$\qquad\qquad = \quad \beta_{left \; y, \; right \; \delta}$$

for some $\beta$, $y$, and $\delta$. It is fairly clear that $y$ should be $\alpha$ —if *outleft*'s argument is $(left \; x)$ then $\alpha$ is the context that applies to $x$— but what should $\delta$ be? If *outleft*'s argument is of the form $(right \; y)$, then the whole program will crash, so we can safely take $\delta$ to be the bottom element of the context domain. For example, in the case of strictness analysis we have

$$outleft_1 \; \alpha \quad = \quad \alpha_{left \; \alpha, \; right \; S} \, .$$

(On the basis of this an optimizing compiler would evaluate a call such as *outleft* (*right* (1/0)) by computing 1/0 before calling *outleft*, causing a division-by-zero error that would not occur in an unoptimized implementation. This doesn't matter because the program fails anyway —with a pattern-matching-failure— and we consider one run-time error to be as good as another.)

Using these rules we can derive context functions from single equations, but how should we treat functions defined by several alternative equations? Such definitions take the form

$$f\, p_{11} \ldots p_{1n} \quad = \quad E_1$$

$$\vdots$$

$$f\, p_{m1} \ldots p_{mn} \quad = \quad E_m.$$

We know that, in any particular call, one of these equations is used to determine the result of the function— we just don't know which equation it will be. There is a close analogy here with conditional expressions, where we know that either the **then** or the **else** branch will be used, but we don't know which. Just as we expressed this uncertainty using ⊔ in the case of conditional expressions, we can define the context functions associated with this kind of definition by taking the least upper bound of the contexts derived from each equation separately:

$$f_i\, \alpha \;=\; \alpha \xrightarrow{E_1} p_{i1} \;\sqcup\; \cdots \;\sqcup\; \alpha \xrightarrow{E_n} p_{in}.$$

For example, let us strictness-analyze

$$isleft\, (left\, x) \quad = \quad \mathbf{true}$$

$$isleft\, (right\, y) \quad = \quad \mathbf{false}.$$

Applying its context function to $S$, we find

$$isleft_1\, S$$

$$= \; S \xrightarrow{\mathbf{true}} left\, x \;\sqcup\; S \xrightarrow{\mathbf{false}} right\, y$$

$$= \; S_{left(S \xrightarrow{\mathbf{true}} x),\, right\, S} \;\sqcup\; S_{left\, S,\, right(S \xrightarrow{\mathbf{false}} y)}$$

$$= \; S_{left\, L,\, right\, S} \;\sqcup\; S_{left\, S,\, right\, L}$$

$$= \; S_{left\, L,\, right\, L}\,,$$

so the argument is evaluated, but its component is not, whichever variant it turns out to be. Notice that, because we use the bottom of the context domain for the contexts of patterns that don't match, and then combine the results from different equations using ⊔, each equation contributes only to the context of the variant that it matches.

### 6.3 *Recursive Types*

Using the above ideas we can construct a finite context domain corresponding to any nonrecursive Miranda data type. However, if we try to do the same thing for a recursive data type we obtain an infinite number of contexts. For example, consider lists, which might be defined by

$$List * ::= [] \mid * : List * .$$

Lists have two variants, so list contexts should have two subscripts, and they should be of the form

$$\alpha_{[\,],\,\beta:\gamma} ,$$

where $\alpha$ applies to the list itself, and if the list is nonempty then $\beta$ applies to its head and $\gamma$ to its tail. However, since the first subscript has no components we will omit it and just write

$$\alpha_{\beta:\gamma} .$$

But $\gamma$ is itself a list context, with its own subscripts, and clearly the depth of subscripts is infinite.

We can derive a finite domain of list contexts by restricting ourselves to those in which every head context and every tail context is the same— that is, contexts of the form

$$\alpha_{\beta:\gamma_{\beta:\gamma_{...}}}$$

(note that we do not insist that $\alpha$ and $\gamma$ should be equal— this would forbid strict and lazy versions of the same context). We write infinite contexts finitely by omitting all but the first subscripts; for example the context above is written

$$\alpha_{\beta:\gamma} .$$

So, for example, in the case of strictness analysis the (strict) list contexts are

$S_{S:S}$ all heads and tails of a list in this context are evaluated, so no closures need be used in its representation.

$S_{L:S}$ a *tail-strict* context— the spine of any list in this context is evaluated, but the elements may not be. Only the heads of cons-cells need contain closures.

$S_{S:L}$ a *head-strict* context— the head of any evaluated cons-cell is also evaluated, so only the tails of cons-cells need contain closures. Notice that this depends on the refined interpretation of component contexts introduced in Section 6.1.2.

$S_{L:L}$ nothing can be said about either heads or tails, all of which have to be represented by closures.

Of course, application of the analysis rules given in previous sections may produce contexts that do not satisfy the restriction we have made. As an example, let us calculate

$$S_{S:L} \ \& \ S_{L:S}$$
$$= S_{S:L_{S:L}...} \ \& \ S_{L:S_{L:S}...}$$
$$= (S \ \& \ S)_{S \& L:L_{S:L}... \& S_{L:S}...}$$
$$= S_{S:L_{S:L}... \& S_{L:S}...} \ .$$

Notice that, at the next level, we are *not* combining the same two contexts that we started off with. Continuing the calculation, we use the rule for applying & to lazy contexts to derive

$$= S_{S:(L \& S)_{L \sqcup (L \& S), S... \sqcup (L... \& S...)}}$$
$$= S_{S:S_{L:L}... \& S...} \ ,$$

and the calculation now repeats, so the final answer is

$$S_{S:S_{L:S}}$$

(using the convention that a missing subscript denotes an infinite repetition at the second level). Whenever this situation arises, and we obtain a context of the wrong form, we approximate it as follows:

$$\alpha_{\beta:\gamma_{\beta':\gamma'}} \implies \alpha_{(\beta \sqcup \beta'):(\gamma \sqcup \gamma')} \ .$$

So in this particular example we take

$$S_{L:S} \ \& \ S_{S:L} = S_{L:S} \ .$$

(Our notation tempts us to assume that the subscripts on infinite contexts can be treated just like those on finite ones, but the example shows this is not the case; if lists were a nonrecursive type the result in this example would be $S_{S:S}$.)

## 6.4 *Example: Analyzing Append*

In this section we present a slightly more substantial example: We will perform strictness and lifetime analysis of the well-known function *append*. We take as our starting point the following definition:

$$append\,[\,]\,y \quad = \quad y,$$
$$append\,(a:x)\,y \quad = \quad a:append\,x\,y.$$

Its context functions are

$$append_1\,\alpha \quad = \quad \alpha \xrightarrow{y} [\,] \;\sqcup\; \alpha \xrightarrow{a:append\,x\,y} (a:x),$$
$$append_2\,\alpha \quad = \quad \alpha \xrightarrow{y} y \;\sqcup\; \alpha \xrightarrow{a:append\,x\,y} y.$$

The second is clearly

$$append_2\,\alpha \quad = \quad \alpha \sqcup append_2(:_2\,\alpha),$$

while the exact definition of the first depends on the kind of analysis we are doing. In the case of strictness analysis,

$$\alpha \xrightarrow{y} [\,] \;=\; S_{S:S},$$

remembering that we can assume $\alpha$ to be strict, and that the contexts of components that do not match a pattern are the bottom of the context domain ($S$ in this case). So we find

$$append_1\,\alpha = S_{S:S} \sqcup S_{\alpha \xrightarrow{a:append\,x\,y} a\,:\,\alpha \xrightarrow{a:append\,x\,y} x}$$
$$= S_{S:S} \sqcup S_{(:_1\,\alpha):(append_1(:_2\,\alpha))}$$
$$= S_{(:_1\,\alpha):(append_1(:_2\,\alpha))}\,.$$

Now since $append_1$ is recursive, we should tabulate it by a fixed-point iteration. Rather than construct the whole table, we will look at two particular cases. First we analyze a call of *append* in a completely strict context, by evaluating $append_1\,S_{S:S}$ and $append_2\,S_{S:S}$. We begin with the first argument:

$$append_1\,S_{S:S} \quad = \quad S_{(:_1\,S_{S:S}):append_1(:_2\,S_{S:S})}\,,$$

and since $(:_1\,\alpha_{\beta:\gamma}) = \beta$ and $(:_2\,\alpha_{\beta:\gamma}) = \gamma$, we have

$$append_1\,S_{S:S} \quad = \quad S_{S\,:\,append_1\,S_{S:S}}\,.$$

This is a recursive equation for $append_1\,S_{S:S}$, so we can solve it by iteration.

The first approximation is the bottom of the list context domain, which is $S_{S:S}$, and the second is

$$S_{S:S_{S:S}} \,,$$

which is, of course, exactly the same. So we have reached the fixed point and shown that the first argument of *append* is also in a completely strict context.

To determine the context of the second argument we must compute

$$append_2 \, S_{S:S} \quad = \quad S_{S:S} \sqcup append_2 \, (:_2 S_{S:S})$$
$$= \quad S_{S:S} \sqcup append_2 \, S_{S:S} \,,$$

and a similar iteration shows that this is also $S_{S:S}$, so the second argument is also completely evaluated.

As another example, let us analyze a call of *append* in a head-strict context $S_{S:L}$. We find

$$append_1 \, S_{S:L} \quad = \quad S_{(:_1 S_{S:L}):append_1(:_2 S_{S:L})}$$
$$= \quad S_{S:append_1 L_{S:L}} \,.$$

This doesn't give us a recursive equation for $append_1 \, S_{S:L}$ directly, but we know that

$$append_1 \, L_{S:L} \quad = \quad ABSENT \sqcup append_1 \, S_{S:L}$$
$$= \quad L_{S:S} \sqcup append_1 \, S_{S:L} \,,$$

which gives us a recursive equation we can solve by iteration. The first approximation is $S_{S:S}$ again, and the second is

$$S_{S:L_{S:S} \sqcup S_{S:S}}$$
$$= \quad S_{S:L_{S:S}}$$
$$\implies \quad S_{S:L} \,,$$

which turns out to be the fixed point— so the first argument of *append* is also in a head-strict context.

Moving on to the second argument,

$$append_2 \, S_{S:L} \quad = \quad S_{S:L} \sqcup append_2(:_2 S_{S:L})$$
$$= \quad S_{S:L} \sqcup append_2 \, L_{S:L}$$
$$= \quad S_{S:L} \sqcup L_{S:S} \sqcup append_2 \, S_{S:L}$$
$$= \quad L_{S:L} \sqcup append_2 \, S_{S:L} \,.$$

Solving by iteration, the first approximation is (as always) $S_{S:S}$, and the second is

$$L_{S:L} \sqcup S_{S:S}$$

$$= \ L_{S:L} \, ,$$

which is the fixed point. So the second argument may not be evaluated at all— but if it is, it will be evaluated head-strictly.

As a final example, we will perform a lifetime analysis of a call of *append* in a persistent context $P_{P:P}$ (the result of *append*, and all its heads and tails, may persist for a long time). The context functions we derive for lifetime analysis are

$$append_1 \ \alpha \ = \ T_{(:_1 \alpha) \, : \, append_1(:_2 \alpha)} \, ,$$

$$append_2 \ \alpha \ = \ \alpha \sqcup append_2(:_2 \ \alpha) \, ,$$

and so, for a call in a persistent context, we have

$$append_1 \ P_{P:P} \ = \ T_{(:_1 P_{P:P}) \, : \, append_1(:_2 P_{P:P})}$$

$$= \ T_{P \, : \, append_1 \ P_{P:P}} \, ,$$

$$append_2 \ P_{P:P} \ = \ P_{P:P} \sqcup append_2 \ (:_2 P_{P:P})$$

$$= \ P_{P:P} \sqcup append_2 \ P_{P:P} \, ,$$

which can be solved by iteration. Since $T \sqsubseteq P$, the bottom of the list context domain is $T_{T:T}$. This is the first approximation in each case; the second approximation to $append_1 \ P_{P:P}$ is

$$T_{P:T_{T:T}}$$

$$\implies \ T_{P \sqcup T \, : \, T \sqcup T}$$

$$= \ T_{P:T} \, ,$$

and the second approximation to $append_2 \ P_{P:P}$ is

$$P_{P:P} \sqcup T_{T:T}$$

$$= \ P_{P:P} \, .$$

In each case the second approximation turns out to be the limit. So the first argument to append has a transient spine, although its elements may persist; but the second argument may persist in its entirety.

## 7 *Related Work*

Abstract interpretation was first applied to functional languages by Mycroft, who in 1980 published the strictness analysis algorithm sketched in Section 3 [18]. His analysis was restricted to first-order programs and could not usefully analyze lazy data structures. Nevertheless, it remained the state of the art for five years. Then in 1985, Burn, Hankin, and Abramsky showed how abstract interpretation could be extended to higher-order programs in a monomorphically typed language, and described a higher-order strictness analysis method [4]. A different approach to higher-order programs suitable for untyped languages was discovered by Hudak and Young [10]. Abramsky went on to show how the method could be applied to polymorphic programs, by taking advantage of the fact that the analysis gives the same results for every instance of a polymorphic function [1]. Then Wadler solved the problem of analyzing lazy data structures, finding finite abstract domains for lists by approximating every element by the same abstract value [19]. Strictness analysis could now give good results when analyzing realistic functional programs. Meanwhile Clack and Peyton Jones tackled the inefficiency of abstract interpretation by representing functions cleverly— their *frontiers* are typically much smaller than a tabulation of the function they represent [5]. This idea has been extended to higher-order strictness analysis by Martin and Hankin [17]. A collection of papers on abstract interpretation may be found in [2].

Backwards analysis of functional programs has almost as long a history— a backwards strictness analyzer like that in Section 5.1 was developed by Johnsson in 1981 [15], although not under that name. In 1985 Wray implemented a strictness-and-absence analyzer as part of the Ponder compiler [21]. Wray's analyzer is notable both for its speed (never more than 5% of compilation time) and for its ability to analyze second-order functions. In the same year I published a backwards strictness analyzer that could analyze lazy data structures using structured contexts [12]. It did not use finite domains and so was obliged to solve recursive context equations symbolically. At this stage backwards analyzers had no theoretical foundation; Dybjer provided one based on *inverse images* of open sets [6], and I developed another based on regarding a context as a set of possible continuations [13]. Later, Wadler and I published a theory that models contexts by *projections* and applied Wadler's idea to find finite context domains for data structures [20]. At the same time, Hall and Wise developed a backwards strictness analyzer that also generates multiple versions of each function to be called in different contexts [8]. I attempted to give a framework for backwards analysis, and generalized Wray's idea to extend any backwards analysis to functions of any order, in [14].

Strictness analysis has received more attention than any other analysis problem, but not to the exclusion of all else. Hudak and Bloss developed an analysis to avoid unnecessary copying of functional arrays [9, 11] and have also developed *path analysis*, a refinement of strictness analysis that offers information about the ordering of events [3]. Goldberg invented a sharing analysis based on abstract interpretation, which he applied to optimize super-combinator abstraction [7]. Other novel analyses will follow.

# 8  *Conclusion*

Forwards analysis and backwards analysis are two natural ways to analyze functional programs, and in fact both are variants of abstract interpretation. When contextual information is desired, backwards analysis is a convenient approach, with good efficiency. Moreover, an analysis developed with atomic values in mind can easily be extended to analyze data structures also. Backwards analysis holds much promise for the future.

## *Acknowledgements*

I am grateful to the many friends and colleagues who have discussed backwards analysis with me over the years, in particular to Phil Wadler, Stuart Wray, and Peter Dybjer; and to Mary Sheeran, who read my drafts carefully; also to the Science and Engineering Research Council, who funded my work in this area; and finally to Ham Richards, without whom this paper would not have been written.

## *References*

[1] Abramsky, S. "Strictness analysis and polymorphic invariance". In *Proceedings of the Workshop on Programs as Data Objects* (Copenhagen), H. Ganzinger and N. Jones, eds. Lecture Notes in Computer Science, vol. 217. Springer-Verlag, Berlin, 1985.

[2] Abramsky, S. and Hankin, C. (eds.). *Abstract Interpretation of Declarative Languages*. Ellis-Horwood, 1987.

[3] Bloss, A. and Hudak, P. "Variations on strictness analysis". *Proceedings of the ACM Conference on Lisp and Functional Programming* (Boston). ACM Press, New York, 1986.

[4] Burn, G., Hankin, C., and Abramsky, S. "The theory of strictness analysis for higher-order functions". In *Proceedings of the Workshop on Programs as Data Objects* (Copenhagen). H. Ganzinger and N. Jones, eds. Lecture Notes in Computer Science, vol. 217. Springer-Verlag, Berlin, 1985.

[5] Clack, C. and Peyton Jones, S. "Strictness analysis— A practical approach". In *Functional Programming Languages and Computer Architecture* (Proceedings, Nancy, France, September), J.-P. Jounannaud, ed. Lecture Notes in Computer Science, vol. 201. Springer-Verlag, Berlin, 1985.

[6] Dybjer, P. "Computing inverse images". *Proceedings of the International Conference on Automata, Languages and Programming*, 1987.

[7] Goldberg, B. "Detecting sharing of partial applications in functional programs". In *Functional Programming Languages and Computer Architecture* (Proceedings, Portland, Oregon, September). G. Kahn, ed. Lecture Notes in Computer Science, vol. 274. Springer-Verlag, Berlin, 1987.

[8] Hall, C. and Wise, D. S. "Compiling strictness into streams". In *Proceedings of the ACM Conference on Principles of Programming Languages* (Hamburg). ACM Press, New York, 1987.

[9] Hudak, P. and Bloss, A. "The aggregate update problem in functional programming systems". In *Proceedings of the ACM Conference on Principles of Programming Languages*. ACM Press, New York, 1985.

[10] Hudak, P. and Young, J. "Higher-order strictness analysis for untyped lambda calculus". In *Proceedings of the ACM Conference on Principles of Programming Languages*. ACM Press, New York, 1986.

[11] Hudak, P. "A semantic model of reference counting and its abstraction". In [2].

[12] Hughes, J. "Strictness detection in non-flat domains". In *Proceeedings of the Workshop on Programs as Data Objects* (Copenhagen). H. Ganzinger and N. Jones, eds. Lecture Notes in Computer Science, vol. 217. Springer-Verlag, Berlin, 1985.

[13] Hughes, J. "Analysing strictness by abstract interpretation of continuations". In [2].

[14] Hughes, J. "Backwards analysis of functional programs". In *Proceedings of the IFIP Workshop on Partial Evaluation and Mixed Computation* (Ebberup, Denmark). To appear.

[15] Johnsson, T. "Detecting when call-by-value can be used instead of call-by-need". Programming Methodology Group Memo PMG-14, Institutionen för Informationsbehandling, Chalmers Tekniska Högskola, Göteborg, 1981.

[16] Lieberman, H. and Hewitt, C. "A real-time garbage collector based on the lifetime of objects". *Communications of the ACM 23*, 6 (June 1983), pp. 419–429.

[17] Martin, C. and Hankin, C. "Finding fixed points in finite lattices". In *Functional Programming Languages and Computer Architecture* (Proceedings, Portland, Oregon, September). G. Kahn, ed. Lecture Notes in Computer Science, vol. 274. Springer-Verlag, Berlin, 1987.

[18] Mycroft, A. "The theory and practice of transforming call-by-need into call-by-value". *Proceedings of the International Symposium on Programming*. Lecture Notes in Computer Science, vol. 83. Springer-Verlag, Berlin, 1980.

[19] Wadler, P. "Strictness analysis on non-flat domains". In [2].

[20] Wadler, P. and Hughes, J. "Projections for strictness analysis". In *Functional Programming Languages and Computer Architecture* (Proceedings, Portland, Oregon, September). G. Kahn, ed. Lecture Notes in Computer Science, vol. 274. Springer-Verlag, Berlin, 1987.

[21] Wray, S. C. "A new strictness detection algorithm". *Proceedings of the Workshop on Implementations of Functional Languages* (Aspenäs, Sweden). L. Augustsson et al., eds. Programming Methodology Group Report 17, Institutionen för Informationsbehandling, Chalmers Tekniska Högskola, Göteborg, 1985.

# Functional Programming and Databases

# 6

**Peter Buneman**
University of Pennsylvania

## 1 Introduction

I would like to invite people interested in functional programming to apply some of their ideas to databases. This is especially true of the two areas of functional programming that have really borne fruit in the past few years: data types and implementation techniques. Researchers in programming languages and databases have worked almost independently of one another for the past twenty years—a sad state of affairs when one considers that most software is developed for database access. In general, database programming involves either a language with external subroutine calls or an embedded language: a sublanguage with limited expressive power. In either case, communication with the database is subject to an "impedance mismatch" [17] in which the data structures in the host language do not match those in the database. As a result, communication with the database takes place through primitive data types: *integer, string,* etc., a communication channel that is both un-wieldy and potentially inefficient, being nothing more than the well-known "von-Neumann" bottleneck [4].

The problem is, of course, to match the structures in the database with those in the programming language. If one looks back at database research, its main purpose has been to find a good data model—a data type—for a large class of conventional data processing tasks. The first data models (network and hierarchical) were criticized for being insufficiently abstract, and this led to the development of the relational data model [11]: the first data model to correspond to an abstract data type in that it was specified by the functions that operate on relations rather than by its implementation. Over the past ten years, so much technology has been thrown at making relational operations efficient that we now see relations as concrete data types from which we can implement more sophisticated data models such as entity-relation [10], complex-object [5, 1], and higher-order relations [20].

In this paper I would like to do two things. I want to convince functional programmers, first, that there is an obvious application of their techniques to the implementation of database programming languages and, second, that there is a close connection between the semantics of databases and the se-mantics of programming languages. It is possible that this connection will yield a richer type system for databases and for programming languages that exploit inheritance [9]. A glaring omission will be any discussion of update. There are a few observations to be made about this. Many transactions against databases are *queries*, which are, as we shall see, applicative in nature. Up-date transactions are, in most systems, made through different mechanisms and through different forms of interaction with the user. We shall naturally concentrate on the first of these. Another point is that whatever type system we develop for databases should be equally applicable to update and query languages. But I think it is an outstanding challenge to functional program-mers to represent update in such a way that it can be handled within some functional programming framework and without completely destroying the elegance of the language.

## 2  *Queries as Functional Programs*

Rather than go into the details of data models —they are all well estab-lished in the database literature— let us look informally at what database queries are like and how one might formulate them in a functional language. Consider a simple single relation such as

| Name | Age | Sal | Mgr |
|------|-----|------|------|
| Joe  | 34  | 12000 | Jane |
| Jane | 32  | 20000 | Sue  |
| Fred | 25  | 8000  | Joe  |
| Jim  | 31  | 14000 | Sue  |

A typical relational query against this relation—this is SQL [13]—looks like

SELECT   *Name, Age*

FROM     *Employee*

WHERE    *Sal* ≥ 10000

whose intent, even if one is not acquainted with the relational model, is reasonably obvious. Equally obvious is a translation of this into a functional language such as Miranda [21]:

[(*Name e, Age e*) | *e* ← *Employee*; *Sal e* ≥ 10000] .

Moreover, we can use Miranda to define functions such as

*Underlings e* =

*e* : [*f* | *u* ← *Employee*; *Mgr u* = *Name e*; *f* ← *Underlings u*] ,

which are not possible in languages such as SQL. Recently, considerable effort has been expended in the technology of implementing recursive queries such as this in logic programming [6]; for practical purposes, however, much further research is still required on the use of functions and sets in logic programming. Some illustrations of this are given in [3].

If we look more closely at the Miranda examples, we see that the database appears to contain two kinds of entity: sets, such as *Employee*, and functions, such as *Name, Sal*, etc., which are defined over database sets. Such functions are presumably defined extensionally; i.e., they are implemented through the data structure that represents *Employee*. We might note here that, by using Miranda, we have slightly abused the relational model, which, strictly speaking, is expressed in terms of sets rather than sequences; but relational query languages such as SQL commit the same offense, so we shall set aside this objection until it becomes important — as it will.

Some time ago, Rishyur Nikhil, Bob Frankel, and I [7] designed and implemented a functional query language, FQL, which exploited this idea of treating the database as a collection of sets and functions. Loosely based on

Backus's FP [4], the language was based on a few combinators of which the four most important were the familiar *map, filter*, and function composition (∘) found in most functional languages, and a higher-order combinator *tuple*, defined as $tuple(f_1, f_2, ..., f_n)\, x = (f_1 x, f_2 x, ..., f_n x)$. Using these, our first Miranda example can be easily expressed as a function:

$$!Employee \circ filter(tuple(Sal, 10000) \circ (\geq)) \circ map(tuple(Name, Age))\,,$$

where the notation for composition is reversed $[(f \circ g)\, x = g(f\, x)]$ and *!Employee* stands for a set of values (of type *Employee*). In fact we used a somewhat terser syntax that, arguably, made the language more readable; but it was intended more as a concrete syntax for the definition of a database machine rather than as a "friendly" query language.

Syntactic considerations aside, the use of such a language in connection with databases has a number of important advantages, notably:

**1.** The expressive power is considerably greater than most database query languages.

**2.** The use of lazy evaluation —often criticized for the computational overhead it imposes— is, generally speaking, an optimizing technique where database queries are involved. The main computational demands, and delays, are in reading from the database. If lazy evaluation, as is generally the case, avoids unnecessary i/o, these savings dominate the cost of a lazy implementation.

**3.** The use of an appropriate set of combinators is important in performing high-level optimization of a program. A simple example is $map\, f \circ map\, g \equiv map(f \circ g)$; others are described in [7]. When such high-level transformations can be recognized, they are usually the most powerful of all optimizing techniques.

**4.** We can exploit the techniques of type-checking and inferencing that are available for functional languages. Surprisingly, because of the need to talk to the database through one of the interfaces mentioned in the introduction, type-checking in most database programming is low level and often performed dynamically.

To summarize, functional languages appear to be an ideal medium for database queries. This was our own experience with FQL, which was actually used for building interfaces to the now unfashionable but still widely used Codasyl systems (which are naturally represented as functional databases). It also appears that functional languages are again enjoying a resurgence as interfaces for "object-oriented" and "complex-object" databases.

However, it is not entirely clear that a type system built around the kinds of sets and functions I used in the Miranda examples is entirely appropriate for these new languages, nor does it give a complete account of relational databases. One difficulty with FQL and with the examples I have given in Miranda is that the results of the queries were not of the same general type as the structures over which they were defined. For example, our query

$$[(Name\ e,\ Age\ e)\mid e \leftarrow Employee;\ Sal\ e \geq 10000]$$

returns a sequence of pairs of type *string* × *int*, but to be consistent with the database, we would like it to return some set or sequence upon which the functions *Name* and *Age* are defined. An alternative way of expressing this, assuming the existence of some record type in Miranda, would be

$$[\{Name = (Name\ e),\ Age = (Age\ e)\}\mid e \leftarrow Employee;\ Sal\ e \geq 10000]\ .$$

As we shall see, however, the introduction of record types together with operations for extending or combining them introduces a new set of issues into how we deal with database values in a programming language. It is these issues that I shall address in the next section.

## 3 *Records, Inheritance, and Sets*

While many of the operations usually defined on relations are set operations such as union, difference, etc., there are two—*projection* and *natural join*—that are not. Projection is an operation that removes columns from a relation; natural join connects two relations on columns with common names. For example, consider the following:

| Name | Sal | Dept |
|------|-----|------|
| Joe  | 20k | Sales |
| Jane | 20k | Sales |
| Fred | 10k | Mktg |
| Jim  | 15k | Rsrch |

| Dept | Mgr |
|------|-----|
| Sales | Sue |
| Mktg | Joe |
| Dev | Bert |

$$R_2$$

$$R_1$$

The natural join, $R_1 \bowtie R_2$, is formed by concatenating the rows of $R_1$ and $R_2$ that agree on the common *Dept* column. It is

| Name | Sal | Dept | Mgr |
|------|-----|------|-----|
| Joe | 20k | Sales | Sue |
| Jane | 20k | Sales | Sue |
| Fred | 10k | Mktg | Joe |

The projection $\Pi_{\{Sal,\ Dept\}}R_1$ is formed by extracting the *Sal* and *Dept* fields from $R_1$. It is

| Sal | Dept |
|-----|------|
| 20k | Sales |
| 10k | Mktg |
| 15k | Rsrch |

Note that these operations apply to, and produce, sets rather than sequences.

To understand these operations better, we need a formal definition of a relation. A tuple of a relation (or record) is simply a function defined on a set of labels $\mathcal{L}$ that take on values in some space $\mathcal{V}$. A relation is a set of such functions; i.e., it is a subset of $\mathcal{L} \to \mathcal{V}$. If we have two relations, $R_1 \subseteq \mathcal{L}_1 \to \mathcal{V}$ and $R_2 \subseteq \mathcal{L}_2 \to \mathcal{V}$, the natural join $R_1 \bowtie R_2$ is that subset of $(\mathcal{L}_1 \cup \mathcal{L}_2) \to \mathcal{V}$ whose members satisfy the property $t \in R_1 \bowtie R_2$ iff $t|\mathcal{L}_1 \in R_1$ and $t|\mathcal{L}_2 \in R_2$, where $t|\mathcal{L}$ stands for restriction of the domain of $t$ to $\mathcal{L}$. Projection is also defined by the obvious restriction of the domain of a tuple.

At this point it is worth remarking that one of the most basic assumptions of the relational data model, the "first normal form" assumption, is that relations are essentially flat. The domain $\mathcal{V}$ of values consists of what, in a programming language, would be called base types. One of the advantages of languages with polymorphic types is that we can parameterize types by other types and write general-purpose code for such parameterized types. If we are to have databases—more specifically relational databases—as values in our language, we would like to see whether we can relax the first-normal-form assumption and, more generally, the assumption that relations are sets of records, and see if we can still define operations such as projection and join.

To obtain a more general approach to relations, we first observe that records may be treated as partial functions on some large domain of labels. As such they are partially ordered; we can think of the tuples of a relation being ordered by the amount of information they provide. For example, {*Name*= '*Joe'*}

$\sqsubseteq$ {*Name*= *'Joe'*,*Age*=21}; moreover, we can extend this ordering to nonflat records when the space $\mathcal{V}$ of values is partially ordered. For example

{*Name*= *'Joe'*, *Address*={*City*= *'Austin'*}}

$\sqsubseteq$

{*Name*= *'Joe'*, *Address*={*City*= *'Austin'*, *Zip*=12345}} .

This ordering is similar to that suggested for orderings on types proposed by Cardelli [9] and Aït-Kaci [2], but here we are looking at the effect on values. An important property of these orderings is that they possess least upper bounds. Given two partial functions in $\mathcal{L} \rightarrow \mathcal{V}$, where $\mathcal{V}$ is flat, their join is their union (treating the functions as graphs) provided the union is functional. For example,

{*Name*= *'Joe'*, *Age*=21} $\sqcup$ {*Name*.= *'Joe'*, *Sal*=20000}

=

{*Name*= *'Joe'*, *Age*=21, *Sal*=20000} .

If, however, the two records differed on the *Name* field, the join would not exist. It is clear that each tuple in the natural join of two relations is the join of tuples in those relations.

What we now do is to relax our ideas about the structure of records. We shall assume simply that our database values are points in some partially ordered space which has least upper bounds. Since we shall deal only with finite structures, the only technical assumption we shall want to make is that our domains of database values are *bounded complete*: any set that is bounded above has a least upper bound. Were we to want to describe recursive record structures such as those that can be defined in languages with lazy evaluation, we would need to make additional assumptions about the domain (see [8] for details).

If our values are chosen from some partially ordered space, can we similarly order sets of values? The study of nondeterminism and concurrency in programming languages provides us with three such orderings. If $A$ and $B$ are sets in some partially ordered space, we can write:

$A \sqsubseteq^{\flat} B$      for      $\forall a \in A \; \exists b \in B . a \sqsubseteq b ,$

$A \sqsubseteq^{\sharp} B$      for      $\forall b \in B \; \exists a \in A . a \sqsubseteq b ,$

$A \sqsubseteq^{\natural} B$      for      $A \sqsubseteq^{\flat} B$ and $A \sqsubseteq^{\sharp} B .$

These are called, respectively, the Hoare, Smyth, and Egli-Milner orderings. As it stands these are not orderings (antisymmetry does not hold), but if we make the assumption that our sets are *cochains* then $\sqsubseteq^\flat$ and $\sqsubseteq^\sharp$ become partial orders, for which joins always exist; i.e., they give rise to lattices. (A set $S$ is a cochain if no two elements in it are comparable: if $a, b \in S$ and $a \sqsubseteq b$ then $a = b$.) Thus, if we have domain $\mathcal{D}$, we can use $C(\mathcal{D})$ for the cochains in $\mathcal{D}$ and get our first interesting connection with relational databases.

## Proposition 1

When relations $R_1$ and $R_2$ are interpreted as cochains in $C(\mathcal{L} \rightharpoonup \mathcal{V})$, the natural join $R_1 \bowtie R_2$ is $R_1 \sqcup^\sharp R_2$.

The union $\sqcup^\sharp$ is the least upper bound in the Smyth ordering, which, by our previous remarks, always exists. An immediate question to ask is whether the other orderings, $\sqsubseteq^\flat$ and $\sqsubseteq^\sharp$, have any meaning in databases. Indeed, they do: $\sqcup^\flat$ is sometimes called the *null join*, which is studied in connection with databases with missing information; and while least upper bounds do not necessarily exist in $\sqsubseteq^\sharp$, if two relations have a bound in this ordering then they have a *lossless join*. Lossless joins are important in the theory of relational database design [16].

With these initially promising connections between domain theory and relational databases, we might be tempted to drop the idea that relations are sets of records an d ask whether we can generalize them to sets of values taken from some partially ordered space. If we can do this, we will have a good start in our search for a more "generic" relational data type. Before doing this I want to digress for a moment on semantics of databases. I think it is reasonable to claim that values in a database describe "things" in the real world. Using this simple-minded notion of semantics, we can say that the denotation $[\![x]\!]$ of a database value $x$ is the set of "things" described by $x$. Moreover, we can write $x \sqsupseteq y$ if $x$ is more informative than $y$, i.e., if $[\![y]\!] \subseteq [\![x]\!]$. Now in the mundane [sic] subject of databases, the real world is somewhat elusive. We probably have only a finite set of labels; we can deal only with structures that are finite; and we may have constraints on the kinds of structure that we are allowed to build. Thus, rather than describe thesemantics of database values as a collection of real-world objects, we shall describe it in terms of the "best" approximations we can make in our space of database values, namely, the maximal elements of our domain $\mathcal{D}$ of database values. That is, we write

$$[\![x]\!]_{\mathcal{D}} \quad \text{for} \quad \{y \mid y \text{ maximal in } \mathcal{D} \text{ and } y \sqsupseteq x\}.$$

The notation $[\![x]\!]_{\mathcal{D}}$ to indicate the denotation with respect to a domain $\mathcal{D}$ will be needed when we discuss mappings between domains. It is interesting to note that this idea of database semantics is extremely close to that invented by Imielinski and Lipski [14] in describing an interpretation for null or missing values in a relation.

The reason for introducing this definition of denotation is to try to make sense of the second of our database operators, projection. Looking at the example of projection above, it is clear that projection "throws away" information. Moreover, projection can be defined for individual records:

$$\pi_{\{Name,Sal\}}(\{Name= \text{'}Joe\text{'}, Dept= \text{'}Sales\text{'}; Sal=20000\})$$

$$= \{Name= \text{'}Joe\text{'}, Sal=20000\} \ ,$$

and projection $\Pi_{\{Name,Sal\}}$ for sets of records can be defined by extension.

Thinking of our domain not as a set of records, but as some partially ordered space, what do we want to say about projection? It is a monotone, decreasing, idempotent function $f$; i.e., $f$ satisfies for all $x, y$,

$$f(x) \sqsubseteq f(y) \quad \text{whenever } x \sqsubseteq y$$

$$f(x) \sqsubseteq x$$

$$f(f(x)) = f(x) \ .$$

These properties characterize a "projection" when the term is used in connection with partial orders. What we need to know first is whether the partial order definition of projection adequately characterizes the database definition. We should first note that any cochain in S in a domain $\mathcal{D}$ defines a (partial order) projection by

$$p_S(x) = \sqcup\{y \in \underline{S} \mid y \sqsubseteq x\}$$

where $\underline{S}$ is the downward closure of S, $\{d \in D \mid \exists s \in S.d \sqsubseteq s\}$. For example, if we take S as $\{\{Name=n, Age=i\} \mid i, n \in \mathcal{V}\}$ then the projection function $p_S$ will be the projection defined for records $\pi_{\{Name,Sal\}}$. Obviously any relational database projection can be defined in this way. But if we were to allow arbitrary sets to define projections, there would be nothing to stop us projecting onto a set such as $\{\{Name= \text{'}Joe\text{'},Age= 21\}, \{Name= \text{'}Sue\text{'}, Sal= 20000\}\}$. Now this gives rise to some surprising consequences if we consider our ideas about semantics. Consider

$$p_S(\{Name= \text{'}Bob\text{'}, Age=21, Sal=200000\}) \ ,$$

which is $\{Age=21, Sal=200000\}$. This does not lie in $\underline{S}$. We cannot use the maximal elements of $\underline{S}$, i.e., S (recall that S is a cochain) as a "real world" for the elements in $\underline{S}$. We really need $\underline{S}$ to be a (bounded complete) domain in its own right.

Another "semantic" condition which one might want to impose is that the maximal elements of $\mathcal{D}$ should be mapped by $p_S$ into $S$. The following result shows that these two conditions are really the same.

## Proposition 2

For any cochain $S$, $p_S^*(\max \mathcal{D}) \subseteq S$ iff $\underline{S}$ is closed under join, where $f^*$ is the pointwise extension of $f$ over sets.

Downward closed, join closed sets are called *ideals*.

The reasons for imposing this condition are admittedly vague; the underlying reason comes from database design theory, where one deals with *functional dependencies*. There is no point in going into this textbook material [22, 15, 13] in any detail. Roughly speaking, a relation $R$ satisfies a functional dependency $(A, B)$, where $A, B$ are sets of column names, if the relation determines a function from records on $A$ to records on $B$. A more precise characterization, following [12], is to consider a relation $R$ defined over some set of column names $U$. If $A \subseteq U$, we can define an equivalence relation $E_A$ on $R$ by $E_A(t_1, t_2) \equiv \pi_A(t_1) = \pi_A(t_2)$. $R$ satisfies $(A, B)$ iff $E_A \subseteq E_B$. There is a well known set of inference rules, called Armstrong's axioms, that derive new functional dependencies from old ones. For example, if $R$ satisfies $(A, B)$ and $(C, D)$, and $C \subseteq B$, then $R$ must satisfy $(A, D)$. The set of all functional dependencies that can be inferred from a given set is sometimes called an *FD-scheme*. FD-schemes are the basic components of database design.

If we try to carry this idea into our more general domains and maintain the view that relations are arbitrary cochains, then in order to treat functional dependencies properly we are forced to take the restricted view of projection described above. In doing this we must also relax our definition of functional dependencies to work in terms of partial equivalence relations. Having done this, however, things fall into place rather naturally. In particular, the following result generalizes the basic properties of functional dependencies.

## Proposition 3

FD-schemes are closures in $I(\mathcal{D})$, the domain of ideals of $D$ ordered by inclusion.

A *closure* is an upside-down projection: it is a monotone, idempotent, *increasing* function. We should also note that the ordering of ideals determines the Hoare ordering, $\subseteq^b$, on their maximal elements.

These observations get us some way to generalizing relational database concepts to arbitrary domains, but our restriction on projection is still not strong enough. How strong we want to make it depends, of course, on how much database theory we want to capture. However, there is an additional assumption that comes up in some database design, especially that based on universal relations, concerning the interaction of projection and join; it is $\Pi_A(R) \bowtie R \sqsupseteq^\flat R$. Since (by the definition of $\bowtie$ as $\sqcup^\sharp$) $\Pi_A(R) \bowtie R \sqsupseteq^\sharp R$, we are asking that $\Pi_A(R) \bowtie R \sqsupseteq^\natural R$. To make this work, we need once again to resort to our ideas about semantics.

The restriction of database projection to projection onto ideals can still leave us with some unpleasant structures. For example, consider the downward closure of

$$\{\{Name = n\} \mid n \in \mathcal{V}, n \neq \text{'Joe'}\} \cup \{\{Name = \text{'Joe'}, Age = a\} \mid a \in \mathcal{V}\}.$$

It is certainly an ideal, but projections onto it throw away information in a nonuniform way; specifically, they fail to preserve the interaction with natural join that we have just demanded. To eliminate sets such as this, we impose an additional constraint on projection, namely, that it "commutes" with semantics, i.e., that the projected domain acts like a microcosm of the real world:

$$\forall x \in \mathcal{D}.p_S^*(\llbracket x \rrbracket_\mathcal{D}) = \llbracket p_S(x) \rrbracket_S.$$

We call a set $S$ that satisfies this condition as well as the ideal condition a *scheme* by analogy with the database term for sets of column names. Projection using schemes guarantees us that the join condition holds and that the orderings on schemes enjoy the following nice property.

## Proposition 4

If $S_1$ and $S_2$ are schemes then $S_1 \sqsubseteq^\flat S_2$ iff $S_1 \sqsubseteq^\sharp S_2$.

Thus schemes are ordered by the Egli-Milner ordering, $\sqsubseteq^\natural$. Note that the sets $\max(\mathcal{D})$ and $\{\bot_\mathcal{D}\}$ are always schemes.

In [8], Atsushi Ohori and I tried to show that with this notion of schemes, one could capture a great deal of what is usually called relational database theory: they appear to be the "right" generalization of sets of column names. In particular, one can discuss universal relations and other ideas in database design using schemes. But how general are they? There would not be much point to them if they were so restrictive that we get only flat relations.

## Proposition 5

If $S_1$ is a scheme in $D_1$ and $S_2$ is a scheme in $D_2$, then $S1 \times S2$ is a scheme in $D_1 \times D_2$ and $injl(S_1) \cup injr(S_2)$ is a scheme in $D_1 + D_2$, where $\times$ and $+$ stand for the separated product and sum.

What this means is that we can generalize the operations of relational algebra, and much of database design, to work over domains of Pascal-like record
structures of arbitrary complexity. Moreover, if we suitably extend our definition of a domain as suggested at the beginning of this section, we can also
deal with recursive records and the "infinite" structures that are so attractive
in lazy evaluation. It is an open question as to whether schemes can be built
up in any other interesting way.

## 4 *Some Thoughts on Data Types*

In the previous section, I have attempted to show that one can use the
apparatus of domain theory to define relational databases independently of
any particular representation of relations as, say, sets of records. Since we
are using the same theory that has been established to provide semantics of
programming languages, we may naturally ask whether this helps us in our
goal of integrating databases and programming languages, especially where
data types are concerned. The answer is, I think, yes, but one must exercise
a great deal of caution in attempting to identify too closely the domains that
we use in the two areas. Here are some thoughts, many of them half-baked,
on the problems of representing databases as typed objects.

In [19] some of the preceding analysis is carried out in a typed domain
that includes record and set types. This allows us to assign data types to
joins, projection, etc., but this may not be the most general domain in which
we can do this. In particular, we should be able to extend the type system
to sums, which would presumably be realized as records with some form
of discriminated union. In order to get around the problem of working in
a universal domain of partial records, i.e., the space $\mathcal{L} \rightharpoonup \mathcal{V}$ (which is very
close to the universal relation assumption), one can introduce the notion of
typed missing or *null* values. Specifically, each base type such as *int, bool,...*
is augmented with an undefined value $\perp_{int}, \perp_{char},....$ Using this as a basis,
one can build up the notion of partial records of a given type and then define
an ordering and the operations above to work over such partial records.

It is important to note that values such as $\perp_{int}$ are not undefined values
in the usual sense of nonterminating computations. They are values that one
may want to hand to the user, and they may be used in what we would regard as nonmonotonic computations. For example, *if* $x = \perp_{int}$ *then* 0 *else i* is
a common form of database computation even if it has, in some general sense,
undesirable properties. In any case, it has nothing to do with termination.

Another possibility that needs to be considered is performing type inferencing in some language that contains sets, projections, and joins. In [23]
Wand describes an extension to the type inferencing system of ML for a lan-

guage with record variables and constructs for extending records. It works by the ingenious device of introducing a separate system of type variables that range over record types. Unfortunately, this language does not have the same kinds of information-combining operations that we have needed to define database operations. Wand's operation for adding information to a record overrides fields that are already defined. Thus {*Name*= *'Joe'*, *Age*=20} *with* {*Age*=21} results in {*Name*= *'Joe'*, *Age*=21}, whereas a language based on the constructs we have defined would require {*Name*= *'Joe'*, *Age*=20}⊔{*Age*=21} to be undefined or *nonexistent* if it were used in a programming language. Now we have made the requirement that we can compute joins, which presupposes the existence of an equality predicate over database values. But if—as seems essential for databases — we are going to use sets, we need equality in any case, so that we cannot expect our database types to be fully general. Practical implementations of ML [18] and Miranda cope quite well with equality even though it is not a polymorphic function.

Finally, in database work it is common to want to deal with sets of heterogeneous values. In early database management systems and, more recently, in object-oriented database systems, one wants to think of the database as a collection of objects of varying types and to have functions that extract all the objects that have a given type. Again, abusing Miranda notation, one wants to say something like:

$$[e \mid e \leftarrow mydatabase; e : Person],$$

meaning, presumably, extract all those things from the database which have at least type *Person*. Notice that this should be a superset of

$$[e \mid e \leftarrow mydatabase; e : Employee]$$

if we assume that *Employee* is a subtype of *Person* in some ordering on types. The ability to do this (see [3]) would considerably simplify database programming languages that exploit some form of inheritance. At present, such languages require a special class of types that have associated extents, and such types are not treated uniformly within the language. The view of types that seems to be required to make the expressions above work is one of *upward-closed* subsets of the domain of values, for which the Smyth powerdomain is the appropriate ordering. This is in contrast to the more usual ideal representation of data types. Whether our ideas of *schemes*, which reconcile these two views, can be exploited remains to be seen.

## Acknowledgments

The research reported in this chapter was supported in part by NSF IRI86–10617, NSF MCS 8219196–CER, ARO DAA6–29–84–k–0061, DAA29–84–9–0027, and a grant from AT&T's Telecommunications Program at the University of Pennsylvania.

## References

[1] Abiteboul, S. and Hull, R. "IFO: A formal semantic database model". In *Proceedings Third ACM SIGACT-SIGMOD Symposium on Principles of Database Systems* (Waterloo, Canada), April 1984.

[2] Aït-Kaci, H. "A lattice theoretic approach to computation based on calculus of partially ordered type structures". PhD thesis, University of Pennsylvania, 1985.

[3] Atkinson, M. and Buneman, P. "Types and persistence in database programming languages". *ACM Computing Surveys 19*, 2 (June 1987), pp. 105–190.

[4] Backus, J. "Can programming be liberated from the von Neumann style? A functional style and its algebra of programs". *Communications of ACM 21*, 8 (August 1978), pp. 613–641.

[5] Bancilhon, F. and Khoshafian, S. "Calculus for complex objects". In *Proceedings Fifth ACM SIGACT-SIGMOD Symposium on Principles of Database Systems*, March 1986.

[6] Bancilhon, F. and Ramakrishnan, R. "An amateur's introduction to recursive query processing strategies". *Proceedings ACM SIGMOD* (Washington, DC, May), pp. 166–176. ACM, New York, 1986.

[7] Buneman, P., Frankel, R., and Nikhil, R. "An implementation technique for database query languages". *ACM Transactions on Database Management Systems 7*, June 1982.

[8] Buneman, P. and Ohori, A. "Using powerdomains to generalize relational databases". *Theoretical Computer Science.* To appear.

[9] Cardelli, L. and Wegner, P. "On understanding types, data abstraction, and polymorphism". *ACM Computing Surveys  17*, 4 (August 1985), pp. 471–522.

[10] Chen, P. "The entity-relationship model: Towards a unified view of data". *ACM Transactions on Database Systems 11*, March 1976.

[11] Codd, E. "A relational model for large shared databanks". *Communications ACM 13*, 6 (June 1970), pp. 377–387.

[12] Cosmodakis, S., Kanellakis, P., and Spyratos, N. "Partition semantics for relations". Technical Report, Brown University, Digital Equipment Corporation, 1985.

[13] Date, C. J. *An Introduction to Database Systems* (3rd edition). Addison-Wesley, Reading, Mass., 1981.

[14] Imielinski, T. and Lipski, W. " Incomplete information in relational databases". *Journal of the ACM*, Oct. 1984.

[15] Korth, H. and Silberschatz, A. *Database System Concepts*. McGraw-Hill, New York, 1986.

[16] Maier, D. *The Theory of Relational Databases*. Computer Science Press, 1983.

[17] Maier, D. "Why database programming languages may be a bad idea". In *Proceedings of the Roscoff Workshop on Database Programming Languages*, Altaïr - CRAI, September 1987. Available as a technical report from CIS Department, University of Pennsylvania, Philadelphia, PA 19104, or from Altaïr, BP 105 Rocquencourt, 76153 LeChesnay Cedex, France.

[18] Milner, R. "A proposal for standard ML". *Polymorphism 1*, December 1983.

[19] Ohori, A. "Orderings and types in databases". In *Proceedings of the Roscoff Workshop on Database Programming Languages*, Altaïr - CRAI, September 1987. Available as a technical report from CIS Department, University of Pennsylvania, Philadelphia, PA 19104, or from Altaïr, BP 105 Rocquencourt, 76153 LeChesnay Cedex, France.

[20] Ozsoyoglu, Z. and Yuan, L. "A new normal form for nested relations". *ACM Transactions on Database Systems 12* (March 1987), pp. 111–136.

[21] Turner, D. "Miranda: A non-strict functional language with polymorphic types". *Functional Programming Languages and Computer Architecture* (Nancy, France, Sept. 1985), J.-P. Jouannaud, ed. Lecture Notes in Computer Science, vol. 201, pp. 1–16. Springer-Verlag, Berlin, 1985.

[22] Ullman, J. *Principles of Database Systems*, Second Edition. Pitman, 1982.

[23] Wand, M. "Complete type inference for simple objects". *Proceedings of the 1987 Conference on Logic in Computer Science*, pp. 37–44. IEEE, New York, 1987.

# Lazy Evaluation and the Logic Variable

# 7

**Keshav K. Pingali**
Cornell University

## Abstract

$F$unctional languages can be enriched with logic variables to provide new computational features such as incremental construction of data structures. In this paper, we present a novel application for logic variables that highlights their importance: we argue that they are essential for efficient implementations of pure functional languages. This point is made by demonstrating that logic variables are required for explicating the process of demand propagation in lazy evaluation of functional programs. There are two applications of this result. For dataflow researchers, it offers a simple and efficient implementation of laziness on dataflow machines. For researchers investigating lazy graph reduction, it suggests new strictness analysis algorithms in which logic variables play an important role.

## 1 *Introduction*

In a functional language, an identifier obtains its value as the result of evaluation of a single applicative expression. In contrast, a *logic variable* in logic programming languages obtains its value incrementally by the intersection of successively applied constraints. The incorporation of logic variables into an otherwise functional language provides the programmer with a powerful tool for writing elegant and efficient programs for problems such as the construction of large arrays in scientific programming [5], owner-coupled sets in database programming [17], etc., which are difficult to write in a purely functional language.

In this paper, we argue that logic variables play a key role in compile-time analysis and implementation of modern functional languages, i.e., functional languages that support *nonstrict* data constructors. Informally, a constructor is said to be nonstrict if it can produce some output even if one or more of its inputs are undefined. The classic example of such a constructor is the nonstrict *cons* introduced by Friedman and Wise [8]. If *cons* is nonstrict, the expression $car(cons(1, e))$, where $e$ is some nonterminating computation, returns 1; in contrast, this expression would be undefined in a language like LISP in which *cons* is strict. In conjunction with higher-order functions, nonstrict data constructors can be used to write modular and elegant programs[23], and they are an important feature of most modern functional languages. Unfortunately, nonstrict constructors are considerably more difficult to implement than their strict counterparts. Using nonstrict constructors, a programmer can define infinite data objects such as infinite lists and trees (e.g., in the Miranda program $x = 1 : x$, where (:) is the nonstrict infix *cons* operator, $x$ is an infinite list of 1's). A naive implementation would attempt to construct the entire list, resulting in dire consequences! A more successful strategy is to use lazy evaluation. Although $x$ is an infinite list, it may be the case that only a few of its elements are required to produce the output of the program. A lazy evaluator computes only those elements, not the entire list. This is achieved by suspending computations until it is established that they are needed to produce the output of the program. The process of determining which computations are required to produce the output is called *demand propagation*. During the course of program execution, the result of a suspended computation may be demanded more than once. To avoid repeated evaluation, most lazy interpreters use the principle of *graph reduction*—the first time a suspended computation is demanded, it is evaluated and its code is overwritten by the result. No computation is done on subsequent demands.

Considerable experience has been gained over the past few years in implementing sequential and parallel lazy evaluators [9, 13, 15, 16, 19, 24].

This experience has revealed two problems. First, there is a definite space and time penalty associated with suspending computations. When a computation is suspended, its environment must be saved, and this takes up storage. Moreover, every access to the result of a suspended computation involves a check to ensure that the computation has been performed and the result is available. A second problem is that lazy evaluation of a program usually does not exhibit much parallelism [6]. One way to ameliorate these problems is to avoid delaying computations whenever it is safe to do so: Instead of being completely lazy, the interpreter performs some computations eagerly and some lazily. To identify those computations that need not be delayed, the compiler performs *strictness analysis* to locate computations that are definitely required in order to produce the output of the program. At run time, the interpreter evaluates these computations eagerly. Unfortunately, the complexity of algorithms that have been proposed for strictness analysis is exponential in the size of the program [6, 10].

In this paper, we present a different approach to the efficient implementation of lazy evaluation. Rather than start with a lazy interpreter and attempt to compile in eagerness by means of strictness analysis, we start with an eager (data-driven) interpreter and compile in laziness. To do so, we formalize the notions of demand and demand propagation, and we introduce code for demand propagation into programs explicitly rather than burying it in the interpreter. Interestingly enough, there are two very different ways of introducing demand propagation code. The first method is "functional" in the sense that all the operators required for demand propagation are pure functions from inputs to outputs. This method is described in Section 3 of this paper and is similar to the algorithm described in [20] where it was presented as a program transformation. A surprising aspect of this transformation is the need for a least-upper-bound operator that behaves very much like unification (which is the least upper bound in the domain of first-order terms under the instantiation ordering). The need for such an operator can be understood by analogy with Milner's algorithm for compile-time type-checking. To deduce the type for a formal parameter of a function, Milner's algorithm examines the body of the function to see how the parameter is used; each use (occurrence) of the parameter contributes some type information, and a type is inferred for the formal parameter by "merging" all this information using unification. The algorithm for introducing demand-propagation code is similar: Each use of a formal parameter contributes some demand information, and the overall demand for the parameter is obtained by merging all this information using an operation similar to unification. What is surprising about this is that conventional lazy evaluators based on graph reduction do not need unification to perform demand propagation at run time. Is the need for such an operator an unavoidable result of making demand propagation code explicit (rather than burying it in the interpreter), or is it a peculiarity of the method we chose for demand propagation? In this paper, we provide a somewhat paradoxical answer to this puzzle. In Section 4, we present a new algorithm for introducing demand propagation code; this algorithm can also be thought of as a program transformation, but the target language is a "hybrid" language in which logic variables are integrated into a functional language. Surprisingly enough, transformed programs are a subset of programs in this language that do not need the full power of unification! Moreover, there is a close connection between this transformation and demand propagation in conventional parallel graph reduction interpreters such as the one of Keller et al. [16].

One advantage of formalizing demand propagation and introducing demand-propagation code into programs explicitly is that it becomes subject to standard program optimizations. This has been studied by Amamiya et al. [18], who use conventional global optimization techniques such as constant propagation and value subsumption to eliminate demand-propagation code wherever possible. There appears to be a close connection between this approach and a recent algorithm for strictness analysis called "backward analysis" [11, 12]. We believe that this algorithm can be improved and simplified by viewing strictness analysis as an optimization of demand-propagation code. There are also reasons to believe that the complexity of such an algorithm would be far better than that of conventional algorithms for strictness analysis [11]. Moreover, the need for logic variables in explicating demand propagation suggests new backward-analysis algorithms in which logic variables play an important role.

The rest of the paper is organized as follows. In Section 2, we introduce a simple first-order functional language F, and show how F programs can be executed on an abstract data-driven interpreter. In Section 3, we show how demand-propagation code can be introduced into F programs. This is presented as a transformation on F programs which is similar to that described in [20]. In Section 4, we describe the new demand-propagation algorithm, presenting it as a transformation of F programs to programs in a hybrid language with logic variables. Although the target language has logic variables, transformed programs are a special subset which do not need the full power of unification. We extend the technique to handle higher-order functions. In Section 5, we discuss two applications of this transformation. First, we show how it can be used to implement laziness on a concrete dataflow architecture, and contrast the resulting system with the graph reduction approach. Second, we discuss some implications for strictness analysis.

## 2  A Simple First-order Functional Language

The techniques described in this paper are very general and apply to any functional language such as Miranda [22] or LML [13]. To focus attention on the main issues, however, we will consider a simple "desugared" functional language called F. The main aspect of the desugaring is that every expression in an F program has a name. As we will see, this makes the discussion of demand propagation easier to describe and comprehend.

### 2.1  Syntax of F

The syntax of F programs is shown in Figure 1. An F program consists of a set of function definitions $(f_1, ..., f_m)$ and a function invocation (of some function $f_k$) whose result is the output of the program. The body of a function is a single **letrec** in which there is a definition for each identifier introduced in its scope and a list of identifiers whose values are to be returned as the outputs of the function. Expressions are built from constants and identifiers by the

---

**Figure 1.**  Syntax of language F.

$program ::=$  $f_1(id, ..., id) =$ **letrec** $def ... def$ **in** $id, ..., id$

$...$

$f_m(id, ..., id) =$ **letrec** $def ... def$ **in** $id, ..., id$

$\Rightarrow f_k(constant, constant, ..., constant)$

$def ::= id, ..., id = exp$

$exp ::=$  $constant \mid id \mid id\ op\ id \mid$ **if** $id$ **then** $id$ **else** $id \mid$

$cons(id, id) \mid car(id) \mid cdr(id) \mid$

$f_j(id, ..., id) \mid$

$fork\text{-}i(id)$

---

application of predefined and user-defined functions. Predefined functions include the usual operators like +, *, etc.; in addition, we provide a data constructor *cons* which is nonstrict in both of its arguments. The functions *car* and *cdr* are the destructuring operators. In F programs, a unique name must be given to every *use* of an identifier. This is accomplished by the introduction of *fork* operators—for each integer *i* greater than 1, the operator *fork-i* is the identity operator with *i* outputs. To clarify the point of this desugared syntax, it is useful to consider how a program in a language like LML can be translated into an F program. If we ignore higher-order functions for the moment, we can obtain the translation quite simply by drawing the abstract syntax graph for the expression, giving a name to each arc in the graph (i.e., to each subexpression in the original program) and creating a definition for each name. An example of such a translation is shown in Figure 2. Nodes that have more than one arc pointing to them (such as the node labeled *y*) correspond to names in the original program whose value is used in more than one place: to give each use a different name, we introduce *fork* operators. The resulting F program is shown in Figure 2 (b). We will not describe this translation formally since we will work only with F programs.

## 2.2 *Operational Semantics of F Programs*

F programs can be given an operational semantics using dataflow. Although there are a wide variety of dataflow models [3, 7], the differences between them, for the most part, are not relevant to our discussion. Therefore we carry out our development without reference to any particular model, and in the final section we discuss an implementation on the tagged-token dataflow interpreter [3]. The dataflow graph for a function in an F program is obtained by drawing a node for each definition in the body of the function, labeling the node with the function on the right-hand side of the definition, labeling its outputs with the identifiers on the left-hand side of the definition, and connecting these outputs to nodes that use them. For definitions of the form $x = y$, the node is labeled with the *identity* operator. For expository purposes, we will assume that nodes that represent application of a user-defined function, such as $f_k$, are labeled *apply* $f_k$. Figure 2 (b) shows the dataflow graph for the F program considered earlier.

The operational behavior of dataflow graphs is specified by means of "firing rules", which describe the actions of nodes when they receive tokens on one or more of their inputs. Rather than describe the firing rules formally, we will use the graph of Figure 2 (b) to explain the operational behavior of dataflow graphs. Suppose that function $f$ is called with two arguments $e1$ and $e2$. These arguments are evaluated in parallel until one of them (say $e2$) produces a value—i.e., generates a token. When the *apply f* operator receives this token, it creates a copy of the dataflow graph for *f* and assumes responsibility for the forwarding of arguments and the returning of results—in effect, the dataflow graph for *f* gets spliced into the original graph in place of the *apply f* operator. Once this is done, operators in the body of *f* can begin to execute. The token carrying the value of *y* is duplicated by the *fork*-2 operator and sent to the

**Figure 2.**   Translating a conventional functional program into an F program.

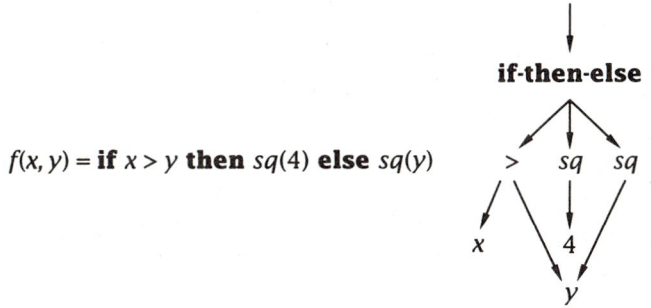

$f(x, y) = $ **if** $x > y$ **then** $sq(4)$ **else** $sq(y)$

(a) LML program and parse tree

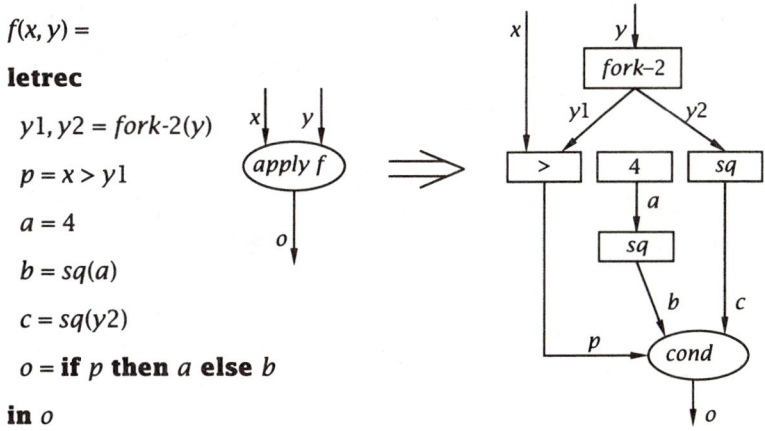

$f(x, y) =$

**letrec**

$y1, y2 = fork\text{-}2(y)$

$p = x > y1$

$a = 4$

$b = sq(a)$

$c = sq(y2)$

$o = $ **if** $p$ **then** $a$ **else** $b$

**in** $o$

(b) Corresponding F program and dataflow graph

> operator and the *sq* operator. The *sq* operator can execute, producing a token carrying the value of *c*. When the constant operator labeled 4 executes, it produces a token carrying the value 4 as output[1]—this value is squared to produce a token carrying the value of *b*. When the > operator receives the values of *x* and *y*1, it fires, computing the value of the predicate *p*. Depending on the value of the predicate, the *cond* operator produces a token carrying either the value of *b* or the value of *c*. This value is returned to the caller as the result of the function application. It is important to realize that *cond* is nonstrict—for example, if *p* is *true* and the value of *b* has been produced, the *cond* operator can produce the output without waiting for the value of *c*. If and when the value of *c* is computed, the *cond* operator executes again and simply absorbs the token at its input without producing any output.

We now discuss the implementation of the data structure operations. The *cons* operator requires careful treatment in dataflow to ensure that nonstrict semantics are respected. Consider a definition $x = cons(a, b)$, where *b* is the output of some nonterminating computation. To be faithful to nonstrict semantics, the value of *a* must be available to the consumers of *x* even though the value of *b* is never produced. Thus, the *cons* operator cannot wait for both of its inputs before firing. This difficulty is circumvented by allocating storage for data structures in a special structure storage called *I-structure storage* [2]. The first time a *cons* operator receives an input, it allocates a *cons* cell in I-structure storage, stores the value it received in the appropriate field of this cell, and outputs a token carrying the address of the cell. Subsequently, if a token is received on the other input, its value is stored in the other field of this cell. A *car* or a *cdr* operation executes when it receives a token carrying the address of some cell in structure memory—the appropriate field of this cell is read and the value is output. There is potential for a read-before-write hazard here since a *car* or a *cdr* operation may be executed on a *cons* cell before a value has been stored in that field. This hazard is avoided with the help of a smart structure controller: If an attempt is made to read an empty field, the controller defers the access until the corresponding write occurs.

Notice that at most one token flows down an arc in the dataflow graph. We will exploit this fact when we discuss a concrete implementation on the tagged-token dataflow machine.

## 2.3 *Denotational Semantics*

A denotational semantics for F programs is straightforward. Let $\mathcal{A}$ be the domain of atoms and let *V* be the domain that satisfies the equation $V = \mathcal{A} \oplus V \times$

---

1. The implementation sends a dummy token to each constant operator in a function graph when the function is invoked, which causes it to fire and produce the appropriate constant.

$\mathcal{V}$. The coalesced sum is required because there is no difference operationally between $\bot$ and $cons(\bot, \bot)$ (storage is allocated for a *cons* cell only if at least one of its inputs has been produced). Let the operators $+, *, cons, car, cdr$, etc. have their usual interpretation in this domain. The operator *fork-n* is interpreted as a function from $V$ to $V^n$ which acts as the identity function on each component of its range. A function $f_k$ with $i$ inputs and $j$ outputs can be interpreted as a monotonic and continuous function from $V^i$ to $V^j$. The program is interpreted as a set of equations to be solved for the denotations of $f_1, f_2, \ldots, f_m$. It is a standard result that such a set of equations has a least solution, which gives the meaning of the program.

Using a result of Kahn [14], it can be shown that the results produced by a dataflow interpretation of an F program are consistent with the program's denotational semantics. This is subject to two caveats. The first caveat is that there must be some notion of fair scheduling: The execution of a node that is ready to fire cannot be postponed indefinitely. The second caveat has to do with constant functions—i.e., user-defined functions that produce some constant value as output regardless of their inputs. The firing rule that we have described for function application invokes the function when at least one of its actual parameters has been computed. This means that a function application of the form $f(a)$, where $a$ is the output of some nonterminating computation, would never be performed; if $f$ is a constant function, this would not be in consonance with the denotational semantics of $f$. This is not a serious problem since such functions can always be compiled to take an additional parameter that is a constant supplied by the implementation (a "trigger"). Thus, the dataflow interpreter is faithful to nonstrict semantics and will produce correct results. However, this is cold comfort—if the programmer uses the nonstrict *cons* to define infinite data objects, the dataflow interpreter may eventually produce the results of the program, but it would perform an unbounded amount of computation over what would have been performed by a lazy interpreter! We will fix this problem over the next few sections.

## 3 *Functional Demand Propagation*

To give the reader an intuitive feel for our techniques, we first show how unnecessary computation can be avoided in the program of Figure 2. We then discuss our transformation, which is a systematic way of achieving this effect for any F program. This transformation is similar to the one discussed in [20].

### 3.1 *Introducing Demand Propagation Code*

To prevent the dataflow interpreter from performing unnecessary computation, it is necessary to control the flow of data in such a way that an operator receives data on its inputs only if it has been established that its output is required for production of the program's result. Let us see how this can be achieved for the program in Figure 2. To avoid unnecessary computation, the *sq* operator whose output is *b* must receive a token carrying the value 4 only if the predicate *p* is *true*. The value of *y* is needed to compute *p*, but a token carrying this value should be sent to the *sq* operator that produces the value of *c* only if *p* is *false*. This is achieved by the transformed program shown in Figure 3, which mimics the way a lazy interpreter propagates demands. The backward graph, called the demand graph, is responsible for demand propagation. For every line *x* in the original graph, there is a demand line labeled *dx* (demand line for *x*). Demand lines are shown as thick lines to distinguish them from data lines. Tokens carrying a distinguished value 'd' (for demand) flow on lines in the demand graph. The transformation ensures that a data token flows on line *x* only if a demand token has been produced on line *dx*. To reduce the complexity of the figures, *fork* and *identity* operators in the demand graph are not shown explicitly—an implicit *fork* operator is present wherever there is fan-out in the demand graph.

Let us work through the execution of the transformed program. The original function *f* had two inputs and one output; the transformed function *Tf* has one new in put (the demand line for the output of the function) and two new outputs (demand lines for the inputs of *f*). When the *apply Tf* operator receives a demand token on line *do*, it creates a copy of the graph of the transformed function *Tf* and forwards the demand token to the body of the function. This causes a demand token to be generated on line *dp* which generates demand tokens on lines *dx* and *dy*1. The token on line *dx* is returned to the caller where it causes the value of *x* to be computed. The token on line *dy*1 causes the *lub*-2 operator to fire. The *lub*-2 operator combines demands for the outputs of the *fork* into demand for the input of the *fork*. It produces a demand token at its output the first time it receives a demand token on one of its inputs. Subsequently, tokens received on other inputs are consumed without any output (as we will see, this operator can be described denotationally by the least-upper-bound function). Thus, a demand token is produced on line *dy*, which causes the value of *y* to be computed. The token carrying the value of *y* must be sent to the > operator but not to the operator labeled *sq* unless the predicate *p* turns out to be *false*. This is accomplished by the *gate* operators shown as ⋈ in the graph. The *gate* operator behaves like a *K* combinator that is strict in both of its arguments: It has two inputs, and it outputs the token it receives on its first input when it receives a token its second input. Thus, a token carrying the value of *y* is output on line *y1* but not on line *y2*. Once the predicate is computed, a demand token must be sent on either line *db* or line *dc*. This is accomplished by the *switch* operator, which uses the predicate *p* to output the demand token at its input on either line *db* or line *dc*. This results in the computation of either *b* or *c*, and that value is output by the *cond* as the result of the function application.

The effect of lazy evaluation has been obtained by program transformation: Data-driven evaluation of the transformed program performs only those computations that would have been done by a lazy evaluation of the original program. Suspension of computations is achieved by controlling the flow of data, and no data value is computed more than once. How was the transformed program obtained in the first place? A systematic method for generating it is shown in Figure 4. Each definition in the source program is replaced with new definition(s) as shown in this figure.[2] We leave it to the reader to

---

2. We have permitted ourselves a little flexibility in the syntax of transformed programs—we do not introduce *fork* operators explicitly on demand lines. In the actual implementation, *constant*

---

**Figure 3.** Introducing demand-propagation code into the program of Figure 2 (b).

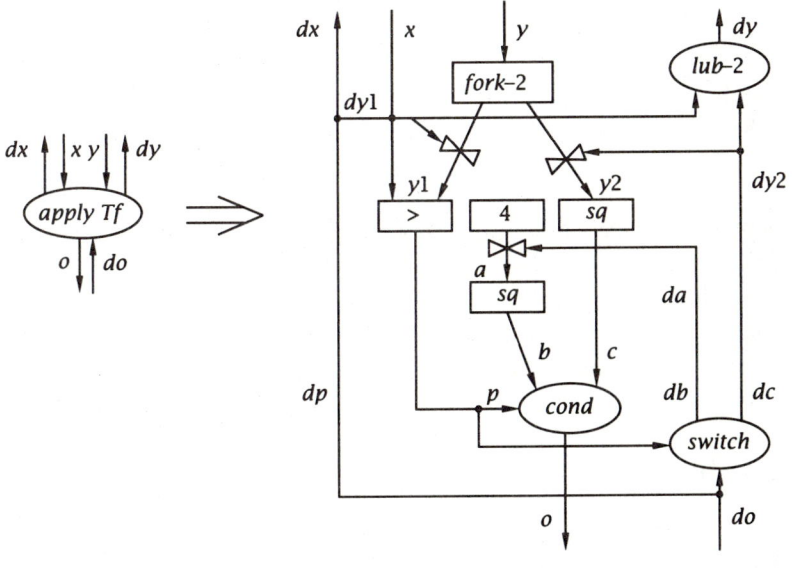

verify that the dataflow graph shown in Figure 3 is obtained by applying this transformation to the program in Figure 2. It is obvious from Figure 3 that there is considerable scope for optimization in the demand graph. These optimizations and their relation to strictness analysis will be discussed in Section 4.

The approach introduced above can be extended easily to data structures built from the nonstrict *cons*. Demand for an atomic value (such as an integer or boolean) was represented by a token carrying the atomic value 'd'. Similarly, a structure consisting of 'd' values can be used to represent demand for the elements of a data structure. For example, if $x$ is the data structure *cons*(1, *cons*(2, *cons*(3, ...))) (i.e., an infinite list of integers), the demand structure *cons*('d', *cons*($\perp$, *cons*('d', $\perp$))) represents demand for the first and third elements of $x$.[3] Given this intuition, the demand propagation code shown for data structure operations in Figure 4 should be easy to comprehend. If $dx$ is the demand for the output of the *cons*, *car*($dx$) gives the demand for the left input of the *cons*, and *cdr*($dx$) gives the demand for the right input of the *cons*. The *car* operator never makes a demand for the *cdr* of its input; therefore, if $dx$ is the demand for its output, the demand for its input is simply *cons*($dx$, $\perp$). Similar considerations apply to the *cdr* operator. *Lub* operators, which were introduced to combine demands at *forks*, must be extended to work on demand structures: for example, if *cons*('d', $\perp$) and *cons*($\perp$, *cons*($\perp$, *cons*('d', $\perp$))) are the demands for the outputs of a *fork*, the *lub* operator must combine them and produce the demand structure *cons*('d', *cons*($\perp$, *cons*('d', $\perp$))) as the demand for the input of the *fork*.

To give an abstract semantics for transformed programs, let $\mathcal{DA}$ be the two-element domain given by the set $\{\perp, \text{'d'}\}$ where $\perp \sqsubseteq$ 'd', and let $\mathcal{D}$ be the domain that satisfies the equation $\mathcal{D} = \mathcal{DA} \oplus \mathcal{D} \times \mathcal{D}$. It is natural to interpret the *lub* operator as the least-upper-bound function in this domain. Unfortunately, two elements in this domain need not have a least upper bound (consider the elements 'd' and *cons*('d', 'd')). This problem arises operationally only in programs that are not type-correct—if one output of a *fork* receives a demand for a scalar while another receives a demand for some elements of a data structure, the demands cannot be merged in any sensible way. To handle this technically, we add an over-defined element $\top$ to $\mathcal{D}$ which is above all elements of $\mathcal{D}$. If we let $D$ be this new domain, the operators *gate, switch,* and *lub-n* can be interpreted as follows:

---

operators are handled a little differently—in Figure 3, the line *da* would actually be input to the operator labeled 4, and this operator would produce a token carrying the value 4 when it received a 'd' token on its input. To avoid having to introduce yet another operator in transformed programs, we have chosen the current presentation.

3. There is no notion of issuing a single atomic demand for all the elements of a data structure.

**Figure 4.** Functional transformation for introducing demand propagation code.

| Definition in Source | Definition in Transformed Program |
|---|---|
| $x = constant$ | $x = gate(constant, dx)$ |
| $x = y$ | $x = y$ <br> $dy = dx$ |
| $x = y\ op\ z$ | $x = y\ op\ z$ <br> $dy = dx$ <br> $dz = dx$ |
| $x = $ **if** $a$ **then** $b$ **else** $c$ | $x = $ **if** $a$ **then** $b$ **else** $c$ <br> $da = dx$ <br> $db, dc = switch(a, dx)$ |
| $x = cons(y, z)$ | $x = cons(y, z)$ <br> $dy = car(dx)$ <br> $dz = cdr(dx)$ |
| $x = car(y)$ | $x = car(y)$ <br> $dy = cons(dx, \perp)$ |
| $x = cdr(y)$ | $x = cdr(y)$ <br> $dy = cons(\perp, dx)$ |
| $x_1, \ldots, x_n = fork\text{-}n(y)$ | $t_1, \ldots, t_n = fork\text{-}n(y)$ <br> $x_1 = gate(t_1, dx_1)$ <br> $\cdots$ <br> $x_n = gate(t_n, dx_n)$ <br> $dy = lub\text{-}n(dx_1, \ldots, dx_n)$ |
| $x_1, \ldots, x_n = f_i(y_1, \ldots, y_m)$ | $x_1, \ldots, x_n, dy_1, \ldots, dy_m = Tf_i(y_1, \ldots, y_m, dx_1, \ldots, dx_n)$ |

$$gate : V \times D \rightarrow V$$

$$gate(x, y) = \textbf{if } y = \perp \textbf{ then } \perp \textbf{ else } x$$

$$switch : V \times D \rightarrow D \times D$$

$$switch(b, x) = \textbf{if } b \textbf{ then } x, \perp \textbf{ else } \perp, x$$

$$lub\text{-}n : D^n \rightarrow D$$

$$lub\text{-}n(x_1, \ldots, x_n) = x_1 \cup \cdots \cup x_n .$$

The operators *cons*, *car*, *cdr*, and *fork-n* are treated as overloaded symbols that are interpreted in $D$ as well as in $V$. Each operator in the transformed program is a monotonic and continuous function; therefore, transformed programs can be assigned meanings using the standard techniques discussed in Section 2.

The *lub* operator is similar to the unification operator on first-order terms in logic programming languages. Consider the set of first-order terms built out of a two-place constructor *cons* and an atom 'd'. A demand structure such as $cons($'d'$, cons(\perp, cons($'d'$, \perp)))$ can be translated to a first-order term by replacing each occurrence of $\perp$ with a unique variable (say $cons($'d'$, cons(x, cons$ ('d'$, y))))$. It is easy to verify that the *lub* operator on demand structures corresponds to unification on such first-order terms. Strictly speaking, this operation is a special case of unification (like pattern matching) since *co-referencing*, the occurrence of a variable more than once in a term, cannot happen.

To demonstrate the correctness of the transformation, we would have to show that a dataflow interpretation of the transformed program performs the same computations as a lazy interpreter does on the original program. This measure excludes work done in demand propagation. We refer the reader to [20], where a similar result is shown for a stream language.


## 3.2 *Discussion*

The transformation described in this section has demonstrated that the various aspects of lazy evaluation, such as suspension of computations, demand propagation, and ensuring that suspended computations are done at most once, can be achieved in the dataflow model by introducing explicit demand-propagation code into programs. On the other hand, the need for demand structures and for a *lub* operator that, in effect, performs unification of demand structures is puzzling because these notions are absent in reduction-based implementations of lazy evaluation. A plausible conclusion is that lazy evaluation is tied up intimately with the notion of reduction, so any attempt to model it in a system that does not permit over-writing of code with data must introduce some idiosyncrasies that are a reflection of the system rather than of the phenomenon being modeled. However, this "fatalistic" conclusion does not provide any insight and in fact is overly pessimistic. In the next section, we show that the need for demand structures arises from the functional nature of the transformation of Figure 4; a new transformation for which the target language is a functional language enriched with logic variables eliminates the need for demand structures and their unification.

## 4 *Using Logic Variables for Demand Propagation*

Logic variables can be incorporated into functional languages in a variety of styles. In this section, we adopt the approach taken in our earlier work on *Id Nouveau* [5]. We then show how these variables can be used profitably for demand propagation.

### 4.1 *Logic Variables and Functional Languages*

In a functional language, a data structure is a value which is defined as the result of evaluating a single applicative expression. For example, the evaluation of the ML expression *val x = {name = 'Miranda', age = 2, used = true}* allocates storage for a record with three fields *name*, *age*, and *used*, stores the specified values into these fields, and binds the identifier *x* to this record. Once the record has been created, it cannot be mutated. In imperative languages, on the other hand, the usual programming style is to use a command to allocate storage for a data structure and then to use other commands to write into this storage. Moreover, the freedom to "side-effect" a data structure is absolute, and an element of a data structure may hold many different values over the lifetime of the data structure. Logic variables are a compromise between these two extremes; intuitively, they provide the programmer with write-once storage. As in imperative languages, storage for a data structure may be allocated without specifying the values of its elements. However, once an element of a data structure has acquired a value, it cannot be reassigned another value later in the program. For example, in a language like Id Nouveau, the programmer can write

```
. . .
x = {name =?, age =?, used =?};
. . .
x.name = 'Miranda';
. . .
```

*x.age* = 2;

· · ·

*x.used* = *true*;

· · ·

Storage for the record is allocated by the first statement, while the values of its fields are defined by the other statements. In logic programming parlance, this is explained using logic variables: When the record is allocated, the fields are initialized to logic variables (say $L1$, $L2$, and $L3$), that are initially unbound. Logic variables are bound to values as the result of execution of other statements in the program. The scope of these bindings is global—for example, if a record is passed as a parameter to a function that defines some of its fields, the bindings stay in effect even after the execution of the function has terminated. This has the flavor of call-by-reference parameter binding in imperative languages. Unlike variables in imperative languages, however, a logic variable cannot be redefined once it has acquired a value. Looked at another way, each statement in the program is a constraint that gives partial information about the value of $x$, and the intersection of these constraints defines the value of $x$. Thus, the first statement is a constraint that is satisfied by any record with three fields *name*, *age*, and *used*. The second statement is a constraint that is satisfied by any record whose *name* field contains the string 'Miranda'. A similar interpretation holds for the other statements. By intersecting these constraints, we can deduce that $x$ must be the record {*name* = 'Miranda', *age* = 2, *used* = *true*}. Thus, the record obtains its value not by the evaluation of a single expression but by the combined effect of a number of statements in the program. The viewpoint of constraints provides a nice rationale for the prohibition of multiple assignments to record fields: if the programmer wrote *x.age* = 2; *x.age* = 3, the program should return the value "error" since there is no record that satisfies both constraints. A benign case of multiple assignment occurs when a constraint occurs more than once in the program. It is permitted to write *x.age* = 2 in two places in the program since there is no contradiction in repeating the same constraint. Appropriately enough, we will call these data structures *monotonic records*: they are objects whose state changes as the program executes, but each state change increases the information in the object.

To understand how programs in such a language can be executed, let us replace the functional *cons* in language F with monotonic records and discuss how these programs can be executed on a dataflow interpreter. For our purpose, we do not need general records; therefore, we will introduce a single kind of monotonic record with four fields *car*, *cdr*, *d-car*, and *d-cdr*. The role of the *d-car* and *d-cdr* fields will become clear later in this section. Figure 5 shows the syntax of this hybrid language, which we call FL. A record is allocated by the *L-cons* operation (for *Logical cons*). Unlike the functional *cons* operation, this operation does not have any arguments since the values of the fields of a monotonic record do not have to be specified at the time of allocation. If *x* is a monotonic record, its fields may be read by the selection operations *x.car*, *x.cdr*, *x.d-car*, and *x.d-cdr*. The fields may be given values by definitions of the form *x.car* = *e* where *e* is some expression.

To implement FL programs on a dataflow interpreter, we need a structure memory similar to *I-structure memory*, which was discussed in Section 2.2, and dataflow nodes for allocating, reading, and writing monotonic records. The *L-cons* operation is translated to a node labeled *allocate* in the dataflow graph, which allocates a record in structure memory and returns a pointer to it. The definition *x.car* = *y* is translated into a node labeled *store-car* which has two inputs *x* and *y*. When this node receives tokens on both its inputs, it executes, sending a write request to the structure memory. If the *car* field of record *x* is empty, the structure memory simply writes the value of *y* into that field; otherwise, it unifies this value with the value stored in the *car* field. If unification fails, the entire program aborts. The *store-car* operator has no

---

**Figure 5.**   Syntax of language FL.

$program ::=$  $f_1(id, \ldots, id) =$ **letrec** $def \ldots def$ **in** $id, \ldots, id$

   . . .

   $f_m(id, \ldots, id) =$ **letrec** $def \ldots def$ **in** $id, \ldots, id$

   $\Rightarrow f_k(constant, constant, \ldots, constant)$

$lhs ::= id \mid id.car \mid id.cdr \mid id.d\text{-}car \mid id.d\text{-}cdr$

$def ::= lhs, \ldots, lhs = exp$

$exp ::=$  $constant \mid id \mid id \; op \; id \mid$ **if** $id$ **then** $id$ **else** $id \mid$

   $L\text{-}cons() \mid id.car \mid id.cdr \mid id.d\text{-}car \mid id.d\text{-}cdr \mid$

   $f_j(id, \ldots, id) \mid$

   $fork\text{-}i(id)$

---

output since its purpose is to store a value into the *car* field of a record. The expression *x.car* is translated into a dataflow node labeled *car* with input *x*. When this operator receives a pointer to a record, it executes and sends a read request for the *car* field of *x*. If the *car* field has not been written into, the structure memory delays this request until the write happens.[4] The translation of operations on the other fields of a record are similar.

We are currently working on a denotational semantics for this language. This semantics uses the viewpoint of constraints described earlier to give abstract meanings to programs.

## 4.2 *Demand Propagation*

To understand the relevance of monotonic records to demand propagation, it is useful to consider the following analogy. A graduate student has a committee of three professors, and to get his degree he has to fulfill the demands that all three professors make on him. How does he go about figuring out what the professors demand of him? One way is to let each professor make up a list of his demands. Some activities may be demanded by more than one professor (presumably, "write your thesis" is in all three lists) while others may be in only one list ("teach CS999 while I'm away"). To figure out the requirements for graduation, the student must merge all the three lists together, eliminating duplicate demands. This is analogous to the functional solution of Figure 4. How can the merging of demand lists be avoided? One way is for the student to make out a single checklist of all the activities he can perform, with a box next to each item on this list. This list is circulated to all three professors, who make their demands known by placing an X in the appropriate boxes. To figure out what is expected of him, the student can simply read this checklist—by eliminating separate demand lists, he eliminates the need for merging them.

How can we use this analogy for the problem of propagating demands in F programs? Instead of requiring that each of a data structure's consumers generate a separate demand structure, there must be a single demand structure, which is defined co-operatively by all the consumers. In fact, we can go further and combine the data structure and the demand structure into a single, composite structure that has both data values and demand values in it. This is achieved by implementing a *cons* cell as a monotonic record of four fields *d-car*, *car*, *d-cdr*, and *cdr* (for *d*emand for *car*, *car*, etc.). This record should be thought of as a mailbox that is shared by the producer and the consumers. The mailbox is allocated by the producer, and a pointer to it is

---

4. There is a close connection between read operations on monotonic records and unification of read-only variables in Concurrent Prolog [21].

passed to any consum er that wishes to make a demand. The *d-car* and *d-cdr* fields of the mailbox are read by the producer to monitor demands from the consumers. A consumer that wants the value of the *car* field stores the value 'd' in the *d-car* field and reads the *car* field of the record. The 'd' value stored in the *d-car* field is read by the producer, that propagates this demand to the computation responsible for producing the value of the *car* field. When this value is computed, the producer stores it in the *car* field of the mailbox, where it is read by the consumer. Multiple demands for the *car* or *cdr* of a *cons*-cell show up as multiple writes of the value 'd' into the *d-car* or *d-cdr* field. This can be handled by a trivial case of unification that checks that these constants are indeed the same.

With this intuitive picture in mind, let us examine the new transformation shown in Figure 6, which shows how demand propagation code is introduced into F programs. As before, if $x$ is an atomic value, a demand token on line $dx$ represents a demand for its value. If $x$ is the output of a *cons* operation, a demand token on line $dx$ represents a demand for allocation of the mailbox through which demands and data are to be communicated. There are no demand structures—so the problem of unifying them does not arise. Not surprisingly, the differences between this transformation and the earlier one shown in Figure 4 show up only in the demand propagation code for data structures. Let us look at the code for the *cons*. The mailbox is allocated when a demand arrives for the output of the *cons*, and a pointer to this mailbox is produced as output. Read requests are sent to the *d-car* and *d-cdr* fields to monitor demands from the consumers; if and when these fields are written into by the consumers, these demands are propagated to $y$ and $z$, respectively. Once $y$ or $z$ is computed, its value is stored in the appropriate field of the mailbox. Note that the *car* and *cdr* fields are written into at most once. Let us now examine the code for the *car* operation. A demand for the output of the *car* operation is propagated as a demand for the input of the *ca*—i.e., a demand is made for the allocation of the mailbox. When a pointer to this mailbox is received, a 'd' value is stored into the *d-car* field and a read request is sent for the *car* field. If the *d-car* field was empty (i.e., this is the first demand for the *car* field), the *d-car* field gets set to the value ' d', the producer reads this value, and the computation for the *car* field is begun. If the *d-car* field already had the value 'd' in it, the write request is discarded. The value of the *car* field is returned when it is written into by the producer.

Figure 7 shows a fragment of an F function and the dataflow graph for the transformed program. The *allocate* operator executes when the function is invoked producing a pointer to a record in structure memory. Let us refer to this record as $R$. The token carrying this pointer is held at the *gate* operator until a demand is made either for $p$ or for $q$. Suppose a demand is made for $p$.

**Figure 6.**  Using logic variables for demand propagation.

| Definition in Source | Definition in Transformed Program |
|---|---|
| $x = constant$ | $x = gate(constant, dx)$ |
| $x = y$ | $x = y$ <br> $dy = dx$ |
| $x = y\ op\ z$ | $x = y\ op\ z$ <br> $dy = dx$ <br> $dz = dx$ |
| $x = $ **if** $a$ **then** $b$ **else** $c$ | $x = $ **if** $a$ **then** $b$ **else** $c$ <br> $da = dx$ <br> $db, dc = switch(a, dx)$ |
| $x = cons(y, z)$ | $x = gate(L\text{-}cons(), dx)$ <br> $x.car = y$ <br> $x.cdr = z$ <br> $dy = x.d\text{-}car$ <br> $dz = x.d\text{-}cdr$ |
| $x = car(y)$ | $x = y.car$ <br> $dy = dx$ <br> $y.d\text{-}car = d$ |
| $x = cdr(y)$ | $x = y.cdr$ <br> $dy = dx$ <br> $y.d\text{-}cdr = d$ |
| $x_1, \ldots, x_n = fork\text{-}n(y)$ | $t_1, \ldots, t_n = fork\text{-}n(y)$ <br> $x_1 = gate(t_1, dx_1)$ <br> $\ldots$ <br> $x_n = gate(t_n, dx_n)$ <br> $dy = lub\text{-}n(dx_1, \ldots, dx_n)$ |
| $x_1, \ldots,_n = f_i(y_1, \ldots, y_m)$ | $x_1, \ldots, x_n, dy_1, \ldots, dy_m = Tf_i(y_1, \ldots, y_m, dx_1, \ldots, dx_n)$ |

The demand token on line *dp* is propagated by the *lub*-2 operator to the *gate* operator, which causes a token carrying a pointer to $R$ to appear on line $x$ and then on line $x_1$. A 'd' value is stored in the *d-car* field of $R$, thereby posting a read request for the *car* field. This value is read by the *d-car* operator, and a demand token is produced on line *da*. As a result, a token carrying the value 5 is sent to the *store-car* operator. This operator executes, storing the value 5 in the *car* field of $R$. This value is returned to the *car* operator, which produces a token carrying the value 5 on line $p$. Subsequently, if a demand token is sent on line $q$, a token carrying a pointer to $R$ is produced on line $x_2$. The value 'd' is written into the *d-car* field of $R$, but this write is ignored. The *car* operator executes, producing the value 5 on line $q$.

The use of logic variables for demand propagation provides a nice example of what Lindstrom has called the action-at-a-distance feature of logic variables[17].

## 4.3 *Discussion*

Transformed programs do not need the full power of unification. Since the source language is a functional language, multiple writes cannot occur in the *car* and *cdr* fields of monotonic records in transformed programs. Monotonic records' *d-car* and *d-cdr* fields may be written into more than once; since the value being written is always the atomic constant 'd', this can be handled by ignoring multiple writes. Although transformed programs do not need the full power of unification, we do not see any way to mimic this style of demand propagation in a purely functional language. Monotonic records acquire their values by the co-operative effort of a number of statements in the program, and we have put this feature to use in eliminating demand structures from the demand-propagation algorithm. However, one can ask whether a compiler might be able to analyze a program produced by the functional transformation and optimize it to produce the program that would have resulted from the new transformation. We leave this as an open question.

It is straightforward to extend the transformation of Figure 6 to other constructs such as a *nil* constructor and higher-order functions. Let us enrich the source language with a constructor *nil* and an *is-nil?* function, which returns *true* if its argument is *nil* and *false* otherwise. Suppose $x = is\text{-}nil?(y)$ is a definition in the source program and $y$ is the output of a *cons* operator. How would a demand for $x$ be propagated to a demand for $y$? The functional demand propagation algorithm runs into difficulties because demands can be made only for the elements of $y$, but these elements are of no interest to the *is-nil?* function. Using the new approach, demand propagation is straightforward— the demand propagation code is simply $dy = dx$. Propagating a demand token

**Figure 7.**   Propagating demands using the new algorithm.

$$\dots$$

$$a = 5$$

$$x = cons(a, b)$$

$$x1, x2 = fork\text{-}2(x)$$

$$p = car(x1)$$

$$q = car(x2)$$

$$\dots$$

(a) Fragment of source program

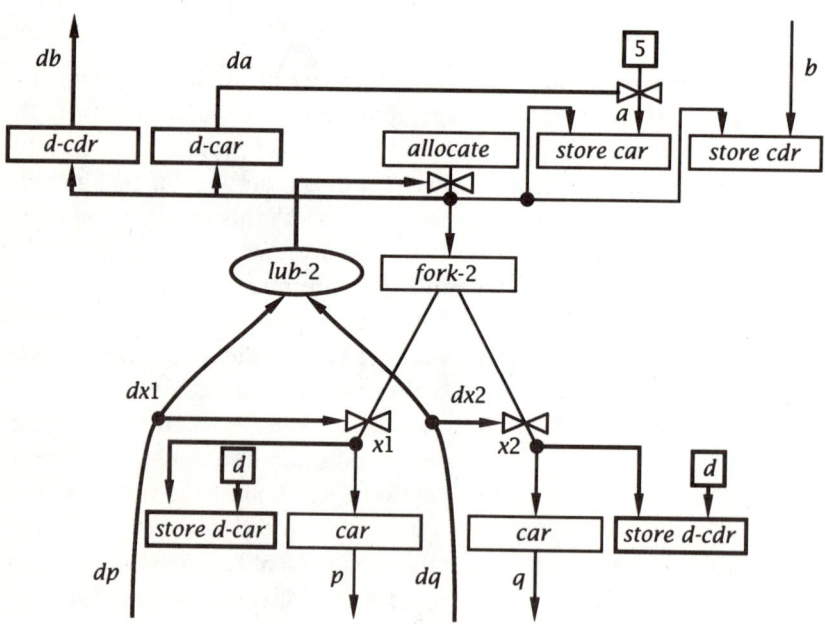

(b) Program transformed according to Figure 6

on line $dy$ will cause the address of a mailbox to be produced on line $y$ and the *is-nil?* operator executes, producing *false* as the output.

Higher-order functions pose no problems since they can be treated like the *cons* operation. We assume that all functions are curried and that lambda-lifting has been done [13]. If $(f\ a)$ is a partial application, a demand for its output is propagated as a demand for $f$. When the value of $f$ is obtained, its arity is checked. If the arity is one, the function application is carried out; otherwise, a mailbox is allocated (this is like an *apply* node in the G-machine) and the value of $f$ is written into the *car* field of the mailbox. The *d-cdr* and *cdr* fields are used to communicate data and demand for the argument $a$.

## 5  *Applications*

In this section, we describe two applications of the transformation of Figure 6. First, we show how this transformation can be used to implement lazy evaluation on a real dataflow machine. Second, we discuss some connections with algorithms for strictness analysis.

### 5.1  *Implementing Lazy Evaluation on a Dataflow Machine*

Apart from two minor complications, it is straightforward to implement the transformation described in the previous section on the tagged-token dataflow machine [2]. I-structure memory as originally defined did not permit multiple writes into the fields of a record. The transformation described above requires multiple writes into the *d-car* and *d-cdr* fields to be handled by a trivial case of unification (unification of constants). This involves a minor change to I-structure memory. Secondly, dataflow instructions in this machine do not have any local state associated with them that carries information from one firing to the next. Examining the transformation of Figure 6, we see that there are two operators which do have such state: *cond* and *lub*. As we have described it, *cond* fires twice, once to produce the output and once to absorb the input that was not needed. This means that the value of the predicate must be stored somewhere from one firing to the next. Notice, however, that under lazy evaluation, the *cond* operator is not required since a token will arrive only at the input that is needed to produce the output of the *cond* operator. Thus, in the implementation, the *cond* operator is eliminated and its two data inputs are tied together (i.e., they become the same line in the dataflow graph). Similarly, the *lub* operator cannot be implemented as a primitive since information that a 'd' token has been produced must be carried from one firing to the next. The *lub* operator is implemented using the *d-car* field of a record in memory. A definition of the form $x = lub(a, b)$ is implemented as the scheme

> $r = L\text{-}cons()$;
>
> $r.d\text{-}car = a$;
>
> $r.d\text{-}cdr = b$;
>
> $x = r.d\text{-}car$;

The tagged-token dataflow machine permits different invocations of a function to share the same code by tagging tokens to distinguish tokens belonging to one activation from those belonging to another. The execution of programs produced by the transformation of Figure 6 is compatible with tag manipulation on the dataflow machine—notice that during function invocation, at most one token flows down an arc in the function's dataflow graph.

Garbage collection poses an interesting problem in this implementation. Dataflow graphs for data-driven execution have the self-cleaning property [4]—once computation has terminated in some function activation, no tokens are left behind. This is useful because tokens are held in an associative store (called the waiting-matching section), and space in this store is limited. Unfortunately, dataflow graphs generated by our transformation are not self-cleaning—for example, if a demand is made only by one output of a fork but not the other, a token will sit at the *gate* operator unless it is "garbage collected". While it is possible to come up with schemes for collecting such tokens, recent developments in the architecture have made the problem moot. To circumvent the problem of building a large associative store, the tagged-token dataflow machine has been redesigned so that a waiting-matching section is not required. Instead, an *activation record* in ordinary memory is assigned to each function activation. This is very much like a stack frame in conventional implementations of sequential languages, and it holds operand values during the execution of the function activation. In this architecture, activation records can be garbage collected with structure memory.

### 5.2 *Comparison with Graph Reduction*

The seminal work on parallel, lazy graph reduction interpreters was done by Keller and Lindstrom in their AMPS and Rediflow projects [16, 15]. This work has inspired much of the current effort in parallel implementations of lazy evaluation. In their system, the program is stored as a directed graph of instructions which gets over-written by data as the program executes. Each instruction has an opcode, pointers to other instructions that produce its operands, and two bits, called the *demand* bit and the *ready* bit. The output of an instruction is demanded by putting its address on a global demand list (task queue). A free processor picks up this instruction, sets its demand bit, and attempts to execute it. If the operands have not been computed, their addresses are placed on the demand list and the instruction is discarded. When an instruction is evaluated, it is over-written by the result and its ready bit is set. Addresses of other instructions that are waiting for this result are placed on a result list and are then rescheduled for execution. The demand bit is used to ensure that an instruction is not queued multiply on the demand queue.

This approach differs from the one described in this paper in several ways. In our approach, instructions are not over-written by data. This permits different invocations of a function to share the same copy of code, provided that tokens are tagged to distinguish tokens belonging to one activation from those that belong to other activations. It may be possible to achieve this in the AMPS model by separating operand storage from instruction storage and giving each function invocation its own activation record for storing operands. This would represent a step away from graph reduction. In our approach, data and demands are treated uniformly—these values are carried on tokens, and an instruction is scheduled when it receives a token regardless of whether the token represents data or demand. In essence, we have merged the demand list and result list, which simplifies the design of the processor. The *d-car* and *d-cdr* fields in our approach play a role similar to demand bits in AMPS. However, we introduce them only at *fork*s and in data structures, i.e., where data are shared, rather than in every instruction. Checking the demand bit does not have to be part of the instruction execution cycle. In some sense, ours is a "RISC" approach to lazy evaluation! In a processor designed to implement lazy graph reduction, the interpretation of instructions is complicated by the fact that an instruction must be processed in two different ways: One set of actions must be taken if the instruction is being processed in response to a demand, while a different set of actions must be taken if the instruction is being processed because its inputs have arrived. In our approach, the processor is freed from these concerns since demand propagation code is exposed by the compiler.

### 5.3 *Connections with Strictness Analysis*

One problem with completely lazy evaluation is that parallelism is limited [6]. We emphasize that this is as much a problem in our implementation as in an implementation based on graph reduction. On the other hand, the advantage of exposing demand propagation code is that this code becomes subject to standard program optimization, which can take the place of strictness analysis. Examining the program in Figure 3, we see that there is considerable scope for optimization. At run time, a 'd' token must flow on line *do* to indicate demand for the output of the function. Using constant propagation, we see that the *lub*-2 operator and the *gate* operator on line $y_1$ can be removed, and that the demand on line *do* can be propagated directly to *dx* and *dy*. A similar conclusion can be drawn using strictness analysis [6, 10] of this program. Traditionally, strictness analysis algorithms have been based on abstract interpretation, but their complexity can be exponential in the size of the program. We believe that it should be possible to view strictness analysis as an optimization of the demand propagation graph, using standard techniques such as constant propagation and value subsumption [1]. Results in this direction are reported by Amamiya et al., who have used global dataflow analysis to optimize the demand propagation code generated by our functional transformation [18].

Interestingly enough, support for this thesis comes also from a new strictness analysis algorithm called backward strictness analysis [11, 12]. This algorithm exhibits much better complexity than the traditional algorithms based on abstract interpretation, and it uses a technique similar to our functional transformation. Backward analysis is presented using contexts, which correspond roughly to what we have called demands. Strictness analysis is performed by associating a context transformer with each function; context transformers correspond to demand-propagation code. The formalization of contexts and context transformation appears to require a fair amount of mathematical machinery such as lifted domains and projections. It is possible that viewing backward analysis in terms of optimization of demand propagation code may simplify the presentation. Moreover, the improved demand propagation algorithm shown in Figure 6 suggests that this analysis might profitably be performed in a language with logic variables. We are currently investigating this problem.

## 6 *Conclusions*

We have argued that logic variables are required in order to explicate the process of demand propagation in lazy evaluation of pure functional languages. This result provides a new approach to the old problem of efficient analysis and implementation of laziness. It offers a simple, RISC-like parallel implementation of lazy evaluation in which data and demands are handled uniformly by the processor. In addition, it suggests that strictness analysis could be viewed fruitfully as conventional optimization of demand propagation code.

## *Acknowledgments*

The author is supported by an IBM Faculty Development Award and by NSF grant CCR–8702668.

## *References*

[1] Aho, A., Sethi, R., and Ullman, J. *Compilers: Principles, Techniques, and Tools.* Addison-Wesley, Reading, Mass., 1986.

[2] Arvind and Culler, D. "Dataflow architectures". Technical Report C.S.G. memo TM–294, M.I.T. Laboratory for Computer Science, February 1986.

[3] Arvind and Gostelow, K. "The U-interpreter." *Computer*, February 1982.

[4] Arvind, Gostelow, K., and Plouffe, W. "An asynchronous programming language and computing machine." Technical Report 114a, University of California, Irvine, December 1978.

[5] Arvind, Nikhil, R., and Pingali, K. "I-structures: Data structures for parallel computing." Technical Report 87–810, Cornell University, February 1987.

[6] Clack, C. and Peyton Jones, S.L. "Strictness analysis — a practical approach." *Functional Programming Languages and Computer Architecture* (Nancy, France, September), J.-P. Jouannaud, ed., pp. 35–49. Lecture Notes in Computer Science, vol. 201. Springer-Verlag, Berlin, 1985.

[7] Dennis, J. B. "First version of a data flow procedure language." *Proceedings of the Colloque sur la Programmation*, pp. 362–376. Lecture Notes in Computer Science, vol. 19. Springer-Verlag, Berlin, 1974.

[8] Friedman, D. and Wise, D. "Cons should not evaluate its arguments." In *Automata, Languages and Programming*, 1976.

[9] Goldberg, B. and Hudak, P. "Alfalfa: Distributed graph reduction on a hypercube multiprocessor." *Graph Reduction* (Santa Fé, NM, October), pp. 94–113. Lecture Notes in Computer Science, vol. 279. Springer-Verlag, Berlin, 1986.

[10] Hudak, P. and Young, J. "Higher-order strictness analysis in untyped lambda calculus." In *Proceedings of the 13th ACM Symposium on Principles of Programming Languages*, 1986.

[11] Hughes, J. and Wadler, P. "Projections for strictness analysis." *Functional Programming Languages and Computer Architecture* (Portland, Ore., September), G. Kahn, ed., pp. 385–407. Lecture Notes in Computer Science, vol. 274. Springer-Verlag, Berlin, 1987.

[12] Hughes, J. "Compile-time analysis of functional programs". This volume (Chapter 5).

[13] Johnsson, T. "Efficient compilation of lazy evaluation." *Proceedings of the ACM SIGPLAN '84 Symposium on Compiler Construction. SIGPLAN Notices 19*, 6 (June

1984), pp. 58–69.

[14] Kahn, G. "The semantics of a simple language for parallel programming." *Proceedings of the IFIP Congress 74*, pp. 471–475, 1974.

[15] Keller, R. "Rediflow multiprocessing." In *Proceedings of Compcon 84*, 1984.

[16] Keller, R., Lindstrom, G., and Patil, S. "A loosely-coupled applicative multi-processing system." *AFIPS National Computer Conference Proceedings 48* (1979), pp. 861–870.

[17] Lindstrom, G. "Functional programming and the logical variable." In *Proceedings of the 12th ACM Symposium on Principles of Programming Languages*, 1985.

[18] Ono, S., Takahashi, N., and Amamiya, M. "Optimized demand-driven evaluation of functional programs on dataflow machines." In *Proceedings of the 1986 ICPP*, pp. 421–428, 1986.

[19] Peyton Jones, S.L. *The Implementation of Functional Programming Languages*. Prentice-Hall International, Englewood Cliffs, N.J., 1986.

[20] Pingali, K. and Arvind. "Efficient demand-driven evaluation. Part 1." *ACM Trans. Programming Languages and Systems 7*, 2 (April 1985), pp. 311–333.

[21] Shapiro, E. "A subset of concurrent Prolog and its interpreter." Technical Report TR–003, Institute for New Generation Computer Technology, 1983.

[22] Turner, D. "Miranda: A non-strict functional language with polymorphic types." *Functional Programming Languages and Computer Architecture* (Nancy, France, September), J.-P. Jouannaud, ed., pp. 1–16. Lecture Notes in Computer Science, vol. 201. Springer-Verlag, Berlin, 1985.

[23] Turner, D. "The semantic elegance of functional languages." In *Proceedings of the 1981 Conference on Functional Programming Languages and Computer Architecture* (Portsmouth, N.H.), 1981.

[24] Turner, D. "A new implementation technique for applicative languages." *Software — Practice and Experience 9*, 1 (January 1979), pp. 31–49.

**David Turner**
University of Kent

## 1 Overview

This chapter reports some of the initial results of a research project at the University of Kent for the construction of an operating system written entirely in a functional language. We are here primarily concerned with the internal structure of the operating system, seen as a network of communicating processes. The description in purely functional terms of such a network has until recently posed logical problems, a solution to which was proposed by W. Stoye in 1984. We have developed a refinement of Stoye's model which has stronger synchronization properties and permits each process to run in a separate address space, facilitating a distributed implementation. By introducing the concept of a wrapper-function, we enable message passing code to be statically type checked.

This chapter describes the state of the KAOS project at the end of 1987 (when the Texas meeting took place). For an account of subsequent developments, and a more detailed treatment of the structure of the KAOS system as it finally emerged, the reader is referred to [2, 3, 4].

## 2 *Background: The KAOS Project*

The aim of the KAOS (Kent Applicative Operating System) project is to build a multiuser operating system written entirely in a purely applicative language.

We can see an operating system as being composed of three (essentially independent) components.

1. *Kernel.* This is always running, it manages resources, and it is the "real" operating system.

2. *Tools.* Editor(s), compiler(s), spelling checkers, games, etc. Each of these is a separate program. The essential minimum is an editor and a compiler, but you can have as many other tools as you want. In a well designed operating system most of the code is here, and most of the functionality of the operating system is provided at this level.

3. *Shell.* This is the operating system as seen by the user when he or she logs on. This provides the language in which the user interacts with the computer.

There can be different shells for different users, presenting (perhaps very) different interfaces to the operating system. We are interested in developing a shell that provides a good programming environment for an applicative language, but there could be another shell that implements BASIC. The structure of the operating system as seen through a shell can be substantially different from the structure of the operating system as seen by the person who wrote the kernel (and can differ from one shell to another).

Note that one essential function of a general purpose shell (we leave aside special purpose shells, for example, one that runs on a particular terminal and permits its user only to consult a timetable) is that it must provide the user with a set of data structures that persist from session to session, and *some commands for updating them.*

This implies that the language of the shell must be an imperative language, at least in certain respects. An attempt to pretend otherwise can only result in confusion.

Does this mean that the project of producing a complete operating system written in a functional language is somehow doomed to failure? Not at all. It is entirely possible to write an interpreter for an imperative language (the shell in this case) in an applicative one. The aim of the project is that all the code that *implements* the operating system (at each of the three levels discussed above) be written in a functional language.

As the language vehicle for this project we are using Miranda. The advantages of Miranda for our purposes are that it is purely functional, that it is statically type-checked (which we regard as essential for any large-scale programming project), that it is a complete and well defined language, and that it is coming to be reasonably widely used (at the time of writing it is running at around 300 sites). We didn't use ML [12], although it has a somewhat stronger claim to be a standard vehicle, because it is not a functional language (it has assignment and other referentially opaque features). We also wanted a language with lazy evaluation, which Miranda supports and ML doesn't.

The notation of Miranda is based on higher-order recursion equations and is similar to that of a number of other modern functional languages. We assume this style of notation is by now reasonably well known; for a more specific discussion of the features of Miranda the reader is referred to [17, 18].

The current status of the project, very briefly, is that we have some of the essential tools (level 2) written. There is a full screen editor, medit, written in Miranda [5], and a Miranda compiler in Miranda also exists. We have experimented with some simple shells written in Miranda.

The purpose of this paper is to report on the progress that has been made in designing a framework for the internal structure of the operating system, which involves communicating processes, traditionally a difficult area for functional programming.

It is an essential requirement of an operating system (even a single-user system) that it must pay attention to several tasks concurrently. For example, we might expect it to run shells for several users and perform background compilations, all at the same time. Even a very simple, single-user, one-job-at-a-time system must be ready to pay attention to interrupts at the same time as running the user's job.

The best model for this seems to be to structure the operating system as a number of independent processes. The processes run concurrently and send each other messages (and of course some processes receive messages from, or send messages to, the outside world). Some processes are always present and constitute the kernel;, other processes go in and out of existence under the control of the kernel (for example, user shells).

Each process has internal state (that is, it is not destined always to respond in the same way on receiving the same message), but there is no explicit global state (i.e., the global behavior is simply the product of the local behaviors). How may such a network of communicating processes be described in a functional language? We take this question in two parts: first the description of the individual process, then the way in which they are connected together.

## 3 *Processes as Functions over Infinite Lists*

If we consider the behavior of a process as the association of output events with individual input events, it is clearly not a function, since the output depends not only on the input event but also on the internal state. However, the internal state is itself a function of (some initial state and) the previous input history. It is therefore the case (at least for a deterministic process) that the output history, taken as a whole, is a function (determined by the initial state) of the input history, taken as a whole.

Such a process can be programmed in a functional language in the following way. For simplicity we take the case of a process with a single input channel and a single output channel. Let the input messages be of type $\alpha$ and the output messages of type $\beta$. Let $s0$ be the initial state, let $trans :: \alpha \rightarrow state \rightarrow state$ be the state transition function, and let $out :: \alpha \rightarrow state \rightarrow [\beta]$ give the (perhaps empty) list of output messages in response to a particular input message:

> $process :: [\alpha] \rightarrow [\beta]$
> $process\ =\ p\ s0$
> > **where**
> > $p\ s\ (a : x) = out\ a\ s \mathbin{+\!\!+} p\ (trans\ a\ s)\ x$

The notation used here (and in other examples in the paper) is that of Miranda.

That processes with internal state can be programmed in this way in a (lazy) functional language is now quite an old idea, current since at least the mid 70's (see, e.g., [10, 16]).

Networks of such processes can also be described. For example if we also have $process' :: [\beta] \rightarrow [\alpha]$, and it is connected in a loop with the above process, this can be programmed as

> $chanA :: [\alpha]$
>
> $chanB :: [\beta]$
>
> $chanA = process'\ chanB$
>
> $chanB = process\ chanA$.

If this is not to be deadlocked one of the processes must be a net producer (and allowing for this possibility requires a slight modification to our earlier schema for a process).

A typical example of programming in this style is shown by the Miranda program for the well known communicating-process solution to the Hamming numbers problem (see Fig. 1). The problem is to print in ascending order all numbers of the form $2^a 3^b 5^c$, where $a$, $b$, and $c$ can be any natural numbers. There is a nice solution to this problem in the form of a network of communicating processes, sketched at the top of the figure. Below the diagram we show the functional program, written in Miranda, which describes this network.

To summarize the preceding paragraphs: Concurrent networks of communicating sequential processes can be programmed in a (lazy) functional language, elegantly and even efficiently, as recursions over infinite lists, and this fact has been known for about ten years. Does this then mean that the problem of how to describe the internal structure of an operating system in a functional language is essentially solved? Unfortunately not, for there is an

**Figure 1.**  A solution to the Hamming-numbers problem.

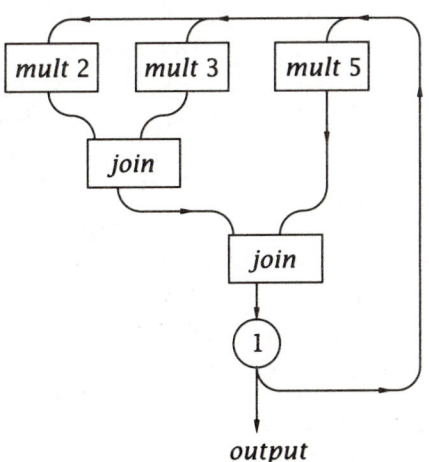

$$output = 1 : join \ (join \ (mult \ 2) \ (mult \ 3)) \ (mult \ 5)$$
$$\textbf{where} \ \ mult \ n = map \ (n\times) \ output$$
$$join \ (a : x) \ (b : y) = a : join \ x \ (b : y), \ a < b$$
$$= b : join \ (a : x) \ y, \ a > b$$
$$= a : join \ x \ y, \quad \ \ a = b$$

important restriction on the behavior of networks that can be described in this way: They must be *deterministic* (as must the individual processes).

That this must be so is immediately apparent from very basic properties of a functional notation. Given a network with a certain number of input lists, and a specified initial state, the list(s) of output messages must be uniquely determined by the given lists of input messages. Otherwise we shall be in the position of attempting to use a functional language to describe a relation that is not a function, an exercise that cannot succeed.

In particular this means that the output behavior of the network cannot depend on the relative speed of arrival of input messages along different channels. We can describe only networks whose output is independent of the relative speeds of the processes of which it is composed (and likewise independent of the relative speeds of arrival of messages on different input ports of the whole network).

For an operating system this is quite unacceptable. We need to be able to deal with certain events, e.g., requests for resources, in the order in which they arise (this concept need not be precise — if two events occur "almost at the same time" we should be allowed to make an arbitrary decision as to which happened first). This means that the output behavior of the network must be not independent of, but dependent on, the relative speeds of the processes of which it is composed. How can we modify the above method of describing networks of processes to permit us to program this?

The most straightforward approach is to modify our representation of channels, as lists of messages, to add information representing the passage of time. We can pad out the lists with neutral elements called "hiatons" (because they represent a hiatus in activity on the channel). A slow process will have many hiatons between the messages on its output list, and a fast process will have very few, or none. The way is now open to describe time-sensitive behavior in a referentially transparent manner. This approach to the description of nondeterministic networks in a functional language has been most consistently advocated by W. Wadge [private communication], and the term "hiaton" is due to him.

From a theoretical point of view this is a rather principled approach and has much to commend it. The programming details become unattractive, however, and so far as I am aware no one has yet constructed a functional operating system along these lines. There are two main problems. The first is that to carry the proposal through, *every* process in the network (including therefore those inside user programs) becomes enmeshed in the obligation to emit hiatons to mark the passage of time; otherwise the operating system cannot time the process out if it "takes too long". This seems a highly undesirable complication, and it appears to violate some principles of modularity.

The second problem is that we have what operating-system people call "busy waiting" — at any given time a significant proportion of the processes in the network will be "counting hiatons", which seems a highly inefficient use of resources. In effect we have no real-time interrupts, and are doing everything by polling.

We have therefore rejected the hiaton approach for the KAOS project. An alternative approach is to add to our functional language some new primitives that permit the description of nondeterministic behavior. For example we can add a nondeterministic operation *merge* that takes two (possibly infinite) lists and returns a list containing their elements "in order of arrival". Thus

$$merge\ (a:x)\ y\ \Rightarrow\ a:merge\ x\ y$$

$$merge\ x\ (b:y)\ \Rightarrow\ b:merge\ x\ y.$$

The intention here is that the machine will use whichever of the above two reduction rules first becomes applicable. (*Warning*: this is not Miranda notation — the definition of *merge* is not possible in Miranda, nor in any other functional language. Read as a system of equations, the above definition of *merge* is just *inconsistent*.)

We also require that *merge* be "fair" at least in the weak sense that every item on either input list is present eventually in the result list. It turns out that all of the other nondeterministic primitives that have been proposed can be programmed in terms of fair merge. So adding *merge* to our functional language is in some sense enough to describe all nondeterministic networks. (Again we refer to results that have been known in the functional programming community for some years.)

The use of *merge* to create operating-system-like behavior is described in [7]. We give a sketch in Figure 2 of how a two-client/one-server situation is programmed. The use of *merge*, or an equivalent primitive, to program substantial aspects of operating system behavior in an otherwise functional language has been described by a number of authors, for example, [9, 1, 6].

It seems to us that there are two basic objections to this approach — one practical, the other theoretical.

**1.** The communication paths within the network must be programmed in detail by numerous uses of *merge/unmerge*, leading to what Backus has called "spaghetti programming" [private communication]. We lack the concept of an "ether" permitting a process to send a message to any other process whose name is known.

**2.** *merge* is not a function. It does not have side effects, but a call to *merge* can return different results on different occasions, even when the arguments are the same. (Recall that two arguments are semantically the same if they compute the same value, regardless of by what method.) Referential transparency, that is the ability to employ equational reasoning in programs, has been destroyed. We may still be programming "in a functional style", but this is no longer functional programming in any real sense.

A simple and ingenious scheme that overcomes both of these difficulties has recently been proposed by William Stoye of Cambridge University [14], and it is upon this that our approach is based.

## 4 The Sorting Office — A Global Interconnection Scheme

A sketch of Stoye's scheme is shown in Fig. 3. The important change that has taken place here (and the step by which Stoye has advanced beyond the path opened up by Henderson et al.) is that there is now only a single (infinitary) occurrence of *merge* in the whole system, and it is *outside the language* (in Stoye's implementation it is part of the microcode that supports the abstract machine).

Each process has a single input list and a single output list. This is not a significant restriction since the input items can be labeled with information about their origin, and the output messages are always labeled with their intended destinations (so there would be no increase in power by allowing multiple output channels from each process). A significant restriction, of course, is that each process must be *sequential*; that is, its output list must be uniquely determined by the sequence of arrival of messages on its input list; otherwise the process could not be described in a functional language, for the reasons discussed above.

[Note that this does not exclude the possibility of fine-grain parallelism in-

---

**Figure 2.** Using nondeterministic *merge* to schedule a resource between two clients.

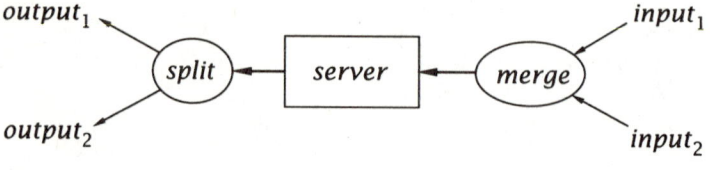

side the implementation of each process; this would be "and-parallelism", of the kind that arises from, for example, evaluating both sides of a *plus* operation in parallel, which is not a source of nondeterminism. This consideration is orthogonal to the kind of parallelism we are discussing here.]

The output messages from each process are merged together and placed in the input lists of their addressees by a piece of apparatus called the sorting office. This is part of the abstract machine, and plays the role of the ether.

The output list of each process arises from the application of a certain list-to-list function (which we will call the process body) to the corresponding input list. In Stoye's scheme new processes are created by sending messages to a special process called, the process-creation process. The contents of such a message is a function, namely, the process body. On receiving it the process-creation process applies the body to a newly created input list (thus creating the desired process) and sends the address of the new input list back to the requesting process as a reply.

The process-creation process is also part of the abstract machine, and everyone knows its address (it is process number zero, say). Since new processes can arise dynamically, the number of processes in the system is unbounded in the general case, which is why we said earlier that the implied occurrence of *merge* inside the sorting office is in fact an infinitary merge.

Stoye implemented this scheme on SKIM 2 (a microcoded combinator reduction machine constructed at Cambridge) and used it to program a simple but quite usable operating system for this machine. The reduction machine was modified to time-slice itself among a set of reduction tasks (one for each process in existence) and to route messages to the correct destinations. The interested reader is referred to Stoye's thesis [15] for details.

The important point for us about Stoye's scheme is that (given the rather simple modifications to the abstract machine) all of the code that describes

---

**Figure 3.**  The structure of Stoye's functional operating system.

the structure of the operating system can now be written in a purely functional language. We are therefore using this method (with certain modifications described below) for our operating system, KAOS, now being written in Miranda. A fundamental design aim of the project was that we should carry the task through without compromising the functional nature of Miranda by adding referentially opaque features, such as *merge*, whence the decision to follow this route.

Each process in the operating system can be written in perfectly ordinary (deterministic) Miranda code. In fact, to define the operating system we actually have to write code for the body of just one process — namely, the boot process, which creates all the other processes and thus calls the operating system into being!

[*Aside*: some people have argued that Stoye's scheme is really cheating, because *merge* is still "in there somewhere", even if it is not visible in any of the functional code. Our response is that because there is now only a single invocation of *merge* in the whole life history of the system, it is possible to write down a purely declarative account of the behavior of the whole network and not merely of each individual process. We will not pursue this matter further here.]

## 5  *Some Refinements to the Model*

We now discuss some more-detailed design decisions and their consequences. First, how can we satisfy the requirements of static type-checking, a pervasive (and extremely valuable) feature of Miranda? In Stoye's thesis each message is a pair, consisting of the address to which it is being sent and some data item. Since there are no restrictions on the type of items that can be sent (so long as sender and receiver are in agreement about the nature of the transaction) Stoye's compiler did not attempt to type-check code that did message handling.

### 5.1  *Type Security*

In our scheme the interfaces between processes are (statically) type secure. We sketch how this is accomplished. We have that all processes produce the *same* output type, namely,

[*message*]

i.e., "list of *message*". An object of type *message* is opaque (that is, you cannot take it apart to find out what is in it); the only thing a process can usefully do with a message is to put it in its output list. A data object is turned into a message by applying a wrapper function (sometimes just "wrapper" for short). A wrapper function for objects of type $\alpha$ is called an $\alpha$-wrapper and is of type $\alpha \rightarrow message$.

Each process expects a specific kind of input item (not normally *message*, but some useful data item, say *num*, or *tree*, or whatever). In the interests of static type checking we require that any given process has a single type of items in its input list (of course, this could be a union type, so there is no real loss of power). A process requiring its input list to be of type $\alpha$ is called an $\alpha$-process. So we have many different kinds of process, e.g., *num*-process, *tree*-process, and so on. Notice that in the interests of clarity we call the things that appear in input lists items, *not* messages (messages are the opaque objects in output lists). Note also that the body of an alpha-process is a function of type

$$[\alpha] \rightarrow [message].$$

Associated with each process is a wrapper function that can be used to send it messages. If it is an $\alpha$-process the associated wrapper will be an $\alpha$-wrapper (and it is this discipline that enables us to ensure statically that processes receive only items of the right type in their input lists). The wrapper function carries, then, two pieces of information — its type, saying what kind of object it is willing to wrap (this is for the use of the compiler only, since in a strongly typed language, such as Miranda, type information does not exist at run time) and the intended destination of the messages created by its use (this is for the use of the sorting office).

When a message passes through the sorting office, its wrapper function is stripped off, and the data item it contained is placed in the input list of the destination process that was specified by the wrapper.

As the reader will by now realize, *message* is for us an abstract data type associated with wrapper functions. The underlying representation type (i.e., what a message "really looks like" to the machine) is for us, as for Stoye, essentially just a (*destination, item*) pair. We will show later in this paper (after we have introduced the mechanism by which new processes are created) how the abstract data type *message* can be formally created from the concrete message apparatus by a Miranda **abstype** definition.

The underlying concrete message type we will call *premessage*, for clarity. The constructors of this type are not in scope for ordinary processes (e.g., we do not wish them to have access to process addresses directly). All normal communication takes place using wrappers.

## 5.2 *Synchronization*

The next group of issues concerns the nature of the buffering and the degree of interprocess synchronization in message passing. A closely related issue is, what kind of items it should be permitted to pass in a message (e.g., should we allow a message to contain an infinite object, such as the list of all prime numbers?).

We can take Stoye's decisions on these questions as a starting point. First, he allows arbitrary objects to be sent in messages, including both functions and infinite lists. This gets full marks for orthogonality, but has some not necessarily desirable implications for storage management. Both functions and lazy lists are closure objects; that is, they can contain embedded references to any other item in the heap space of the process that created them. The implication is that in the general case the data structures of different processes will be inextricably intertwined, meaning that we are probably committed to a single monolithic heap space, shared by all processes. (Since Stoye was programming for a monoprocessor with a single global address space, this was presumably not a disadvantage.)

On synchronization and buffering, Stoye has the abstract machine simultaneously demanding output from all active processes, so there are no output queues, but each process can accumulate an unbounded queue of input items (implying that communication is completely asynchronous). Again these are not necessarily bad decisions (Stoye's system worked and was even quite efficient), but for several reasons we have decided to do things differently.

We are concerned to avoid "dragging problems" in the communication between processes (meaning unbounded space requirements for as yet unevaluated expressions), and we also wish to support interprocess synchronization. The latter, although still possible, is a somewhat unnatural activity in a system allowing unbounded input buffers. One is reminded of Keynes's remark about the difficulty of controlling something by "pushing on a piece of a string". Our decisions on these matters are outlined in the following subsections.

**Communication is Synchronous** If process $A$ attempts to send a message to process $B$ (by placing a message created with $B$'s wrapper on its output list) and process $B$ has not yet demanded an input item, then process $A$ is *deactivated* until $B$ is ready. This makes communication symmetrical between sender and receiver in its synchronization properties — both must be ready to make the transaction. It also eliminates the need for any queues or buffers in the communication system — there will be no storage needs associated with the sorting office or with input or output lists.

An important consequence of this is that we can now program *data driven* concurrency (for example, to program one-producer/two-consumer situations without introducing dragging problems). Trying to program data drive in a system with input buffers is the "pushing on a piece of string" puzzle referred to earlier. Since it has been argued [13] that the occurrence of dragging problems is one of the most important obstacles standing in the way of a more general use of lazy functional languages, this seems an important advantage.

It is also worth pointing out that almost all recent theoretical work on communicating processes [11, 8] assumes synchronous communication, and it may be useful to be able to draw on this body of knowledge.

**Communication is Hyperstrict**   Some terminology. We say that function $f$ is *strict* just when

$$f \perp = \perp$$

where $\perp$ (pronounced "bottom") is the imaginary value deemed to be the result of expressions whose evaluation fails to terminate.

We say that $f$ is *hyperstrict* if

$$f x = \perp$$

whenever $x$ is not *totally defined*. For example, if the argument of $f$ is a tree, $f$ *hyperstrict* means that $f$ fails if there is a $\perp$ anywhere in the tree.

We make wrapper functions hyperstrict. This means that items are fully evaluated before transmission to another process in a message. (Stoye's system evaluates messages to top level only, so he has message passing strict but not hyperstrict.) Our decision implies that only *discrete* (i.e., finite, total) objects can be passed in messages, and hence not functions or, for example, infinite lists.

This decision further strengthens the synchronization properties of the system. The major reason for the decision however is the following:

Each process can have a separate heap space, which may be garbage collected independently of the heap space of every other process. Communication consists in copying a fully evaluated subgraph from one heap into another.

This brings many benefits, including at least the following.

(i) The need for global garbage collection is eliminated.

(ii) Processes that run amok in their space requirements can be easily identified, observed, and dealt with. In view of the fact that we still lack a good understanding of the space behavior of functional programs, this is very desirable. By contrast, in a system with a monolithic heap containing intertwined data structures of all processes, the question, "how much space is this process using?" is not even meaningful.

**(iii)** Mapping the operating system onto a loosely coupled network of computers, each with its own local address space, becomes a relatively trivial exercise. (Actually the first implementation of KAOS is likely to be on a single large computer, but knowing that it can be easily moved to a distributed implementation later is a definite plus.)

There is, of course, an associated disadvantage, namely, the loss of orthogonality with respect to the types of items in messages. Certain values, specifically functions and infinite (lazy) objects, can no longer be transmitted in messages. We remind the reader that the view of the operating system seen by the user through the shell need bear no simple relation to the internal structure of the operating system as supported by the kernel. So our decision *does not imply* that, for example, functions will be in any way second-class citizens as seen by the user. This means we may have to do some work in the intervening layers of the operating system, but operating systems already have to solve problems that are at least as hard as this one.

**Process Creation**   We do have, however, an immediate problem, namely, how new processes can come into being. Stoye's method is to transmit a message containing a process body to a special address (that of the process-creation process). Since a process body is a function, this method is no longer open to us. We use instead an entirely different method (directly borrowed from UNIX).

In the situation where a process requires to initiate a new process, the code for the continuation of the current process and the process body of the new process must both be present in the heap space of the current process. The process emits a special premessage, *FORK*, on its output list (this premessage should be considered as addressed to the abstract machine, rather than to another process).

The response of the machine to *FORK* is to duplicate the emitting process, by making a second copy of its heap image. The two processes distinguish themselves, each from the other, by reading the next item on their (now separated) input lists. Associated with each process is a small integer, which is its *process-id* (hereafter *pid* for short). In the case of one process (the parent) the next item on its input list is the *pid* of the child, while in the case of the child the next item on its input list is (say) 0, which is recognizable as not being a possible *pid* for a child.

All the processes in the system are descended, via invocations of *FORK*, from an initial boot process (with *pid* = 0, say). We are now ready to describe the nature of premessage passing as supported directly by the abstract machine. At this level we are working in terms of *pid*s, not wrapper functions, and we don't yet have type security (this comes at the next stage, when we define the abstract type *message* as supported by wrapper functions).

The data type of physical messages as supported by the machine is

> *premessage* ::= *SEND pid item* |
>
> *FORK* |
>
> *WRITEDEV devid item* |
>
> *READDEV devid* |
>
> *KILL pid* |
>
> *CLOSE pid* .

Here *item* denotes a fully evaluated data object of arbitrary type, while *pid* and *devid* are just numbers. At any given time there are a number of processes in existence, each with its own heap space and an associated *pid* number. Each process can receive items on its input list and evaluates to a list of type

> [*premessage*] .

Some processes will be *active* and others *suspended*. The active processes are subjected to simultaneous (in fact, time-sliced) demand for their output by the machine.

An active process becomes suspended

> if it tries to read the next item in its input list when nothing has been transmitted,
>
> if it tries to *SEND* to a process that is not yet demanding input,
>
> if it issues a *READDEV* to a device with no ready data,
>
> it sends a *WRITEDEV* to a device that is not ready to write.

It becomes reactivated when the relevant data transfer is able to take place.

The action of the *FORK* premessage in creating new processes has already been described above. A process ceases to exist, and its resources can be immediately reclaimed, if it receives the *KILL* premessage (clearly only certain very privileged processes should be allowed to send a *KILL*, but this security is a matter for higher levels of the system). The resources of a process can also be reclaimed if it terminates itself by returning [ ] (the empty list) as the remainder of its output list.

Sending *CLOSE* to a process causes the remainder of its input list to become [ ]. This is a somewhat more polite way of asking a process to leave than sending it a *KILL*. The process will discover, next time it tries to read its input list, that there are no more inputs, but it has the option of then doing some tidying up.

The above is (in outline) a description of the lowest level of the system, as implemented in the abstract machine. In fact the type *premessage* is not in scope for normal Miranda scripts, not even those that constitute the kernel of the operating system. Apart from a few processes that do lowest-level communication with external devices, the sole use of *premessage* in a Miranda script is in the definition of the abstract type *message*, shown in Fig. 4.

The abstract type *message* provides the type-secure framework for inter-process communication in the rest of the system. It is implemented by a high-level *fork*, which is applied to three continuations (functional arguments) for parent, child, and failure, respectively (the failure continuation is invoked if the fork cannot take place, e.g., because some resource is exhausted). Note that the parent continuation is supplied with the wrapper function for the child. Note also that the type of the high-level *fork* operation allows for the fact that parent and child will in general require input lists of two different types.

The function *changetype* (definitely not permitted in normal Miranda scripts) is semantically equivalent to the identity function but has type $* \rightarrow **$ so it can be used to smuggle things past the type-checker. Its purpose here is to permit the definition of (type-secure) *fork*, in terms of (not type-secure) *FORK* to be accepted as legal by the compiler. Our current view is that there is only one other place in the operating system where the use of *changetype* will be necessary, namely, in the loader (the program that converts compiled code to "function").

Readers unfamiliar with the Miranda **abstype** mechanism will find an account of it in [17]. The point to note here is that the distinction between abstract types and their representations exists only at compile time. At run time, messages and premessages are indistinguishable. This means that the apparatus of wrapper functions, by which we have added type security to Stoye's scheme, has no associated run-time overhead. As far as the author is aware, Miranda's method of defining abstract data types is unique in having this property.

There are a number of points of detail we haven't discussed here for lack of space. One issue is the apparently asymmetrical nature of the communications established by *fork*, in that the parent is handed the child's wrapper but not vice versa. Seemingly, this would permit only downwards communications, from ancestors to descendants. However, recall that the process body of the child is a function arising in the parent's name space. The child may therefore inherit, as free variables, names for any and all wrapper functions known to the parent. This allows networks of arbitrary topology to be created.

## 6  *Conclusions*

Taking the requirements of the Kent operating-system project as )ackground, we have sketched a history of some of the methods by which p ople have sought to represent communicating processes in a functional program-

---

**Figure 4.**  The Miranda script defining the abstract type *message* and the type-secure *fork* function in terms of the underlying *FORK* primitive.

**%export** *message fork*

**%include** *<sys.private/changetype>*

**%include** *<sys.private/premessage>*

|| *process* and *wrapper* are synonym types, defined for convenience
|| only

*process * == [*] → [message]*

*wrapper * == * → message*

**abstype** *message*

**with** *fork* :: (*wrapper** → process *) → process ** → process *
                *→ process **

|| the implementation equations for the abstract type *message* follow

*message == premessage*

*fork parent child fail* (*a : input*)

=  *switch* (−1) = *fail input*

    *switch* 0    = *child* (*changetype input*)

    *switch n*    = *parent* (*changetype* (*SEND n*)) *input*

---

ming language. It seems to us that the scheme of William Stoye is the first that permits the description of nondeterministic behavior without violating the requirements of referential transparency. We have described our own modifications to the Stoye scheme, permitting static type security in messages, synchronous communication, and separately garbage-collected heap spaces.

The scheme described here — with some interesting further modifications (of which the most important is switching from streams to continuations for the communication mechanism) — has since been used to construct a small but complete working operating system. For further details the reader is referred to the thesis of Cupitt [4].

From a theoretical point of view an important remaining challenge is to show that equational reasoning can be applied to scripts involving *fork* in a way that allows useful inferences about the behavior of the processes.

## Acknowledgements

Much of the above design emerged during a long series of discussions with Robert Duncan (formerly of the University of Kent, now of the University of Sussex). I am extremely grateful to Robert for his inputs. In particular, the definition of *fork* in terms of *FORK* was first worked out by him. I am also grateful to John Cupitt of the University of Kent for discussions of many of the above issues. The KAOS project is supported by the Science and Engineering Research Council of Great Britain under grant number GR/D/26825. I am also indebted to ICL for financial support during the period of this research.

An earlier draft of this paper appeared in the proceedings of the first Conference on Parallel Architectures and Languages Europe (PARLE), Eindhoven, The Netherlands, June 1987 (see Lecture Notes in Computer Science, Springer-Verlag, vol. 259.).

## References

[1] Abramsky, S. and Sykes, R. "SECD-M: A virtual machine for applicative programming". In *Proceedings of the IFIP International Conference on Functional Programming Languages and Computer Architecture* (Nancy, France, September). Lecture Notes in Computer Science, vol. 201. Springer-Verlag, Berlin, 1985.

[2] Cupitt, J. "Another new scheme for writing functional operating systems". Technical Report No. 52, University of Kent Computing Laboratory, March 1988.

[3] Cupitt, J. "A brief walk through KAOS". Technical Report No. 58, University of Kent Computing Laboratory, February 1989.

[4] Cupitt, J. "The design and implementation of an operating system in a functional language". Ph.D. Thesis, University of Kent, October 1989.

[5] Duncan, R. J. "Using the Miranda screen editor MEDIT". Computing Laboratory, University of Kent, 1986.

[6] Friedman, D. P. and Wise, D. S. "Applicative multiprogramming". Technical Report 72, Computer Science Department, Indiana University, January 1978.

[7] Henderson, P. "Purely functional operating systems". In *Functional Programming and its Applications*, J. Darlington, P. Henderson, and D. Turner, eds. Cambridge University Press, 1982.

[8] Hoare, C. A. R. *Communicating Sequential Processes.* Prentice-Hall International, 1985.

[9] Jones, S. B. "Abstract machine support for purely functional operating systems". Technical Monograph 34, Programming Research Group, Oxford University, August 1983.

[10] Kahn, G. and MacQueen, D. B. "Coroutines and networks of parallel processes". In *IFIP 77*, North-Holland, Amsterdam, 1977.

[11] Milner, R. *A Calculus of Communicating Systems.* Lecture Notes in Computer Science, vol. 92. Springer-Verlag, Berlin, 1980.

[12] Milner, R. "The standard ML core language". Department of Computer Science, University of Edinburgh, October 1984.

[13] Peyton Jones, S. L. *The Implementation of Functional Programming Languages.* Prentice-Hall International, Hemel Hempstead, U.K., March 1987.

[14] Stoye, W. R. "A new scheme for writing functional operating systems". Technical Report 56, Computer Laboratory, Cambridge University, 1984.

[15] Stoye, W. R. "The implementation of functional languages using custom hardware". Ph.D. Thesis, Cambridge University, December 1985.

[16] Turner, D. A. "SASL language manual". Department of Computational Science, St. Andrews University, December 1976.

[17] Turner, D. A. "Miranda: A nonstrict functional language with polymorphic types". In *Proceedings of the IFIP International Conference on Functional Programming Languages and Computer Architecture* (Nancy, France, September). Lecture Notes in Computer Science, vol. 201. Springer-Verlag, Berlin, 1985.

[18] Turner, D. A. "An overview of Miranda". *SIGPLAN Notices*, December 1986. [Reprinted in this volume.]

# An Introduction to the Programming Language FL

## 9

**John Backus**
**John H. Williams**
**Edward L. Wimmers**
IBM Almaden Research Center

## 1 Note Added in Proof—Language Changes

The following paper was written in 1987 and describes the FL language of 1987. In the intervening years the language has been changed rather extensively, and Parts 1 and 2 of a new, completely rewritten manual [3] describing the current FL language is now available; Part 3, describing the denotational semantics of FL, is forthcoming. This manual makes obsolete the earlier preliminary manual [2] cited in this paper. Nevertheless, the present paper is a good general description of the essence of FL, and it provides a good description of the semantics of FL, which may be helpful until Part 3 of the new manual is available.

### 1.1 *Additions to FL*

The three principal changes to the language described herein are briefly described below (for details see [3]). In addition, there are a number of smaller changes and simplifications in the language that make a few details of the present paper inaccurate for the current language.

**Exceptions, Treatment of Errors**   In the earlier language all errors were semantically equivalent to bottom (undefined), and error reporting was extra linguistic. In the current version of FL, if a function is applied to an inappropriate argument and terminates, the result is an *exception* that contains information about the name of the function, the argument, and any special circumstances. All FL functions preserve exceptions; thus errors (which may be detected either at compile time or at run time) are informative as to their source. Moreover, the new language has a combining form (catch), which permits backtracking and user-defined error recovery and exception handling.

**Lambda expressions**   To simplify the definition of new combining forms and higher-order functions, lambda expressions based on FL patterns are provided.

**Operations on environments**   A complete set of operations for combining environments is provided; these make it possible for one set of definitions to make use of other definition sets in a completely general way.

## 2 *Overview*

FL is intended to be a programming language in which it is easy to write clear, concise, and efficient programs[1]. It is designed around a set of functional forms for combining existing programs to construct new ones. This emphasis on programming at the function level results in programs that have a rich mathematical structure and that may be transformed and optimized according to an underlying algebra of programs.

FL is an interactive language. It incorporates an implicitly controlled history component for dealing with input–output operations and for maintaining a persistent store. This history component provides a mechanism for the localized and disciplined handling of storage and I/O.

---

1. This chapter is a revised excerpt from a preliminary version of the FL language manual [2]. The revisions represent changes (mostly deletions) to the language described therein. Note that this preliminary manual has now been made obsolete by a new one [3].

FL programs can be higher order. In addition to the primitive combining forms provided, the language includes powerful mechanisms for defining new higher-order functions. There are primitive operators for currying functions and for lifting functions to functionals; these are useful for writing closed-form, combinatorial definitions of higher-order functions.

FL is a statically scoped language. An FL program consists of an expression together with a list of definitions to be used in evaluating that expression. A definition list entry may itself be a nested definition list that exports only some of its definitions. This provides a convenient hiding mechanism which, together with the facility for programmer defined data types, provides a powerful technique for making encapsulated type definitions. The definition of local function names is further facilitated by a powerful pattern-matching mechanism that allows patterns to be constructed out of user defined predicates.

FL has a hierarchical, dynamic type system that divides the value domain into subsets called types. The type system is based on a particular class of predicates that enables many type errors to be discovered at compile time. New data types can be implemented as tagged objects of an underlying representation type. The language is designed so that all such tagged objects are initially in the domain of FL values, thus giving the programmer a convenient, concrete way of thinking about and manipulating data types. Moreover, these tagging operations can be hidden *via* the scoping mechanism, thereby providing the capability for abstract data type definitions.

The meaning of FL programs is specified by an operational semantics that uses rewrite rules *and* by an equivalent denotational semantics that uses an unusually simple domain of values as its basis. The rewrite rule semantics employs a novel scheme for combining higher-order function definitions with call-by-value evaluation order. The denotational semantics is presented in a way that allows the programmer to think about the values denoted by expressions without having constantly to be aware of the usual mathematical complexities of the actual domains. Thus, the denotational semantics is a useful tool for the programmer as well as for the language analyst.

## 3 *Introduction*

FL is a function-level functional programming language. The key component of the language is a collection of operations called *combining forms*, operations for building new programs from old programs. These combining forms are carefully chosen to have rich, mutually distributive properties, so that programs written using one combining form as the main connective can often be transformed into an equivalent program whose main connective is some other combining form. These mutually distributive properties form the basis for an *algebra of programs,* a rich collection of identities that hold between different representations of functions in FL. This algebra of programs underlies a program transformation system, which is used both to reason about programs and to provide a basis for an optimizing compiler for FL.

In addition to the combining forms, there are three other fundamental design considerations that distinguish FL from many other programming languages:

**1.** the emphasis on function level programming,

**2.** a specific history component for handling I/O and memory,

**3.** a denotational semantics designed to be a useful tool for programmers.

### 3.1 *Function Level Programming*

The language design is based on the fundamental tenet that clarity is achieved when programs are written at the function level, i.e., by putting together existing programs to form new programs, rather than by manipulating objects and then abstracting from those objects to produce programs. This premise is embodied in the name of the language, F(unction) L(evel). For example, to define a program sumprod to compute the sum and product of two numbers, one doesn't proceed by beginning with two objects x and y, constructing the object $\langle x + y, x * y \rangle$ (note that the sequence of objects $x_1, \ldots, x_n$ is written $\langle x_1, \ldots, x_n \rangle$), and then abstracting with respect to x and y (e.g., Def sumprod $\equiv \lambda x, y.\langle x + y, x * y \rangle$), but rather by beginning with the functions + and * and by applying the combining form *construction* ([ ]), which is defined so that for any functions $f_1, \ldots, f_n$, the function $[f_1, \ldots, f_n]$ applied to x produces the *n*-element sequence whose *i*th element is $f_i$ applied to x; i.e., $[f_1, \ldots, f_n]: x = \langle f_1 : x, \ldots, f_n : x \rangle$ (note that the application of f to x is written f: x). This results in the function level definition Def sumprod $\equiv [+, *]$.

### 3.2 *I/O and Persistent Memory*

In order to accommodate interactive input and output and to facilitate the writing of programs that require persistent storage, all FL programs are required to map pairs into pairs. The first component of the pair can be any FL value, but the second component is required to be a *history:* an FL sequence that contains the current value of the file system and the current status of all input and output devices. Thus, the functionality of any FL program f is f: $\langle val, history \rangle \rightarrow \langle val', history' \rangle$.

Most of the primitive functions are completely independent of the history component and leave it unchanged. For example, tl: $\langle\langle 1, 2, 3\rangle$, history$\rangle = \langle\langle 2, 3\rangle$, history$\rangle$ no matter what the contents of history may be. These functions are called type A.

A few of the primitives depend on the contents of history but do not change the file system or the status of any device; e.g., get retrieves the most recent file system from the history. These primitives are called type B.

Finally, some primitives both depend on the contents of the history and alter it; e.g., in maps $\langle$dev, history$\rangle$ into $\langle$next_inp, history$'\rangle$, where next_inp is the next value from device dev and the history is changed to reflect the fact that dev has been read (the precise details are given in [2]). These primitives are called type C.

It is important to note that without the history as an explicit argument, a primitive such as in could not be a function, since in: reader could return different values depending on when it was called. Including the history as an explicit argument permits a functional treatment of input–output and file system fetches. This implies that *all* programs must be viewed as mapping pairs to pairs, even type A programs such as tl. However, if the history component were to be added explicitly, it would then be possible to treat it like any other object, e.g., to make multiple copies of it and to apply different operations to the various copies. Such manipulations would not be consistent with the intended use of the history component as representing *the* current status of the I/O devices and the file system.

Therefore, some methodology is required whereby exactly one history is in existence at any given time. This is accomplished in FL by making the history component *implicit*. Thus there is no possibility of FL programs treating the history in a way inconsistent with the methodology, since the history component may be accessed or changed only by built-in primitives such as get, put, in, and out, and these primitives are guaranteed to preserve the consistency of the history component.

Whenever possible in this chapter the history component will not be mentioned explicitly. For example, in the next section tl (a type A function) is discussed as though it simply mapped values to values. This suppression of the history component except where necessary for understanding a program is the result of an attempt to reintroduce the notion of an underlying state into an otherwise basically functional language in a disciplined way. Thus, this language can be viewed as an experiment in combining the convenience of languages in which dependence on an underlying state is always implicit (e.g., Pascal, PL/I, etc.) with the mathematical properties of languages in which all functional dependencies must be explicitly written when they are required by the program's specification (e.g., pure functional languages such as FP [1] and SASL [4]).

The difficulty with the entirely procedural approach of Pascal, etc., is that the underlying state is pervasive and encourages a style of programming in which essentially all programs depend on and alter the state. The undisciplined use of an underlying state and side effects results in programs that are difficult to understand and reason about. On the other hand, the difficulty with the explicitly functional approach of FP, SASL, etc., is that the increased complexity of a program's functionality becomes a notational nuisance, which masks the primary purpose of the program. For example, an interactive SASL program to correct misspelled words in a file using an (updatable) dictionary has the primary purpose of mapping an in_file to a corrected_file but has the proper functionality

⟨in_file, dictionary, keyboard⟩ →
⟨corrected_file, dictionary', screen, rest_of_keyboard⟩

(Note that the program must be given keyboard as input to receive responses to interactive queries it puts on screen, and it must return the "rest" of the keyboard input for use by subsequent programs).

FL is an attempt to combine the advantages (and avoid the problems) of these two approaches by (semantically) attaching an explicit history component to the functionality of all programs and (syntactically) suppressing consideration of that component. The success of this approach will be measured by the extent to which programmers can use the convenience of treating the history component implicitly, thus keeping their program notations uncluttered, and still be able to write clear programs. (For a comparison of the underlying algebraic properties of FL and pure FP see [5].)

### 3.3  *The Semantics of FL*

To understand a program it is sometimes convenient to think about *how* the program computes; at other times it is more convenient to consider *what* it computes. For example, to understand the temporal dependencies of I/O it may be more illuminating to describe the *process* of computation, whereas the meaning of new higher-order combining forms may be better understood by considering the functions *denoted* by those forms. For this reason, the meanings of FL programs are specified both by an operational semantics based on rewrite rules and by a complementary and precisely equivalent denotational semantics.

**The Operational Semantics**  The model of a typical computing machine consists of two parts, a computation engine (usually called a CPU) and a set of input–output and permanent storage devices (such as keyboards, screens, and disks). Similarly, the model of computation for FL consists of two parts, an expression that is worked on by the CPU and a history component that maintains a chronological record of the activities of the I/O and permanent storage devices. Computation proceeds by transforming the expression by means of rewrite rules. Initially the CPU contains rewrite rules for each of the primitive functions of the language; e.g., the rule id: $x \rightarrow x$ allows the CPU to simplify expressions containing applications of the identity function id. Other rules may be added to this initial set as the result of programmer defined functions. For example, the definition Def f $\equiv$ E results in the rule f: $x \rightarrow$ E: x being added to the set of rewrite rules that can be applied by the CPU.

The computation process (also called the rewriting or reduction process) consists of locating a subexpression that is an instance of the left-hand side of some rewrite rule and replacing it by the corresponding right-hand side. For example, the CPU will rewrite the expression ⟨id: 2, id: 3⟩ to ⟨2, 3⟩ using two applications of the rewrite rule id: $x \rightarrow x$.

As part of the computation process, evaluation of the expression will sometimes request information from or send information to an I/O device. When this occurs, an appropriate notation is added to the history stream as part of the rewriting process. For example, the expression out: ⟨'screen', 12⟩ rewrites to ⟨'screen', 12⟩ (the result of a successful output operation is just its argument), and the notation ⟨'outflag', ⟨'screen', 12⟩⟩ is added to the end of the history stream to indicate that the output 12 has occurred on the device screen. Of course, the history stream is just a formalism used in describing the rewriting process; this output event is actually implemented by printing the number 12 on the screen.

Since I/O can occur as the result of applying a rewrite rule, it is crucial that the order of rewriting be specified precisely. In order to simplify the semantics, FL is designed so that the process that locates the next subexpression to be reduced is always required to select the leftmost innermost such expression. To satisfy this requirement and to allow for the definition of recursive higher-order functions requires a novel treatment of programmer defined functions. As described above, the definition Def f $\equiv$ E results in the rule f: $x \rightarrow$ E: x being added to the set of rewrite rules. This will treat recursive definitions such as Def f $\equiv$ E(f) correctly, since the CPU will not attempt to rewrite the recursive occurrence of f within E(f) until it actually gets applied to some argument, i.e., until E(f): x gets rewritten to some expression that has f: x as the leftmost innermost subexpression.

However, if the recursive definition of a higher-order function such as Def H $\equiv$ E(H) were to produce the rewrite rule H: f $\rightarrow$ E(H): f, then in reducing an expression such as (H: f): x, the leftmost innermost reducible expression would always be located in the subexpression (H: f), and the process would diverge, forever developing the function H: f and never getting around to applying it to the argument x. To avoid this problem, definitions can be marked as being second level by writing $Def_2$ H $\equiv$ E(H). This results in the rewrite rule H: f: x $\rightarrow$ E(H): f: x. Using this rule, a higher-order function application such as H: f will not be reduced to E(H): f unless it occurs in a context where the resulting function is being applied to some argument. This device permits the convenient definition of higher-order functions within a strict (call by value) semantics.

**The Denotational Semantics** Every FL expression is considered to denote some semantic object, its *meaning*. This is the case for all syntactic objects, from the simplest such as atoms (the expression 1 has the meaning 1) to the more complex such as applications (tl: ⟨id, 3⟩ denotes ⟨3⟩). Moreover, the meaning of a compound expression is expressed as a function of the meanings of its components; in the above example, the meaning of tl is a function *tl*, which when applied to a nonempty sequence of semantic objects and a history *h* produces the tail of that sequence and the same *h* (e.g., *tl*: ⟨⟨id,3⟩, h⟩ = ⟨⟨3⟩, h⟩).

$\mathcal{H}$ is used to denote the set of all possible histories. The semantic domain $\mathcal{D}$ of FL is the smallest set that contains the element $\perp$ (representing the "undefined" element), the atoms $\mathcal{A}$, and the functions $\mathcal{F}$ (e.g., *tl* and *add*) from $\mathcal{D} \times \mathcal{H} \rightarrow \mathcal{D} \times \mathcal{H}$, and is closed under the operations of sequence formation (e.g., ⟨tl, 3⟩) and tagging with strings (e.g., ┤'gram', 17├). Strictness requires that $\perp$ cannot appear in a sequence or a tagged pair.

This domain is sufficiently rich so that the meaning of any FL expression can be given by a *meaning function* $\mu$. Just as the operational semantics deals with two components, an expression and a history, $\mu$ maps an expression and a history into a meaning and a history; i.e., the functionality of $\mu$ is

$$\mu:\ \text{expr} \times \mathcal{H} \rightarrow \mathcal{D} \times \mathcal{H}.$$

The history component can be conveniently thought of as a (potentially) infinite sequence of objects from $\mathcal{D}$. For example, $\mu$(out: ⟨'screen', add: ⟨1, 2⟩⟩, h) = ⟨⟨'screen', 3⟩, h'⟩ where h' is h with ⟨'outflag', ⟨'screen', 3⟩⟩ appended to the end.

(Note to language specialists: Special care has been taken to design $\mathcal{D}$ so that simple concepts have simple representations. Retracts, isomorphisms, and inverse limits are not required in order to understand the meaning of sequences. The machinery to make the domain mathematically sound is hidden in the representation of functions like *tl*, where the programmer needn't be concerned with them. Concentrating the set theoretic machinations of the domain within the function representations complicates their mathematical structure, but it results in a domain that is a natural, intuitively appealing tool that programmers can use to understand and reason about their programs.)

Because $\mathcal{D}$ is closed under tagging, it contains representations for all the new data objects that might ever be defined in FL programs. This provides programmers with a convenient mental representation for expressions that evaluate to (abstract) data types without requiring them to think of such expressions as denoting function closures or special hiding mechanisms in the semantic domain.

### 3.4 *Examples of FL Programs*

In presenting these examples, language constructs are used without giving complete definitions or descriptions of them in the hope that seeing a few sample programs will serve to give the flavor of the language (and to motivate the following section in which the language is described precisely). Each example consists of a program, an instance of its use, and some brief comments.

**1.** A program to compute the sum and product of two numbers.

   $[+, *]$

   $[+, *] : \langle 2, 3 \rangle \rightarrow \langle +: \langle 2, 3 \rangle, *: \langle 2, 3 \rangle \rangle \rightarrow \langle 5, 6 \rangle.$

   This program uses the combining form *construction* ([ ]) which is defined so that in general $[f_1, \ldots, f_n] : x \rightarrow \langle f_1 : x, \ldots, f_n : x \rangle.$

**2.** A simple function definition.

   Def second $\equiv$ s1 $\circ$ tl

   second: $\langle 2, 3, 4 \rangle \rightarrow$ (s1 $\circ$ tl): $\langle 2, 3, 4 \rangle \rightarrow$ ( $\circ$: $\langle$s1, tl$\rangle$): $\langle 2, 3, 4 \rangle \rightarrow$ s1 : (tl: $\langle 2, 3, 4 \rangle) \rightarrow$ s1: $\langle 3, 4 \rangle \rightarrow 3.$

   In general si is the primitive function that selects the $i$th element of a sequence, and *tl* is the primitive function that returns all but the first element of a sequence. Thus second is defined to be the same as the primitive s2. This is a simple example of the use of infix notation in expressions. The functional $\circ$ (which is defined so that ($\circ$: $\langle$f, g$\rangle$): x = f: (g: x)) is applied to the two arguments s1 and tl. In general, f op g means op: $\langle$f, g$\rangle$.

**3.** A recursive factorial program.

> Def fact ≡ id = ˜0 → ˜1; id ∗ fact ∘ subl
>
> fact: 5 → 120

The fact function is built by applying the combining forms *composition* (∘), *constant* ( ˜ ), and *conditional* to the primitive functions =, id, ∗, and the (recursive) function name fact. As noted above, composition is defined so that (f ∘ g): x = f: (g: x). Constant is defined so that ˜x: y = x (provided that y terminates), and conditional is defined so that (p → f; g): x = f: x if p: x is true, and g: x otherwise. Thus, fact: 5 rewrites to 5 ∗ (fact: 4)(since 5 = 0 is false), etc.

**4.** Another version of factorial.

> ∗ ∘ ints_to
>
> ∗ ∘ ints_to : 5 → ∗: (ints_to: 5) → ∗:⟨1, 2, 3, 4, 5⟩ → 120

ints_to is a primitive function such that ints_to: n = ⟨1, ..., n⟩ provided n is a positive integer. Note that ∗ maps a sequence of numbers into the product of those numbers (∗:⟨⟩ = 1).

**5.** A program to compute the length of a sequence.

> + ∘ α:˜ 1
>
> (+ ∘ α:˜ 1) : ⟨a, b, c⟩ → + : (α: ˜1:⟨a, b, c⟩)
> → +:⟨˜1: a, ˜1: b, ˜1: c⟩ → +:⟨1, 1, 1⟩ → 3

This program works by simply replacing each element of the sequence by a 1 and then adding them up. The combining form α (for *apply to all*) is defined so that (α: f) : ⟨$x_1$, ..., $x_n$⟩ = ⟨f: $x_1$, ..., f: $x_n$⟩. Note that : associates to the left (i.e., x: y: z = (x: y): z) so that α: ˜1: a means (α: ˜1): a.

**6.** A program to compute the average of a sequence of numbers.

> Def ave ≡ (+ ÷ length where Def length ≡ + ∘ α: ˜1 end)
>
> ave:⟨3, 4, 8⟩ → (+ ÷ length) : ⟨3, 4, 8⟩ → (+:⟨3, 4, 8⟩) ÷ (length : ⟨3, 4, 8⟩) →
> 15 ÷ 3 → 5

Any expression (in this case the right-hand side of the definition of ave) can have an associated list of definitions (in this case the single definition Def length ≡ + ∘ α: ˜1). Such definitions are *local*; i.e., their scope of definition is limited to the expression to which they are attached.

**7.** An order n log n sorting program.

$$\text{Def sort} \equiv \text{tree}: \langle \text{merge}, \langle\rangle \rangle \circ \alpha: [\text{id}]$$

$$\text{sort}: \langle 8, 4, 2, 3 \rangle \;\rightarrow\; (\text{tree}: \langle \text{merge}, \langle\rangle \rangle \circ \alpha : [\text{id}]) : \langle 8, 4, 2, 3 \rangle$$
$$\rightarrow \text{tree}: \langle \text{merge}, \langle\rangle \rangle : (\alpha: [\text{id}]: \langle 8, 4, 2, 3 \rangle)$$
$$\rightarrow \text{tree}: \langle \text{merge}, \langle\rangle \rangle : \langle\langle 8\rangle, \langle 4\rangle, \langle 2\rangle, \langle 3\rangle\rangle$$
$$\rightarrow \text{merge}: \langle \text{merge}: \langle\langle 8\rangle, \langle 4\rangle\rangle, \text{merge}: \langle\langle 2\rangle, \langle 3\rangle\rangle\rangle$$
$$\rightarrow \text{merge}: \langle\langle 4, 8\rangle, \langle 2, 3\rangle\rangle \rightarrow \langle 2, 3, 4, 8 \rangle$$

tree is a primitive combining form that takes a function and an object and produces a function such that $\text{tree}: \langle f, z\rangle: \langle x_1, \ldots, x_n\rangle$ rewrites to z if $n = 0$, $x_1$ if $n = 1$, and $f: \langle \text{tree}: \langle f, z\rangle: \langle x_1, \ldots, x_m\rangle, \text{tree}: \langle f, z\rangle: \langle x_{m+1}, \ldots, x_n\rangle\rangle$ if $n > 1$ (where $m = \text{ceil}: (n \div 2)$). merge is a primitive function that merges two sorted sequences of numbers into a single sorted sequence; e.g., $\text{merge}: \langle\langle 3, 6\rangle, \langle 1, 3, 5\rangle\rangle = \langle 1, 3, 3, 5, 6\rangle$. (Notice that $\alpha: [\text{id}]$ maps an *n*-element sequence into a sequence of $n$ singleton sequences.)

**8.** A program for doing a "protected" divide.

$$\text{Def safediv}_1 \equiv \text{ispair} \rightarrow ((\text{isnum} \circ \text{s1} \wedge (\text{isnum} \wedge \text{not} \circ \text{iszero}) \circ \text{s2}) \rightarrow \text{s1} \div \text{s2}; \; \sim \text{`diverror'}); \; \sim \text{`diverror'}$$

$$\text{safediv}_1 : \langle 8, 4\rangle \rightarrow 2$$

$$\text{safediv}_1 : \langle 8, 4, 2\rangle \rightarrow \text{`diverror'} \;\; (\text{since } \langle 8, 4, 2\rangle \text{ is not a pair})$$

$$\text{safediv}_1 : \langle 8, 0\rangle \rightarrow \text{`diverror'} \;\; (\text{since } \text{s2}: \langle 8, 0\rangle \text{ is } 0)$$

safediv first checks that its argument is a pair, then that the first element of the pair is a number and the second element of the pair is a nonzero number; if so, it divides the first by the second, otherwise it returns `diverror`.

**9.** An equivalent program that uses a *pattern* to create function names for the arguments.

$$\text{Def safediv}_2 \equiv [\![ \text{n., m.} ]\!] \rightarrow ((\text{isnum} \circ \text{n} \wedge (\text{isnum} \wedge \text{not} \circ \text{iszero}) \circ \text{m}) \rightarrow \text{n} \div \text{m}; \; \sim \text{`diverror'}); \; \sim \text{`diverror'}$$

$$\text{safediv}_2 : \langle 8, 4\rangle \rightarrow 2$$

$$\text{safediv}_2 : \langle 8, 4, 2\rangle \rightarrow \text{`diverror'} \;\; (\text{since } \langle 8, 4, 2\rangle \text{ fails to match the pattern } [\![ \text{n., m.} ]\!])$$

$$\text{safediv}_2 : \langle 8, 0\rangle \rightarrow \text{`diverror'} \;\; (\text{since } \text{not} \circ \text{iszero is false for m})$$

The pattern mechanism is defined so that $\text{safediv}_2$ is just a notational shorthand for $\text{safediv}_1$. That is, the pattern $[\![ \text{n., m.} ]\!]$ produces a predicate that tests for the structure of the pattern (ispair in this case) and also defines the function names indicated by "." (n and m in this case) to be selector functions that correspond to their places in the structure (in this case s1 and s2, respectively). These resulting function definitions are local; their scope is limited to the "true" and "false" arms of the conditional.

**10.** Another equivalent version of safediv that uses embedded predicates within the pattern.

Def safediv$_3$ ≡ ⟦n.isnum, m.isnum ∧ not ∘ iszero⟧ → n ÷ m; ˜ 'diverror'

safediv$_3$ : ⟨8, 4⟩ → 2

safediv$_3$ : ⟨8, 0⟩ → 'diverror' (the pattern fails to match, since not ∘ iszero is false for 0)

Again, the pattern mechanism is defined so that safediv$_3$ is exactly equivalent to safediv$_1$. To match a pattern with embedded predicates, not only must the argument have the proper structure, but its (sub)components must match the corresponding predicates as well. This ability to embed predicates in patterns greatly increases the usefulness of the pattern-matching mechanism for writing terse, easy to read function definitions. Note that the precedence of the infix operators ., ∧, and ∘ is such that m.isnum ∧ not ∘ iszero means m.(isnum ∧ (not ∘ iszero))

**11.** An interactive program to prompt for two numbers and print their sum.

Def adder ≡ out_screen ∘ (˜ 'sum = ' ++ + ∘getnums)

    where

        Def out_screen ≡ out ∘ [˜ 'screen', id]

        Def getnums ≡ [prompt ∘ ˜ 'enter a' ,

          prompt ∘ ˜ 'enter b' ]

        Def prompt ≡ in ∘ ˜ 'keyboard' ∘ out ∘

          [˜ 'screen', id]

    end

        {(This is a comment) ++ catenates strings}

adder : 'x'

    → (out_screen ∘ (˜ 'sum = ' ++ + ∘ getnums)): 'x'

→ out_screen: (++: ⟨ 'sum = ' , +: (getnums: 'x' )⟩)

→ out_screen: (++: ⟨ 'sum = ' , +: ⟨prompt: 'enter a' ,
  prompt: 'enter b' ⟩⟩)

→ out_screen: (++: ⟨ 'sum = ' , +: ⟨1, prompt: 'enter b' ⟩⟩)

> (assuming that the user types 1 in response to the
> prompt message enter a)

→ out_screen: (++: ⟨ 'sum = ' , +: ⟨1, 2⟩⟩)

> (assuming that the user types 2 in response to the
> prompt message enter b)

→ out_screen: (++: ⟨ 'sum = ' , 3⟩)

→ out_screen: 'sum = 3'

→ (out ∘ [~ 'screen' , id]): 'sum = 3'

→ out: ⟨ 'screen' , 'sum = 3' ⟩

→ ⟨ 'screen' , 'sum = 3' ⟩ (and sum = 3 appears on the screen)

This program is independent of the value to which it is applied ('x'
in this case). Its real purpose is to prompt for two numbers and
output their sum. out is a primitive function that, when applied to
a pair ⟨devicename, x⟩, evaluates to ⟨devicename, x⟩ and causes x to
be written on the output device named devicename. in is a primitive function that, when applied to an argument devicename, reads
the next input token from the device named devicename and evaluates to that input token. Thus, prompt : 'enter a' rewrites to (in ∘
~ 'keyboard' ): (out: ⟨ 'screen' , 'enter a' ⟩), which rewrites to (in ∘~
'keyboard' ): ⟨ 'screen' , 'enter a' ⟩), which writes enter a on the device named 'screen' . This latter expression then rewrites to in:
'keyboard' , which gets the next input from the device named
'keyboard' and rewrites to that input value. Note that ++, the
primitive for catenating strings, will coerce nonstring arguments
(in this case the integer 3) into strings automatically. Like the primitives + and *, ++ is *multilevel*; i.e., when applied to *objects* it performs the catenation function, but when applied to *functions* (e.g.,
++: ⟨f, g⟩), it rewrites to ++ ∘[f, g], thus avoiding the need to do explicit lifting (see Section 3). Text enclosed in { } pairs is a comment
and is lexically equivalent to a blank space.

## 4 *Simple Programs*

To describe the syntax and semantics of FL expressions, it is convenient to proceed in stages, beginning with a primitive kernel language called *core expressions*, whose syntax and semantics are easily described. Although it is universal (in the sense that any computable function is expressible in it), this kernel is extremely Spartan and has no concessions to ease of programming or readability. In fact, it doesn't even contain the notion of auxiliary program definitions; all core expressions must be written solely in terms of primitive functions.

The first step in enriching core expressions is to include some convenient syntactic abbreviations for some of the commonly occurring forms and to allow expressions to be built up from programmer defined functions as well as primitive functions. Such enriched expressions are called *simple expressions*, which when combined with a simple list of declarations for programmer defined functions (known as a *simple declaration list*), becomes a *simple program*, i.e., an expression of the form simple_expr where simple_decl_list end.

Simple programs form a conceptually appealing half-way point in the development of complete FL expressions. They provide the programmer with a sufficiently rich syntax so that most small to medium sized programs can be expressed clearly and conveniently as simple programs, and, at the same time, allow the continued use of the relatively straightforward semantic techniques for core expressions in reasoning about programs.

Finally, simple programs are extended to allow declarations to be nested within expressions and other declaration lists and to allow function definitions to create local "names" for their arguments. These extensions result in the collection of full FL *expressions*; an FL program is such an expression. Rather than enhance the semantic mechanisms to handle such issues as definition hiding and nested scopes, the semantics of full FL is given by first describing how to map all FL expressions to their core expression equivalents and then applying the easy to understand semantics of core expressions.

The description of this development is divided into two sections. The development up through simple programs is given in this section, and the remainder is given in Section 4. The rest of this section is organized into the following subsections:

**1.** The Syntax of Core Expressions

**2.** The Semantics of Core Expressions

**3.** Simple Expressions

**4.** Simple Programs

## 4.1 *The Syntax of Core Expressions*

A *core expression* is (recursively) one of the following:

**1.** An atom (which may be a char, a number, or a truth value)

**2.** A primitive function name

**3.** ? (which is used to indicate an error)

**4.** A sequence. If $x_1, \ldots, x_m$ are core expressions, then the *sequence* $\langle x_1, \ldots, x_m \rangle$ is a core expression. The empty sequence $\langle \rangle$ is a core expression. A sequence of chars is called a *string*, which may be abbreviated as described below.

**5.** An application. If $x_1, x_2$ are core expressions, then the *application* $x_1 : x_2$ is a core expression.

**6.** A tagged pair. If $x_1$ is a string and $x_2$ is a core expression, then the *tagged pair* $\dashv x_1, x_2 \vdash$ is a core expression.

Expressions may contain comments (described below). The following describes the syntax of atoms, function names, abbreviations for strings, and comments.

**Atoms** The set of *atoms* is the union of three disjoint sets: the chars, the numbers, and the truth values.

A *char* is any single printable letter, symbol, or punctuation mark preceded by the double quote symbol ("). For example, "a and "" are chars.

A *number* has the form sIFE where s represents a sign and is either +, −, or empty, I represents an integer and is a string of (zero or more) digits (0 through 9), F represents a fractional part and is either empty or a period (.) followed by a string of (zero or more) digits, and E represents an exponent and is either empty or an (upper- or lower-case) e followed by something of the form sI. At least one of the strings I or F in sIFE must have at least one digit. For example, −40500e − 2 is the integer −405, 3. is the integer 3, and −.2056E1 is the real number −2.056.

A *truth value* is one of the symbols <u>true</u> or <u>false</u>.

A sequence that is a *string* may be abbreviated by juxtaposing the chars in the sequence and removing the double quote marks. For example, ⟨"a, "b⟩ is abbreviated 'ab'. The symbol " is used as an escape character so that ' or " may appear in a string. For example, ⟨"a, "', "", "b⟩

is abbreviated `a"′ ""b′`. Note that ⟨⟩ and `''` both denote the empty string (i.e., the empty sequence).

**Function Names**  A *function name* is either one of the symbols

$$\circ + * \div - = \leq < \geq >) \neq /\backslash \vdash \dashv \wedge \vee ++$$

or the juxtaposition of one or more of the following:

all upper- or lower-case Roman letters,

all upper- or lower-case Greek letters,

the digits 0, 1, . . ., 9,

the special characters !, \$, ¢, %, #, ¬, ∇, □, –,

provided that the initial character is not a digit. There are about 70 primitive functions in FL. The complete list is given in [2].

**Comments**  A *comment* is any sequence of characters and/or symbols enclosed in braces { }. Comments may be nested. A comment may appear anywhere in an expression that a blank space may appear; lexically it is equivalent to a blank space.

**Objects**  It is useful to identify a special subset of core expressions. An *object* is an atom or (recursively) a sequence of objects.

### 4.2  *The Semantics of Core Expressions*

**The Denotational Semantics**  The *meaning* of a core expression is provided by the denotational semantics of FL. Section 2 has already explained how the meaning function $\mu$ maps a pair (expr,$h$) into $(d_1, h_1)$, where $h$ is the initial history that provides the I/O and file system environment in which the expression expr is to be evaluated, and $d_1$ and $h_1$ are the element of the semantic domain $\mathcal{D}$ and the set of histories $\mathcal{H}$, respectively, that result from evaluating the expression expr with the history $h$.

The semantic domain $\mathcal{D}$ for FL is unusual in that it actually *contains* the set $\mathcal{A}$ of atoms, not some isomorphic image of them. (But $\mathcal{A}$ contains only the "canonical forms" of numbers.) Thus $\mathcal{D}$ contains the set of atoms, $\mathcal{A}$, an isomorphic copy of the set $\mathcal{F}$ of "good" functions that map $\mathcal{D} \times \mathcal{H}$ into itself, and $\perp$, and it is closed under sequence formation and tagging with strings. $\mathcal{H}$ is the set of all "semantic histories", i.e., those that contain the semantic counterparts of values (e.g., the semantic counterpart of the function value id is the mathematical function *id* such that $id(d, h) = (d, h)$; the counterpart of the string value 'abc' is just that string itself). The following gives, informally, the denotational semantics of core expressions.

The meaning of an atom is the canonical form of that atom. (Every non-number atom is in canonical form; every number has a canonical form, which is a number.)

The meaning of a function name corresponds to a function from $\mathcal{D} \times \mathcal{H}$ into itself. For example, the meaning of tl is the function *tl*, where $tl(\langle x_1, \ldots, x_n\rangle, h) = (\langle x_2, \ldots, x_n\rangle, h)$

The meaning of ? is $\perp$.

The meaning of the sequence $\langle x_1, \ldots, x_n\rangle$ is the sequence of the meanings of its components except in the case that one of the components has meaning $\perp$. More formally, $\mu(\langle x_1, \ldots, x_n\rangle, h_1) = (\langle y_1, \ldots, y_n\rangle, h_{n+1})$ where $\mu(x_i, h_i) = (y_i, h_{i+1})$, provided no $y_i$ is $\perp$. If some $y_i = \perp$, then $\mu(\langle x_1, \ldots, x_n\rangle, h_1) = (\perp, h_{k+1})$ provided $y_k = \perp$ and $y_j \neq \perp$ for $j < k$.

The meaning of the application $x_1 : x_2$ is the result of applying the function that is the meaning of $x_1$ to the meaning of $x_2$. More formally, $\mu(x_1 : x_2, h_1) = y_1(y_2, h_3)$ provided $y_1$ is a function (mapping $\mathcal{D} \times \mathcal{H}$ to itself) where $\mu(x_i, h_i) = (y_i, h_{i+1})$. If $y_1$ is not a function and not $\perp$, then $\mu(x_1 : x_2, h_1) = (\perp, h_3)$. If $y_1 = \perp$, then $\mu(x_1 : x_2, h_1) = (\perp, h_2)$.

The meaning of the tagged pair $\dashv x_0, x_1 \vdash$ is the meaning of $x_1$ tagged by $x_0$. (Recall that $x_0$ must be a string.) More formally, $\mu(\dashv x_0, x_1 \vdash, h_1) = (\dashv x_0, y_1\vdash, h_2)$ where $\mu(x_1, h_1) = (y_1, h_2)$. Tagged pairs may be created only by the rewriting system itself and may *not* be written by the programmer (since tagged pairs are designed for use in the implementation of data types).

### *The Operational Semantics of Core Expressions*

**The Operational Semantics of Core Expressions** The operational semantics of FL is based on a rewriting process. In such a process, an expression is rewritten to another according to a set of rewrite rules. This process continues until it is not possible to rewrite the expression any further. An expression that cannot be rewritten is called a *value* and represents the (fully evaluated) "answer" for the original expression. As a consequence of the rewrite rules for FL, every atom is a value, any sequence all of whose components are values is a value, and any tagged pair with a value as its second component is a value. The only other kind of values are irreducible function expressions (i.e., expressions to which no rewrite rules apply and whose meanings are functions) such as $\circ : \langle tl, tl\rangle$. An expression x is said to have the value v iff v is a value and x rewrites to v. Not all expressions have values since it is possible for the rewriting process to continue forever; in this case, the expression has meaning $\perp$.

The rewriting process is *sound*: it preserves the (denotational) meaning of expressions. If $e_1$ can be rewritten to $e_2$, then the meaning of $e_2$ is the same as the meaning of $e_1$; moreover, if $e_2$ is an object, then it *is* the meaning of $e_1$ (provided numbers are in canonical form). Furthermore, the rewriting process is *complete*; this implies that if the meaning of $e_1$ is the object $e_2$, then the rewriting process will rewrite $e_1$ to $e_2$.

The rewriting process consists of locating a redex (i.e., a subexpression matching the left-hand side of some rewrite rule), replacing it by the corresponding right-hand side, and repeating until there are no more redexes in the final expression. For example, the rewrite rule for the identity function id is id: $x \to x$, indicating that the function id when applied to the value x rewrites to x. Another example of a rewrite rule is cons: $\langle f_1, \ldots, f_n \rangle: x \to \langle f_1 : x, \ldots, f_n : x \rangle$ indicating that cons when applied to a sequence of n functions yields a function that always produces a sequence of length n as its answer.

Since the evaluation of an expression can require I/O operations, it is important to specify the order in which the rewrite rules are applied. The redex chosen is always the leftmost innermost redex. This requires that all proper subexpressions of the left-hand side of a rewrite rule be values and that rewriting be done left to right. So in order to rewrite $x_k$ in the expression $\langle x_1, \ldots, x_n \rangle$, it is necessary that each $x_i$ be a value for $i = 1, \ldots, k-1$. Similarly, in order to rewrite $x_2$ in the expression $x_1 : x_2$, it is necessary that $x_1$ be a value. So, for example, the expression $\langle \text{out}: \langle \text{`screen'}, \text{`hi'} \rangle, \text{out}: \langle \text{`screen'}, \text{`bye'} \rangle \rangle$ is first rewritten to $\langle\langle \text{`screen'}, \text{`hi'} \rangle, \text{out}: \langle \text{`screen'}, \text{`bye'} \rangle \rangle$ causing "hi" to appear on the screen and then is rewritten to $\langle\langle \text{`screen'}, \text{`hi'} \rangle, \langle \text{`screen'}, \text{`bye'} \rangle \rangle$ causing "bye" to appear on the screen. This final expression is a value.

The complete list of the rewrite rules and an informal description of all the primitive functions are given in [2]. In general, these functions act by rewriting the expression and adding some notations (if appropriate) to the history stream to indicate their actions.

The rewriting process has been presented as one of rewriting expressions. However, the purpose of this process is to transform a pair (expr, hist) into (expr$_1$, hist$_1$), since the rewriting of expr may involve a history change. The pair transformation associated with any rewrite rule is just that of applying the rule to rewrite expr to obtain expr$_1$ and to make any additions to hist that the rule requires to obtain hist$_1$. For example, $(\langle \text{id}: 3, 4 \rangle, \text{hist})$ is transformed by the rewrite rule for id into $(\langle 3, 4 \rangle, \text{hist})$. Observe that, if e is an expression that does I/O but rewrites forever, then $(e, h)$ will have the meaning $(\perp, h_1)$ and the (potentially infinite) history $h_1$ is an accurate record of the I/O activity of e.

As a result of the rewrite rule $? \to ?$, once the rewriting process causes ? to appear in an expression, the rewriting process will forever rewrite ? to itself. Thus, ? has meaning $\perp$ and is used to indicate that some sort of error has occurred. For example, the whole sequence $\langle a, ?\rangle$ has meaning $\perp$ (and rewrites to itself forever) since its second component (?) has meaning $\perp$(and rewrites to itself forever). Error handling is an extra-language notion, and the exact manner in which errors are handled is implementation-dependent. It is envisioned that implementations will handle errors by informing the user about the nature of each error.

## 4.3 *Simple Expressions*

Although the primitive functions provided in [2] are sufficient to express any computable function, it is important to have a more convenient notation for expressing functions. Therefore, the language provides special notations for some of the commonly used combining forms, and it provides a convention for infix notation, designed to improve the readability of function expressions. In addition, to reduce the need for parenthetical groupings, the language also employs precedence conventions for these special forms. (All the rewrite rules for these combining forms can be found in [2].)

### *Special Notation for Combining Forms*

1. **Prime:** $f'$ abbreviates lift: $f$ and is useful in infix notation (see below). For example, $f': \langle x, y\rangle$ has the same meaning as both $x f' y$ and $f \circ [x, y]$.

2. **Construction:** $[^{(n)}f_1, \ldots, f_m]$ abbreviates $cons^{(n)}: \langle f_1, \ldots, f_m \rangle$ where the superscript $n$ indicates the number of primes. Thus, $[f_1, \ldots, f_m]: x$ rewrites to $\langle f_1 : x, \ldots, f_m : x\rangle$.

3. **Predicate-Construction:** $[\![^{(n)}f_1, \ldots, f_m]\!]$ abbreviates $pcons^{(n)}: \langle f_1, \ldots, f_m\rangle$ where the superscript $n$ indicates the number of primes. Predicate-construction is a predicate combining form such that $[\![f_1, \ldots, f_m]\!]$ is true just for sequences of length $m$ whose elements satisfy, one-for-one, the predicates $f_i$. Thus, $[\![f_1, \ldots, f_m]\!]: \langle x_1, \ldots, x_k\rangle$ rewrites to and: $\langle f_1 : x_1, \ldots, f_m: x_m\rangle$, provided $m = k$; otherwise if $m \neq k$ it rewrites to <u>false</u>. The expression and: $\langle f_1: x_1, \ldots, f_m: x_m\rangle$ rewrites to <u>true</u> provided no $f_i: x$ is <u>false</u>; otherwise it rewrites to <u>false</u>.

4. **Constant:** $\tilde{}x$ abbreviates $K: x$. Thus, $\tilde{}2$ abbreviates $K: 2$, and $\tilde{}$ `abc` : y rewrites to `abc` (provided y does not have meaning $\perp$).

5. **Conditional:** $(p \rightarrow^{(n)} f; g)$ abbreviates $cond^{(n)}: \langle p, f, g\rangle$ where the superscript $n$ indicates the number of primes. Informally,

$$(p \rightarrow f; g): x = \begin{cases} f: x & \text{if } p: x \neq \underline{\text{false}} \text{ or ?} \\ g: x & \text{if } p: x = \underline{\text{false}} \\ ? & \text{otherwise} \end{cases}$$

Because it occurs so frequently, FL also allows $p \rightarrow f$ as an abbreviation for $(p \rightarrow f; err)$. (This produces a "dangling else" phenomenon, which is resolved below in the discussion of precedence conventions.) Note that conditional allows predicates $p$ such that $p: x$ is true if it is any value except $\underline{\text{false}}$, and false only if it is $\underline{\text{false}}$. However, all primitive predicates yield $\underline{\text{true}}$ or $\underline{\text{false}}$.

**Multilevel Functions**  For a few commonly used functions $f$ whose arguments are always sequences of *objects* (e.g., +), it is useful to extend their domain to include sequences of functions by adding the rewrite rule

$$f: \langle g_1, \ldots, g_n \rangle \rightarrow f \circ [g_1, \ldots, g_n] \text{ if all the } g_i\text{'s are } \textit{functions}.$$

With this extension $f$ is called a *multilevel* function; for example, + is multilevel, so that if $g$ and $h$ are functions, then $+: \langle g, h \rangle: x = + \circ [g, h]: x = +: \langle g: x, h: x \rangle$. Multilevel functions are particularly convenient in connection with infix notation as described below. The multilevel functions are: $+ - * \div < \leq > \geq$ ++.

**Infix Notation**  In addition to the extensions described so far, the language includes a convention for infix notation in which op: $\langle f, g \rangle$ can be written simply $f$ op $g$. Thus, $\circ: \langle \circ: \langle f, g \rangle, h \rangle$ can be expressed in the more legible form, $f \circ g \circ h$. (The primitive $\circ$, composition, has the rewrite rule $\circ: \langle f_1, \ldots, f_n \rangle: x \rightarrow f_1: (f_2: \ldots (f_n: x) \ldots)$; rules for the precedence and associativity of infix functions are described below.) Since + and other common functions are multilevel functions, the following properties of such infix operations apply (using + as an example):

$$1 + 2 = 3 \text{ since } 1 + 2 = +: \langle 1, 2 \rangle$$

$$(f + g): x = f: x + g: x \text{ if } f \text{ and } g \text{ are functions}.$$

**Precedence**  All of the abbreviations just introduced have a precedence. The precedence rules are realized by fully parenthesizing an arbitrary expression in accordance with the following precedence list. The parenthesizing algorithm is: find the smallest, leftmost, nonparenthesized subexpression that has the form of the first entry in the precedence list (i.e., e ') and put parentheses around it; repeat until all subexpressions with the given form have been parenthesized. The algorithm then repeats this process for each entry in the precedence list in order, except that for the conditional entry, the search is for the smallest *rightmost* nonparenthesized conditional. (Thus all the forms are left associative except conditional, which is right associative.)

$e'$

$e_1 : e_2$

$\tilde{}e$

$e_1 \circ e_2$

$e_1 * e_2$ or $e_1 \div e_2$

$e_1 + e_2$ or $e_1 - e_2$

$e_1 = e_2$

$e_1 \mapsto e_2$ or $e_1 \dashv$ (See Patterns in the next section for the definitions of $\mapsto$ and $\dashv$.)

$e_1 \wedge e_2$ or $e_1 \vee e_2$

$e_1\ e_2\ e_3$ provided this form is not covered by any other case

$p \rightarrow f, g$ or $p \rightarrow f$ (This is the only right-associative case.)

$e_1$ where dl endlet dl in $e_1$

$fn \equiv e_1$

Some examples of parenthesized expressions:

| Before Parenthesizing | After Parenthesizing |
|---|---|
| $a \rightarrow b; c \rightarrow d; e$ | $(a \rightarrow b; (c \rightarrow d; e))$ |
| $a \rightarrow b; c \rightarrow d$ | $(a \rightarrow b; (c \rightarrow d))$ |
| $a \rightarrow b \rightarrow c; d$ | $(a \rightarrow (b \rightarrow c; d))$ |
| $a \rightarrow b \rightarrow c$ | $(a \rightarrow (b \rightarrow c))$ |
| $f + g = \tilde{}h' \circ k$ | $((f + g) = ((\tilde{}(h')) \circ k))$ |

**Simple Expressions** The *simple expressions* are just the core expressions with two differences:

1. All function names are allowed in simple expressions rather than just the primitive function names.

2. All the special notation described in this subsection is allowed in simple expressions.

Thus, the simple expressions are a superset of the core expressions.

## 4.4 *Simple Programs*

**Simple Declaration Lists** A simple declaration list has the form

$$\text{Def } g_1 \equiv e_1 \; \ldots \; \text{Def } g_n \equiv e_n$$

where $e_1, \ldots, e_n$ are simple expressions and $g_1, \ldots, g_n$ are distinct function names. Def $g \equiv e$ is a *definition* that defines g. (Other kinds of declarations and additional ways of making definitions are introduced in Section 4.) The definitions in the declaration list may be (mutually) recursive. For example, Def fact $\equiv$ id $=\tilde{\ }0 \rightarrow\tilde{\ }1$; id $*$ fact $\circ$ subl recursively defines the factorial function (where subl is the function that subtracts one).

**Simple Programs** A *simple program* has one of three forms:

e

e where deflist end

let deflist in e

where e is a simple expression and deflist is a simple declaration list. The last two are equivalent.

Since simple programs are a superset of core expressions, it is natural to extend the semantics of core expressions to handle simple programs. This can be done by adding new rewrite rules for each of the function names defined in the simple declaration list; i.e., the definition Def f $\equiv$ e in deflist produces the rule f: x $\rightarrow$ e: x. The value of e where deflist end can then be obtained by rewriting e with this augmented set of rewrite rules. Such an extension provides a conceptually simple treatment of the semantics of simple programs and is correct provided that the program evaluates to an object and that only objects are read from or written into the history. However, simple programs can contain operations that do not satisfy this proviso.

***The Representation of Functions*** If a program outputs a function, exactly how will it be represented? If a function is printed, how will it appear? For example, if the simple program out:⟨'printer', f⟩ where Def f ≡ tl end causes "f" to be printed, that might be meaningful to the writer of the program, who might know that f denotes the function tl. However, if the representation f were used to store that function in the file system and later that representation were to be recalled and applied to form f: x in another program with a different definition list, then the function applied to x might not be the same as the one originally stored.

Such considerations make it necessary to represent a function as an expression that is not context dependent, i.e., that has no free function names. Therefore, in the above example, instead of the expression f, the expression f where Def f ≡ tl end would be printed.

This completes the development of simple programs. In fact, most of the examples in Section 2 were written using simple programs.

## 5 *Additional Language Constructs*

This section contains features useful for higher-order programming as well as useful ways for defining functions. As with simple programs, rather than extend the operational and denotational semantics to cover these new features, their meaning is in terms of their core expression equivalents.

### 5.1 *Patterns*

It often happens that one wants to write a conditional that tests whether an argument has a particular structure, and if so, to apply a function to the various components of that structure. This can be accomplished using the primitive selector functions, but it is convenient to have a mechanism that at once tests for structure *and* permits the local definition of functions for accessing those components. For this reason the language provides an additional syntactic construct, *patterns*, which can appear only in the first position of a conditional. Thus conditional is extended to include the form pattern → $e_1$ ; $e_2$.

A pattern is a structured expression that (a) denotes a predicate that is true for arguments whose structure is similar to that of the pattern, and (b) defines function names to select argument elements whose positions in the argument are those of the defined function names in the pattern. For example, the pattern ⟦x.isstring, ⟦y.isint, z.isint⟧ ⟧ tests its argument to make sure it is a pair whose first element is a string and whose second is a pair of integers. The functions x, y, and z are defined by the pattern (indicated by

".") to be functions that select the parts of their argument that occupy the same positions that they themselves occupy in the pattern. Thus the pattern denotes the predicate ⟦isstring, ⟦isint, isint⟧ ⟧ and makes the definitions Def x ≡ s1, Def y ≡ s1 ∘ s2, and Def z ≡ s2 ∘ s2. The predicate denoted by a pattern is called its *predicate part*, and the set of definitions it makes is called its *definition part*.

The most elementary patterns define a function name; thus the pattern x. denotes the identically true predicate T and defines x to be the identity function id. The pattern x.isint denotes the predicate isint and defines x to be id. Compound patterns are built from elementary ones using *predicate combining forms*. A pattern can also be built by composing a pattern with a function. (See the following table that gives the predicate and definition parts for patterns.)

The predicate combining forms are: ⟦...⟧ (predicate-construction), ↦ (predicate append left), ⊣ (predicate append right), and ∧ (Boolean and). ⟦$p_1$,..., $p_n$⟧ is true only for a sequence of length n for which each $p_i$ is true of the *i*th element; p ↦ q is true for a nonempty sequence for which p is true for its first element and q is true for its tail; p ⊣ q is true for a nonempty sequence for which q is true for its last element and p is true for its tail-right.

When patterns are combined with predicate combining forms, the resulting pattern denotes a predicate that is the combination of the predicates denoted by its constituents; the functions it defines are those its constituent patterns would have defined individually, but modified to reflect their positions in the new pattern. There must be only one instance of each defining function name in a pattern. Thus in ⟦x.isstring, ⟦y.isint, z.isint⟧ ⟧, while the elementary pattern x.isstring alone defines x to be id, this compound pattern defines x to be the function that selects the first element of a sequence (i.e., id ∘ s1) and it defines y to select the first element of the second element of a sequence (i.e., id ∘ s1 ∘ s2).

The fundamental tenet of FL, that programs be written at the function level, means that patterns can take advantage of the power of FL without having to depend on a subsidiary unification algorithm. Thus, as in the example, in addition to just giving a pattern to denote structures of the form ⟨x, ⟨y, z⟩⟩, qualifying predicates for x, y, and z can also be included, as well as other predicates for the whole argument or for its parts.

The predicate and definition parts of an arbitrary pattern are given in Table 1. Since patterns are defined recursively, the following notational conventions are used: $p_i$ is the predicate part of the sub-pattern $P_i$ ; *Defs* (P) is the definition part of the pattern P (in which a typical definition is d ≡ D); fname denotes an arbitrary function name, and e denotes an arbitrary expression (which usually denotes a predicate).

---

**Table 1.**  Patterns' predicate and definition parts.

| Pattern | Predicate Part | Definition Part |
|---|---|---|
| fname. | T | {fname ≡ id} |
| fname.P | p | {fname ≡ id} ∪ *Defs* (P) |
| e | e | {} |
| $\llbracket P_1, \ldots, P_n \rrbracket$ | $\llbracket p_1, \ldots, p_n \rrbracket$ | $\cup_{i=1}^{n} \{d \equiv D \circ si \mid (d \equiv D) \in Defs(P_i)\}$ |
| $P_1 \mapsto P_2$ | $p_1 \mapsto p_2$ | {d ≡ D ∘ sl \|(d ≡ D) ∈ *Defs* (P$_1$)} <br> ∪ {d ≡ D ∘ tl \| (d ≡ D) ∈ *Defs* (P$_2$)} |
| $P_1 \dashv P_2$ | $p_1 \dashv p_2$ | {d ≡ D ∘ tlr \| (d ≡ D) ∈ *Defs* (P$_1$)} <br> ∪ {d ≡ D ∘ rl \| (d ≡ D) ∈ *Defs* (P$_2$)} |
| P ∘ e | p ∘ e | {d ≡ D ∘ e \|(d ≡ D) ∈ *Defs* (P$_1$)} |
| $P_1 \wedge P_2$ | $p_1 \wedge p_2$ | *Defs* (P$_1$) ∪ *Defs* (P$_2$) |

---

Patterns may appear only in the predicate part of conditionals, and the definitions they make may be seen only in the two arms of the conditional. The meaning of a conditional $(P \rightarrow e_1 ; e_2)$ with a pattern P in the predicate position is exactly the same as the conditional $p \rightarrow e_1$ where *Defs*(P) end; $e_2$ where *Defs*(P) end (assuming that the names in the right-hand sides of the definitions of *Defs*(P) never refer to the functions defined in *Defs*(P)). Note that the scope of the functions defined by the pattern includes the false arm; it is sometimes useful to use the definitions there even though the argument does not match the pattern.

Table 2 gives some examples of expressions written using patterns and their equivalent simple expressions.

This use of patterns must not be mistaken for a kind of λ-abstraction. Notice that $\llbracket x., y. \rrbracket \rightarrow x \circ y$; err abbreviates $\llbracket T, T \rrbracket \rightarrow sl \circ s2$; err, which, if applied to ⟨f, ⟨g, h⟩⟩, rewrites to g. Contrast this with λx, y . x ∘ y, which, if applied to ⟨f, ⟨g, h⟩⟩, would produce f ∘ ⟨g, h⟩ (which is equivalent to err, since ⟨g, h⟩ is not a function).

**Enhanced Definitions**  FL includes some special syntactic notation for enhancing the readability of defined functions. There are two kinds of en-

**Table 2.**  Examples of expressions written using patterns.

| Expression Using Patterns | Equivalent Simple Expression |
|---|---|
| ⟦x., isnum, y.isint⟧ → <br> f ∘ [x, g ∘ [id, y]]; x | ⟦T, isnum, isint⟧ → <br> f ∘ [s1, g ∘ [id, s3]]; s1 |
| ⟦T, x.isnum⟧ ∘ s1 → <br> f ∘ x; g ∘ x | ⟦T, isnum⟧ ∘ s1 → <br> f ∘ s2 ∘ s1; g ∘ s2 ∘ s1 |
| (x.isnum ⊢ y.) → <br> (f ∘ x) al ' (g ∘ y); h | (isnum ⊢T) → <br> (f ∘ s1) al ' (g ∘ tl); h |

hanced definitions. The first is useful for defining higher-order functions; it causes application of the defined function to be delayed until the appropriate number of arguments is available. The second allows patterns to be written on the *left* side of a function definition to limit the kinds and shapes of actual arguments for which the function is defined and to name selectors for parts of a valid argument.

Both kinds of enhanced definitions correspond in a simple way to an ordinary definition. The following table shows how to reduce any enhanced definition to an ordinary one by using the correspondences it gives. The primitive function args has the rewrite rule args: n: f: $x_1$ : ... : $x_n$ → f: $x_1$ : ... : $x_n$. In the table, P is a pattern, F is an "enhanced" left-hand side (i.e., a function name or, recursively, F ← P), E is an expression, and i is a nonnegative integer.

| Enhanced Definition | Corresponding Definition |
|---|---|
| $Def_i$ f ≡ E | Def f ≡ args: i: E |
| $Def_i$ F ← P ≡ E | $Def_i$ F ≡ (P → E; err) |

For example, using the rules in the table, the enhanced definition $Def_2$ ReverseComp ← ⟦f., g.⟧ ≡ g ∘ ' f reduces to $Def_2$ ReverseComp ≡ (⟦f., g.⟧ → g ∘ ' f; err) by using the second rule, which in turn reduces to the simple definition Def ReverseComp ≡ args: 2: (⟦f., g.⟧ → g ∘ ' f; err) by using the first rule. (Further elimination of the pattern and the ' symbol gives the function Def ReverseComp ≡ args: 2: (⟦T, T⟧ → ∘ ∘[s2, s1]; err); the presence of args: 2

prevents ReverseComp from rewriting except in the context ReverseComp: $x_1$ : $x_2$.)

### 5.2 *Nesting Declaration Lists*

Since it is frequently useful to make auxiliary definitions that are visible only to a few select functions, declaration lists can be nested to allow this capability.

Instead of enclosing a nested declaration list with the keywords where and end, such a nested declaration list can begin with one of the following key phrases (and is always ended with the keyword end):

**1.** begin (indicating that all the functions defined in the declaration list are visible in the containing declaration list),

**2.** export($f_1, \ldots, f_n$) (indicating that only the function names $f_1, \ldots, f_n$ are visible in the containing declaration list),

**3.** hide($f_1, \ldots, f_n$) (indicating that all but the function names $f_1, \ldots, f_n$ = are visible in the containing declaration list).

To aid the programmer in catching misspellings, the functions named in the export or hide clause must be distinct and must be a subset of the function names that are given definitions in the nested declaration list.

For example, the Table 3 shows an expression before simplification and an equivalent expression with a simple declaration list. In the table, $E(x_1, \ldots, x_n)$ represents an expression with the function names $x_1, \ldots, x_n$ occurring in it. Notice that, in the second column, the h in the main expression refers to the primitive definition supplied by the system if h is the name of a primitive function; and if h is not the name of a primitive function, then h is given the implicit definition Def h $\equiv$ err.

It is envisioned that the programming environment (e.g., the operating system, an editor, a language preprocessor, etc.) will provide the capability of including one file in another by means of an "include" or "embed" command. This command would probably insert the contents of one file into the file where the include command was located; a file representing an expression could then "include" another containing a declaration list. Since this is a feature of the programming environment, it is not described in this chapter as part of the language itself.

### 5.3 *Expressions*

Section 4 has introduced several additional constructs to the expressions of the complete FL language. It is helpful to review the structure of expressions

---

**Table 3.**  Example of expression simplification.

| Expression with Enhanced Definitions | Equivalent Simple Expression |
|---|---|
| $E_0(f, g, h)$ where | $E_0(f_1, g_2, h)$ where |
| export$(f, g)$ | Def $f_1 \equiv E_1(f_1, g_2, h_1)$ |
| Def $f \equiv E_1(f, g, h)$ | Def $f_2 \equiv E_2(f_2, g_2, h_1)$ |
| hide$(f)$ | Def $g_2 \equiv E_3(f_2, g_2, h_1)$ |
| Def $f \equiv E_2(f, g, h)$ | Def $h_1 \equiv E_4(f_1, g_2, h_1)$ |
| Def $g \equiv E_3(f, g, h)$ | end |
| end | |
| Def $h \equiv E_4(f, g, h)$ | |
| end | |
| end | |

---

that incorporate these new constructs.

If se is a simple expression, $e, e_1, \ldots, e_n$ are expressions, and declist is a declaration list, then the following are FL *expressions*:

se
$\langle e_1, \ldots, e_n \rangle$
$e_1 : e_2$
$e'$
$[^{(m)}e_1, \ldots, e_n]$
$[\![^{(m)}e_1, \ldots, e_n]\!]$
$\tilde{}e$
pattern $\rightarrow e_1 ; e_2$
pattern $\rightarrow e_1$
$e_1 \rightarrow^{(n)} e_1 ; e_2$
$e_1 \ e_2 \ e_3$ (infix notation)
$e$ where declist end
let declist in $e$

**The Semantics of FL Expressions** As discussed in Section 3, the semantics of an expression can be given indirectly, by rewriting the expression to its core language equivalent. The value/meaning of this core expression is then, by definition, the value/meaning of the original program, and the history it produces is, by definition, the one that the original program produces. As described in Section 3, the value (and resulting history) of a core expression is obtained by the rewrite rules of the operational semantics, and its meaning (and history) by the denotational semantics. An informal description of this rewriting process was given for each additional construct as it was introduced. A more formal description is given in [2].

## References

[1] Backus, J. "Can programming be liberated from the von Neumann style? A functional style and its algebra of programs". *Communications of the ACM 21*, 8 (August, 1978), pp. 613-641.

[2] Backus, J., Williams, J. H., and Wimmers, E. L. "FL language manual," (preliminary version). Report RJ 5339, IBM Almaden Research Center, November, 1986.

[3] Backus, J., Williams, J. H., Wimmers, E. L., Lucas, P., and Aiken, A. "FL language manual, Parts 1 and 2". Report RJ 7100, IBM Almaden Research Center, October 1989.

[4] Turner, D. A. "Recursive equations as a programming language". *Functional Programming and its Applications*, J. Darlington et al. (editors), Cambridge University Press, Cambridge, UK, 1982.

[5] Williams, J. H. and Wimmers, E.L. "Sacrificing simplicity for convenience: Where do you draw the line?" *Proceedings of the 15th ACM Conference on Principles of Programming Languages*. ACM, New York, 1988.

# Interactive Functional Programs

## A Method and a Formal Semantics

# 10

## Simon Thompson
University of Kent

## Abstract

$I$n this chapter we present a model of interactive programs in a purely functional style. We exploit lazy evaluation in the modeling of streams as lazy lists. We show how programs may be constructed in an *ad hoc* way, and then we present a small set of interactions and combinators that form the basis for a disciplined approach to writing such programs.

One of the difficulties of the *ad hoc* approach is that the way in which input and output are interleaved by the functions can be unpredictable. In the second half of the chapter we use traces, i.e., partial histories of behavior, to explain the interleaving of input and output, and we give a formal explanation of our combinators. We argue that this justifies our claim that the combinators have the intuitively expected behavior, and finally, we contrast our approach with another.

## 1 *Introduction*

This chapter explains an approach to describing interactive processes in the lazy functional programming language Miranda [7].

Functional programming is based on *expression evaluation*, where expressions will, in general, contain applications of system- and user-defined functions. Lazy evaluation is a particular strategy for expression evaluation (as there is a *choice* of the way in which we perform the process), which means that

> The values of arguments to functions are evaluated only when they are *needed*.

> Moreover, if an argument is a composite data object, like a list, the object is evaluated only *to the extent that is needed* by the function applied to it. One of the simplest examples of this is the head function (*hd*) on lists, which necessitates the evaluation of only the first item in the argument list.

The chapter consists of two parts. In the first we develop our model of interactive programs in the lazy Miranda system. Since the lazy evaluation strategy is somewhat subtle, we were prompted to try to understand it using formal means; the result is the second half of this chapter.

In the first part, after an introductory discussion of lazy evaluation, we introduce the type of interactions and present a number of examples. These are developed in an *ad hoc* way, which may lead to unexpected interleaving behavior. We then present a small collection of primitives from which we can build interactions in a disciplined way. We aim to avoid the unexpected by using these primitives alone; nevertheless, we find there are subtle points that need to be elucidated. This is the purpose of the second part of the chapter.

In the second half we aim to give a foundation to the development of interactive processes under the lazy streams approach. We concentrate on a slightly simplified type, which omits the state information included in the first half, since the crucial *interleaving* properties of interactions can be studied more easily in the simpler setting.

After giving a summary of our notation, we introduce, informally at first, the idea of a *trace*. Traces describe the possible histories of a process (more information about the use of traces to describe processes can be found in [3]). One of the basic ideas in the first part was that of an incomplete or partial interaction; such interactions are the building blocks from which we build full interactive processes. These are reintroduced in Section 9, which is followed by a discussion of lazy evaluation and our first attempt at a formal definition of traces. As should be clear, we have tried to *motivate* the eventual definition of traces by retracing our steps towards its final formulation. Section 11 contains a note on the precise nature of print-driven evaluation; in Section 12 we introduce the formal definitions of *weak pretraces* and *weak traces*, following in Section 13 with a number of examples.

To underline that we are dealing with *deterministic* processes, we prove a theorem in Section 14 that all the processes described by our model *are* deterministic. The proof is constructive and shows, incidentally, how we derive the (weak) trace set of a particular process.

Weak traces and pretraces contain sufficient information to describe the behavior of processes in isolation. Given that we combine processes to build more complex ones, this may not be sufficient, and indeed we show that we have to incorporate more information about *termination* into our description. This is the aim of Section 15, which supplies the definition of *pretraces*, *traces*, and *terminal traces*. We revisit our examples in the following section.

A fundamental process combinator is *sq*, which is intended to perform *sequential composition* of processes. In Section 17 we describe how the trace sets of two processes are combined sequentially. The subtlety of lazy evaluation, which we mentioned above, manifests itself here— we see how termination and laziness interact to give an interesting effect when processes are combined: The laziness of reading allows some writing to "overtake" reading. Our definition of sequential composition is justified in Section 18, where we prove that *sq* implements sequential composition as described. This means that we can *predict* the behavior of interactive processes when placed in a (sequential) environment, allowing us to write robust and reliable interactive programs in Miranda.

In the final section, we draw some conclusions about the anomalies we have found and the methodology we have recommended, and we argue that the methodology does indeed lead to reliable programming. We also contrast our approach with that of the FP/FL school, and finally, we make some acknowledgements.

We should stress that the trace method adopted here will be applicable to *any* process (i.e., any stream or lazy-list processing program) and not only to interactive processes.

## *Part I*

## 2 *Lazy Evaluation*

A feature of a number of modern functional programming languages such as Miranda is that they embody *lazy evaluation*. By this we mean that arguments are passed to functions *unevaluated*. If we look at the function *const* (from the Miranda standard environment), which is defined by

   *const a b = a* ,

then the application

   *const* (16 + 1) *f*

will return the result (17) without the expression *f* being evaluated. An argument is evaluated only if its value is required by the function.

   Suppose we say

   *dconst a b = a + a*

and evaluate

   *dconst* (16 + 1) *b* ;

we get the result 34. In deriving this we may have made no gain, as in evaluating

   *a + a*

we may have replaced a single evaluation of 16 + 1 by two evaluations. A naïve approach to demand-driven evaluation might do this, but under lazy evaluation we ensure that the result of evaluating an argument is *shared* by all its instances.

   A more subtle manifestation of lazy evaluation arises when we consider composite arguments. Once we begin to evaluate a numerical argument, for instance, we evaluate it completely. On the other hand, a composite argument may be evaluated only *partially*. The simplest example is given by the function

   *hd* (*a* : *x*) = *a* ,

which returns the first, or *head*, item *a* of a list (*a* : *x*). If we pass

   *nums* 17

to *hd* where the function *nums* is defined by

$$nums\ n = n\ :\ nums\ (n+1),$$

then in order for the application to return the result 17 we require only that *nums* 17 evaluate partially to

$$17\ :\ nums\ 18\ .$$

As illustrated above, lazy evaluation has an effect on the membership of various of the data types of the language, such as *lists*. In the example above we see that the *infinite* list *nums* 17 receives exactly the same treatment as a finite list such as

$$[17, 18, \ldots, 23]\ .$$

In fact, in order for *hd l* to return 17, all that we need to know about *l* is that its first member is 17; the rest, or *tail*, of the list may be undefined. We usually write $\perp$ for the undefined list (indeed we write it for the undefined object of any type). Using this notation we see that

$$hd\ (17 : \perp) = 17\ ,$$

so *partial* lists, which have undefined final segments, are legitimate lists in our lazy scheme of things.

Input and output are often thought of as *streams*. Given the discussion above we can see that streams can be identified with lazy lists.

> The operation of testing whether a stream contains any items corresponds to *pattern matching* the list with the pattern $(a : x)$. In case this is successful, the list's first item will be bound to *a* and the remainder of the stream (which may be empty) to *x*.

> On the other hand, given an item *b*, the expression

$$b : y$$

> specifies a stream whose first element is *b* and whose remainder consists of *y*. We can thus view the list-construction operation ":" as an output operation, placing an item onto a stream.

> We would like to know the effect of evaluating an expression such as

$$nums\ 17$$

or

$$nums'\ 17\ 100$$

when

$$nums'\ n\ m\ =\ [\ ],\qquad\qquad\qquad n > m$$
$$=\ n\ :\ nums'\ (n+1)\ m,\quad \textbf{otherwise}\ .$$

Output will be produced in an incremental fashion: The first element of the list will be evaluated and printed, then the second, and so on. Portions of the output will be printed before the evaluation is complete. In particular, if the result being printed is a function application, it is the need to print that will drive the evaluation of the function's arguments. As we hinted above, lazy evaluation can be seen as a *species* of demand-driven dataflow. We discuss this further in the context of interactive programming in Section 10.

## 3 *A Type of Interactions*

An interactive program is designed to read from a stream of input and to write to a stream of output. As we have already observed, we can view streams as *lists*, so if we say

    *input* == [*char*]

    *output* == [*char*] ,

then the type of functions

    *input* → *output*

forms a simple model of interactive processes. For instance, a process that double-spaces its input can be written thus:

$$double\text{-}space\ (a : x)\ =\ a : double\text{-}space\ x,\qquad a \neq newline$$
$$=\ a : a : double\text{-}space\ x,\quad \textbf{otherwise}$$
$$double\text{-}space\ [\ ]\qquad =\ [\ ],$$

and a process which simply copies (or echoes) its input is written

    *echo y = y* .

These equations describe how the output stream depends upon the input stream. In an interactive context we are likely to be interested not only in the input–output relation but also in the way that the two streams are *interleaved* temporally, for example, on a terminal screen. Recall our lists' laziness, and recall our discussion of the way in which lists are printed. We mentioned in that account that output will begin to be produced as soon as possible, and that further output is generated similarly, contingent upon the presence of sufficient input. In printing the result of

> *echo stdin*

(*stdin* denotes *standard input*), a character can be echoed as soon as it is typed at the terminal, since an item is placed on the output stream as soon as it appears on the input stream. (Users of real systems will perhaps observe something different, as most terminals *buffer* their input into lines before transmitting it to a host. In such a situation *echoing* happens as promptly as possible, i.e., line by line.)

In most cases laziness has the effect we would intend. Nonetheless, it can have some unpredicted effects. We return to this in Section 6.

Before we continue we should emphasize that our model is sufficiently powerful to capture processes that have an *internal state*. A particular item on the output stream will depend on as much of the input stream as has thus far been read, and so will depend on the whole *history* of the input to the process. Just to give a brief example, we can write a program that either single spaces or double spaces its input, where $ is used to toggle between the two modes. The function, which we call *option-on*, starts off in double-spacing mode.

$$
\begin{array}{lll}
\text{\textit{option-on}}\ (a:x) & =\ \text{\textit{option-off}}\ x, & a = \text{`\$'} \\[4pt]
 & =\ a:a:\text{\textit{option-on}}\ x, & a = \textit{newline} \\[4pt]
 & =\ a:\text{\textit{option-on}}\ x, & \textbf{otherwise} \\[6pt]
\text{\textit{option-off}}\,(a:x) & =\ \text{\textit{option-on}}\ x, & a = \text{`\$'} \\[4pt]
 & =\ a:\text{\textit{option-off}}\ x, & \textbf{otherwise}
\end{array}
$$

## 4  *Partial Interactions*

An interactive process *in isolation* is specified by a function of type

> *input → output*

which describes the form of the output in terms of the input. In general, however, we wish to combine simple interactions into composite ones. If we think of following one interaction by another, we need to be able to pass the portion of the input stream unexamined by the first on to the second. Such *partial* interactions must therefore return the unconsumed portion of the input stream as a part of their results. These partial interactions will therefore be of type

> *input → (input, output)* .

Consider an interaction that reads a line of input and outputs its length:

*line-len* :: *input* → (*input, output*)

*line-len in*

= (*rest, out*)

   **where**

   *out = show (#line)*

   (*line, rest*) = *get-line* [ ] *in*

   *get-line front* (*a* : *x*)

      =   *get-line* (*front* ++ [*a*]) *x*,   *a* ≠ *newline*

      =   (*front, x*),                         **otherwise** .

The function *get-line* is used to get the first line from the input stream. It returns a result consisting of the *line* paired with the remainder of the input, *rest*. The first parameter of *get-line* is used to *accumulate* the partial line, and *show* is a function converting a number to a printable form.

We need to make one further refinement to the model. As we are now contemplating building interactions from simpler components, we may want to pass (state) information from one interaction to another. In general we think of an interaction as being supplied with a value, of type *, say, on its initiation and returning a value of a possibly different type, **, say, on termination. This gives a general type of partial interactions:

*interact* * ** == (*input*, *) → (*input*, **, *output*) .

To summarize

   Interactions are modeled by a function type, parameterized on two type variables *, **.

   The domain type is (*input*, *); items of this type are pairs consisting of

      input streams

      initial state values.

   The range type is (*input*, **, *output*), items of which are triples consisting of

      the portion of the input stream unexamined by the interaction

      the final state value

      the output produced during the interaction.

There are natural examples of interactions for which ∗ and ∗∗are different. For instance, if *get-number* is meant to get a number from the input stream, then its natural type would be

> *interact () num* .

Here () is the one-element type whose single member is (), the empty tuple; its use here signifies that no prior state information is required by the process.

To give an example of an interaction of this type, we might consider modifying *line-len* so that after each line it will print an accumulated total number of characters, as well as the length of the line itself:

> *line-len-deluxe* :: *interact num num*

> *line-len-deluxe (in, tot)*

>     =  *(rest, newtot, out)*

>       **where**
>
>       *(line, rest) = get-line [ ] in*
>
>       *len = # line*
>
>       *newtot = tot + len*
>
>       *out = show len ++ show newtot*

The state information passed in by the interaction is modified by the addition of the current line length.

## 5  *Combining Interactions*

Up to this point we have considered primitive interactions, built in an *ad hoc* way. In this section we look at some functions that enable us to combine interactions in a disciplined way, with the consequence that their interactive behavior will be more predictable.

First we introduce a number of basic interactions, and then we present some combining forms or *combinators* that build complex interactions from simpler ones.

### 5.1 *Basic Interactions*

First, to read single characters we have

> *get-char* :: *interact* ∗ *char*

$$get\text{-}char\ ((a : x), st) = (x, a, [\,])$$

and to write single characters,

$$put\text{-}char :: char \rightarrow interact\ *\ *$$

$$put\text{-}char\ ch\ (in, st) = (in, st, [ch])\,.$$

We can also perform internal actions, applying a function to the state value:

$$apply :: (* \rightarrow **) \rightarrow interact\ *\ **$$

$$apply\ f\ (in, st) = (in, f\ st, [\,])\,.$$

These are three atomic operations from which we can build all our interactions using the combinators that follow. That these are sufficient should be clear from the fact that they give the atomic operations on input, output, and internal state.

## 5.2 *Sequential Composition*

The type of the sequential composition operator *sq* is given by

$$sq :: interact\ *\ ** \rightarrow interact\ **\ *** \rightarrow interact\ *\ ***\,.$$

The operation *sq first second* should have the effect of performing *first* and then *second*, so

$$sq\ first\ second\ (in, st)$$

$$=\ (rest, final, out\text{-}first ++ out\text{-}second)$$

**where**

$$(rem\text{-}first, inter, out\text{-}first)\ =\ first\ (in, st)$$

$$(rest, final, out\text{-}second)\ =\ second\ (rem\text{-}first, inter)\,.$$

Here *first* is applied to $(in, st)$, resulting in output *out-first*, new state *inter*, and remainder of the input *rem-first*. The last of these, paired with *inter*, is passed to *second*, with result

$$(rest, final, out\text{-}second)\,.$$

The input remaining after the composite action is *rest*, the final state value is *final*, and the overall output produced is the concatenation of the output produced by the individual processes,

$$out\text{-}first ++ out\text{-}second\,;$$

and so we return the triple of these values as the result of the combination. We explore the precise interleaving behavior of this combinator in the second part of this chapter.

## 5.3 *Alternation and Repetition*

To choose between two alternative interactions according to a condition on the initial state, we use the *alt* combinator:

$$alt :: cond * \rightarrow interact * ** \rightarrow interact * ** \rightarrow interact * **$$

$$alt\ condit\ inter1\ inter2\ (in, st) \quad = \quad inter1\ (in, st), \quad condit\ st$$

$$= \quad inter2\ (in, st), \quad \textbf{otherwise}\,.$$

The type $cond * == * \rightarrow bool$ is the type of predicates or *conditions* over the type $*$. The effect of *alt* is to evaluate the condition on the input state, $condit\ st$, and according to the truth or falsehood of the result to choose to invoke the first or second interaction.

The *trivial* interaction

$$skip :: interact * *$$

does nothing:

$$skip\ (in, st) = (in, st, [\,])\,.$$

(Observe that we could have used *apply* to define *skip* since it is given by *apply id*.) Using *sq*, *alt*, *skip*, and *recursion* we can give a high-level definition of iteration:

$$while :: cond * \rightarrow interact * * \rightarrow interact * *\,,$$

which we define by

> *while condit inter*
>
> = *loop*
>> **where**
>> *loop = alt condit (inter $sq loop) skip*.

Depending on the condition, either we perform *inter* and re-enter the loop or we *skip*, i.e., do nothing to the state and terminate forthwith. Note, incidentally, that we have prefixed *sq* by $ to make it an infix operator. Using *while*, we can define a repeat loop:

$$repeat :: cond * \rightarrow interact * * \rightarrow interact * *$$

> *repeat condit inter*
>
> = *inter $sq (while not-condit inter)*
>> **where**
>> *not-condit = (~).condit*.

Because ~ is the boolean negation function, *not-condit* is the converse of the *condit* condition.

### 5.4 *Using the Combinators*

In this section we give an example of a *full* interaction, that is, an interaction of type

> *input → output*

which is built from partial interactions using the combinators. The program inputs lines of text repeatedly until a total of at least one thousand characters has been input, at which point it halts. After each line of input the length of the line and the total number of characters seen thus far is printed. Define the numerical condition

> *sufficient n* = $(n \geq 1000)$ .

Letting

> *rep-inter*   ::   *interact num num*
>
> *rep-inter*   =   *repeat sufficient line-len-deluxe* ,

then we can define our full interaction,

> *full-inter* :: *input → output* ,

by

> *full-inter in*
>
> =   *out*
>
> **where**
>
> (*rest, final, out*) = *rep-inter* (*in*, 0) .

It should be obvious why we have chosen the starting value for the state to be zero: At initiation of the process, no characters have been read.

## 6 *Two Cautionary Examples*

We mentioned that interaction functions that we define may not always behave as we expect. The two examples we present here illustrate two different ways in which that can happen.

## 6.1 *Pattern Matching*

Pattern matching can delay output. We might write a function that prompts for an item of input and then echoes it thus:

$$try\ (a : x) = \text{``}\texttt{Prompt:}\ \ \text{''} ++ [a]\ .$$

Unfortunately, the prompt will be printed only *after* the item has been input. This is because the evaluator can begin to produce output only when the match with the pattern $(a : x)$ has succeeded, and that means precisely when the item has entered the input stream. We can achieve the desired effect by writing

$$again\ x = \text{``}\texttt{Prompt:}\ \ \text{''} ++ [hd\ x]$$

The prompt will appear before any input has been entered, as nothing needs to be known about the argument $(x)$ for that portion of the output to be printed.

## 6.2 *Lazy Reading*

Consider the process

$$while\ (const\ True)\ get$$

where

$$get\ ::\ interact\ *\ *$$

$$get\ (in, st)\ \ =\ \ (tl\ in, st, \text{``}\texttt{Prompt:}\ \text{''})\ .$$

What is the effect? We first envisage that it repeats the interaction *get* indefinitely, and that the effect of *get* is to prompt for an item input and then to read it. In fact we see that the prompt is printed indefinitely, and at no stage does input take place. As we explained above, output is driven by the need to print, and the output from this interaction can be derived without any information about the input stream, with the consequent effect that no input is read.

The phenomenon illustrated by the second example —lazy reading— causes a major headache. We shall see presently precisely how writes can overtake reads, and in the conclusion to the chapter we argue that this will not happen under the disciplined approach advocated here.

## 7 *Miscellany and Conclusions*

We have shown how interactive programs can be written in a disciplined way in a functional system. Central to this enterprise are

**streams,** implemented here as lazy lists, but available in other languages as objects distinct from lists, and

**higher-order functions.** The type *interact* ∗ ∗∗ of interactions is a function type, and so our interaction combinators are inescapably higher order.

We need not be limited in our definitions to sequential combinators. We can, for example, reset a state to its initial value after an interaction, which means that, for instance, we can perform a "commutative" or "pseudo-parallel" composition of processes. Such combinations of processes can be useful when we write input routines for structured objects.

We can view the type *interact* ∗ ∗∗ in a slightly different way. We can see the type as one of *functions* which read input and produce output: These pseudo-functions are of type ∗ → ∗∗, and they return as part of their results the input stream after their application, together with the output produced. This gives us another perspective on the combinators defined above.

Observe also that not every member of the type *interact* ∗ ∗∗ is a natural representative of an interaction. All the interactions $f$ we have seen so far have the property that if

$$f\,(in, st) = (rest, st', out)\,,$$

then *rest* will be a final segment of *in* (i.e., will result from removing an initial portion from *in*).

This seems to be the place to make a polemical point. Much has recently been made of the notion of multiparadigm programming; the present work can be seen as an antidote to this. We have seen that the functional paradigm allows us to model another paradigm (the imperative) in a straightforward way, without sacrificing the elegant formal properties of the functional domain. A naïve combination of the two sacrifices the power and elegance which each possesses individually.

In the next part of the chapter we explore a formal *trace* semantics for interactions, in order to resolve any difficulties we may have had with interleaving.

## *Part II*

## 8 *Notation*

Here we introduce notation we shall use in the remainder of the document. The reader may wish to skip the section on first reading and refer back to it if and when it is necessary. The identifiers $tr, tr', \ldots$ will range over *sequences*, that is, finite lists that are terminated by [ ] and not by $\perp$. We say

$$tr \subseteq tr'$$

if $tr$ is an initial segment of $tr'$, i.e.,

$$\#tr \leq \#tr'$$

(where # gives the length of a list), and

$$\forall n \leq \#tr . tr!n = tr'!n .$$

We write

$$tr \subset tr'$$

if and only if $tr \subseteq tr'$ and $tr \neq tr'$.

Most of our sequences will consist of objects of three kinds. These will be input objects, tagged with $r$ (for *r*ead), output objects, tagged with $w$ (for *w*rite) and the object $\sqrt{}$ (pronounced 'tick'), which we use to indicate termination (we explain this further in the body of the chapter). We write

$$tr \subset_c tr'$$

if and only if $tr \subset tr'$ and the element that follows the initial segment $tr$ in $tr'$ is not an output object (tagged with $w$). We call these initial segments *complete* because they are complete with respect to writing.

Often we wish to look at the input or output portions of the sequences separately. We write

$$tr \upharpoonright in$$

$$tr \upharpoonright out$$

for these restrictions. For example, if

$$tr = [r2, r3, w5, \sqrt{}, r7] ,$$

then

$tr \upharpoonright in = [2, 3, 7]$

$tr \upharpoonright out = [5]$ .

We use a number of standard list functions in the sequel. Each nonbottom list is of the form [ ] or $(a : x)$ for some *head* element $a$ and *tail* list $x$. We write our definitions using pattern matching over these cases:

$hd (a : x) \; = \; a$ ,

$tl (a : x) \quad = \; x$ ,

$hd [\,] \qquad = \; \perp$ ,

$tl [\,] \qquad = \; \perp$ .

Finally, note that we use ++ as list (or sequence) concatenation, so

$[3, 4] ++ [5, 6] = [3, 4, 5, 6]$ .

## 9 *Traces*

Our aim is to describe the semantics of interactive programs by means of *traces* of their behavior. These traces will be sequences of actions, which can be of three kinds:

1. $r\, a$ is a read, or input, action — the item $a$ is read from the input stream,

2. $w\, a$ is a write, or output, action — the item $a$ is written to the output stream,

3. $\sqrt{}$ is an (invisible) action that signals that the process has completed its output — we shall say some more about this below, including a discussion of *why* we need such an action in our descriptions.

We say that a sequence *tr* is a trace of a process $P$ if and only if the sequence of actions in *tr* is a possible behavior of the process $P$. For example, a process that

prompts for an item by writing a prompt,

reads an item from the input stream, and

echoes the item read

will have

$[w\, prompt, r\, a, w\, a]$

as one of its traces. In fact, if the process terminates after echoing the item read, the full set of traces will be

[ ]

[*w prompt*]

[*w prompt, r a*]

[*w prompt, r a, w a*]

[*w prompt, r a, w a,* $\sqrt{}$] .

Further details of a calculus of processes and their associated trace semantics can be found in [3]. We shall use the set of traces of a process as the means by which we *specify* a process, and our aim in this chapter will be to describe Miranda processes by means of their trace sets. There is an associated problem of describing these sets of traces, one solution of which may be provided by temporal logic [4]; we do not address that problem in this chapter.

How do we model interactive programs in Miranda? As we saw above, we consider the programs to be mappings between the *streams* of input and output. We model a complete interaction as a function

$input \rightarrow output$ ,

where *input* and *output* are lists of items. The interaction we specified above is described by the function

$example_1 \ x = [prompt, hd \ x]$ .

Note that

[*w prompt, r a, w a,* $\sqrt{}$] $\restriction$ *out* = [*prompt, a*]

and

[*w prompt, r a, w a,* $\sqrt{}$] $\restriction$ *in* = [*a*] ,

and that the portion of the input read from a list $(a : x)$ will be [*a*], so that the trace

[*w prompt, r a, w a,* $\sqrt{}$]

is an *interleaving* of the input consumed and the output written by the function *example*$_1$ (together with the termination information given by $\sqrt{}$). We discuss below the formal means by which we find the traces of functional interactions.

In the first part of the chapter we saw that in general we need to consider *partial* interactions, i.e., objects of type

$$interact == input \rightarrow (input, output),$$

which return unconsumed input as a part of their result. Our model of the example interaction above is now

$$example_2\ x = (tl\ x, [prompt, hd\ x]),$$

where we see that the tail of the list $x$, i.e., $tl\ x$, is the remainder of the input stream, passed to a succeeding interaction, if any.

In the first part we also added state information to the model; we do not do that here, as our purpose is to concentrate on input–output behavior.

Recall that we combine two interactions sequentially thus:

$$sq\ ::\ interact \rightarrow interact \rightarrow interact$$

$$sq\ inter_1\ inter_2\ in\ =\ (rest, out_1 ++ out_2)$$

$$\textbf{where}$$

$$(betw, out_1) = inter_1\ in$$

$$(rest, out_2) = inter_2\ betw$$

How do we explain this? The output of the combined process is the second component of the pair, and is the concatenation of the outputs $out_1, out_2$ produced, respectively, by the processes $inter_1$ when supplied with input *in* and $inter_2$ when supplied with input *betw* (for *between*), the input *remaining* after the first interaction. We shall give a formal justification for this explanation later.

## 10  *Lazy Evaluation Revisited*

The evaluation of an expression written in the Miranda language is driven by the need to write or produce the result— evaluation is *demand* driven, and function arguments are evaluated only if and when they need to be. Such a scheme is called lazy evaluation. When arguments and results are structured, in particular when they are *lists*, laziness means that

> the component parts of lists are *written* as soon as they are available, so we can see *writing is eager*, in a sense;

> the component parts of an argument list are read only as they are needed.

Consider the example of $example_1$ from Section 9. The first item of the output list, *prompt*, can be written without any examination of the input list *x*. On the other hand, the second item is the head of the input list, and so this item needs to be read before writing can proceed further. Once it is read it can be output, with no further examination of the input list.

This analysis justifies our claim that

$$[w \; prompt, r \; a, w \; a]$$

is a trace of the function $example_1$. How could we show this rigorously? We do this by means of our language's denotational semantics [2, 6]. In particular we analyze the behavior of our function on *partial* lists, i.e., lists that are terminated by the bottom element $\perp$. The element $\perp$ represents the state of our *knowing nothing* about a value, so the partial list

$$[2, 3] ++ \perp$$

represents a list about which we know nothing except its first two elements.

What is the semantics of $example_1$? Recall the definition of *hd* (from Section 8) and note that

$$hd \perp = \perp .$$

(this should be an obvious truth — we can deduce it from the monotonicity of the semantic interpretation, which we shall discuss further below). Now,

$$
\begin{aligned}
example_1 \perp \;\; &= \;\; [prompt, hd \perp] \\
&= \;\; [prompt] ++ \perp
\end{aligned}
$$

$$
\begin{aligned}
example_1([a] ++ \perp) \;\; &= \;\; [prompt, hd \, ([a] ++ \perp)] \\
&= \;\; [prompt, a] .
\end{aligned}
$$

We see, in the two cases, that the input sequences [ ], [*a*] give rise to the output sequences [*prompt*], [*prompt*, *a*]. (We shall have something more to say about these functions in Section 11.) If we write $\rightsquigarrow$ instead of "gives rise to", we can make our first attempt at defining traces.

**Definition** (attempt 1)    We say that *tr* is a trace of *f* if for each initial segment *tr'* of *tr*,

$$f \, tr' \! \upharpoonright in \;\; \rightsquigarrow \;\; tr' \! \upharpoonright out .$$

This definition contains the essence of the definition we shall end up with in

Section 12. Our definition states that

$$f \, tr \upharpoonright in \ \rightsquigarrow \ tr \upharpoonright out$$

and that, moreover, this holds for every initial segment of *tr*. Clearly we need this second condition, since *any* merge $tr_1$ of the sequences $tr \upharpoonright in$, $tr \upharpoonright out$ satisfies

$$tr_1 \upharpoonright out \ = \ tr \upharpoonright out ,$$

$$tr_1 \upharpoonright in \ = \ tr \upharpoonright in .$$

It is not hard to see that asking for the property to hold of every initial segment *tr'* of *tr* means that we are asking for a particular interleaving of the sequences, namely the one embodied by *tr*. This is reflected in our definition and theorem on determinacy in Section 14. In Section 12 we refine our attempted definition, but first we say something about approximation and monotonicity. The ordering $\sqsubseteq$ on the domain of interpretation is an ordering of *increasing information*. For example, for every *x*,

$$\bot \sqsubseteq x$$

and for two finite sequences *s*, *t*,

$$s \subseteq t$$

if and only if

$$s ++ \bot \sqsubseteq t ++ \bot .$$

The interpretation of this equivalence is revealing. Extending the defined portion of a stream, from *s* to *t*, gives more information about the stream. Conversely, more information about partial streams terminated by $\bot$ is given by extending the defined portion, that is, by providing more input items.

We say that a function is *monotone* if for all *x, y*,

$$x \sqsubseteq y \ \Rightarrow \ f x \sqsubseteq f y .$$

In words: If we give more information about the argument, we can only get more information about the result.

We should note that if the sequences *s* and *t* are finite, $s \sqsubseteq t$ if and only if $s = t$. This is because the lists are *definite*: They cannot be extended as they are fully defined. Note however that

$$s ++ \bot \sqsubseteq s$$

for every *s*.

The reader should have no difficulty now in seeing that the only possible value for $hd \, \bot$ (and indeed for $tl \, \bot$) is $\bot$.

## 11 *A Note on Printing*

In the previous section we stated that

$$example_1 \perp = [prompt, hd \perp]$$
$$= [prompt] ++ \perp .$$

The second equality is *not* in fact true! We shall see here, however, that as far as the printing device, or evaluator, is concerned they are equivalent.

How does the printer print values that are lists? A list is printed one item at a time, starting from the head. If at any point one of the items of the list is not (so far) defined, then no further output will be produced. We can write this as a Miranda function *print*. For the rest of the chapter we shall assume that our functional interactions produce output that is "printable" directly; we can ensure this by composing them with *print* if we wish. The function *print* is defined in [5], which also contains an example of two denotationally *unequal* functions whose printable behavior is equivalent. These functions are

$$example_3 x = [prompt] ++ outx$$

$$\textbf{where}$$

$$out (a : z) = a$$

## 12 *Weak Pretraces and Traces*

We made our first attempt at a definition of the trace of a complete inter-action on page 267. In this section we refine the definition in the light of our example, $example_3$, which we saw in the previous section, and also adapt it to *partial* interactions, i.e., objects of type *interact*.

We saw in the earlier section that the example has the same printing be-havior as $example_1$, which we already know has traces

$$[ \ ] ,$$

$$[w \ prompt] ,$$

$$[w \ prompt, r \ a] ,$$

$$[w \ prompt, r \ a, w \ a] .$$

Does each of these sequences have the property that

$$example_3 \ sq \upharpoonright in \rightsquigarrow sq \upharpoonright out \ ?$$

We work through them in turn:

$example_3\ ([\,] ++ \bot)\ =\ [prompt] ++ \bot\ ,$

$example_3\ ([a] ++ \bot)\ =\ [prompt, a]\ .$

Interpreting these, we find that

$example_3\ [\,]\ \rightsquigarrow\ [prompt]\ ,$

$example_3\ [a]\ \rightsquigarrow\ [prompt, a]\ ,$

so that

$example_3\ tr'\upharpoonright in\ \rightsquigarrow\ tr'\upharpoonright out$

only for the sequences [*w prompt*] and [*w prompt, r a, w a*], and *not* for the other two initial segments of [*w prompt, r a, w a*], namely, [ ] and [*w prompt, r a*]. Why should this be? Remember that the language's implementation uses lazy evaluation, and as we observed in Section 10, this means that *writing is eager*. The input portion of the trace

[*w prompt, r a*]

is sufficient to allow the writing of the item *a*. This fact is not registered by the initial segment [*w prompt, r a*], as it is not "complete" with respect to writing. We say that a proper initial segment *tr'* of *tr* is *complete*, i.e.,

$tr' \subset_c tr\ ,$

if and only if $tr' \subset tr$ and the element following *tr'* in *tr* is not a *w* element. As we see in the example above, we can expect the property

$f\,tr'\upharpoonright in\ \rightsquigarrow\ tr'\upharpoonright out$

only for complete initial segments of a potential trace.

If we consider the process described by *example_3* as a *partial* interaction, we should record the input consumed by the interaction. We saw in Section 9 that we could do this by returning the remainder of the input as one component of the result, the other being the (partial) output. The natural way that we modify the example function is

$example_3\ x\ =\ (tl\ x\ ,\ [prompt] ++ out\ x)$

**where**

$out\ (a : z) = a\ .$

This registers that the interaction consumes only the first item of the input stream. Now we define the relation "*gives rise to*".

## Definition

   $f\ insq \mapsto outsq$

if and only if

   $f\,(insq ++ \perp)$

is equal to

   $(\perp, outsq ++ \perp)$

or

   $(\perp, outsq)\,,$

or in the case that *outsq* is $\perp$,

   $\perp\,.$

In each of these cases, we register that the portion of input presented, *insq*, is read fully by requiring that the remainder of the input returned is $\perp$ — if an item in *insq* had not been read then it would form part of the sequence returned.

**Definition** (*weak trace* and *pretrace*)    A sequence *tr* is a *weak pretrace* of *f* if and only if

   $f\ tr \upharpoonright in \mapsto tr \upharpoonright out$

and for every *complete* initial segment *tr'* of *tr*

   $f\ tr' \upharpoonright in \mapsto tr' \upharpoonright out\,.$

A sequence *tr* is a *weak trace* of *f* if and only if it is an initial segment of a weak pretrace of *f*.

(**Aside:** If we look at our previous definitions of *example*$_3$ and of traces we see that

   $f\ insq \rightsquigarrow [a]$

for *any insq* that begins with *a* — no account is taken by this definition that the input is not read beyond the first item.)

We shall examine the definition of weak traces and give the full definition of traces in Section 15. First we examine some examples in detail.

## 13 *The Weak Traces of Some Examples*

In this section we look at a number of example interactions, describing their weak traces and pretraces.

### Example 1        $write\ in = (in, [message])$

We want to find the sequences *insq* and *outsq* such that

$write\ insq \mapsto outsq$ .

Note first that there is no $x$ such that

$write\ x = \perp$ .

Now,

$write\ x = (\perp, y)$

if and only if $x = \perp$ and $y = [message]$, so

$write\ [\ ] \mapsto [message]$ .

This means that $[w\ message]$ is a candidate weak pretrace, if all its complete initial segments have the same property. The sequence $[\ ]$ is the only proper initial segment, and this is not complete, so the condition is satisfied vacuously. The set of weak traces will be

$\{[\ ], [w\ message]\}$ .

### Example 2        $read\ (a : x) = (x, [\ ])$

This example has the weak pretraces

$\{[\ ], [r\ a]\}$ ,

which are exactly the weak traces too.

### Example 3        $echo\ (a : x) = (x, [a])$

This interaction has the set of weak traces

$\{[\ ], [r\ a], [r\ a, w\ a]\}$ .

We begin to see the subtlety of the analysis in the contrast between the following pair of examples.

### Example 4        $promptin_1\ (a : x) = (x, [prompt])$

We have

$promptin_1\ y = \perp$

if $y = \perp$ or $y = [\ ]$, implying that

$promptin_1\ [\ ] \mapsto [\ ]$,

which makes [ ] a weak pretrace. Similarly,

$promptin_1\ [a] \mapsto [prompt]$,

and as above, the possible pretraces are

$$tr_1\ =\ [r\ a, w\ prompt]\,,$$
$$tr_2\ =\ [w\ prompt, r\ a]\,.$$

Sequence $tr_1$ is a weak pretrace, since its only complete initial segment is [ ], but $tr_2$ *fails* to be; this is a surprise, as we might expect the prompt to precede the input of the item. The delay is caused by the fact that the right-hand side is produced only after a successful pattern match, and this can take place only after an input item is present. We should contrast this with the next example.

## Example 5 $\qquad promptin_2\ y = (tl\ y, [prompt])$

This interaction has the weak trace set

$\{[\ ], [w\ prompt], [w\ prompt, r\ a]\}$.

It is worth contrasting this with the previous example: Here we see the effect of removing pattern matching, which we first came across in Section 6.

We shall see in Section 15 that the set of weak traces is insufficient to describe the behavior of one of these interactions *when it is embedded in a context*. First we look at a result on the determinacy of our functional interactions.

## 14 *Determinacy*

Using the functional approach, we write interactive processes as functions:

$input \rightarrow (input, output)$.

Functions associate their results with their arguments deterministically, and this carries over to our functional processes — a result that we formulate and prove in this section.

**Theorem  1** (Determinacy)
For all sequences *insq*, *outsq*, if

$$f\ insq \mapsto outsq\,,$$

then there is a unique weak pretrace *tr* of *f* with $tr \restriction in = insq$ and $tr \restriction out = outsq$.

In other words, if an input sequence *insq* gives rise to an output sequence *outsq*, then there is a unique interleaving *tr* of the two which forms a behavior of the process; that is, the order in which the actions of input and output take place is *determinate*.

**Proof**   The full proof is contained in [5]. It is a constructive proof: We build a weak pretrace by induction and then show that it is unique. The uniqueness depends upon our use of *functions* to model our interactions.   □

## 15 *Traces*

We have seen how the behavior of an interaction *in isolation* can be described by the collection of *weak traces*. In this section we look at an example that exposes the limits of this approach, and then we introduce the full definition of *traces*, which extend the descriptive information available.

We start with our example:

$$read_1\ (a : x)\ =\ (x, [\,])\,,$$
$$read_2\ y\ \quad =\ (tl\ y, [\,])\,.$$

Each of these processes reads a single item from the input stream and produces no output. Examining the formal details, we see that

$$read_1\ \perp\quad\ =\ \perp\,,$$
$$read_1\ (a : \perp)\ =\ (\perp, [\,])\,,$$
$$read_2\ \perp\quad\ =\ (\perp, [\,])\,,$$
$$read_2\ (a : \perp)\ =\ (\perp, [\,])\,,$$

which means that each has the set of traces

$$\{[\,], [r\ a]\}\,.$$

How do the two interactions differ? If we interpret

$$read_2\ \perp = (\perp, [\,])\,,$$

we can see that the process produces no output, and moreover *output terminates before any input is read.* Indeed, if we follow the interaction by a process that writes, e.g.,

$$write\ y = (y, [message]),$$

then the message will be output before any input is read. On the other hand, if we follow $read_1$ with *write*, reading precedes writing. We justify these assertions by examining the compositions

$$rw_1 \quad = \quad sq\ read_1\ write,$$

$$rw_2 \quad = \quad sq\ read_2\ write,$$

where we compose the processes using *sq* as defined in Section 9.

On one hand,

$$rw_2 \perp \quad = \quad (rest, out_1 ++ out_2)$$

$$\textbf{where}$$

$$(betw, out_1) = read_2 \perp$$

$$(rest, out_2) = write\ betw$$

Now,

$$(betw, out_1) \quad = \quad (\perp, [\ ]),$$

$$(rest, out_2) \quad = \quad (\perp, [message]),$$

so

$$rw_2 \perp = (\perp, [message]),$$

which implies that

$$rw_2 [\ ] \mapsto [message].$$

This means that writing precedes reading in this case.

On the other hand,

$$rw_1 \perp \quad = \quad (rest, out_1 ++ out_2)$$

$$\textbf{where}$$

$$(betw, out_1) = read_1 \perp$$

$$(rest, out_2) = write\ betw$$

Now, $read_1 \perp = \perp$ so $out_1 = \perp$, and therefore

$$rw_1 \perp = (\perp, \perp),$$

$$rw_1 \, [\,] \mapsto [\,],$$

which shows that writing *does not* precede reading in this case.

The moral of this example is that our traces should contain some information about the point at which output terminates (if indeed it does). Given a trace *tr*, output can terminate only after all the *w* actions have taken place, but it can terminate *at any point after that*. We use the symbol $\sqrt{}$ to indicate that output has (just) terminated. Intuitively, our traces for $read_1$ and $read_2$ will be

$$\{[\,], [r\, a, \sqrt{}]\},$$

and

$$\{[\,], [\sqrt{}], [\sqrt{}, r\, a]\},$$

respectively, showing how the two processes differ. We now show how the check marks are added to the weak traces, and we also introduce the notion of a terminal trace.

We now make the definition of a pretrace, on which the definition of trace is based. First we establish some notation. We write

$$f \, insq \downarrow outsq$$

when $f(insq \,{+}{+}\, \perp) = (\perp, outsq)$. This is the situation in which $f \, insq \mapsto outsq$ *and* the output has terminated. This is signalled by the fact that the output sequence is *definite* and not terminated by $\perp$. We also say that a sequence is *completed* if it contains $\sqrt{}$ (the choice of terminology should be obvious, as a check mark is intended to mark the point at which output terminates). Because of this, we have the following definition.

**Definition**     A sequence *tr* is a *pretrace* of *f* if and only if all of the following hold:

**1.** *tr* is a weak pretrace,

**2.** if *tr* is completed, then $f \, tr \upharpoonright in \downarrow tr \upharpoonright out$ and

$$f \, tr' \upharpoonright in \downarrow tr' \upharpoonright out$$

for all *completed* complete initial segments *tr'* of *tr*,

**3.** for all initial segments *tr'* of *tr*, if $f \, tr' \upharpoonright in \downarrow tr' \upharpoonright out$, then *tr'* either is a completed initial segment of *tr* or is immediately followed by $\sqrt{}$ in *tr*.

**Definition**    A sequence *tr* is a *trace* of *f* if and only if it is an initial segment of a pretrace of *f*.

The preceding definitions succeed in capturing sufficient information about the termination of the output of a process, as we shall see from the examples in the next section. There is another issue dual to output termination: Can we find out the point at which the remainder of the input can be passed to a succeeding process? This information is contained in the terminal traces, which we now define.

**Definition**    A sequence *tr* is a *terminal trace* of *f* if and only if both of the following hold:

**1.** *tr* is a completed pretrace of *f*

**2.** for all lists *x*,

$$f((tr \upharpoonright in) ++ x) = (x, (tr \upharpoonright out)).$$

The second condition means that whatever follows the input portion of *tr* in the input stream is actually passed to a succeeding process. This implies

$$f \, tr \upharpoonright in \downarrow tr \upharpoonright out$$

but the two are *not necessarily equivalent*. Consider the examples

$$null \, x \quad = \quad (x, [\,]) \,,$$
$$coy \, x \quad = \quad (\bot, [\,]) \,.$$

Each has as collection of traces

$$\{[\sqrt{}]\}$$

since

$$null \, \bot \quad = \quad (\bot, [\,]) \,,$$
$$coy \, \bot \quad = \quad (\bot, [\,]) \,.$$

but the *null* process passes the remainder of the input stream and so has terminal trace [√], whereas *coy* will not ask for more input and yet will not pass the remainder. Hence [√] is a terminal trace of *null*, but not of *coy*.

## 16  *The Examples Revisited— Traces and Terminal Traces*

In this section we re-examine the examples from Section 13, and look at their traces. In this chapter we merely describe the traces; we show their derivations in more detail in [5]. During the discussion two points emerge:

The *weak* pretraces of a process are insufficient to characterize the process's behavior in context. We demonstrate this point with Examples 5 and 6, which have the same weak pretraces but different behaviors in context.

The $\sqrt{}$ symbol can appear in a trace only after all the *write* items. Clearly it would be counterintuitive for this to fail, but we exhibit a proof of the fact in Example 3.

## Example 1          *write in = (in, [message])*

The set of traces is

$$\{[\,], [w \; message], [w \; message, \sqrt{}]\}\,.$$

Are there any terminal traces? If we refer to the defining equation, we can see that

$$write \; ([\,] ++ in) = (in, [message])\,,$$

so that [*w message*] is indeed one. It is the only one.

## Example 2          *read (a : x) = (x, [ ])*

We saw that the weak pretraces are

$$\{[\,], [r \; a]\}\,,$$

and so, since the $\sqrt{}$ must follow all writes, we have two possible pretraces: [$\sqrt{}, r \; a$] and [$r \; a, \sqrt{}$]. We can see that completion *does* occur at some point, since the output is [ ]. For the first possibility, we need to show that

$$read \; [\,] \downarrow [\,]$$

since [$\sqrt{}$] is a completed initial segment of [$\sqrt{}, r \; a$]. Looking back at Section 13 we see that this is not the case. What about the second candidate? The only completed initial segment is the sequence itself, and we have that

$$read \; [a] \downarrow [\,]\,,$$

assuring us of the pretrace property. In fact,

$$read([a] ++ x) = (x, [\,])\,,$$

so that this pretrace will be terminal too.

## Example 3    $echo\ (a : x) = (x, [a])$

Interaction *echo* has [ ] and [$r\ a, w\ a$] as its weak pretraces. What are its potential pretraces? We claimed that a check mark could only follow all the writes in a pretrace; intuitively this is clear, but can we see a formal reason for it? If $\sqrt{}$ precedes the writing of some item, $b$ say, then there are two sequences $outsq_1$ and $outsq_2$, the first a proper initial segment of the other, which will contain $b$, with corresponding input sequences

$$insq_1 \subseteq insq_2$$

and

$$f(insq_i ++ \perp) = (\perp, outsq_i)\,.$$

Since $insq_1 \sqsubseteq insq_2$ we should have by monotonicity $outsq_1 \sqsubseteq outsq_2$, but this is not the case, as $outsq_2$ is a *proper* extension of $outsq_1$, a contradiction.

This means that there is only one possible completed pretrace, [$r\ a, w\ a, \sqrt{}$], and this will indeed be one, since

$$echo\ [a] ++ \perp = (\perp, [a])\,,$$

that is,

$$echo\ [a] \downarrow [a]\,.$$

Also we have

$$echo\ [a] ++ x = (x, [a])$$

for every $x$, making the pretrace terminal. As the complete initial segment [ ] is not completed, the fact that it is a weak pretrace makes it a pretrace immediately.

## Example 4    $promptin_1\ (a : x) = (x, [prompt])$

An analysis similar to the one above leads us to conclude that the traces take the form

$$\{[\ ], [r\ a], [r\ a, w\ prompt, \sqrt{}]\}$$

with the final trace being terminal.

## Example 5    $promptin_2\ y = (tl\ y, [prompt])$

This interaction has the set of traces

$$\{[\ ], [w\ prompt, \sqrt{}], [w\ prompt, \sqrt{}, r\ a]\}\,.$$

Observe that

$$promptin_2 [a] ++ x = (x, [prompt])$$

for every $x$, so that the final trace will be terminal.

## Example 6

$$promptin_3 \ x \quad = \quad (y, [prompt] ++ rest)$$

**where**

$$(y, rest) = (tl \ x, [\ ]) \ , \quad existstail \ x$$

$$existstail \ (b : z) = True$$

This provides a variant of the two preceding functions. Functions *promptin₂* and *promptin₃* have the same *weak* pretraces (an exercise for the reader), but their pretraces will be *different*. In particular, [*w prompt*, $\sqrt{}$] is not a pretrace, since that would require that

$$promptin_3 [\ ] \downarrow [prompt] \ ,$$

which is not the case. Now, the only possible candidate pretrace is

[*w prompt, r a,* $\sqrt{}$] .

It has a single completed initial segment which we can check has the right property, making this a pretrace (because [*w prompt*] is not a completed initial segment, we require only its *weak* pretrace property).

The last two examples serve to emphasize that weak traces and pretraces are insufficient to characterize the behavior of processes in context.

## 17 *The Definition of Sequential Composition*

This section introduces the operation of sequential composition *on trace sets* and proceeds to prove that the *sq* function (defined in Section 9), which combines interactions, is sound with respect to this operation. We find that the operation has some subtlety, and we will show why we needed to introduce the machinery of check marks and terminal traces.

We saw in Section 15 that processes complete their behavior in two different ways:

The output is completed, and a definite list is returned as the output portion of the result;

The remainder of the input is passed to a succeeding process.

Recall also the discussion in Section 10, in which we explained how evaluation was driven by the need to print, i.e., that evaluation is *demand driven*. How does this affect the sequential composition of two processes using the *sq* function

$$sq\ f_1\ f_2\ in\ =\ (rest, out_1 ++ out_2)$$
$$\textbf{where}$$
$$(betw, out_1) = f_1\ in$$
$$(rest, out_2) = f_2\ betw$$

The output produced by the function is $out_1 ++ out_2$. The printer will demand the item-by-item evaluation of $out_1$, to be followed on its completion by a similar evaluation of $out_2$. Note that $out_2$ is examined only if and when $out_1$ is *completed*. Once this happens, the printer begins to take output from the second process.

What does this suggest about the traces of the process

$$sq\ f_1\ f_2\ ?$$

Clearly any trace of $f_1$ should be a trace of the composite, and we would expect that if (and only if) a trace $tr_1$ of $f_1$ is completed, its effect can be followed by one described by a trace $tr_2$ of $f_2$. In other words, we might expect that $tr = tr_1 ++ tr_2$ would be a trace of the composite. This is roughly right, except for two provisos:

**1.** As we remarked in Section 10, writing is eager, and *a write at the start of $tr_2$ may overtake a read at the end of $tr_1$*. This will indeed happen after the output of $f_1$ is completed, so any read after the check mark ($\sqrt{}$) will be overtaken by a write from the front of $tr_2$.

**2.** We have not demanded that the trace $tr_1$ be terminal, i.e., that $f_1$ pass the remainder of its input to $f_2$. In case $tr_1$ is not terminal, none of the reads in $tr_2$ (nor any of the writes that follow such a read) can be performed. Writes at the front of the sequence can and will be performed (before any reads following the check mark, as in 1). On the other hand, if a trace $tr_1$ is terminal, then *all* the following actions can be performed.

We can now formulate our definition. Suppose that $t_1$ is a completed trace and $t_2$ is a pretrace. Trace $t_1$ takes the form

$$t_1 = t_{11} ++ [\sqrt{}] ++ t_{12} ,$$

where $t_{12}$ consists exclusively of reads (by the monotonicity argument we gave in Example 3 of Section 16). Pretrace $t_2$ takes the form

$$t_2 = t_{21} ++ t_{22},$$

where $t_{21}$ consists entirely of writes and $t_{22}$ begins with either a read or a $\sqrt{}$. We define the *sum* of $t_1$ and $t_2$,

$$t_1 \oplus t_2,$$

to be

$$t_{11} ++ t_{21} ++ t_{12} ++ t_{22}$$

except when $t_{22} = [\sqrt{}] ++ t_{22}'$, in which case it is

$$t_{11} ++ t_{21} ++ [\sqrt{}] ++ t_{12} ++ t_{22}'.$$

In words: The reads following the check mark in $t_1$ are overtaken by the writes that begin $t_2$. Output terminates at the same point, unless that point immediately follows the initial block of writes that overtake $t_{12}$. In this case, output will terminate immediately after the block of writes and *before* $t_{12}$. Note that if either $t_{12}$ or $t_{21}$ is empty, that is, if $t_1$ ends with a check mark (which will certainly happen if its last action is to write) or if $t_2$ begins with a read, then

$$t_1 \oplus t_2 = t_1 ++ t_2.$$

We also define the *partial sum* of $t_1$ and $t_2$,

$$t_1 \otimes t_2,$$

to be

$$t_{11} ++ t_{21} ++ t_{12}$$

except when $t_{22} = [\sqrt{}] ++ t_{22}'$, in which case it is

$$t_{11} ++ t_{21} ++ [\sqrt{}] ++ t_{12}.$$

Again, to explain the definition, this is a case where the reads at the end of $t_1$ are overtaken by the writes at the front of $t_2$; the rest of $t_1$, however, is lost. This combinator models the combination of traces when $t_1$ is not terminal, the case we discussed in point 2 above.

**Definition** We define the *sum* $S_1 \oplus S_2$ of sets of pretraces $S_1, S_2$ to consist of

1. the noncompleted members of $S_1$, $tr_1$, say,

2. the sums $tr = tr_1 \oplus tr_2$ of terminal traces $tr_1$ from $S_1$ with members $tr_2$ of $S_2$,

3. the partial sums $tr = tr_1 \otimes tr_2$ of nonterminal completed traces $tr_1$ from $S_1$ with members $tr_2$ of $S_2$.

We now look at the proof that this sum embodies the "lazy" sequential combination of processes.

## 18 *Proving the Correctness of Sequential Composition*

In this section we prove that the *sq* function implements sequential composition, as defined in the previous section. This has the formal statement:

## Theorem 2
If $S_i$ is the set of pretraces of $f_i$, then $S_1 \oplus S_2$ is the set of pretraces of *sq* $f_1 f_2$.

**Proof**   Here we give only an outline of the proof; the full proof is to be found in [5].

We prove the result in two parts. In the first part we show that every member of $S_1 \oplus S_2$ is a pretrace of the composition of $f_1$ and $f_2$ and that each such pretrace is a member of the sum set.

The second part aims to show the converse— that every pretrace of the composite is a member of the sum set. In this part of the proof we rely on the determinacy theorem given in Section 14. This theorem can be extended to pretraces proper, rather than to weak pretraces; we leave this extension as an exercise for the reader. We then proceed by examining the general form of the definition of *f* and sequences *insq*, *outsq* so that

$$f\, insq \mapsto outsq\,.$$

The proof again splits into a number of cases, which we look at in turn.

During the course of the proof we make two assumptions:

**1.** For all interactive functions, *g*, and all input streams *x*, if

$$g\, x = (rest, out)\,,$$

then *rest* is a final segment of *x*, or is $\perp$, which can be considered to be the degenerate final segment.

**2.** If *insq*, *outsq* are sequences, then if

$$f\, insq \mathbin{++} \perp = (betw, outsq \mathbin{++} \perp)\,,$$

then *betw* = $\perp$. This is discussed further in [5].   $\square$

## 19 *Conclusions*

We have explored the general behavior of our streams-as-lazy-lists model for interactions, and we have shown how the behavior of sequential composition can be explained in terms of trace sets. If we ensure that output termination, as signalled by $\sqrt{}$, occurs only at the end of terminal traces, we can be sure that no overtaking takes place and that composition of traces is simply concatenation. On the other hand, we have the formal means by which we can explain more exotic interactions. As can be seen from the first part of the chapter, *sq* is the crucial combinator as, together with a simple choice combinator, primitive reading and writing operations, and recursion, it enables us to define all the other higher-level combinators.

**Definition**   We call a process, *f* say, *read-strict* if for no trace of *f* does $\sqrt{}$ precede an input item (and therefore $\sqrt{}$ precedes *no* other items).

It is not difficult to show that the basic operations of Section 5 are read-strict and that the combining forms introduced there preserve read-strictness; the only nontrivial case is that of *sq*, and that result follows from our analysis of *sq* above. Now, if we take the sequential composition of two read-strict processes we can see that no overtaking of reads by writes can take place (again, by our analysis of *sq*), and so we claim that the interleaving behavior of the functions of Section 5 *is* predictable as we suggested. On the other hand, as we saw from the examples in Section 6, it is all too easy to go astray if we adopt an *ad hoc* approach.

Another approach to I/O in a functional language is suggested by Backus, Williams, and Wimmers in [1] and followed up in [8]. In the latter paper they suggest that the lazy stream, or "pure", approach we adopt here is less convenient to use than one in which every function is taken to have a side effect on the *history* of the I/O devices. We prefer to see our approach as complementary to theirs. Indeed, as we explained in Section 4, we can see our type

> *interact* * **

as a type of functions with side effects on I/O.

As Williams and Wimmers remark, many functions fail to affect the history. This phenomenon is manifested here by the *apply* operation,

> *apply* :: (* → **) → *interact* * ** ,

which turns a "true" function into one with (trivial) I/O side effects. Once we realize this we can see that properties of many functions will carry over, just as Williams and Wimmers suggest.

The major advantage that we see in our approach is that we have a *purely functional* model of I/O, and so one to which we can apply the accepted methods of reasoning. As we remarked in the conclusion to the first part of the chapter, we see no need to combine the functional one with any other in order to describe interactive I/O.

## Acknowledgments

I am grateful to my colleagues at the University of Kent for various discussions about interactions and processes, and for using the interaction combinators supplied in the earlier paper and giving me valuable feedback about their behavior.

## References

[1] Backus, J., Williams, J. H., and Wimmers, E. L. "FL language manual", (preliminary version). Technical Report RJ 5339 (54809) 11/7/86, IBM Research Division, 1986.

[2] Cartwright, R. and Donahue, J. "The semantics of lazy (and industrious) evaluation." Technical Report CSL–83–9, Xerox Palo Alto Research Center, 1984.

[3] Hoare, C. A. R. *Communicating Sequential Processes.* Prentice-Hall International, 1985.

[4] Pnueli, A. "Applications of temporal logic to the specification and verification of reactive systems: A survey of current trends." In *Current Trends in Concurrency: Overviews and Tutorials*, J. W. de Bakker, W.-P. de Roever, and G. Rozenberg, eds. Springer Verlag, Berlin, 1986.

[5] Thompson, S. J. "Interactive functional programs." Technical Report 48, Computing Laboratory, University of Kent at Canterbury, 1987. (An extended version of this chapter, containing further discussion of the examples and full proofs of the theorems.)

[6] Thompson, S. J. "A logic for Miranda." Computing Laboratory, University of Kent at Canterbury, March 1987.

[7] Turner, D. A. "Miranda: A non-strict functional language with polymorphic types." *Functional Programming Languages and Computer Architecture* (Nancy, France, September), J.-P. Jouannaud, ed., pp. 1–16. Lecture Notes in Computer Science, vol. 201. Springer-Verlag, Berlin, 1985.

[8] Williams, J. H. and Wimmers, E. L. "Sacrificing simplicity for convenience: Where do you draw the line?" In *Proceedings of the 15th ACM Conference on Principles of Programming Languages.* ACM, New York, 1987.

# A
# *Calculus of Functions for Program Derivation*

# 11

## R. S. Bird
Oxford University

## 1 *Introduction*

This paper is about how to calculate programs. We introduce a notation for describing functions, outline a calculus for manipulating function descriptions, and prove two general theorems for implementing certain functions efficiently. Like useful calculi in other branches of mathematics, the calculus of functions consists of a body of knowledge expressed as basic algebraic identities, technical lemmas, and more general theorems. We illustrate the calculational approach to program construction by posing and solving a simple problem about coding sequences.

In presenting this work we wish to argue:

**1.** that some, perhaps many, algorithms can be derived by a process of systematic calculation from their specifications;

**2.** that an appropriate framework for this activity can be based on notation
for describing functions, notation that is wide enough to express both
specifications and implementations;

**3.** that an effective calculus of program derivation must be built upon useful
general theorems relating certain forms of expression to common patterns
of computation, theorems which —in the main— we still lack.

By way of motivation, we start in Section 2 by posing the problem we
want to solve. The notational framework is introduced in Section 3. In that
section we also state (mostly without proof) a number of simple algebraic laws
about functions. In Section 4 we apply these laws to our example problem
until we arrive at a point where a more substantial theorem is required. This
theorem is stated, together with a second theorem, in Section 5. We believe
that these two theorems are of the kind that will eventually prove important
in establishing a useful calculus for program derivation.

## 2  *Run-length Encoding*

The problem we will use to illustrate our approach is that of run-length
encoding. The idea behind run-length encoding is to represent a sequence of
values (usually characters) in a compact form by coding each "run" of equal
values by a pair consisting of the common value and the length of the run.
For example,

$$\text{\textit{code} "AABCCAAA"} = [(\text{'A'}, 2), (\text{'B'}, 1), (\text{'C'}, 2), (\text{'A'}, 3)]$$

The algorithm for computing *code* contains no surprises or subtleties. Our
objective, however, is to derive the algorithm from its specification, using
essentially the same kind of reasoning that a mathematician might employ
in solving a problem in, say, formal integration.

To specify *code*, consider the inverse function, *decode*. A sequence of pairs
can be decoded by "expanding" each pair to a sequence of values and concatenating the results. Given *decode*, we can specify (*code x*) as the *shortest*
sequence of pairs that decodes to *x*.

To make this idea precise, suppose we define the *generalized inverse* $f^{-1}$
of a function $f$ by the equation

$$f^{-1}x = \{w \mid f\,w = x\}.$$

Using notation from [1] (discussed further in the next section) we can now
specify *code* as follows:

$$code \quad :: \quad [\alpha] \rightarrow [(\alpha, N^+)]$$

$$code \quad = \quad \sqcap_{\#}/ \cdot decode^{-1}$$

$$decode \quad = \quad +\!\!+\!/ \cdot exp*$$

$$exp\,(a, n) \quad = \quad K_a * [1..n].$$

The first line of the specification gives the type of *code* as a function from lists of $\alpha$-values to lists of pairs, each pair consisting of an $\alpha$-value and a positive integer. The second line says that *code* is the functional composition of a function ($\sqcap_{\#}/$) that selects the shortest in a set of sequences, and the generalized inverse of *decode*. The third line defines *decode* as the composition of a function ($+\!\!+\!/$) that concatenates a list of lists together, and a function ($exp*$) that applies *exp* to every element of a list. Finally, $exp\,(a, n)$ is obtained for a positive integer $n$ by applying the constant-value function $K_a$ to each element of the list $[1..n]$, thereby giving a list of $n$ copies of $a$.

We shall return to this specification in Section 4. First we need to discuss notation in more detail, as well as introduce some of the basic algebraic identities employed in the derivation.

## 3 *Notation*

Our notation is basically that of [1] (see also [4, 5, 6]) with some additions and modifications. In particular, functions are curried, so function application associates to the left, and simple function arguments are written without brackets.

### 3.1 *Lists and Sets*

We shall use square brackets, [ and ], to denote lists, and braces, { and }, for sets. The symbol $+\!\!+$ denotes list concatenation, and $\cup$ denotes set union. The functions $[\cdot]$ and $\{\cdot\}$ return singleton lists and sets, respectively. Thus

$$[\cdot]\,a \quad = \quad [a],$$

$$\{\cdot\}\,a \quad = \quad \{a\}.$$

To avoid clumsy subscripts, we shall use $a°$ rather than $K_a$ to describe the function that always returns the value $a$. In particular, $[\,]°$ denotes the function defined by the equation

$$[\,]°a = [\,].$$

A similar function for sets is used below. We use $\#x$ to denote the length of the list $x$ (or the size of the set $x$).

### 3.2 *Conditionals*

We shall use the McCarthy conditional form $(p \rightarrow f, g)$ to describe the function

$$(p \rightarrow f, g)\, x \;=\; f x, \quad \textbf{if } p x$$
$$=\; g x, \quad \textbf{otherwise}.$$

For total predicates $p$ we have the following well-known identity:

$$h \cdot (p \rightarrow f, g) \;=\; (p \rightarrow h \cdot f, h \cdot g). \tag{1}$$

Equation (1) is referred to as the dot-cond law.

### 3.3 *Map*

The operator $*$ (pronounced "map") takes a function on its left and a list (or set) on its right. Informally, we have

$$f * [a_1, a_2, \ldots, a_n] = [f a_1, f a_2, \ldots, f a_n],$$

with an analogous equation holding for sets. We can specify $*$ over lists by the three equations

$$f * [] \;=\; [],$$
$$f * [a] \;=\; [f a],$$
$$f * (x + y) \;=\; (f * x) + (f * y).$$

These equations can also be expressed as identities between functions:

$$f * \cdot []^{\circ} \;=\; []^{\circ}, \tag{2}$$
$$f * \cdot [\cdot] \;=\; [\cdot] \cdot f, \tag{3}$$
$$f * \cdot +\!/ \;=\; +\!/ \cdot (f*) * . \tag{4}$$

We will refer to (2) as the map-empty law, to (3) as the map-single law, and to (4) as the map-concat law. Equation (4) makes use of the reduction operator $/$, discussed below. Similar equations hold for the definition of $*$ over sets. In particular, the analogue of (4) (in which $+$ is replaced by $\cup$) is called the map-union law.

**Note on syntax:** In [1], laws like the above were written with more brackets. For example, the map-concat law—called map promotion in [1]—was written

$$(f*) \cdot (+\!/) \;=\; (+\!/) \cdot ((f*)*).$$

In the present paper we avoid these additional brackets by assuming functional composition $(\cdot)$ has lowest precedence.

Another useful identity is provided by the fact that $*$ distributes over functional composition—the dot-map law:

$$(f \cdot g)* \;=\; f* \cdot g * . \tag{5}$$

### 3.4 *Reduce*

The reduction operator $/$ takes a binary operator $\oplus$ on its left and a list (or set) on its right. Informally, we have

$$\oplus/[a_1, a_2, \ldots, a_n] = a_1 \oplus a_2 \oplus \cdots \oplus a_n .$$

More formally, we can specify $\oplus/$ on nonempty lists by the equations

$$
\begin{aligned}
\oplus/[a] \quad &= \quad a , \\
\oplus/(x \mathbin{+\!\!\!+} y) \quad &= \quad (\oplus/x) \oplus (\oplus/y) .
\end{aligned}
$$

For the second equation to be unambiguous we require that $\oplus$ be an associative operator (because $\mathbin{+\!\!\!+}$ is). These equations can also be expressed as functional identities (the reduce-single and reduce-concat laws):

$$\oplus/ \cdot [\cdot] \;=\; id , \tag{6}$$
$$\oplus/ \cdot \mathbin{+\!\!\!+}/ \;=\; \oplus/ \cdot \oplus/ * . \tag{7}$$

Similarly, we can define $\oplus/$ over nonempty sets by the equations

$$
\begin{aligned}
\oplus/\{a\} \quad &= \quad a , \\
\oplus/(x \cup y) \quad &= \quad (\oplus/x) \oplus (\oplus/y) .
\end{aligned}
$$

In particular, the function level equivalent of the second equation is the reduce-union law:

$$\oplus/ \cdot \cup/ \;=\; \oplus/ \cdot \oplus/ * . \tag{8}$$

In order for the application of $\oplus/$ to a set to be unambiguous, we require $\oplus$ to be an associative, commutative, and idempotent operator (because $\cup$ is). For example,

$$\oplus/x = \oplus/(x \cup x) = (\oplus/x) \oplus (\oplus/x) ;$$

and so $\oplus$ must be idempotent.

## 3.5 *Identity Elements*

If $\oplus$ has an identity element $e$, then we can also define

$$\oplus/[\,] = \oplus/\{\,\} = e\,.$$

Equivalently, the reduce-empty law says

$$\oplus/\cdot[\,]^{\circ} = e^{\circ}\,. \tag{9}$$

It is often useful to invent fictitious identity elements for operators that do not possess them. For example, we can introduce the fictitious value $\infty$ to serve as the identity element of $\sqcap$, the binary operator which returns the smaller of its two (numeric) arguments. By making $\infty$ the zero element of $+$, we can then express the property that $+$ distributes over $\sqcap$ as the assertion that

$$\sqcap/\cdot(x+)* = (x+)\cdot\sqcap/\,.$$

holds for all $x$. Provided certain care is taken, fictitious identity elements can always be adjoined to a domain (see [1] for a more complete discussion).

## 3.6 *Selection*

Suppose $f$ is a numeric-valued function. The binary operator $\sqcap_f$ selects its left or right argument, depending on which has the smaller $f$-value:

$$
\begin{aligned}
x\sqcap_f y \;&=\; x, \quad \textbf{if } fx < fy \\
&=\; y, \quad \textbf{if } fy < fx\,.
\end{aligned}
$$

Unless $f$ is an injective function on the domain of values of interest, the operator $\sqcap_f$ is under-specified: If $x \neq y$ but $fx = fy$, then the value of $x\sqcap_f y$ is not specified (beyond the fact that it is one of $x$ or $y$). For example, the value

$$\text{``bye''}\sqcap_{\#}\text{``all''}$$

is under-specified since both arguments have the same length.

   This under-specification of $\sqcap_f$ can be very useful in formulating problems in computation. However, without further information about how the indeterminacy is resolved, the only properties of $\sqcap_f$ we can assume are that it is associative, idempotent, commutative, selective, and minimizing in the sense that

$$f(x\sqcap_f y) = fx \sqcap fy\,.$$

To emphasize the dangers of assuming too much, here is an intuitively obvious law that happens to be false:

$$\sqcap_{\#}/ \cdot (f*)* \;=\; f* \cdot \sqcap_{\#}/. \tag{10}$$

To see that (10) is false, take $f$ to be the function that negates its argument, and apply both sides to the set $\{[1],[-1]\}$. The left-hand side gives $\sqcap_{\#}/\{[1],[-1]\}$, while the right-hand side gives $f*\sqcap_{\#}/\{[1],[-1]\}$. These values cannot be equal, no matter how $\sqcap_{\#}$ is interpreted. On the other hand, equation (10) is valid when applied to a set that contains a unique shortest sequence. This fact is used below.

If we want to appeal to additional properties, then further information about the interpretation of $\sqcap_f$ must be supplied. For example, the condition that $+\!\!+$ distributes through $\sqcap_{\#}$, that is,

$$x +\!\!+ (y \sqcap_{\#} z) = (x +\!\!+ y) \sqcap_{\#} (x +\!\!+ z),$$

does not hold in general, but does hold if we interpret $x \sqcap_{\#} y$ for equal length sequences $x$ and $y$ as the lexicographically smaller of $x$ and $y$. If we introduce $\omega$ as the fictitious identity element of $\sqcap_{\#}$, and make $\omega$ the zero of $+\!\!+$, then the above distributivity condition can be expressed in the equivalent form

$$\sqcap_{\#}/ \cdot (x+\!\!+)* = (x+\!\!+) \cdot \sqcap_{\#}/.$$

## 3.7 *Homomorphisms*

Functions of the form $\oplus/ \cdot f*$ describe homomorphisms over lists (or sets) and are discussed in [1] (see also [3]). Each homomorphism $h = \oplus/ \cdot f*$ over lists satisfies the promotion law

$$h \cdot +\!\!+/ \;=\; \oplus/ \cdot h*. \tag{11}$$

The following proof of this result shows the way we shall lay out the steps of a calculation:

$$h \cdot +\!\!+/$$
$$= \text{ definition of } h$$
$$\oplus/ \cdot f* \cdot +\!\!+/$$
$$= \text{ map-concat (4)}$$
$$\oplus/ \cdot +\!\!+/(f*)*$$
$$= \text{ reduce-concat (7)}$$
$$\oplus/ \cdot \oplus/ * \cdot (f*)*$$

$= \quad$ dot-map (5)

$\quad \oplus/ \cdot (\oplus/ \cdot f*)*$

$= \quad$ definition of $h$

$\quad \oplus/ \cdot h*$

A similar result holds for homomorphisms over sets.

There are three particular homomorphisms that will be needed below: generalized conjunction, filter, and cartesian product.

**1.** *Generalized conjunction.* For a boolean-valued function $p$ we define *all $p$* by the equation

$$all\ p = \wedge/ \cdot p* \, ,$$

where $\wedge$ denotes logical conjunction. Thus (*all $p$ $x$*) returns true if every element of the list (or set) $x$ satisfies $p$, and false otherwise. One simple law (all-and) is

$$all\ (p \wedge q) \quad = \quad all\ p \wedge all\ q \, . \tag{12}$$

**2.** *Filter.* The operator $\triangleleft$ (pronounced "filter") is defined for sets by the equation

$$p \triangleleft = \cup/ \cdot (p \rightarrow \{\cdot\}, \{\}^\circ) * \, .$$

Thus, ($p \triangleleft$) is a homomorphism on sets. A similar equation holds for lists. In effect, ($p \triangleleft x$) returns the subset of elements of $x$ that satisfy $p$. This subset is obtained by replacing each element $a$ of $x$ by $\{a\}$ if $p\ a$ holds, or $\{\}$ if $p\ a$ does not hold, and taking the union of the resulting set of sets.

The filter-union law says that

$$p \triangleleft \cdot \cup/ \quad = \quad \cup/ \cdot (p\triangleleft) * \, . \tag{13}$$

This law is an immediate consequence of (11).

For total predicates $p$ and $q$, we have the and-filter law:

$$(p \wedge q)\triangleleft \quad = \quad p \triangleleft \cdot q \triangleleft \, . \tag{14}$$

Another identity (reduce-cond) involving $\triangleleft$ is as follows. Suppose $\oplus$ has identity element $e$; then

$$\oplus/ \cdot (p \rightarrow f, e^\circ)* \quad = \quad \oplus/ \cdot f* \cdot p \triangleleft \, . \tag{15}$$

Here is the proof:

$$\oplus/ \cdot f* \cdot p\triangleleft$$

=    definition of $\triangleleft$

$$\oplus/ \cdot f* \cdot +\!/ \cdot (p \rightarrow [\cdot], [\,]^\circ)*$$

=    promotion (11)

$$\oplus/ \cdot (\oplus/ \cdot f* \cdot (p \rightarrow [\cdot], [\,]^\circ))*$$

=    dot-cond (1)

$$\oplus/ \cdot (p \rightarrow \oplus/ \cdot f* \cdot [\cdot], \oplus/ \cdot f* \cdot [\,]^\circ)* \ .$$

Now we argue that

$$\oplus/ \cdot f* \cdot [\cdot]$$

=    map-single (3)

$$\oplus/ \cdot [\cdot] \cdot f$$

=    reduce-single (6)

$$f$$

and also that

$$\oplus/ \cdot f* \cdot [\,]^\circ$$

=    map-empty (2)

$$\oplus/ \cdot [\,]^\circ$$

=    reduce-empty (9)

$$e^\circ ,$$

completing the calculation.

3. *Cartesian product.* The third homomorphism is a function $cp$ (short for cartesian product) with type

$$cp :: [\{\alpha\}] \rightarrow \{[\alpha]\} .$$

Thus, the cartesian product of a list of sets is a set of lists. Informally we have

$$cp\,[S_1, S_2, \ldots, S_n] = \{[a_1, a_2, \ldots, a_n] \mid a_j \in S_j\} .$$

Formally we can define $cp$ as the homomorphism

$$cp = +\!\!\!\!+^\circ/ \cdot ([\cdot]*)* ,$$

where

$$S +\!\!+^\circ T = \{x +\!\!+ y \mid x \in S; \, y \in T\}.$$

Note that $+\!\!+^\circ$ is an associative operator. For example, we can calculate

$$cp\, [\{a, b\}, \{c\}, \{d, e\}]$$
$$= \quad +\!\!+^\circ / [\{\{[a], [b]\}, \{[c]\}, \{[d], [e]\}\}]$$
$$= \quad \{[a], [b]\} +\!\!+^\circ \{[c]\} +\!\!+^\circ \{[d], [e]\}$$
$$= \quad \{[a, c, d], [a, c, e], [b, c, d], [b, c, d]\}.$$

Two identities involving $cp$ are the cp-single and cp-cond laws:

$$cp \cdot \{\cdot\}* \quad = \quad \{\cdot\}, \tag{16}$$
$$cp \cdot (p \to f, \{\}^\circ)* \quad = \quad (all\ p \to cp \cdot f*, \{\}^\circ). \tag{17}$$

In effect, the first law says that the cartesian product of a list of singleton sets is a singleton set, while the second law says —in part— that if any set in the argument list is empty, then so is the cartesian product.

### 3.8 *Generalized Inverse*

The generalized inverse of a function $f$ is defined by

$$f^{-1}a = \{b \mid fb = a\}.$$

The dot-inverse and map-inverse laws are

$$(f \cdot g)^{-1} \quad = \quad \cup/ \cdot g^{-1} * \cdot f^{-1}, \tag{18}$$
$$(f*)^{-1} \quad = \quad cp \cdot f^{-1} *. \tag{19}$$

We give a proof of (18):

$$(f \cdot g)^{-1}a$$
$$= \quad \text{definition of inverse}$$
$$\{b \mid f(g\, b) = a\}$$
$$= \quad \text{set theory}$$
$$\cup/\{\{b \mid g\, b = c\} \mid f\, c = a\}$$
$$= \quad \text{definition of inverse}$$
$$\cup/\{g^{-1}c \mid f\, c = a\}$$
$$= \quad \text{definition of } *$$

$$\cup/g^{-1} * \{c \mid f c = a\}$$

= definition of inverse

$$\cup/g^{-1} * f^{-1} a$$

as required.

### 3.9 *Partitions*

Finally, we introduce a special case of generalized inverse. By definition, a *partition* of a list $x$ is a decomposition of $x$ into contiguous segments. A *proper* partition is a decomposition into nonempty segments. The (infinite) set of partitions of $x$ is just $(+\!\!+/)^{-1}x$. The function *parts*, where

$$parts = all\,(\neq [\,]) \triangleleft \cdot (+\!\!+/)^{-1}\,,$$

returns the (finite) set of proper partitions of a sequence. Two theorems about *parts* are given in Section 5.

## 4 *Calculation of code*

Using the identities given in the previous section, we can now begin to calculate an algorithm for *code*. The derivation is almost entirely mechanical: at each step—with one or two minor exceptions—there is only one law that can be applied.

*code*

= definition of *code*

$$\sqcap_{\#}/ \cdot decode^{-1}$$

= definition of *decode*

$$\sqcap_{\#}/ \cdot (+\!\!+/ \cdot exp*)^{-1}$$

= dot-inverse (18)

$$\sqcap_{\#}/ \cdot \cup/ \cdot (exp*)^{-1} * \cdot (+\!\!+/)^{-1}$$

= reduce-union (8)

$$\sqcap_{\#}/ \cdot \sqcap_{\#}/ * \cdot (exp*)^{-1} * \cdot (+\!\!+/)^{-1}$$

= dot-map (5)

$$\sqcap_{\#}/ \cdot (\sqcap_{\#}/ \cdot (exp*)^{-1}) * \cdot (+\!\!+/)^{-1}$$

= introduction of $f$

$$\sqcap_{\#}/ \cdot f * \cdot (+\!\!+/)^{-1}$$

where

$$f = \sqcap_{\#}\!/ \cdot (exp*)^{-1}.$$

The purpose of this last step is just to name the subexpression that will be the focus of future manipulation.

Before calculating $f$, we first consider the function $exp^{-1}$ that will arise during the calculation. This function has values given by

$$exp^{-1}x = \{(a, n) \mid exp\,(a, n) = x\}.$$

For the set on the right to be nonempty, we require that $x$ is a nonempty list of duplicated values (recall that $n$ must be a positive integer). Suppose we define

$$
\begin{aligned}
nedup\,x &= (x \neq [\,]) \wedge dup\,x \\
dup\,x &= all\,(= head\,x)\,x \\
rep\,x &= (head\,x, \#x)
\end{aligned}
$$

where $head\,x$ returns the first element of the nonempty list $x$. It then follows that

$$exp^{-1}x = (nedup\,x \rightarrow \{rep\,x\}, \{\,\}).$$

or, expressed at the function level, that

$$exp^{-1} = (nedup \rightarrow \{\cdot\} \cdot rep, \{\,\}^{\circ})$$

This equation is needed below.

Now we return to calculating $f$:

       f

=   definition of $f$

     $\sqcap_{\#}\!/ \cdot (exp*)^{-1}$

=   map-inverse (19)

     $\sqcap_{\#}\!/ \cdot cp \cdot exp^{-1}*$

=   definition of $exp^{-1}$

     $\sqcap_{\#}\!/ \cdot cp \cdot (nedup \rightarrow \{\cdot\} \cdot rep, \{\,\}^{\circ})*$

=   cp-cond (17)

     $\sqcap_{\#}\!/ \cdot (all\,nedup \rightarrow cp \cdot (\{\cdot\} \cdot rep)*, \{\,\}^{\circ})$

=   dot-cond (1)

$$(all\ nedup \rightarrow \sqcap_{\#}/ \cdot cp \cdot (\{\cdot\} \cdot rep)*, \sqcap_{\#}/ \cdot \{\}^\circ)$$

=    dot-map (5), and introducing $\omega$ as the identity of $\sqcap_{\#}$

$$(all\ nedup \rightarrow \sqcap_{\#}/ \cdot cp \cdot \{\cdot\} * \cdot rep*, \omega^\circ)$$

=   cp-single (16)

$$(all\ nedup \rightarrow \sqcap_{\#}/ \cdot \{\cdot\} \cdot rep*, \omega^\circ)$$

=   reduce-single (6)

$$(all\ nedup \rightarrow rep*, \omega^\circ).$$

Having calculated $f$, we continue with the calculation of *code*:

   *code*

=   calculation so far

$$\sqcap_{\#}/ \cdot f * \cdot (+\!\!+/)^{-1}$$

=   calculation of $f$

$$\sqcap_{\#}/ \cdot (all\ nedup \rightarrow rep*, \omega^\circ) * \cdot (+\!\!+/)^{-1}$$

=   reduce-cond (15)

$$\sqcap_{\#}/ \cdot (rep*) * \cdot all\ nedup \triangleleft \cdot (+\!\!+/)^{-1}$$

=   shortest-map (10)

$$rep * \cdot \sqcap_{\#}/ \cdot all\ nedup \triangleleft \cdot (+\!\!+/)^{-1}$$

=   definition of *nedup*; all-and (12); and-filter (14)

$$rep * \cdot \sqcap_{\#}/ \cdot all\ dup \triangleleft \cdot all\ (\neq[\,]) \triangleleft \cdot (+\!\!+/)^{-1}$$

=   definition of *parts*

$$rep * \cdot \sqcap_{\#}/ \cdot all\ dup \cdot parts.$$

Appeal to the shortest-map law (10) in the above calculation is valid since for all $x$ the set *all nedup* $\triangleleft \cdot (+\!\!+/)^{-1}$ contains a unique shortest member.
We have shown that

$$code\ x = rep * \sqcap_{\#}/all\ dup \triangleleft parts\ x.$$

In words, *code x* can be obtained by taking the shortest partition of $x$ into nonempty segments of duplicated values and representing each segment by its common value and its length. Expressed this way, the derived equation seems entirely reasonable and might even have served as the specification of the problem. Unlike the original specification, the new definition of *code* is executable. The set *parts x* contains a finite number of elements (in fact, $2^{n-1}$ elements, if $n > 0$ is the length of $x$), and these can be enumerated and filtered, and the shortest can be taken. What we now need is a faster method for computing expressions of the above form, and for this we need to consider various algorithms for computing partititons.

## 5 *Algorithms for Partititons*

Expressions of the form

$$\sqcap_f / all \; p \lhd parts \; x$$

arise in a number of applications. For example, in sorting by natural-merging, the input is first divided into runs of nondecreasing values. The function *runs*, which does this division, can be expressed in the form

$$runs \; x \;=\; \sqcap_{\#}/all \; nondec \lhd parts \; x \,.$$

This reads: the shortest partititon of $x$, all of whose components are nondecreasing sequences.

Similarly, the problem of filling a paragraph (see [2]) can be expressed as a problem about partitions:

$$fill \; m \; ws = \sqcap_W /all \; (fits \; m) \lhd parts \; ws \,.$$

This reads: the least wasteful (according to the waste function $W$) partition of a sequence of words $ws$, all of whose component segments (or "lines") will fit on a line of given width $m$.

There are numerous other examples (including, of course, *code*). This leads to the question: Can we find ways of computing solutions to problems of the form

$$\sqcap_f / all \; p \lhd parts \; x$$

efficiently?

### 5.1 *The Greedy Algorithm*

Here is a greedy algorithm for computing a partititon:

$$
\begin{aligned}
greedy \; p \; x \;&=\; [\,], &&\textbf{if } x = [\,] \\
&=\; [y] \mathbin{+\!\!+} greedy \; p \; (x - y), &&\textbf{otherwise} \\
&\quad \textbf{where } y = \sqcup_{\#}/p \lhd inits^+ x
\end{aligned}
$$

In this algorithm, the expression *inits⁺ x* denotes the list of nonempty initial segments of $x$, in increasing order of length, $\sqcup_\#/$ returns the longest sequence in a set of sequences, and $(x \rightharpoonup y)$ is the sequence that remains when the initial segment $y$ of $x$ is deleted from $x$. The operator $\rightharpoonup$ is specified by the equation

$$(u + v) \rightharpoonup u = v$$

for all sequences $u$ and $v$.

It is easy to see that, at each step, the greedy algorithm chooses the longest nonempty initial segment $y$ of the remaining input $x$ that satisfies the predicate $p$. In order for *greedy* to make progress, it is necessary to suppose that $p$ holds for [ ] and every singleton sequence at least. In this way a nonempty portion of the input is "consumed" at each step.

There is a useful condition on $p$ which enables the next segment $y$ to be computed efficiently. Say $p$ is *prefix-closed* if

$$p(x + y) \Rightarrow p x.$$

In words, if $p$ holds for a sequence, then it holds for every initial segment of the sequence (including [ ]). If $p$ is prefix-closed, then there exists a *derivative* function $\delta$ such that

$$p(x + [a]) = p x \wedge \delta a x.$$

For example, with $p = dup$ we have

$$\delta a x = (x = [\,]) \vee (a = head\, x),$$

and with $p = nondec$ we have

$$\delta a x = (x = [\,]) \vee (last\, x \le a),$$

where *last x* returns the last element of a nonempty sequence $x$.

If $p$ is prefix-closed, we can formulate the following version of the greedy algorithm:

$$
\begin{aligned}
greedy\, p\, x \quad &= \quad shunt\, [\,]\, x \\
shunt\, y\, [\,] \quad &= \quad [\,] \\
shunt\, y\, ([a] + x) \quad &= \quad shunt\, (y + [a])\, x, \quad \textbf{if } \delta\, a\, y \\
&= \quad [y] + shunt\, [a]\, x, \quad \textbf{otherwise}
\end{aligned}
$$

This version is linear in the number of $\delta$-calculations.

A related condition on $p$ is that of being *suffix-closed*; i.e.,

$$p\,(x \mathbin{+\mkern-8mu+} y) \Rightarrow p\,y\,.$$

If $p$ is both prefix- and suffix-closed, then $p$ is said to be *segment-closed*. For example, both *dup* and *nondup* are segment-closed. The suffix-closed condition arises in one of the theorems discussed below.

### 5.2 *The Leery Algorithm*

Here is another algorithm for computing partitions:

> *leery f p x*
>
> $= \ [\,],$                                      **if** $x = [\,]$
>
> $= \ \sqcap_f / \{[y] \mathbin{+\mkern-8mu+} \textit{leery } f\, p\, (x \rightarrow y) \mid y \in p \vartriangleleft \textit{inits}^+ x\}$   **otherwise**

This algorithm is a little more "careful" than the greedy algorithm (whence the name "leery"). At each stage, some initial segment $y$ of $x$ is chosen so that (i) $y$ satisfies $p$; and (ii) $f\,([y] \mathbin{+\mkern-8mu+} ys)$ is as small as possible, where $ys$ is the result of adopting the same strategy on the rest of the input. Unlike the greedy algorithm, the leery algorithm will not necessarily choose the longest initial segment of $x$ satisfying $p$ at each stage.

The direct recursive implementation of *leery* is inefficient, since values of *leery* on tail segments of $x$ will be recomputed many times. Instead, *leery* is better implemented by a dynamic-programming scheme that computes and stores the results of applying *leery* to all tail segments of the input. In making a decision about the next component of the partition, these subsidiary results are then available without recomputation. We shall not, however, formulate the efficient version of *leery* here.

We now state two theorems about the greedy and leery algorithms.

### Theorem 1 (The *Leery* Theorem)
If $\mathbin{+\mkern-8mu+}$ distributes through $\sqcap_f$, then

$$\sqcap_f / all\ p \vartriangleleft parts\ x = leery\ f\ p\ x,$$

provided $p$ holds for $[\,]$.

### Proof   We shall need the following recursive definition of *parts*:

> $parts\,[\,] \ = \ \{[\,]\}$
>
> $parts\ x \quad = \ \cup/subparts * inits^+ x,$                       **if** $x \neq [\,]$
>
>             **where**  $subparts\ y = ([y] \mathbin{+\mkern-8mu+}) * parts\ (x \rightarrow y)$

We omit the proof that this definition of *parts* satisfies the specification

$$parts = all\,(\neq[\,]) \lhd \cdot (+\!\!+\!/)^{-1}\,.$$

Let $\theta$ be defined by

$$\theta x = \sqcap_f/all\,p \lhd parts\,x\,.$$

The theorem is proved by showing that $\theta$ satisfies the recursive definition of *leery*. There are two cases to consider.

**Case** $x = [\,]$**.**  The derivation of

$$\theta[\,] = [\,]$$

is straightforward and is omitted.

**Case** $x \neq [\,]$**.**  In the case $x \neq [\,]$, we argue

$$\sqcap_f/all\,p \lhd parts\,x$$

$=$  definition of *parts*

$$\sqcap_f/all\,p \lhd \cup/subparts * inits^+x$$

$=$  filter-union (13); reduce-union (8)

$$\sqcap_f/\sqcap_f/ * (all\,p\lhd) * subparts * inits^+x$$

$=$  dot-map (5)

$$\sqcap_f/(\sqcap_f/\cdot all\,p \lhd \cdot subparts) * inits^+x$$

$=$  introduction of $h$

$$\sqcap_f/h * inits^+x$$

where

$$h\,y = \sqcap_f/all\,p \lhd subparts\,y\,.$$

We continue by calculating $h$ (note that $h$ depends on $x$):

$$\sqcap_f/all\,p \lhd subparts\,y$$

$=$  definition of *subparts*

$$\sqcap_f/all\,p \lhd ([y]+\!\!+) * parts\,(x \rightharpoonup y)$$

$=$  property of *all*

$$\sqcap_f/(p\,y \rightarrow ([y]+\!\!+) * all\,p \lhd parts\,(x \rightharpoonup y),\{\})$$

$=$  dot-cond (1)

$$(p\,y \to \sqcap_f/([y] \mathbin{+\!\!+}) * all\,p \lhd parts\,(x \to y), \sqcap_f/\{\,\})$$

= distributivity assumption

$$(p\,y \to [y] \mathbin{+\!\!+} \sqcap_f/all\,p \lhd parts\,(x \to y), \sqcap_f/\{\,\})$$

= definition of $\theta$

$$(p\,y \to [y] \mathbin{+\!\!+} \theta(x \to y), \sqcap_f/\{\,\})\,.$$

Finally, if we substitute the derived definition of $h$ into the derived equation for $\theta$ and apply the reduce-cond law, we obtain

$$\theta x \;=\; \sqcap_f/\phi * p \lhd inits^+ x$$

$$\textbf{where}\;\; \phi y = [y] \mathbin{+\!\!+} \theta(x \to y)\,.$$

In other words, $\theta$ satisfies the recursive definition of *leery*, completing the proof of the theorem.   □

In order to apply the leery theorem we need to know when there exists an operator $\sqcap_f$ such that $\mathbin{+\!\!+}$ distributes through $\sqcap_f$. It turns out that a necessary and sufficient condition is given by the following definition.

**Definition 1**   A function $f : [[\alpha]] \to N$ is said to be *prefix-stable* if

$$f\,xs \le f\,ys \Rightarrow f\,([x] \mathbin{+\!\!+} xs) \le f\,([x] \mathbin{+\!\!+} ys)$$

for all $x$, $xs$, and $ys$.

We shall omit the proof of the following lemma.

## Lemma 1

A necessary and sufficient condition for there to exist an interpretation of $\sqcap_f$ such that $\mathbin{+\!\!+}$ distributes through $\sqcap_f$ is that $f$ is prefix-stable. One suitable interpretation is to let $xs \sqcap_f ys$ return the smaller of $xs$ and $ys$ under the ordering $\sqsubseteq_f$ defined as follows: $[\,] \sqsubseteq_f ys$ for all $ys$, and

$$xs \sqsubseteq_f ys \;=\; f\,xs < f\,ys$$
$$\lor\;\; f\,xs = f\,ys \land hd\,xs >_L hd\,ys$$
$$\lor\;\; f\,xs = f\,ys \land hd\,xs = hd\,ys \land tl\,xs \sqsubseteq_f tl\,ys$$

for nonempty sequences $xs$ and $ys$. In the definition, $<_L$ denotes the lexicographic ordering on $[\alpha]$, and $hd$ and $tl$ return the head and tail of a sequence, respectively.

The advantage of using the interpretation of $\sqcap_f$ given in Lemma 1 is that it is computationally inexpensive when used with the leery algorithm. If two partitions have the same $f$-value, then the one with the longest first component is chosen.

For the second theorem we need the following definition.

**Definition 2**    A function $f : [[\alpha]] \rightarrow N$ is *greedy* if both the following conditions hold for all $x$, $y$, $z$ and $s$:

$$f([x + y] + s) \leq f([x] + [y] + s),$$

$$f([x + y] + [z] + s) \leq f([x] + [y + z] + s).$$

The first greedy condition says that shorter partitions have a smaller $f$-value than longer ones; the second condition says that, for partitions of equal length, the longer the first component, the smaller is its $f$-value.

**Theorem 2** (The *greedy* theorem)
Suppose $f$ is prefix-stable and greedy, and let $\sqcap_f$ be interpreted as in Lemma 1. If $p$ is suffix-closed, then

$$leery\, f = greedy.$$

**Proof**    Abbreviating *leery f p* by $\theta$, it suffices to prove that

$$[x + y] + \theta z \quad \sqsubseteq_f \quad [x] + \theta(y + z) \tag{20}$$

for all $x$, $y$ and $z$. But since $x + y >_L x$, assertion (20) follows from

$$f([x + y] + \theta z) \quad \leq \quad f([x] + \theta(y + z)). \tag{21}$$

The proof of (21) is by induction on the length of $y$. The base case, $\#y = 0$, is immediate. For the induction step, consider the value of $\theta(y + z)$. There are two possibilities: Either

$$\theta(y + z) \quad = \quad [y + z_1] + \theta(z_2) \tag{case A}$$

for some $z_1 \neq [\,]$ and $z_2$, such that $z = z_1 + z_2$ and $p\,(y + z_1)$ holds or

$$\theta(y + z) \quad = \quad [y_1] + \theta(y_2 + z) \tag{case B}$$

for some $y_1 \neq [\,]$ and $y_2$, such that $y = y_1 + y_2$ and $p y_1$ holds. (This case includes the possibility that $y_2 = [\,]$).

In case A, we reason that $p\, z_1$ holds, since $p$ is suffix-closed, and so by definition of $\theta$,

$$f(\theta z) \leq f([z_1] + \theta z_2).$$

Hence

$$f([x + y] + \theta z)$$

$\leq$ prefix-stability

$$f([x + y] + [z_1] + \theta z_2)$$

$\leq$ second greedy condition

$$f([x] + [y + z_1] + \theta z_2)$$

$=$ case A

$$f([x] + \theta(y + z))$$

as required. $\square$

In case B, we reason

$$f([x + y] + \theta z)$$

$=$ case B

$$f([x + y_1 + y_2] + \theta z)$$

$\leq$ induction hypothesis, as $\#y_2 < \#y$

$$f([x + y_1] + \theta(y_2 + z))$$

$\leq$ first greedy condition

$$f([x] + [y_1] + \theta(y_2 + z))$$

$=$ case B

$$f([x] + \theta(y + z))$$

as required. $\square$

## 6 Application

We give one application of the greedy theorem. Since *dup* is suffix-closed (in fact, segment-closed), and # is prefix-stable and greedy, we have that

$$code = rep * \cdot greedy\, dup$$

is a solution to the problem of run-length encoding.

## Acknowledgements

Much of the calculus presented above was developed in collaboration with Lambert Meertens of the CWI, Amsterdam, to whom I am grateful for both support and friendship. Roland Backhouse pointed out an error in an earlier draft of the paper, in which the the shortest-map law was assumed to hold unconditionally. I am also grateful to Carroll Morgan, Oege deMoor, Bill Roscoe, and Tony Hoare for many enjoyable discussions on the role of indeterminacy in a purely functional calculus.

## References

[1] Bird, R. S. "An introduction to the theory of lists." *Logic of Programming and Calculi of Discrete Design*, M. Broy, ed., pp. 3–42. Springer-Verlag, Berlin, 1987.

[2] Bird, R. S. "Transformational programming and the paragraph problem." *Science of Computer Programming 6* (1986), pp. 159–189.

[3] Bird, R. S. and Hughes, R. J. M. "The alpha-beta algorithm: An exercise in program transformation." *Inf. Proc. Letters 24* (1987), pp. 53–57.

[4] Bird, R. S. and Meertens, L. G. L. T. "Two exercises found in a book on algorithmics." *Program Specification and Transformation*, L. G. L. T Meertens, ed., pp. 451–458. North-Holland, Amsterdam, 1987.

[5] Bird, R. S. and Wadler, P. *An Introduction to Functional Programming.* Prentice-Hall International, Hemel Hempstead, UK, 1988.

[6] Meertens, L. G. L. T. "Algorithmics — Towards programming as a mathematical activity." *Proc. CWI Symp. on Mathematics and Computer Science*, CWI Monographs, North-Holland, 1 (1986), pp. 289–334.

# Higher-Order Functions Considered Unnecessary for Higher-Order Programming

# 12

**Joseph A. Goguen**[1]

Oxford University

and

SRI International

## Abstract

*I*t is often claimed that the essence of functional programming is the use of functions as values, i.e., of higher-order functions, and many interesting examples have been given showing the power of this approach. Unfortunately, the logic of higher-order functions is difficult, and in particular, higher-order unification is undecidable. Moreover (and closely related), higher-order expressions are notoriously difficult for humans to read and write correctly. However, this paper shows that typical higher-order programming examples can be captured with just first-order functions, by the systematic use of parameterized modules, in a style that we call **parameterized programming**. This has the advantages that correctness proofs can be done entirely within

---

1. This paper was written in 1987 while the author was at the Computer Science Laboratory at SRI International.

first order logic, and that interpreters and compilers can be simpler and more efficient. Moreover, it is natural to impose *semantic* requirements on modules, and hence on functions. A more subtle point is that higher order logic does not always mix well with subsorts, which can nonetheless be very useful in functional programming by supporting the clean and rigorous treatment of partially defined functions, exceptions, overloading, multiple representation, and coercion. Although higher order logic cannot always be avoided in specification and verification, it should be avoided wherever possible, for the same reasons as in programming. This paper contains several examples, including one in hardware verification. An appendix shows how to extend standard equational logic with quantification over functions, and justifies a perhaps surprising technique for proving such equations using only ground term reduction.

---

# 1 *Introduction*

Following an introduction to the OBJ language, this paper gives some examples showing how higher-order functions can be avoided by using sufficiently powerful parameterized modules. I do not consider higher-order functions *harmful, useless,* or *unbeautiful*; but I do claim significant advantages for avoiding higher-order functions whenever possible, and I claim that they can be avoided quite systematically in functional programming, by using parameterized programming instead. Of course, higher-order logic is useful in many areas, particularly the foundations of mathematics (e.g., type theory), extracting programs from proofs, describing proof strategies (e.g., LCF tactics), and the semantics of traditional programming languages (e.g., Scott-Strachey); but it too should be avoided whenever possible, and the appendix develops some techniques for reasoning about first-order functions that often make it posssible to do so.

## 1.1 *Parameterized Programming*

A major advantage of functional programming over traditional imperative programming is that it can yield better structured programs [58]. However, a language with sufficiently powerful parameterized modules can achieve highly structured programs without higher-order functions. In particular, the examples given below show that typical higher-order functional programming techniques are easily carried out with OBJ's **parameterized programming**, in ways that seem to me even more structured and flexible. Code is broken into highly parameterized, mind-sized, internally coherent modules, and then new programs are constructed from old ones by instantiating, transforming, and combining these modules. This paper argues that first-order parameterized programming includes the essential power of higher-order programming and even offers certain advantages.

Parameterized programming is a general and powerful technique for software design, production, reuse, and maintenance. This approach involves abstraction through two kinds of module: **objects** to encapsulate executable code, and in particular to define abstract data types; and **theories** to specify both syntactic structure and semantic properties of modules. Each kind of module can be parameterized, where actual parameters are modules, and can also import other modules. Interfaces of parameterized modules are defined by theories and thus include semantic as well as syntactic constraints.[1] For parameter instantiation, a **view** binds the formal entities in an interface theory to actual entities in a module and also asserts satisfaction of the theory by the module. Views are first-class citizens that can be named, can import modules, and can even be parameterized. This integration of objects, theories, and views provides a powerful wide-spectrum capability. A software design is represented as a hierarchy of modules with associated views, and a software system is actually constructed from its components when the design (i.e., the code) is executed. In particular, **module expressions** allow complex instantiations of generics and include commands that transform already defined modules; they can be seen as generalizing the UNIX[TM] **make** command. Maintenance is facilitated by editing and then re-executing such designs. Reusability is enhanced by the flexibility of the parameterization, composition, and transformation mechanisms. **Default views** can greatly reduce the effort of defining views.

All these ideas are illustrated in OBJ, a wide-spectrum, first-order functional programming language that is rigorously based upon **order-sorted** (conditional) equational logic. This logic provides a notion of **subtype** that supports many useful features, including multiple representation, overloading, coercion, multiple inheritance, and exception handling. This rigorous semantic basis allows a declarative, specificational style of programming, eases system design and implementation, and facilitates program verification. Moreover, logical specifications can be directly executed. These points are illustrated in several examples, including a simple hardware verification example.

---

1. The Ada [76] notion of a generic package provides only part of what is needed. In particular, Ada generic packages provide no way to document the *semantics* of interfaces, although this feature can greatly improve the reliability of software reuse and can also help retrieve the right module from a library (as discussed in [30]). Also, Ada provides only very weak facilities for combining modules; for example, only one level of module instantiation is possible at a time.

### 1.2 *Some History*

OBJ was originally designed in 1976 by Joseph Goguen as a language for "error algebras" [28], an attempt to extend algebraic abstract data types to handle errors and partial functions in a simple, uniform way. This first design also used ideas from Clear [7, 9] for parameterized modules. Initial implementations of OBJ were done from 1977 to 1979 at UCLA by Joseph Tardo as OBJ0 and OBJT [86, 47] using error algebras plus an "image" construct for parameterization. David Plaisted implemented OBJ1 by enhancing OBJT, during 1982–83 at SRI; improvements included (an efficient form of) matching modulo associativity and/or commutativity, hash coded memo functions, and a highly interactive environment [45]. OBJ2 [21, 22] was implemented during 1984–85 at SRI by Kokichi Futatsugi and Jean-Pierre Jouannaud, following a design led by Joseph Goguen and José Meseguer, based on order sorted algebra [44, 41, 36] rather than on error algebra; also, OBJ2 provided Clear-like parameterized modules, theories and views, although not in full generality.

The latest version, OBJ3, is available from SRI International, and was developed (using Kyoto Common Lisp) by Joseph Goguen, José Meseguer, Timothy Winkler, Claude and Hélène Kirchner, and Aristide Megrelis; the implementation team was led by José Meseguer. Although OBJ3 has a syntax quite close to that of OBJ2, it has a different implementation based on a simpler and more efficient operational semantics for order sorted algebra [60]. Also, it provides much more sophisticated module expressions, including default views, for which Timothy Winkler deserves special credit. OBJ can be seen as an implementation of Clear for conditional order sorted logic.

Other implementations of OBJ include UMIST-OBJ from the University of Manchester Institute of Science and Technology [16], Abstract Pascal from the University of Manchester [61], MC-OBJ from the Univeristy of Milan [14], and a Franz Lisp OBJ2 from Washington State University [84]. The first two are written in Pascal and the third in C. UMIST-OBJ is available in Britain as a commercial product, called Obj-Ex, and another variant, called Axis [17], is available from Hewlett-Packard Labs in Bristol, UK. In addition, we are extending OBJ in the directions of relational and object-oriented programming, to languages called Eqlog [39] and FOOPS [42], respectively.

The experimental OBJ systems implemented so far have been used for many applications, including debugging algebraic specifications [45], rapid prototyping [37], defining programming languages in a way that immediately yields an interpreter (see [46] and the elegant work of Peter Mosses [72, 73]), specifying software systems (e.g., the GKS graphics kernel system [19], an Ada configuration manager [23], the Macintosh QuickDraw program [74], and OBJ in itself [16]), and hardware specification, simulation and verification (see

[31, 85] and Section 3.2). Many of these applications were produced under an experiment sponsored by the British Alvey Project, and will be collected with some more recent work in a book on the practical use of OBJ [35]. OBJ is also being combined with Petri nets, thus allowing structured data in tokens [2], and it is one language for programming a massively parallel machine that executes rewrite rules directly [62, 43]; in fact, we believe that OBJ on such a machine should greatly out-perform a conventional language on a conventional machine, by direct *concurrent* execution of rewrite rules; however, FOOPS offers some further advantages.

## 2 *Aspects of OBJ*

This section is a rather lengthy, but still incomplete and informal, introduction to OBJ. Readers already familiar with OBJ should skip directly to Section 3 and the appendix. Readers who are already familiar with some other functional programming language should at least skim this section, because OBJ embodies basic design choices that are quite different from those of other programming languages, including other current functional programming languages:

1. It is rigorously based on deduction in **order-sorted equational logic**, which provides a precise semantics for exception handling, multiple inheritance, overloading, and multiple representations for data abstractions. It uses strong sorting with retracts to ease parsing.

2. It supports **parameterized programming**, as sketched above and expanded below.

3. It supports **user-defined evaluation strategies** for each operation separately, rather than imposing a global order of evaluation; this allows both eager and lazy evaluation, as well as more complex options; also, efficient default evaluation strategies are computed by simple strictness analysis if the user does not provide an explicit strategy.

4. It has rewriting **modulo attributes**, including associativity, commutativity, identity, and idempotence.

OBJ is a **logical programming language** in the sense that it is based on inference in a precise logical system, namely, order-sorted equational logic; see [69] for more on logical programming, and [44] for more on order sorted equational logic. As has been well argued by advocates of Prolog, this confers certain important benefits: program simplicity and clarity (which can greatly ease program understanding, debugging, and maintenance); separation of logic and control; and identity of program logic with proof logic. In such a language, a high-level description of what a program does actually is a program; that is, one can execute it. Other logical programming languages include pure Prolog [18], pure Lisp [68], and CDS [4]; such languages can also be considered as efficiently executable specification languages. Some other languages that are based on algebraic semantics include Larch [52], Asspegique [5], Obscure [63] and Act One [20]; it seems fair to say that they have all been significantly influenced by OBJ.

Higher-order functional programming languages like Hope [12], Miranda [87], ML [54] and Haskell [57] can be seen as based either on rewrite rules or on higher-order equational logic, although they tend to have some impure features for efficiency or convenience; for example, ML has assignment and exceptions, while Miranda has *ad hoc* coercions among various kinds of numbers, as well as lazy pattern matching. Standard ML has a powerful parameterized module facility inspired in part by Clear's. Guttag, Horowitz and Musser [53] describe a system for the symbolic execution of algebraic abstract data types, and Levy and Sirovich [64] describe the TEL system for specifying semantics with equations. Other related systems include those due to Hoffmann and O'Donnell [56, 75], Lucas and Risch [65], and Prywes [79], all of which are first order, and the elegant work of Backus [1], which is higher order functional programming for a fixed set of rewrite rules and data types.

This section provides an intuitive introduction to features of OBJ that are needed for understanding our higher-order programming examples. Some important topics are thus omitted, including user-definable evaluation strategies, details of OBJ semantics, and default views.

## 2.1 *Strong Sorting*

To avoid the confusion associated with the many different uses of the word "type," we shall instead use the word "sort" from here on in connection with the many-sorted equational logic based approach of OBJ. Among the advantages of **strong sorting** are: to catch meaningless expressions before they are executed; to separate logically and intuitively distinct concepts; and to enhance readability by documenting these distinctions. With a modern (e.g., structural) editor, it is little trouble to insert sort declarations; many could even be inserted automatically by a compiler or a smart editor.

Ordinary unsorted logic offers the dubious advantage that anything can be applied to anything; for example,

```
first-name(not(age(3 * false)))
```
$$\text{iff } 2^{\text{birth-place(temperature(329))}}$$

is permissible. Although beloved by Lisp and Prolog hackers, unsorted logic is too permissive. However, many-sorted logic is too restrictive, since it does not support overloaded function symbols, such as `_+_` for integer, rational, and complex numbers (where the underbar character `_` serves as a place-holder for arguments). Moreover, strictly speaking, an expression like **(-4 / -2)** ! does not parse in many-sorted logic (assuming that factorial applies only to natural numbers), since **(-4 / -2)** ! parses as a rational rather than a natural. This problem can be solved by extending order-sorted algebra with **retracts**, which provide sufficient expressiveness while still banishing truly meaningless expressions, as discussed in Section 2.3.


### 2.2 *Operation and Expression Syntax*

It seems worth some extra implementation effort and processing time to support syntax that is as flexible, informative, and close to users' intuitions and to standard usage as possible. OBJ users can define any syntax they like for operations, including prefix, postfix, infix, and most generally, **mixfix**, to customize it for any given problem domain; this is similar to ECL [15]. Obviously, there are many opportunities for ambiguity in parsing such a syntax. OBJ's convention is that an expression is **well formed** if and only if it has *exactly* one parse (or more precisely, a unique parse of *least* sort; see Section 2.3). The argument and value sorts of an operation are declared at the same time as its syntactic form. We distinguish two cases. The first is the usual parenthesized-prefix-with-commas functional form. For example,

```
op f : S1 S2 -> S3 .
```

indicates that **f(X, Y)** has sort **S3** when **X** has sort **S1** and **Y** has sort **S2**. The general mixfix case uses place-holders, indicated by an underbar character, as in the prefix declaration

```
op top_ : Stack -> Int .
```

for **top** as used in expressions like **top push(A, B)**. Similarly, the "outfix" form of the singleton set operation, as in **{ 4 }**, is declared by

```
op {_} : Int -> Set .
```

and the infix form for addition, as in **2 + 3**, is

```
op _+_ : Int Int -> Int .
```

while a mixfix declaration for conditional is

```
op if_then_else_fi : Bool Int Int -> Int .
```

Between the : and the -> in an operation declaration comes the **arity** of the operation, and after the -> comes its **value sort** (also called "co-arity"); the ⟨arity,value sort⟩ pair is called the **rank** of an operation.

Operations with the same arity and value sort but with different forms can be declared together, for example,

```
ops zero one : -> S .
ops (_+_)(_*_) : S S -> S .
```

Parentheses are required in the second case, to mark the boundary between the two forms.

The following simple object for bit strings illustrates some basic OBJ syntax:

```
obj BITS is sorts Bit Bits .
   ops 0 1 : -> Bit .
   op nil : -> Bits .
   op _._ : Bit Bits -> Bits .
endo BITS
```

A typical expression using the syntax of this object is 0 . 1 . 0 . nil .

## 2.3 *Subsorts*

To handle cases where things of one sort are also of another sort — for example, all natural numbers are also rational numbers — and cases where expressions may have several different sorts, we use **order-sorted algebra**. This approach involves imposing a partial ordering on the set of sorts, e.g., **Nat** < **Rat**, meaning **Nat** ≤ **Rat** (we use < instead of ≤ for typographical convenience). Then **multiple inheritance** is supported, since a given sort can have more than one distinct supersort, and operation overloading arises by restricting functions to subsorts. The **signature** of an object consists of the sorts, subsort relation, and operations defined in it, including their form, arity, and value sort.

Two happy facts are that order-sorted algebra is only slightly more difficult than many-sorted algebra and that essentially all results generalize from the many-sorted to the order-sorted case without complication. Although this paper omits all technical details, order-sorted algebra is a rigorous mathematical theory. Order-sorted algebra originated in 1978 and is treated comprehensively in [44] and summarized in [41]. Some alternative approaches have been nicely developed by Gogolla [24, 25], Wadge [88], Reynolds [80], and others.

OBJ directly supports *subsort polymorphism*, which is operator overloading consistent under subsort restriction. By contrast, languages like ML [54] and Hope [12] support *parametric polymorphism* [71], following ideas of Strachey. OBJ's parameterized modules provide a similar capability in a different way.

A term over an order-sorted signature is considered **well formed** if and only if it has a unique parse of lowest sort; [44] and [41] show that this occurs under certain mild and natural assumptions. Sometimes subexpressions are not of the expected sort and must be "coerced" to it. This is trivial from a subsort to a supersort; for example, if the operation **+** is defined only for rationals, then **(2 + 2)** is fine even though **2** is a natural number, because **Nat < Rat**. It is less trivial the other way; for example, consider **(-4 / -2)!** where **!** is defined only for natural numbers. At parse time, we cannot know whether the subexpression **(-4 / -2)** will turn out to be a natural number, so the parser must consider it a rational; in fact, the expression **(-4 / -2)!** *does not parse* in the conventional sense. However, we can give it the benefit of the doubt by having the parser insert a **retract**, a special operation symbol (denoted **r:rat > nat** in the example below) that lowers the sort, and is removed at run time if the subexpression really is a natural, but otherwise remains behind as an informative error message. Thus, the parser turns the expression **(-4 / -2)!** into the expression **(r:rat>nat(-4 / -2))!**, which at runtime becomes first **(r:rat>nat(2))!** and then **(2)!**, using the (automatically provided) key equation

```
r:rat>nat(X) = X
```

where **X** is a variable of sort **Nat**. [36] describes the mathematical and operational semantics of retracts.

Exceptions have both inadequate semantic foundations and insufficient flexibility in most programming and specification languages. Algebraic specification languages sometimes use partial functions, which are simply undefined under exceptional conditions. Although this approach can be developed rigorously, as in [59], it is unsatisfactory in practice because it does not allow error messages or error recovery. For some time, we have been exploring rigorous approaches that allow users to define their own exception conditions, messages, and handling. Unfortunately, the original OBJT/OBJ1 error algebra approach [28] sometimes lacks initial models [77], but our current order-sorted algebra approach seems entirely satisfactory. Using subsorts, we can give a somewhat better representation for bit strings than that in the previous subsection:

```
obj BITS1 is sorts Bit < Bits .
   ops 0 1 : -> Bit .
   op _ _ : Bit Bits -> Bits .
endo
```

A typical expression using this syntax is **0 1 0** .

### 2.4 *Semantics*

OBJ has both an abstract denotational semantics based on order-sorted algebra, and a more concrete operational semantics based on order-sorted rewriting.

***Operational Semantics*** Equations are written declaratively and interpreted operationally as rewrite rules, which replace substitution instances of left-hand sides by the corresponding substitution instances of right-hand sides. We can illustrate computation by term rewriting with a simple **LIST-OF-INT** object. (The **protecting INT** line below indicates that the **INT** module, which provides the integers, is imported; module importation is discussed in Section 2.5.)

```
obj LIST-OF-INT is sort List .
   protecting INT .
   subsorts Int < List .
   op _ _ : Int List -> List .
   op length _ : List -> Int .
   var I : Int .
   var L : List .
   eq length I = 1 .
   eq length I L = 1 + length L .
endo
```

A **reduce** command is executed until reaching a term to which no further rules can be applied, called a **normal** (or **reduced**) **form**. (Most functional programming languages require users to declare **constructors** such that a term is reduced if and only if it consists entirely of constructors. OBJ does not make any use of such constructors, thus achieving greater generality; however, constructor declarations could certainly be used to aid with compiler optimization.) For example,

```
reduce length 17 -4 329 .
```

when evaluated in **LIST-OF-INT** gives

```
result Int: 3
```

by the following sequence of rewrite rule applications

```
length 17 -4 329 =>
1 + length -4 329 =>
1 + (1 + length 329) =>
1 + (1 + 1) =>
1 + 3 =>
3
```

where the first step uses the second equation, which has the left-hand side **length I L** matching **I** to **17** and **L** to **-4 329**. The second step also uses this equation, but now matching **I** to **-4** and **L** to **329**; this match works by regarding the integer **329** as a **List**, since **Int** is a subsort of **List**. The third step simply uses the first rule, and the last step uses the built-in arithmetic[2] of **INT**.

Let us now consider a more sophisticated integer list object with associative and identity attributes:

```
obj LIST-OF-INT1 is sorts List NeList .
   protecting INT .
   subsorts Int < NeList < List .
   op _ _ : List List -> List [assoc id: nil] .
   op _ _ : NeList List -> NeList [assoc] .
   op head_ : NeList -> Int .
   op tail_ : NeList -> List .
   var I : Int .
   var L : List .
   eq head I L = I .
   eq tail I L = L .
endo
```

Then

```
reduce 0 nil 1 nil 3 .
result NeList: 0 1 3
```

---

2. OBJ optionally allows users to define functions with Lisp code; this has been used to provide efficient implementations for the various kinds of numbers.

is executed by applying the identity axiom modulo associativity, as follows

```
0 nil 1 nil 3 =>
0 1 nil 3 =>
0 1 3
```

Similarly, we have

```
reduce head(0 1 3) .
result Int: 0

reduce tail(0 1 3) .
result NeList: 1 3

reduce tail(nil 0 1 nil 3) .
result NeList: 1 3
```

One can also explicitly name a module to be used as the context for evaluation, as in

```
reduce in BOOL : true and false .
```

The identity attribute is implemented by adding rules, rather than by pattern matching modulo identity. A subtle point is that sometimes extra rules are needed. For example, the special case **head I = I** of the first equation in **LIST-OF-INT1** with **L = nil** must be added to the OBJ rule base. Also, sometimes it is necessary to generate so-called "associative extension" rules [60].

OBJ has a built-in polymorphic binary infix **Bool**-valued operation_==_ on every sort, to tell whether or not two ground expressions are equal. This is computed by checking syntactic identity of the normal forms of two expressions. For example, _==_ on **Bool** is just _**iff**_. The operation == really is equality on a sort provided that the rules for expressions of that sort are Church-Rosser and terminating with respect to the given evaluation strategy, since these conditions guarantee that normal forms will be reached. The negation =/= of == is also available. Finally, the conditional

```
if_then_else_fi : Bool S S -> S
```

is provided for every defined sort **S**.

OBJ also allows conditional equations, with syntax

```
ceq ⟨exp1⟩ = ⟨exp2⟩ if ⟨exp3⟩ .
```

where ⟨exp3⟩ is **Bool**-valued, meaning operationally that the rewrite is applied only if the condition evaluates to **true**.

***Denotational Semantics*** Whereas the operational semantics of a programming language shows how computations are done, its denotational semantics should give precise meanings to programs in a conceptually clear and simple way that supports proving properties about them. The denotational semantics of OBJ is algebraic, as in the algebraic approach to abstract data types [49, 48, 90, 51]; that is, the denotation of an object is an **algebra**, a collection of sets with functions among them. In a logical programming language like OBJ, the already established proof theory of the underlying logical system applies directly to programs, and complex formalisms like Scott-Strachey denotational semantics and Hoare axiomatic semantics are not needed. **Initial algebra semantics** [27, 48, 70] takes the unique (up to isomorphism) "initial" algebra as the "most representative" model of the equations (there may of course be many other models), i.e., as the representation-independent standard of comparison for correctness. [10] shows that an algebra is **initial** if and only if it satisfies these two properties:

1. **no junk:** every element can be named using the given constant and operation symbols; and

2. **no confusion:** all equations true of the algebra can be proved from the given equations.

If the rule set is Church-Rosser and terminating, then the rewrite rule operational semantics agrees with initial algebra semantics (see [29, 89]). Order-sorted algebra, and thus OBJ, provides a completely general programming formalism, in the sense that any partial computable function can be defined, according to an as yet unpublished theorem of José Meseguer; [3, 70] give similar results for total computable functions.

### 2.5 *Hierarchical Structure*

Conceptual clarity and ease of understanding are greatly facilitated by breaking a program into modules, each of which is mind-sized and has a natural function. This in turn greatly facilitates both debugging and reusability. When there are many modules, it is helpful to keep explicit track of the hierarchical structure of module dependence, showing exactly which modules use which others. The collection of other modules used by a given module, together with the dependence relations among them, constitute the immediate context of the given module. Whenever a module uses sorts or operations declared in another module, that other module must be explicitly imported and also must have been defined earlier in the program. A program developed in this way has the abstract structure of a hierarchy, or more precisely, an **acyclic graph**, of abstract modules.[3] More exactly, a directed edge in an acylic graph of modules indicates that the higher (target) module **imports** the lower (source) module, and the **context** of a given module is the subgraph of other modules upon which it depends, i.e., the subgraph of which it is the top. Parameterized modules can also occur in such a hierarchy and are treated in essentially the same way as unparameterized modules. (This discussion is a bit oversimplified, since OBJ environments must reflect not only submodule relations but also the more general view relations that may hold among modules.)

OBJ has three modes for importing modules, called **using**, **extending**, and **protecting**. By convention, if a module **M** imports a module **M**′ that imports a module **M**″, then **M**″ is also imported into **M**; that is, importing is a *transitive* relation. The meaning of these three import modes is related to initial algebra semantics, in that an importation of module **M**′ by **M** is:

1. **protecting** if **M** adds no new data items of sorts from **M**′ and also identifies no old data items of sorts from **M**′ (no junk and no confusion);

2. **extending** if **M** identifies no old data items of sorts from **M**′ (no confusion); and

3. **using** if there are no guarantees at all.

The **using** mode is implemented by copying the imported module's text, without copying the modules that it imports; if desired, these can also be copied, by listing them after the **using** keyword.

### 2.6 *Parameterization*

The basic building blocks of parameterized programming are theories, views, and module expressions, each of which can be parameterized; the resulting capabilities go well beyond (for example) those of Ada generic modules. As described above, an **object** encapsulates executable code. On the other hand, a **theory** defines the interface of a parameterized module, that is, the structure and properties required of an actual parameter for meaningful instantiation. A **view** expresses that a certain module satisfies a certain theory in a certain way (note that a module can satisfy a given theory in more than one way); that is, a view describes a binding of an actual parameter to a requirement theory. **Instantiation** of a parameterized module to an actual parameter, using a particular view, yields a new module. **Module expressions**

---

3. Such a hierarchy differs from a Dijkstra-Parnas hierarchy of abstract machines because higher-level modules are not *implemented* by lower-level (less abstract) machines; rather, higher-level modules *include* lower-level modules.

describe complex interconnections of modules, possibly adding, renaming, or modifying functionality. All these topics are treated in greater detail below.

**Theories** Theories express semantic properties of modules and module interfaces. In this subsubsection and the next we discuss requirement theories and views, respectively. In general, OBJ theories have the same structure as objects; in particular, theories have sorts, subsorts, operations, variables, and equations, can import other theories and objects, can be parameterized, and can have views. The difference is that objects are executable, while theories just define properties. Semantically, a theory has a *variety* of models, all the (order-sorted) algebras that satisfy it, whereas an object has just *one* model (up to isomorphism), its initial algebra.

Now some example theories. The first example is the trivial theory **TRIV**, which requires nothing except a sort, here designated **Elt**.

```
th TRIV is sort Elt . endth
```

The next theory is an extension of **TRIV**, requiring that models also have a given element of the given sort, here designated **\***.

```
th TRIV* is extending TRIV .
   op * : -> Elt .
endth
```

Of course, this enrichment is equivalent to

```
th TRIV* is sort Elt .
   op * : -> Elt .
endth
```

which may seem clearer.

Next, the theory of preordered sets (which are like partially ordered sets but without the antisymmetric law). Its models have a binary infix **Bool**-valued operation **<=** that is reflexive and transitive.

```
th PREORD is sort Elt .
   op _<=_ : Elt Elt -> Bool .
   vars E1 E2 E3 : Elt .
   eq E1 <= E1 = true .
   ceq E1 <= E3 = true if E1 <= E2 and E2 <= E3 .
endth
```

The theory of an equivalence relation also has a binary infix **Bool**-valued operation; it is denoted **\_eq\_** and is reflexive, symmetric, and transitive.

```
th EQV is sort Elt .
   op _eq_ : Elt Elt -> Bool .
   vars E1 E2 E3 : Elt .
   eq (E1 eq E1) = true .
   eq (E1 eq E2) = (E2 eq E1) .
   ceq (E1 eq E3) = true if (E1 eq E2) and (E2 eq E3) .
endth
```

Finally, the theory of monoids, which will later serve as a parameter requirement theory for a general iterator that in particular gives sums and products over lists.

```
th MONOID is sort M .
   op _*_ : M M -> M [assoc id: e] .
endth
```

The possibility of expressing *semantic* properties, such as the associativity of an operation, as part of the interface of a module is another aspect where parameterized programming has an advantage over traditional functional programming. For example, one can certainly write a (second-order) function to iterate any given binary function (such as integer addition) over lists, but traditional functional programming cannot state the requirement that the binary function must be associative.

**Views** A module can satisfy a theory in more than one way, and even if there is a unique way, it can be arbitrarily difficult to find. We therefore need a notation for describing the particular ways that modules satisfy theories. For example, **NAT** can satisfy **PREORD** with the usual "less-than-or-equal" ordering, but "divides" and "greater-than-or-equal" are also possible; each of these corresponds to a different view. Thus, an expression like **SORTING[NAT]**, where **SORTING** has requirement theory **PREORD** would be ambiguous in the absence of definite conventions for default views.

More precisely now, a view **v** from a theory **T** to a module **M**, indicated with the notation **v: T => M**, consists of a mapping from the sorts of **T** to the sorts of **M** preserving the subsort relation, and a mapping from the operations of **T** to the operations of **M** preserving arity, value sort, and the (meaning of) whatever attributes **assoc, comm, id:**, and **idem** are present, such that every equation in **T** is true of every model of **M**. (A view from one theory to another is what logicians call a theory interpretation [8].) The mappings of sorts and operations are expressed in the respective forms

```
sort S1 to S1'
```

```
sort S2 to S2'
. . .

op o1 to o1'
op o2 to o2'
. . .
```

where **o1**, **o1** ′, **o2**, etc. may be operation forms, or forms plus value sort, or forms plus value sort and arity, as needed for disambiguation; moreover, **o1** ′, **o2** ′, etc. can be derived operations (i.e., terms with variables). Thus, each mapping can be considered a set of pairs. These two sets of pairs together are called a **view body**. The syntax for defining a view at the top level of OBJ adds to this names for the source and target modules, and possibly a name for the view. For example,

```
view NATD from PREORD to NAT is
    sort Elt to Nat .
    op _<=_ to divides .
endv
```

defines a view called **NATD** from **PREORD** to **NAT** using the divisibility relation.

When there is an obvious view to use, it is annoying to have to write out that view in full detail. **Default views** allow writing simple module expressions like **P[NAT, INT]** wherever possible, by capturing the intuitive notion of "the obvious view"; see [32] for details.

*Parameterized Modules*  Let us now consider some parameterized modules. First, a simple parameterized **LIST** object, "abstracting" the previously given **LIST-OF-INT** object.

```
obj LIST[X :: TRIV] is sorts List NeList .
    subsorts Elt < NeList < List .
    op _ _ : List List -> List [assoc id: nil] .
    op _ _ : NeList List -> NeList [assoc] .
    op head_ : NeList -> Elt .
    op tail_ : NeList -> List .
    var X : Elt .
    var L : List .
    eq head X L = X .
    eq tail X L = L .
endo
```

Modules can have more than one parameter. For example, the notation
[X :: TH1, Y :: TH2] indicates two parameters, and if the two theories
are the same, we can just write [X Y :: TH]. Parameterized theories are
also allowed, such as vector spaces over a field F.

Even though the code is very similar to that for LIST, it seems worth doing
STACK as well, since it is well known and has been done in many different
formalisms; in fact, it provides a very good illustration of the power of order-
sorted algebra.

```
STACK[X :: TRIV] is sorts Stack NeStack .
   subsorts Elt < NeStack < Stack .
   op empty : -> Stack .
   op push : Elt Stack -> NeStack .
   op top_ : NeStack -> Elt .
   op pop_ : NeStack -> Stack .
   var X : Elt .
   var S : Stack.
   eq top push(X,S) = X .
   eq pop push(X,S) = S .
endo
```

This seems about as simple a program as one could desire.

***Instantiation*** This subsection discusses instantiating the formal parameters
of a parameterized module with actual modules. This construction requires
a view from each formal parameter requirement theory to the corresponding
actual module. The result of such an instantiation is to replace each requirement theory by its corresponding actual module, using the views to bind
actual names to formal names, without producing multiple copies of shared
submodules. For example, assuming that we are given a parameterized object
SORTING[X :: PREORD], we can form

```
make SORTING-NATD is SORTING[NATD] endm
```

using the explicit view NATD, while

```
make NATLIST is LIST[NAT] endm
```

uses the default view from TRIV to NAT to instantiate the parameterized
module LIST with the actual parameter NAT. Similarly, we might have

```
make REAL-LIST is LIST[REAL] endm
```

where **REAL** is the field of real numbers, using a default view from **TRIV** to **REAL**, or

```
make REAL-VSP is VECTOR-SP[REAL] endm
```

using the default view from **FIELD** to **REAL**. More interestingly

```
make STACK-OF-LIST-OF-REAL is STACK[LIST[REAL]] endm
```

uses two default views. (Note that Ada does not allow such a complex module expression, and would require using two steps.) In general,

```
make M is P[A] endm
```

is equivalent to

```
obj M is protecting P[A] . endo
```

where **A** may be either a module or a view.

Module composition in parameterized programming is more powerful than the purely functional composition of traditional functional programming, in that a single module instantiation can compose many different functions all at once. For example, a generic complex arithmetic module **CPXA** can be easily instantiated with any of several real arithmetic modules as actual parameter:

single-precision reals, **CPXA[SP-REAL]**,

double-precision reals, **CPXA[DP-REAL]**, or

multiple-precision reals, **CPXA[MP-REAL]**.

Each instantiation involves substituting dozens of functions into dozens of other functions. While something similar is also possible in higher-order functional programming by coding up modules as records, it is much less natural. Furthermore, with parameterized programming, the logic can be first-order, so that understanding and verifying the code can be simpler. Moreover, semantic declarations are allowed at module interfaces (given by requirement theories), and module expressions allow many useful transformations and combinations other than application.

Our approach to parameterization was inspired by the Clear specification language [7, 8]. In fact, OBJ can be regarded as an implementation of Clear. In particular, the notion of view was developed in collaboration with Rod Burstall for use in Clear. Clear's approach was in turn inspired by some ideas in general system theory [26]. A key idea is the use of colimits of diagrams of theories to determine the result of module expression evaluation. Although colimits are beyond the scope of this paper, they give a precise foundation for parameterized programming, and moreover, a foundation that is independent of the particular choice of an underlying logical system, by making use of "institutions" [34]. Any logical programming language (in the sense made precise in [69]) can be given the features for parameterized programming described in this paper. This includes Eqlog, FOOPS, and FOOPlog, as well as OBJ, so that the various combinations of functional, relational, and object-oriented programming are all covered.

Environments for ordinary programming languages are assignments of names to values (perhaps with indirection), but environments for parameterized programming languages must also include relations between modules. In Section 2.5 we discussed the submodule inclusion relation that arises from module importation, giving an acyclic graph structure. Views must also be stored in environments, with source and target explicitly indicated, giving rise to a general graph structure. If submodule inclusions are seen as views, then the submodule hierarchy appears as a subgraph of the view graph.

There is an interesting further generalization of instantiation. First, notice that any parameterized module can be seen as a *view* $p : R \Rightarrow B$ from the requirement theory $R$ (or the sum of all requirement theories, if there are more than one) into the body $B$, which necessarily already includes $R$. For example, **STACK[X :: TRIV]** is just the inclusion view

    **STACK** : **TRIV** => **STACKBODY**,

where the **STACKBODY** code is the same as given above for **STACK**, except for replacing the name **STACK[X :: TRIV]** by just **STACKBODY**. Then, given any binding view $b : R \Rightarrow A$ to an actual module $A$, we can form the instantiation $p[b]$, which substitutes $A$ into $B$ after translation by $p$ of $R$; more precisely, the result of the application is given by what is called a "pushout" in category theory, as developed in the semantics of Clear [7, 9]. With this technique, a single body can be parameterized in many different ways. Thus, Ada's idea to separate the "body" and "specification" (really, interface) parts of modules was good, but it is much more flexible if views are added.

**Module Expressions** Module expressions not only permit defining, constructing, and instantiating complex combinations of modules, they also permit modifying modules in various ways, thus making it possible to use a given module in a wider variety of contexts and to improve the efficiency of existing code. The major combination modes are instantiation and sum. Among possible modifications are:

**1. extend** a module, by adding to its functionality;

**2. rename** some of its external interface;

**3. restrict** a module, by eliminating some of its functionality;

**4. encapsulate** some existing code;

**5. modify** the code inside a module.

This approach to program transformation [6, 82, 81] provides a broad range of program transformations right inside of programs, and it also easily takes account of data structure. Although module importation can be seen as a special case of parameter instantiation, it is more convenient to treat it separately; see Section 2.5. It is worth mentioning that modules may also have internal states; although this feature is neither discussed in this paper nor so far implemented, [33, 42] and [38] give further information on our approach to this important issue.

The simplest module expressions are the *constants*, including the built-in data types **BOOL**, **NAT**, **INT**, **QID**, **ID**, and **FLOAT**, plus any user-defined unparameterized modules available in the current environment. The theory **TRIV** is also built in, as are the $n$-ary parameterized **TUPLE** modules, which form $n$-tuples of sorts for any $n > 1$. All the requirement theories of **TUPLE** are **TRIV**. For example, **TUPLE[INT,BOOL]** is a module expression whose principle sort consists of pairs of an integer and a truth value. Another example is **TUPLE[LIST[INT],INT,BOOL]**.

**Renaming** uses a view body (i.e., a sort mapping and an operation mapping) to create a new module from an old one. A renaming is applied to a module expression postfix following * and modifies the syntax of module expression by applying the pairs that are given. To enrich a module expression, we need only import it into a module and then add the desired sorts, operations, and equations; thus, we really do not need explicit enrichment transformations for module expressions. For example, we can use renaming to modify the **PREORD** theory, and then enrich it, as follows:

```
th EQV is using PREORD * (op _<=_ to _eq_) .
   vars E1 E2 : Elt .
   eq (E1 eq E2) = (E2 eq E1) .
endth
```

Another important module-building operation creates a new module that **adds**, **sums**, or **combines** all the information in its summands. (There are actually three modes for the summand modules, just as there are for imported modules; the default is extending.) An important issue here is sharing submodules that are imported by more than one summand. For example, in the sum **A + B**, both **A** and **B** probably protecting import **BOOL**, and they may also protect or extend **NAT**, **INT**, and other modules. The sum should contain only one copy of such multiply imported modules. It is also very useful to sum views; the source of the sum view is the sum of its sources, and the target of the sum view is the sum of its targets. (See[32] for more details.)

## 3 *Higher-Order Programming and Verification*

This section argues that higher-order functions are not needed for higher-order programming. The first subsection shows how some typical higher-order programming techniques can be accomplished in first-order logic with parameterized programming, and it also suggests some advantages of this approach. The second subsection gives a hardware verification example.

### 3.1 *Some Examples*

Higher-order logic is useful in many areas, including the foundations of mathematics (e.g., type theory), extracting programs from correctness proofs of algorithms, describing proof strategies (as in LCF tactics [50]), modeling traditional programming languages (as in Scott-Strachey semantics), and studying the foundations of the programming process. Perhaps the main advantage of higher-order programming over traditional imperative programming is its capability for structuring programs (see [58] for some cogent arguments and examples). However, a language with sufficiently powerful parameterized modules *does not need* higher-order functions. We do not oppose higher-order functions as such; however, we do claim that they can lead to unnecessarily complex programs and that they can and should be avoided in programming languages. We further claim that parameterized programming provides an alternative basis for higher-order programming that has certain advantages. In particular, the following shows that typical higher-order functional programming examples are easily coded as OBJ programs that are quite structured, flexible, and rigorous. Moreover, we can use theories to document any semantic properties that may be required of functions.

One classic functional programming example is motivated by the following two instances: (1) **sigma** adds a list of numbers; and (2) **pi** multiplies them. To encompass these and similar examples, we want a function that applies a binary function recursively over suitable lists. Let's see how this example looks in vanilla higher-order functional programming notation. First, a polymorphic list type is defined by something like:

```
type list(T) = nil + cons(T,list(T))
```

and then the function we want is defined by

```
function iter :  (T -> (T -> T))
                        -> (T -> (list(T) -> T))
axiom iter(f)(a)(nil) => a
axiom iter(f)(a)(cons(c,list))
                        => f(c)(iter(f)(a)(list))
```

so[4] that we can write

```
sigma(list) => iter(plus)(0)(list)
pi(list) => iter(times)(1)(list)
```

For some applications of **iter** to work correctly, **f** must have certain *semantic* properties. For example, if we want to evaluate **pi(list)** with as many multiplications as possible in parallel, then **f** must be associative. (The algorithm first converts **list** into a binary tree and then does all the mulitplications at each tree level in parallel.) Associativity of **f** implies the following "homomorphic" property, which is needed in the correctness proof:

```
(H) iter(f)(a)(append(list)(list'))
          = f(iter(f)(a)(list))(iter(f)(a)(list')
```

for **list** and **list′** of the same type. Furthermore, if we want the empty list **nil** to behave correctly in property (H), then **a** must be an identity for **f**.

Now let's do this example in OBJ. First, using mixfix syntax _*_ for **f** improves readability somewhat; but much more significantly, we can use the requirement theory **MONOID** to assert associativity and identity axioms for actual arguments of a generic iteration module:

```
obj ITER[M :: MONOID] is protecting LIST[M].
   op iter : List -> M.
   var X : M.
   var L : List.
   eq iter(nil) = e.
   eq iter(X L) = X * iter(L).
endo
```

where **e** is the monoid identity. Note that **LIST[M]** uses the default theory view **TRIV => MONOID**. (This code uses an associative **List** concatenation, but it is also easy to write code using a **cons** constructor in OBJ.)

We can now instantiate **ITER** to get our two examples. First,

---

4. Most people find the rank of **iter** rather difficult to understand. It can be simplified by uncurrying with products, and convention also permits omitting some parentheses; but these devices do not help much. Actually, we feel that products are more fundamental than higher-order functions and that eliminating products by currying can be misleading and confusing.

```
make SIGMA is ITER[NAT+] endm
```

sums lists of numbers, while

```
make PI is ITER[NAT*] endm
```

multiplies lists of numbers, where the view **NAT+** views **NAT** as a monoid under addition, while **NAT\*** views **NAT** as a monoid under multiplication. These seem impressively clear and concise programs; moreover, they are written in a rigorous first-order logic.

Any valid instance of **ITER** has the property (H), which in the present notation is written

```
iter(L L') = iter(L) * iter(L')
```

and it is natural to state this fact with a theory and view, as follows:

```
th HOM[M :: MONOID] is
  protecting LIST[M] .
  op h : List -> M .
  var L L' : List .
  eq h(L L') = h(L) * h(L') .
endth
```

```
view ITER-IS-HOM[M :: MONOID]
     from HOM[M] to ITER[M] endv
```

This view is parameterized, because property (H) holds for all instances; to obtain the appropriate assertion for a given instance **ITER[A]**, just instantiate the view with the same actual parameter module **A**. Since semantic requirements on argument functions cannot be stated in a conventional functional programming language, all of this would have to be done *outside* of such a language. But OBJ can not only assert the monoid property, it can even prove that this property implies property (H), using methods described in [31].

Some have argued that it is actually much easier to use higher-order functions and type inference to get such declarations and instantiations automatically. However, the notational overhead of encapsulating a function in a module is really only a few keywords, and these could even be generated automatically by a structural editor from a single keystroke; moreover, this overhead can often be shared among many function declarations. There is also some overhead due to variable declarations. However, it can be reduced to almost nothing by two techniques: (1) let type inference give a variable the highest possible sort; and (2) declare sorts "on the fly" with a qualification notation. (We have not implemented this for OBJ3, because explicit declarations can save *human* program readers much effort in doing type inference.) Sort and operation declarations are needed in any approach, but our notation for them could be slightly simplified if someone thought it worth the trouble. However, our view has been that the crucial issue is to make the *structure* of *large programs* as clear as possible; thus, tricks that slightly simplify notation for small examples are of little importance and are of negative value if they make it harder to read large programs.

On the other hand, our notation for instantiation can often be significantly simplified, for example, if nondefault views are needed, or if renaming is needed to avoid ambiguity when there is more than one instance of some module in a given context. For example,

```
make ITER-NAT is
        ITER[view NAT is op _*_ to _+_ . endv] endm
```

is certainly more complex than `iter(plus)(0)`. However, we could just let `ITER[(_+_).NAT]` denote the above module, and we could go a bit further and let `iter[(_+_).NAT]` denote the `iter` function itself, with the effect of creating the module instantiation that defines it, unless it is already present. Indeed, this is essentially the same notation used in functional programming, and it avoids the need to give distinct names for distinct instances of `iter`. Let us call this *abbreviated operation notation*. It can also be used when there is more than one argument; note that the expression `iter[(_+_).NAT]` uses default view conventions so that `Elt` maps to `Nat` (rather than `Bool`), and `e` maps to `0`. (The abbreviated operation notation has not yet been implemented in OBJ, but the abbreviated view notation has been, and indeed is illustrated in the next example below.)

An alternative is to model polymorphism within order-sorted algebra; here one could declare certain parameterized objects to be polymorphic within some syntactic scope and obtain the usual kind of polymorphism with a first-order logic. However, I am not sure that this is worth the trouble, because it is rare to need many different instantiations of the same function symbol that cannot be handled by very simple module expressions.

For a second example, let us define the traditional function **map**, which applies a unary function to a list of arguments. Its interface theory requires a sort and a unary function on it (more generally, we could have distinct source and target sorts, if desired).

```
th FN is sort S .
    op f : S -> S .
```

```
endth

obj MAP[F :: FN] is protecting LIST[F] .
   op map : List -> List .
   var X : S .
   var L : List .
   eq map(nil) = nil .
   eq map(X L) = f(X) map(L) .
endo
```

We can now instantiate **MAP** in various ways. The following object defines some functions to be used in examples below.

```
obj FNS is protecting INT .
   op sq_ : Int -> Int .
   op dbl_ : Int -> Int .
   op _*3 : Int -> Int .
   var N : Int .
   eq dbl N = N + N .
   eq N * 3 = N * 3 .
   eq sq N = N * N .
endo
```

Our first instantiation of this uses a default view **FN => FNS**, which maps **f** to **sq_**, since **sq_** is the first operation introduced in **FNS**.

```
make TEST1 is MAP[FNS] endm
```

Now a sample reduction:

```
reduce map(0 1 -2 3) .
result NeList: 0 1 4 9
```

Next, some reductions in objects using in-line nondefault views with operation abbreviation:

```
reduce in MAP[(dbl).FNS] : map(0 1 -2 3) .
result NeList: 0 2 -4 6

reduce in MAP[(3).FNS] : map(0 1 -2 3) .
result NeList: 0 3 -6 9
```

The following module does another classical functional programming example, applying a given function twice; some instantiations are also given.

```
obj 2[F :: FN] is
   op 2x : S -> S .
   var X : S .
   eq 2x(X) = f(f(X)) .
endo

reduce in 2[FNS] : 2x(3) .
result Int: 81

reduce in 2[(dbl).FNS] : 2x(3) .
result Int: 12

reduce in (2[2[FNS]]*(op (2x).2[2[FNS]] to g)) : g(3) .
result Int: 43046721
```

Let us consider this example more carefully. Since **2** applies **f** twice, the result function **2x** of the first instantiation applies **sq_** twice, i.e., raises to the 4th power; then the second instantiation applies that twice, i.e., raises to the 16th power. The renaming is given to prevent syntactic ambiguity of **2x** but could be avoided by using qualification.

To summarize, the difference between parameterized programming and higher-order functional programming is essentially the difference between programming in the large and programming in the small. Parameterized programming does not just combine functions, it combines modules. This parallels one of the great insights of modern abstract algebra, that in many important examples, functions should not be considered in isolation, but rather in association with other functions and constants, along with the axioms that they satisfy, and with their explicit sources and targets. Thus, the invention of abstract algebras (for vector spaces, groups, etc.) parallels the invention of program modules (for vectors, permutations, etc.); parameterized programming makes this parallel more explicit and also carries it further, by introducing theories and views to document semantic requirements on function arguments and on module interfaces, as well as to assert provable properties of modules (such as the property (H) above). As we have already noted, it can be more convenient to combine modules then to compose functions, because a single module instantiation can compose many conceptually related functions at once, as in the complex arithmetic (**CPXA**) example mentioned in Section 2.6. On the other hand, the notational overhead of theories and views is excessive for applying just one function. However, this is exactly the case where our abbreviated view and operation notations can be used to advantage. And we should not forget that it can be much more difficult to reason with higher-order functions than with first-order functions; in fact, the undecidability of higher-order unification means that it will be very difficult to mechanize certain aspects of such reasoning. Also, it is much easier to compile and interpret first-order programs. It is worth noting that Poigné [78] has found some significant difficulties in combining subsorts and higher-order functions, and we hope to have been convincing that subsorts are very useful. Finally, note the experience of many programmers, and not just naive ones, that higher-order notation can be very difficult to understand and to use.

### 3.2 *Hardware Specification, Simulation, and Verification*

This subsection develops a computer hardware verification example. The crucial advantage of using a logical programming language here is that reductions really are proofs, because programs really are logical theories. The following propositional calculus decision procedure object is also an excellent example of software reuse, since its original form was written years before we thought of using it for hardware verification [45]:

```
obj PROPC is sort Prop .
   protecting TRUTH + QID .
   subsorts Id Bool < Prop .

   op _and_ : Prop Prop -> Prop [assoc comm prec 2] .
   op _xor_ : Prop Prop -> Prop [assoc comm prec 3] .
   vars p q r : Prop .
   eq p and false = false .
   eq p and true = p .
   eq p and p = p .
   eq p xor false = p .
   eq p xor p = false .
   eq p and (q xor r) = (p and q) xor (p and r) .

   op _or_ : Prop Prop -> Prop [assoc comm prec 7] .
   op not_ : Prop -> Prop [prec 1] .
   op _implies_ : Prop Prop -> Prop [prec 9] .
   op _iff_ : Prop Prop -> Prop [assoc prec 11] .
   eq p or q = (p and q) xor p xor q .
   eq not p = p xor true .
   eq p implies q = (p and q) xor p xor true .
   eq p iff q = p xor q xor true.
```

```
endo
```

Here **and** and **xor** are constructors, subject to the first group of equations, while the second group introduces derived operations. The attribute **prec n** means that the operation it follows has precedence **n**, where lower precedence means tighter binding. The declaration **Id Bool < Prop** prepares the way for overloading all the Boolean operations and also includes identifiers among the propositions for use as "propositional variables."

The code below first defines time for use in bit streams, which are functions from **Time** to **Prop**. A requirement theory **LINE** is defined and then a **NOT** gate using it. The object **F** introduces the variables **t** and **f0**, which are a "generic" time and input stream, respectively. Finally, two **NOT** gates are composed and applied to **F**, using renaming to avoid syntactic ambiguities and some rather nice default views. Note that an expression of the form **t iff t**′ reduces to **true** if and only if **t** and **t**′ reduce to the same thing.

Three extended equations are actually proved, the first of which was described informally above. In more detail, this assertion has the form

$$P \models_\Sigma (\forall \Phi) \, r$$

where $P \models s$ means "*s* is satisfied by the initial algebra of *P*," where $\Sigma$ is the union of the signatures of the OBJ objects **PROPC** and **TIME**, *P* is the union of their equations, $\Phi$ is the signature containing three functions $f_0, f_1, f_2$ from **Time** to **Prop**, and *r* is $(s_1 \wedge s_2) \Rightarrow s_3$, where

$$s_1 = (\forall t)(f_1(s \, t) = \text{not } f_0(t)),$$

$$s_2 = (\forall t)(f_2(s \, t) = \text{not } f_1(t)),$$

$$s_3 = (\forall t)(f_2(s \, s \, t) = f_0(t)).$$

Because some readers may be surprised to see equations with second-order quantifiers proved using just ground-term reduction, some basics needed for the correctness of this verification technique are given in the appendix; details may be found in [31].

```
obj TIME is sort Time .
    op 0 : -> Time .
    op s_ : Time -> Time .
endo

th LINE is
    protecting TIME + PROPC .
```

```
      op f : Time -> Prop .
   endth

   obj NOT[L :: LINE] is
      op g : Time -> Prop .
      var T : Time   .
      eq g(0) = false .
      eq g(T) = not f(T) .
   endo

   obj F is
      protecting TIME + PROPC .
      op t : -> Time .
      op f0 : Time -> Prop .
   endo

   make 2NOT is NOT[NOT[F]*(op g to f1)]*(op g to f2) endm

   reduce f2(s s t) iff f0(t) .
   result Bool: true

   reduce f2(s t) iff not f(t) .
   result Bool: true

   reduce f1(s t) iff not f0(t) .
   result Bool: true
```

Note that parameterized modules make the code much more readable than it would be without them. These techniques seem equally effective for more difficult examples of hardware specification, simulation, and verification, as discussed in [31]. Parameterized programming is attractive for this application, because there can be many instances of just a few kinds of basic gates.

## 4 *Summary and Discussion*

This paper has shown that higher-order functions are not needed for typical higher-order programming techniques, and in fact has shown that there are some advantages to using first-order parameterized programming instead, including greater flexibility and the possibility of imposing semantic requirements on the arguments of functions. Moreover, Poigné [78] has found some significant difficulties to combining subsorts with higher-order functions, and because this paper has argued that subsorts can be very useful, that can be seen as another argument against higher-order functions. Also, it can be much more difficult to reason about properties of higher-order functions; in fact, the undecidability of higher-order unification means that it can be very difficult to mechanize certain aspects of such reasoning. Moreover, it should be easier to compile, optimize, and interpret purely first-order programs. Finally, note the experience of many programmers, and not just naive ones, that higher-order notation can be very difficult to understand and to use. Waxing a bit philosophical, we may say that ordinary computation (manipulating bits according to already given instructions) is inherently first-order, whereas mathematics is inherently higher-order (we can always reason about our reasoning).

The appendix presents a useful extension of equational logic to quantification over functions and, in particular, justifies a perhaps surprising technique for proving second-order quantified equations using just ground-term reduction. This gives a powerful calculus for first-order reasoning about first-order functions, and I think it may capture much of the reasoning that is actually needed for functional programming.

I think we can conclude from all this that it is better to "factorize" code with parameterized modules than with higher-order functions and, in fact, that it is better to avoid higher-order functions whenever possible. From this, one could conclude that the essence of functional programming cannot be the use of higher-order functions and therefore must be the lack of side effects. However, I feel that the true essence may well be having a solid basis in equational logic, because this not only avoids side effects, but more importantly, it supports simple equational reasoning about programs and transformations, as needed for powerful programming environments.

Instead of seeing parameterized programming as a way to supplant higher-order logic, we can see it as an interesting direction in which to generalize higher-order logic, since the calculus of views must confront issues beyond those formalized in the λ-calculus, including the following:

1. The basic "types" (which are the unparameterized modules, including **BOOL**, **NAT**, **MONOID**, and **PREORD**, as well as whatever a user chooses to define) denote not just classes of functions, but *categories* of models (order-sorted algebras in the case of OBJ).

2. Similarly, parameters range not over classes of functions, but over classes of modules, and these classes are subject to semantic constraints (e.g., equations).

3. Modules include both theories and objects.

4. Parameterized modules represent functors between classes of models.

**5.** Views are an entirely new feature, not found in the $\lambda$-calculus.

These points perhaps deserve some elaboration. First, they suggest it might be awkward to "code up" parameterized programming into some form of denotational semantics (e.g., in the style of [66]) or type theory (e.g., in the style of Pebble [11], PX [55] or Martin-Löf's type theory [67]). Even if we had such an encoding, it would not be the sort of notation that programmers should have to deal with in practice but would be somewhat like trying to program with Gödel numbers; however, it could be valuable in theoretical studies. (Of course, one can code up $\lambda$-calculus or type theory in OBJ, but that is quite a different issue.) Moreover, such an encoding of parameterized programming would not emphasize what seem to be the really fundamental entities: just as types play a secondary role as indices for functions in the typed $\lambda$-calculus and objects play a secondary role as indices for morphisms in category theory, so it may be that modules play a secondary role as indices to views in parameterized programming.

Because we claim first order proof theory as a major advantage for OBJ, it is interesting to see how far parameterization can be pushed without endangering this asset. It is possible to achieve the equivalent of parameters that are themselves parameterized through the nesting of parameterized modules. This is a special case of what type theory calls "dependent types." See [33] for further discussion. Whether there are significant applications for some of the more elaborate possibilities that are allowed by type theory remains unclear. It also seems interesting to inquire whether we can find a suitable categorical semantics, in terms similar to the cartesian closed category characterization of the $\lambda$-calculus (of course, the semantics of Clear [8] has already shown how to do everything that this paper needs using colimits of theories). Seeley's locally cartesian closed categories [83] seem relevant, as do Cartmell's S-categories [13], since the **extending** hierarchy of parameterized module inclusions is preserved under instantiation; see also his hierarchical categories. There is also some interesting recent work by John Gray on dependent abstract data types. Altogether, this seems a promising area for future research.

## Acknowledgments

I wish to thank: Professor Rod Burstall for his extended and on-going collaboration on Clear and its foundations, which inspired the parameterization mechanism of OBJ; Dr. José Meseguer for his invaluable contributions to every aspect of OBJ including its theoretical foundations, its implementation, and its applications; Timothy Winkler for his many suggestions concerning the design and theory of OBJ; Professor Jean Pierre Jouannaud for his efforts to educate me on the theory and practice of rewrite rules; Dr. Kokichi Futatsugi for his work on programming methodology using OBJ; and Victoria Stavridou for her efforts to use OBJ3 for hardware specification and verification. I also thank José Meseguer and Timothy Winkler for their very valuable comments on drafts of this paper.

The research reported in this paper has been supported in part by grants from the Science and Engineering Research Council, the National Science Foundation, and the System Development Foundation, as well as contracts with the Office of Naval Research and the Fujitsu Corporation.

## Appendix *Second-Order Quantifiers for First-Order Equations*

This appendix generalizes the **standard case** of equational logic, which quantifies only over constants, to permit quantification over **arbitrary function symbols**. Although this is a kind of second-order quantification, it should be seen as taking first-order equational logic to its limit, rather than as an incursion into the second-order realm; what is essential is that the terms themselves are first-order. We will see that this generalization can be very useful. However, the mathematics is an easy extension of the standard case; indeed, it is hard to see why it has not been thought of before. This appendix includes some new results justifying the use of ground-term reduction to prove equations with second-order quantifiers. The result is a powerful first-order calculus for reasoning about (first-order) functions, which I believe is more satisfactory than trying to use the $\lambda$-calculus or some other more general (and thus less powerful) tool.

Unlike the body of the paper, some familiarity with the basics of universal algebra is probably needed to read this appendix, e.g., [48, 70]. Although OBJ is actually based on order-sorted equational logic, the following discussion uses unsorted equational logic for expository simplicity.

A **signature** $\Sigma$ is a family $\Sigma_n$ of sets, for $n = 0, 1, 2, \ldots$. An element of $\Sigma_n$ is a **function symbol** of **arity** $n$, and in particular, elements of $\Sigma_0$ are **constant symbols**. Given signatures $\Sigma$ and $\Phi$, their **union** is defined by

$$(\Sigma \cup \Phi)_n = \Sigma_n \cup \Phi_n.$$

A $\Sigma$-**algebra** is a set $A$ and an **interpretation function** for $\Sigma$ into $A$, i.e., a family of functions $i_n : \Sigma_n \to [A^n \to A]$ that interpret the function symbols in $\Sigma$ as actual functions on $A$. Since $A^0$ is some one-point set, say $*$, for $c$ in $\Sigma_0$ we can identify $i_0(c)$ with $i_0(c)(*)$, a point in A. Generally, we write just $f$ for $i_n(f)$ in $A$.

Given $\Sigma$-algebras $A$ and $B$, a $\Sigma$-**homomorphism** $h : A \rightarrow B$ is a function $h : A \rightarrow B$ such that

$$h(f(a1, \ldots, an)) = f(h(a1), \ldots, h(an))$$

for each $f$ in $\Sigma_n$ and, in particular, such that $h(c) = c$ for each $c$ in $\Sigma_0$.

Given a signature $\Sigma$, we let $T_\Sigma$ denote the $\Sigma$-algebra of all ground $\Sigma$-terms. Recall that $T_\Sigma$ is **initial** in the sense that given any other $\Sigma$-algebra $A$, there is a *unique* $\Sigma$-homomorphism from $T_\Sigma$ to $A$.

We now define a $\Sigma$-**equation** to consist of a signature $\Phi$ of **variable symbols** (disjoint from $\Sigma$), plus a pair of $(\Sigma \cup \Phi)$-terms. We write such equations abstractly in the form

$$(\forall\ \Phi)\ t = t'$$

and concretely in the form

$$(\forall\ f, g, x, y)\ t = t'$$

where the arities of $f, g, x, y$ can (presumably) be inferred from their uses in $t$ and $t'$.

An example of the power of this kind of equation arises in a denotational style semantics for expressions, where one would normally have to write equations

$$(\forall\ e, e')\ [[e + e']](\rho) = [[e]](\rho) + [[e']](\rho)\,,$$

$$(\forall\ e, e')\ [[e - e']](\rho) = [[e]](\rho) - [[e']](\rho)\,,$$

$$(\forall\ e, e')\ [[e \times e']](\rho) = [[e]](\rho) \times [[e']](\rho)\,, \ldots$$

instead of the following much simpler equation, which quantifies over the binary function symbol $*$,

$$(\forall\ e, e', *)\ [[e * e']](\rho) = [[e]](\rho) * [[e']](p)\,.$$

(This equation actually has a slightly different meaning from the finite set of equations given above, since it asserts the homomorphic property for *any possible* $*$; but we can also get the other semantics by using a conditional equation.)

In the standard case, only $\Phi_0$ can be nonempty, and so $\Phi$ can be identified with a set $X$ of (standard) variables. In this case, the union signature is written $\Sigma(X)$, and such standard equations are written abstractly in the form

$$(\forall\ X)\ t = t'$$

where $t$, $t'$ are $\Sigma(X)$-terms, and concretely in the form

$$(\forall\, x, y, z)\ t = t'.$$

Given a $\Sigma$-algebra $A$ and also an interpretation $f\colon \Phi \to A$ of the variable symbols in $\Phi$ into $A$, there is a unique extension of $f$ to a $(\Sigma \cup \Phi)$-homomorphism, $f^*\colon T_{\Sigma \cup \Phi} \to A$, by the initiality of $T_{\Sigma \cup \Phi}$ where $A$ is regarded as a $(\Sigma \cup \Phi)$-algebra by using $f$ to extend the interpretation function $i$ of $A$ from $\Sigma$ to $\Sigma \cup \Phi$. Then a $\Sigma$-term $t$ with variables in $\Phi$ is just an element of $T_{\Sigma \cup \Phi}$ and a $\Sigma$-algebra $A$ **satisfies** the $\Sigma$-equation $(\forall\, \Phi)\ t = t'$ if and only if for any interpretation $f\colon \Phi \to A$, we have that $f^*(t) = f^*(t')$ in $A$; in this case we write

$$A \models_{\Sigma} (\forall\, \Phi)\ t = t'.$$

A $\Sigma$-algebra $A$ satisfies a set $E$ of $\Sigma$-equations if and only if it satisfies each $e$ in $E$, and in this case we write

$$A \models_{\Sigma} E.$$

A **presentation** $\langle \Sigma, E \rangle$ consists of a signature $\Sigma$ and a set $E$ of $\Sigma$-equations. Any OBJ program $P$ defines a presentation $\langle \Sigma, E \rangle$ where both $\Sigma$ and $E$ are finite and (at present) $E$ is standard; the details of how $P$ yields $\langle \Sigma, E \rangle$, which involve theories, views, colimits, etc., need not concern us here; we simply identify $P$ with its presentation $\langle \Sigma, E \rangle$ and ignore the concrete syntax of OBJ. (Of course, the OBJ program really defines an order-sorted presentation, but here we are restricting attention to the unsorted case.) Since OBJ is both a programming language and a specification language, it admits two kinds of program $P$:

1. objects, whose intended semantics is a *standard model* for $P$; and

2. theories, whose intended semantics is the *variety* of all models for $P$.

The second case generally appears in an auxiliary role, because we are usually interested in defining particular data structures and particular functions over them. A basic intuition for equational logic is that *standard models are initial models*. Reduction techniques cannot be sufficient to prove all properties of initial models and, in particular, should be supplemented with induction techniques.

Now writing

$$E \models_{\Sigma} (\forall\, \Phi)\ t = t'$$

to mean that

$$A \models_{\Sigma} (\forall\, \Phi)\ t = t'$$

for every $A$ such that

$$A \models_\Sigma E ,$$

we have the following theorem.

## Theorem 1

Given disjoint signatures $\Sigma, \Phi$, given a set $E$ of $\Sigma$-equations, and given $t, t'$ in $T_{\Sigma \cup \Phi}$, then

$$E \models_\Sigma (\forall \Phi) \, t = t' \text{ iff } E \models_{\Sigma \cup \Phi} (\forall \varnothing) \, t = t' .$$

where $\varnothing$ is the empty signature.

**Proof**   Each condition is equivalent to the condition

$$f^*(t) = f^*(t')$$

for every $\Sigma \cup \Phi$-algebra $A$ satisfying $E$, where $f^*: T_{\Sigma \cup \Phi} \to A$ is the unique homomorphism.   □

It is pleasing that this proof is so simple and is based entirely on the *semantics* of satisfaction rather than on any particular choice of rules of deduction.

It now follows that if we view $E$ as **rewrite rules** and if $E$ reduces $t$ and $t'$ to the same value, then $E \models_\Sigma (\forall \Phi) \, t = t'$. This helps to justify the hardware proof in Section 3.2; the full details may be found in [31].

The moral of this appendix is that, not only are higher-order functions unnecessary for higher-order programming, but higher-order logic is also unnecessary for reasoning about functional programs. More detail can be found in [31], including a completeness theorem, some induction principles, and techniques for verifying generic modules.

## References

[1] Backus, J. "Can programming be liberated from the von Neumann style?" *Communications of the ACM 21*, 8 (August 1978), pp. 613–641.

[2] Battiston, E., DeCindio, F. and Mauri, G. "OBJSA net systems: A class of high-level nets having objects as domains". In [35].

[3] Bergstra, J. and Tucker, J. "Characterization of computable data types by means of a finite equational specification method". *Automata, Languages and Programming, Seventh Colloquium*, pp. 76–90. Lecture Notes in Computer Science, vol. 81. Springer-Verlag, Berlin, 1980.

[4] Berry, G. and Curien, P.-L. "Theory and practice of sequential algorithms: The kernel of the applicative language CDS". *Algebraic Methods in Semantics*, pp. 35–88. Cambridge University Press, 1985.

[5] Bidoit, M., Choppy, C. and Voisin, F. "The ASSPEGIQUE specification environment — Motivations and design". *Recent Trends in Data Type Specification* (selected papers from the Third Workshop on Theory and Applications of Abstract Data Types), H.-J. Kreowski, ed., pp. 54–72. Springer-Verlag, Berlin, 1985.

[6] Burstall, R. and Darlington, J. "A transformation system for developing recursive programs". *Journal of the ACM 24*, 1 (January 1977), pp. 44–67.

[7] Burstall, R. and Goguen, J. "Putting theories together to make specifications". *Proceedings of the Fifth International Joint Conference on Artificial Intelligence*, R. Reddy, ed., pp. 1045–1058. Department of Computer Science, Carnegie-Mellon University, 1977.

[8] Burstall, R. and Goguen, J. "The semantics of Clear, a specification language". *Proceedings of the 1979 Copenhagen Winter School on Abstract Software Specification*, D. Bjorner, ed., pp. 292–332. Lecture Notes in Computer Science, vol. 86. Springer-Verlag, Berlin, 1980.

[9] Burstall, R. and Goguen, J. "An informal introduction to specifications using Clear". *The Correctness Problem in Computer Science*, R. Boyer and J Moore, eds., pp. 185–213; Academic Press, New York, 1981. Reprinted in *Software Specification Techniques*, N. Gehani and A. McGettrick, eds., pp. 363–390; Addison-Wesley, Reading, Mass., 1985.

[10] Burstall, R. and Goguen, J. "Algebras, theories and freeness: An introduction for computer scientists". *Theoretical Foundations of Programming Methodology* (Proceedings of the 1981 Marktoberdorf NATO Summer School, NATO Advanced Study Institute Series, Volume C91), M. Wirsing and G. Schmidt, eds., pp. 329–350. Reidel, Dordrecht, 1982.

[11] Burstall, R. and Lampson, B. "A kernel language for abstract data types and modules". *Proceedings of the International Symposium on the Semantics of Data Types*, pp. 1–50. Springer-Verlag, Berlin, 1984.

[12] Burstall, R., MacQueen, D. and Sannella, D. "Hope: An experimental applicative language". *Proceedings of the First LISP Conference*, pp. 136–143, Stanford University, 1980.

[13] Cartmell, J. "Formalizing the network and hierarchical data models — An application of categorical logic". *Proceedings of the Conference on Category Theory and Computer Programming*, D. Pitt et al., eds., pp. 466–492. Lecture Notes in Computer Science, vol. 240. Springer-Verlag, Berlin, 1986.

[14] Cavenathi, C., De Zanet, M., and Mauri,G. "MC–OBJ: A C interpreter for OBJ". *Note di Software 36/37*, pp. 16–26, October 1988. In Italian.

[15] Cheatham, T. "The introduction of definitional facilities into higher level programming languages". *Proceedings of the AFIPS Fall Joint Computer Conference*, pp. 623–637. Spartan Books, Cornwell Heights, PA, 1966.

[16] Coleman, D., Gallimore, R. and Stavridou, V. "The design of a rewrite rule inter-

preter from algebraic specifications". *IEE Software Engineering Journal* (July 1987), pp. 95–104.

[17] Coleman, D. *et al.* "The Axis papers". Technical Report HPL–ISC–TR–88–031, Hewlett-Packard Bristol Labs, 1988.

[18] Colmerauer, A., Kanoui,H., and van Caneghem, M. "Etude et réalisation d'un système Prolog". Technical Report, Groupe d'Intelligence Artificielle, U.E.R. de Luminy, Université d'Aix-Marseille II, 1979.

[19] Duce, D. "Concerning the compatibility of PHIGS and GKS". In [35].

[20] Ehrig, H. and Mahr, B. *Fundamentals of Algebraic Specification 1: Equations and Initial Semantics.* Springer-Verlag, Berlin, 1985.

[21] Futatsugi, K., Goguen, J., Jouannaud, J.-P., and Meseguer, J. "Principles of OBJ2". *Proceedings of the 12th ACM Symposium on Principles of Programming Languages,* B. Reid, ed., pp. 52–66. ACM, New York, 1985.

[22] Futatsugi, K., Goguen, J., Meseguer, J., and Okada, K. "Parameterized programming in OBJ2". *Proceedings of the Ninth International Conference on Software Engineering,* R. Balzer, ed., pp. 51–60. IEEE Computer Society Press, New York, March 1987.

[23] Gerrard, C. P. "The specification and controlled implementation of a configuration management tool using OBJ and Ada". In [35].

[24] Gogolla, M. "Partially ordered sorts in algebraic specifications". *Proceedings of the Ninth CAAP (Bordeaux),* B. Courcelle, ed., pp. 139–153. Cambridge University Press, 1984. Also, Forschungsbericht Nr. 169, Universität Dortmund, Abteilung Informatik, 1983.

[25] Gogolla, M. "A final algebra semantics for errors and exceptions". *Recent Trends in Data Type Specification* (selected papers from the Third Workshop on Theory and Applications of Abstract Data Types), H.-J. Kreowski, ed., pp. 89–103. Springer-Verlag, Berlin, 1985.

[26] Goguen, J. "Mathematical representation of hierarchically organized systems". *Global Systems Dynamics,* E. Attinger, ed., pp. 112–128. S. Karger, Basel, 1971.

[27] Goguen, J. "Semantics of computation". *Proceedings of the First International Symposium on Category Theory Applied to Computation and Control,* E. G. Manes, ed., pp. 234–249. University of Massachusetts at Amherst, 1974. Also pp. 151–163, Lecture Notes in Computer Science, vol. 25. Springer-Verlag, Berlin, 1975.

[28] Goguen, J. "Abstract errors for abstract data types". *Proceedings of First IFIP Working Conference on Formal Description of Programming Concepts,* E. Neuhold, ed., pp. 21.1–21.32. MIT, Cambridge, Mass., 1977. Also published in *Formal Description of Programming Concepts,* P. Neuhold, ed., pp. 491–522. North-Holland, Amsterdam, 1979.

[29] Goguen, J. "How to prove algebraic inductive hypotheses without induction: With applications to the correctness of data type representations". *Proceedings of the Fifth Conference on Automated Deduction,* W. Bibel and R. Kowalski, eds., pp. 356–

373. Lecture Notes in Computer Science, vol. 87. Springer-Verlag, Berlin, 1980.

[30] Goguen, J. "Reusing and interconnecting software components". *Computer 19*, 2 (February 1986), pp. 16–28. Reprinted in *Tutorial: Software Reusability*, P. Freeman, ed., pp. 251–263. IEEE Computer Society Press, New York, 1987.

[31] Goguen, J. "OBJ as a theorem prover, with application to hardware verification". *Current Trends in Hardware Verification and Automated Theorem Proving*, V. P. Subramanyan and G. Birtwhistle, eds., pp. 218–267. Springer-Verlag, Berlin, 1989. Also Technical Report SRI–CSL–88–4R2, SRI International, Computer Science Lab, August 1988.

[32] Goguen, J. "Principles of parameterized programming". *Software Reusability, Volume I: Concepts and Models*, T. Biggerstaff and A. Perlis, eds., pp. 159–225. Addison-Wesley, Reading, Mass., 1989.

[33] Goguen, J. "Types as theories". To appear in *Proceedings of the Symposium on General Topology and Applications* (Oxford, June 1989), Oxford University Press, 1990.

[34] Goguen, J. and Burstall, R. "Institutions: Abstract model theory for specification and programming". *Journal of the ACM*, to appear. Report ECS–LFCS–90–106, Computer Science Department, University of Edinburgh, January 1990; preliminary version, Report CSLI–85–30, Center for the Study of Language and Information, Stanford University, 1985.

[35] Goguen, J., Coleman, D., and Gallimore, R., eds. *Applications of Algebraic Specification using OBJ*. Cambridge University Press, 1990. To appear.

[36] Goguen, J., Jouannaud, J.-P., and Meseguer, J. "Operational semantics of order-sorted algebra". In *Proceedings of the 1985 International Conference on Automata, Languages and Programming*, W. Brauer, editor. Lecture Notes in Computer Science, vol. 194. Springer-Verlag, Berlin, 1985.

[37] Goguen, J. and Meseguer, J. "Rapid prototyping in the OBJ executable specification language". *Software Engineering Notes 7*, 5 (December 1982), pp. 75–84. Proceedings of Rapid Prototyping Workshop.

[38] Goguen, J. and Meseguer, J. "Universal realization, persistent interconnection and implementation of abstract modules". *Proceedings of the Ninth International Conference on Automata, Languages and Programming*, M. Nielsen and E. M. Schmidt, eds., pp. 265–281. Lecture Notes in Computer Science, vol. 140. Springer-Verlag, Berlin, 1982.

[39] Goguen, J. and Meseguer, J. "Eqlog: Equality, types, and generic modules for logic programming". *Logic Programming: Functions, Relations and Equations*, D. DeGroot and G. Lindstrom, eds., pp. 295–363. Prentice-Hall, Englewood Cliffs, N.J., 1986. An earlier version appears in *Journal of Logic Programming 1*, 2 (September 1984), pp. 179–210.

[40] Goguen, J. and Meseguer, J. "Extensions and foundations for object-oriented pro-

gramming". *Research Directions in Object-Oriented Programming*, B. Shriver and P. Wegner, eds., pp. 417–477. MIT Press, Cambridge, Mass., 1987. Preliminary version in *SIGPLAN Notices 21*, 10 (October 1986), pp. 153–162. Also Technical Report CSLI–87–93, Center for the Study of Language and Information, Stanford University, March 1987.

[41] Goguen, J. and Meseguer, J. "Order-sorted algebra solves the constructor selector, multiple representation and coercion problems". *Proceedings of the Second Symposium on Logic in Computer Science*, pp. 18–29. IEEE Computer Society Press, New York, 1987. Also Technical Report CSLI–87–92, Center for the Study of Language and Information, Stanford University, March 1987.

[42] Goguen, J. and Meseguer, J. "Unifying functional, object-oriented and relational programming, with logical semantics". *Research Directions in Object-Oriented Programming*, B. Shriver and P. Wegner, eds., pp.s 417–477. MIT Press, 1987. Preliminary version: *SIGPLAN Notices 21*, 10 (October 1986), pp. 153–162.

[43] Goguen, J. and Meseguer, J. Software for the Rewrite Rule Machine. *Proceedings of the International Conference on Fifth Generation Computer Systems 1988*, pp. 628–637. Institute for New Generation Computer Technology (ICOT), 1988.

[44] Goguen, J. and Meseguer, J. "Order-sorted algebra I: Equational deduction for multiple inheritance, overloading, exceptions and partial operations". Technical Report SRI–CSL–89–10, SRI International, Computer Science Lab, July 1989. Given as lecture at Seminar on Types, Carnegie-Mellon University, June 1983; many draft versions exist.

[45] Goguen, J., Meseguer, J., and Plaisted, D. "Programming with parameterized abstract objects in OBJ". *Theory and Practice of Software Technology*, D. Ferrari, M. Bolognani, and J. Goguen, eds., pp. 163–193. North-Holland, Amsterdam, 1983.

[46] Goguen, J. and Parsaye-Ghomi, K. "Algebraic denotational semantics using parameterized abstract modules". *Formalizing Programming Concepts*, pp. 292–309. Lecture Notes in Computer Science, vol. 107. Springer-Verlag, Berlin, 1981.

[47] Goguen, J. and Tardo, J. "An introduction to OBJ: A language for writing and testing software specifications". *Specification of Reliable Software*, M. Zelkowitz, ed., pp. 170–189. IEEE Press, New York, 1979. Reprinted in *Software Specification Techniques*, N. Gehani and A. McGettrick, eds., pp. 391–420. Addison-Wesley, Reading, Mass., 1985.

[48] Goguen, J., Thatcher, J., and Wagner, E. "An initial algebra approach to the specification, correctness and implementation of abstract data types". Technical Report RC 6487, IBM T. J. Watson Research Center, October 1976. *Current Trends in Programming Methodology IV*, R. Yeh, ed., pp. 80–149. Prentice-Hall, Englewood Cliffs, N.J., 1978.

[49] Goguen, J., Thatcher, J., Wagner, E., and Wright, J. "Abstract data types as initial algebras and the correctness of data representations". *Computer Graphics, Pattern Recognition and Data Structure*, A. Klinger, ed., pp. 89–93. IEEE Press, New York,

1975.

[50] Gordon, M., Milner, R., and Wadsworth, C. *Edinburgh LCF*. Lecture Notes in Computer Science, vol. 78. Springer-Verlag, Berlin, 1979.

[51] Guttag, J. "The specification and application to programming of abstract data types". PhD thesis, University of Toronto, 1975. Computer Science Department, Report CSRG-59.

[52] Guttag, J., Horning, J., and Wing, J. "Larch in five easy pieces". Technical Report 5, Digital Equipment Corporation, Systems Research Center, July 1985.

[53] Guttag, J., Horowitz, E., and Musser, D. "Abstract data types and software validation". *Communications of the ACM 21*, 12 (1978), pp. 1048–1064.

[54] Harper, R., MacQueen, D., and Milner, R. "Standard ML". Technical Report ECS-LFCS-86-2, Department of Computer Science, University of Edinburgh, 1986.

[55] Hayashi, S. and Nakano, H. "PX: A computational logic". Technical Report RIMS-573, Research Institute for Mathematical Sciences, Kyoto, Japan, April 1987.

[56] Hoffmann, C. M. and O'Donnell, M. "Programming with Equations". *ACM Transactions on Programming Languages and Systems 1*, 4 (1982), pp. 83–112.

[57] Hudak, P., Wadler, P., Arvind, *et al.* "Report on the functional programming language Haskell". Technical Report YALEU/DCS/RR-666, Computer Science Department, Yale University, December 1988. Draft Proposed Standard.

[58] Hughes, R. J. M. "Why functional programming matters". This volume.

[59] Kaphengst, H. and Reichel, H. "Initial algebraic semantics for non-context-free languages". *Fundamentals of Computation Theory*, M. Karpinski, ed., pp. 120–126. Lecture Notes in Computer Science, vol. 56. Springer-Verlag, Berlin, 1977.

[60] Kirchner, C., Kirchner, H., and Meseguer, J. "Operational semantics of OBJ3". In *Proceedings of the 9th International Conference on Automata, Languages and Programming*. Lecture Notes in Computer Science, vol. 241. Springer-Verlag, Berlin, 1988.

[61] Latham, J. T. "Abstract Pascal: A tutorial introduction". Technical Report Version 2.1, University of Manchester, Department of Computer Science, 1987.

[62] Leinwand, S., Goguen, J., and Winkler, T. "Cell and ensemble architecture of the Rewrite Rule Machine". *Proceedings of the International Conference on Fifth Generation Computer Systems 1988*, pp. 869–878. Institute for New Generation Computer Technology (ICOT), 1988.

[63] Lerman, C.-W. and Loeckx, J. "OBSCURE, a new specification language". *Recent Trends in Data Type Specification* (selected papers from the Third Workshop on Theory and Applications of Abstract Data Types), H.-J. Kreowski, ed., pp. 28–30. Springer-Verlag, Berlin, 1985.

[64] Levy, G. and Sirovich, F. "TEL: A proof-theoretic language for efficient symbolic expression manipulation". Technical Report, IEI, February 1977. Nota Interna B77-3.

[65] Lucas, P. and Risch, T. "Representation of factual information by equations and their evaluation". Technical Report, IBM Research, Yorktown Heights, 1982.

[66] MacQueen, D., Sethi, R., and Plotkin, G. "An ideal model for recursive polymorphic types". *Proceedings of the Symposium on Principles of Programming Languages*, pp. 165–174. Association for Computing Machinery, New York, 1984.

[67] Martin-Löf, P. "Constructive mathematics and computer programming". *Logic, Methodology and Philosophy of Science VI*, pp. 153–175. North-Holland, Amsterdam, 1982.

[68] McCarthy, J., Levin, M., *et al. LISP 1.5 Programmer's Manual*. MIT Press, Cambridge, Mass., 1966.

[69] Meseguer, J. "General logics". In *Proceedings, Logic Colloquium, 1987*, H.-D. Ebbinghaus et al., eds. North-Holland, Amsterdam, 1989.

[70] Meseguer, J. and Goguen, J. "Initiality, induction and computability". *Algebraic Methods in Semantics*, M. Nivat and J. Reynolds, eds., pp. 459–541. Cambridge University Press, 1985.

[71] Milner, R. "A theory of type polymorphism in programming". *Journal of Computer and System Sciences 17*, 3 (1978), pp. 348–375.

[72] Mosses, P. "Abstract semantic algebras!" *Formal Description of Programming Concepts II*, D. Bjorner, ed., pp. 45–70. IFIP Press, 1983.

[73] Mosses, P. "A basic semantic algebra". *Proceedings of the International Symposium on the Semantics of Data Types*, pp. 87–107. Lecture Notes in Computer Science, vol. 173. Springer-Verlag, Berlin, 1985.

[74] Nakagawa, A., Futatsugi, K., Tomura, S., and Shimizu, T. "Algebraic specification of Macintosh's QuickDraw using OBJ2". Technical Report Draft, ElectroTechnical Laboratory, Tsukuba Science City, Japan, 1987. In *Proceedings*, Tenth International Conference on Software Engineering, Singapore, April 1988.

[75] O'Donnell, M. *Equational Logic as a Programming Language*. MIT Press, Cambridge, Mass., 1985.

[76] Department of Defense. "Reference manual for the Ada programming language". Report ANSI/MIL–STD–1815A, United States Government, 1983.

[77] Plaisted, D. "An initial algebra semantics for error presentations". Computer Science Laboratory, SRI International, Menlo Park CA, 1982.

[78] Poigné, A. "On semantic algebras: Higher order structures". Informatik II, Universität Dortmund, 1983.

[79] Prywes, N. and Pnueli, A. "Compilation of nonprocedural specifications into computer programs". *IEEE Transactions on Software Engineering SE–9*, 3 (May 1983), pp. 267–279.

[80] Reynolds, J. "Using category theory to design implicit conversions and generic operators". *Semantics Directed Compiler Generation*, N. D. Jones, ed., pp. 211–258.

Lecture Notes in Computer Science, vol. 94. Springer-Verlag, Berlin, 1980.

[81] Scherlis, W. "Abstract data types, specialization, and program reuse". *Proceedings of the Workshop on Advanced Programming Environments*, R. Conradi, T. Didriksen, and D. Wanvik, eds., pp. 433–453. Lecture Notes in Computer Science, vol. 244. Springer-Verlag, Berlin, 1986.

[82] Scherlis, W. and Scott, D. "First steps towards inferential programming". *Information Processing 83*, R. E. A. Mason, ed., pp. 199–212. Elsevier (North-Holland), Amsterdam, 1983.

[83] Seeley, R. A. G. "Locally cartesian closed categories and type theory". *Mathematical Proceedings of the Cambridge Philosophical Society 95* (1964), pp. 33–48.

[84] Sridhar, S. "An implementation of OBJ2: An object-oriented language for abstract program specification". *Proceedings of the Sixth Conference on Foundations of Software Technology and Theoretical Computer Science*, K. V. Nori, ed., pp. 81–95. Lecture Notes in Computer Science, vol. 241. Springer-Verlag, Berlin, 1986.

[85] Stavridou, V. "Specifying in OBJ, verifying in REVE, and some ideas about time". Technical Report Draft, Department of Computer Science, University of Manchester, 1987.

[86] Tardo, J. "The design, specification and implementation of OBJT: A language for writing and testing abstract algebraic program specifications". PhD thesis, Computer Science Department, University of California, Los Angeles, 1981.

[87] Turner, D. "Miranda: A non-strict functional language with polymorphic types". *Functional Programming Languages and Computer Architecture*, J.-P. Jouannaud, ed., pp. 1–16. Lecture Notes in Computer Science, vol. 201. Springer-Verlag, Berlin, 1985.

[88] Wadge, W. "Classified algebras". Technical Report 46, University of Warwick, October 1982.

[89] Wand, M. "First-order identities as a defining language". *Acta Informatica 14* (1980), pp. 337–357. Originally Report 29, Computer Science Department, Indiana University, 1977.

[90] Zilles, S. "Abstract specification of data types". Technical Report 119, Computation Structures Group, MIT, 1974.

# A Higher-Order Type System for Functional Programming

# 13

**David MacQueen**
AT&T Bell Laboratories

## 1 *Introduction*

My purpose here is to shed light on several of the more subtle issues in the design of modular programming facilities for functional languages. I will base my discussion on the module facilities of the Standard ML programming language, since these represent the culmination of a long development that has been shaped by a number of important lines of research in type theory, semantics, and programming language design and implementation.

I have been thinking about module systems for functional languages for several years, starting with the Hope language [5, 17] and continuing through my work on the design and implementation of modules for Standard ML. This design has been extensively analyzed, leading to a formal semantics of modules that is incorporated in the Standard ML semantics developed by Harper, Milner, and Tofte [15] and a series of papers that discuss the underlying type-theoretic ideas [20, 21, 27]. The design has also undergone the test of implementation: Bob Harper added a prototype implementation of modules to the Edinburgh Standard ML compiler in 1986, David Matthews implemented them in his Poly/ML compiler [24], and they are implemented in the "Standard ML of New Jersey" compiler that my colleagues and I have been developing at Bell Labs and Princeton [1, 19]. We are now beginning to accumulate sufficient experience with the practical use of modules in Standard ML to develop methodological guidelines for their application.

There remains a need for a thorough explanation of some of the fundamental design choices in the Standard ML module system, and I hope to address that need in this paper. My aim will be to highlight some of the basic considerations and principles that have shaped the design.

The module facilities of Standard ML had a long gestation (roughly 1979 to 1987), and during this period our understanding evolved under the influence of several related parallel developments. Initially, the strongest influences were the CLEAR specification language of Burstall and Goguen [3], which was designed to deal with the modular decomposition of large algebraic specifications, and my experience attempting to use the rudimentary modularity features of the POP-2 language [2] in the implementation of the Hope compiler. More recently an influx of ideas from type theory [9, 8, 12, 30, 28, 25, 23] played an important role, particularly the notion of dependent types. Milner's polymorphic type system [10, 26] supplied a starting point and a foundation for the module system, which was conceived as a natural generalization of the core polymorphic type system.

The operational semantics for the full Standard ML[1] language developed by Harper, Milner, and Tofte [15] was extremely helpful in revealing and clarifying some of the subtle issues in the design. This semantics, using the style of Plotkin's structural operational semantics [29], works at a more detailed level than the type-theoretic explanations of the system and proved sufficiently comprehensive to suggest practical strategies for implementing modules. In particular, the SML semantics was designed to address the phenomenon of *generative* declarations that is discussed below.

Related language designs that influenced the SML module design included Hope, which included a crude precursor of the SML module system, the Russell language of Donahue and Demers [11], which was the first language to consciously exploit dependent types, and Pebble, which makes a more explicit and systematic use of dependent types [16], as well as more "conventional" languages like Clu, Modula 2, and Ada. Russell and Pebble both followed the *type as value* approach, in which there exists a type of all types

---

1. Hereafter "Standard ML" will be abbreviated to "SML".

and types are treated as "ordinary" computed values on the same level as, say, integers. It was partly in reaction to the semantic and pragmatic difficulties of this position that I adopted a stratified approach to typing modules (see [25]).

## 2  *Overview of the Module System*

The Standard ML module system has two principle goals. The first, naturally, is to provide the usual benefits of modularity for programming in the large. The main elements are *structures* for packaging a collection of related types and operations so that it can be treated as a unit, *signatures* that specify the type interfaces of structures and mediate their interaction with other modules, and *functors*, which are operations that construct new structures from old, and which supply the glue to construct a large system out of its components.[2]

At a naive level, modules can be explained as a set of constructs for expressing and manipulating environments as objects. A structure consists of a set of named components and is most simply defined by encapsulating a sequence of declarations; the denotation of a structure expression, like the denotation of a declaration, is an environment. A functor defines a new environment in terms of a given parameter environment. A signature is a template defining a class of environments that share a common type scheme. It consists of a sequence of *specifications* that correspond to declarations in a structure definition.

The following SML program illustrates many of the elements of the module system. Like most SML programs, it consists of a sequence of declarations of signatures, structures, and functors.

```
signature ORD =
  sig
    type t
    val le : t * t -> bool
  end

structure S =
  struct
    datatype t = A | B of t
    val least = A
    fun le(A,_) = true
```

---

2. Structures and functors are collectively called modules in the terminology of Standard ML. Structures are the basic kind of module, while functors are the parametric form.

```
      | le(_,A) = false
      | le(B x,  B y) = le(x,y)
   end

 signature LEXORD =
   sig
     structure A : ORD
     val lexord : A.t list * A.t list -> bool
   end

 functor LexOrd(O: ORD)  : LEXORD =
   struct
     structure A = O
     fun lexord([],_) = true
       | lexord(_,[]) = false
       | lexord(x::1,y::m) = ... O.le(x,y) ...
   end

 structure LS = LexOrd(S)
```

This example contains declarations of two signatures, **ORD** and **LEXORD**, two structures, **S** and **LS**, and one functor, **LexOrd**, mapping a structure of signature **ORD** to a new structure of signature **LEXORD**. The structure **LS** is defined as the result of applying **LexOrd** to **S**. We refer to components of a structure using qualified names or paths formed with the usual "dot" notation: e.g., `S.t`, `S.least`, `LS.A.le`.

The **LEXORD** signature and the body of the **LexOrd** functor illustrate that a structure may include other structures among its components. The main reason for doing so is to achieve a kind of self-sufficiency or closure by having a structure explicitly inherit facilities that may be required fully exploit it. It also tends to simplify the interfaces between modules, since it bundles the resources of several structures into one so that they do not have to be separately provided to a client module. On the other hand, in conjunction with functor abstraction, it gives rise to the requirement for sharing constraints discussed below.

## 3 *Signature Matching*

The analog of type-checking for expressions is *signature matching* between structures and signatures. It is a process of comparing the specifications in the signature with the bindings in the structure, "instantiating" the signature template in the process. We say that a structure *matches* a signature if it satisfies the specifications given in the signature. Signature matching is performed in two contexts: (1) when a signature constraint is given in a structure declaration, as in:

```
structure R : ORD = S
```

and (2) when a functor is applied to an argument structure, which must match the signature specified for the formal parameter, as in

```
structure LS = LexOrd(S)
```

where **S** must match **ORD**. Actually, these two contexts are essentially equivalent by Landin's principle of correspondence.

A structure does not have to agree exactly with a signature in order for it to match the signature. For instance, the structure **S** defined above matches the signature **ORD**, even though **S** has an additional value component **least** not specified in **ORD**. In such cases signature matching has a coercive effect, producing a "thinned" structure that exactly agrees with the signature in terms of number of components and their types, but agrees with the matched structure regarding the "identity" of the components. Hence **R** is bound to a thinned version of **S** that does not contain a **least** component; and in the functor application, the formal parameter **O**, and hence the substructure **LS.A**, is also bound to a thinned version of **S**. Another permissible discrepancy is for the value declared in the structure to have a polymorphic type that instantiates to the type specified in the signature, as for example in the following declaration,

```
structure A : sig val f : int -> int end =
  struct
    fun f x = x
  end
```

where the specification requires the monotype **int -> int** and the corresponding structure component has the polymorphic type **'a -> 'a**.[3]

A given structure can match many signatures, differing in the way the formal type components are used, the degree of polymorphism specified for the value components, or the number of components specified. However, Tofte has proved an analog of the Damas-Milner principal types theorem for signature matching [32]. This means there is a most general signature for any structure from which any other signature for that structure can be derived by a combination of "instantiation" and thinning. There is also a kind of "exact"

---

3. Generic type variables in SML are written with an initial apostrophe.

signature that represents the complete static type information associated with a structure, and which is the signature inferred for any structure whose declaration does not specify an explicit signature.

## 4 *The Type-theoretic Basis*

The second goal of the module system was to provide a natural enrichment of the basic polymorphic type system, using functors to provide a more powerful form of type parameterization. In this view, a typical structure embodies an interpreted type or, in other words, a type bound together with operations that give it a particular semantic interpretation, like the integers with an ordering operation. The type-theoretic notion of a dependent sum provides a formalization of this packaging of types with their supporting operations, while the notion of dependent product captures the dependency between a functor's result and its parameter.[4]

At this more abstract level, the module system can explained by translating it into a variant of typed lambda calculus with dependent types, for example the language DL of [20] or the more refined XML of [27]. The key ideas behind such a translation can be summarized as follows:

> Signatures, the types of structures, are represented by a form of dependent sum type.

> The (implicit) signature of a functor is represented by a form of dependent product type, which allows us to express how the result type depends on the argument type, or in other words, how type information is propagated from the argument to the result.

> Types are stratified into two type universes, with "ordinary" types in the first universe ($U_1$) and the dependent types representing structure and functor signatures in the second universe ($U_2$).

> The bound variables in the dependent types range over second universe types ($U_1$ or dependent sum types). This means that types and structures can be components of structures and arguments of functors. Also dependency is asymmetrical; values can depend on types and structures but not the other way around.

> The dependent sum is a *strong* sum, meaning that one can access both components of the pairs that make up the sum type. As a consequence, there is no abstraction or information-hiding effect associated with the

---

4. There is an unfortunate terminological confusion associated with dependent types. What I choose to call a dependent *sum* corresponds to Martin-Löf's *general sum* and what some others [8, 16] call the dependent *product*. My dependent product is Martin-Löf's general product and is also known as a *dependent function space*.

packaging effect of structures.

Ordinary polymorphic types are represented by product types of the form $\Sigma.t : U_1.\tau$ where $\tau$ is in $U_1$. Polytypes are therefore members of $U_2$ and not $U_1$.

The dependencies represented by the dependent sum are simply an expression of the natural dependencies arising from a sequence of definitions. For instance, we define a type and later mention that type in other definitions, which therefore depend on that type. A simple structure expression is an encapsulated sequence of declarations, and the meaning of the structure expression is the environment that results from the normal elaboration of the declaration sequence. To express the type of such an environment (i.e., its signature) requires the use of dependent sum types. For functors, dependent product types naturally express the propagation of type information from the argument to the result of the functor. This dependency also follows from the sequential composition of declarations, except that in this case the declarations in the parameter are "formal" rather than actual. For example, the signature

```
signature SIG =
  sig
    type t
    val f : t -> t
  end
```

translates into the dependent sum type[5]

$$\Sigma t : U_1.t \to t.$$

Here the existence of a type component in the signature is represented by the $\Sigma$-bound variable $t$. Multiple type components would be represented by nested $\Sigma$-bindings. Substructures (structure components of structures) are expressed by $\Sigma$-types whose bound variable itself ranges over a $\Sigma$-type.

The main purpose of the stratification into separate type universes is to keep the world of types separate from the world of values, i.e., to avoid the possibility that the identification of a type depends on the run-time evaluation of a value-denoting expression. This considerably simplifies the implementation of type-checking for the language in comparison with languages like Pebble and Russell, allowing Standard ML to maintain the usual strict separation between compile-time type-checking and run-time evaluation. A

---

5. The name of the value component, "f", has been lost in the translation, but this is a minor nuisance.

strictly limited kind of compile-time or static reduction is involved in elaborating the types of structures, amounting to a static beta-reduction of functor applications (see [19] for details).

The use of a strong dependent sum construct for structure types expresses the transparency of structures. We deliberately separate the issue of abstraction and information hiding from the bundling effect that is the main purpose of forming a structure. In principle, we view type abstraction as a natural consequence of the lambda-abstraction used to form functors.

The idealized typed languages used in this kind of analysis and explanation of the SML module system are actually quite a bit more general and powerful than the module system itself. This extra generality leads the way toward further evolution of the module design, and some early restrictions in the module system have already been relaxed as a consequence.

## 5 *Generative Declarations*

There are other issues that are not evident from this simple summary of the basic module type constructions. One of these is the use of generative declarations in Standard ML. There is a particular class of type declarations, the *datatype* declarations, that generate new, unique type constructors whenever they are elaborated. Structure declarations are also generative. In the case of type constructors, generative declarations are used to avoid difficulties with purely structural identification of recursively defined $n$-ary type constructors (for $n > 0$). In the case of structures, generative declarations also simplify the type-checking problem and particularly the verification of *sharing constraints*, which will be discussed below. Modeling the effects of generative declarations requires a more detailed, less abstract formalism than the idealized typed languages discussed above. Such a formalism is employed in [15].

## 6 *Sharing*

Another subtle but important issue is the interaction between $\Pi$- and $\Sigma$-abstraction that occurs when a functor parameter structure has nested substructures that are required to interact within the body of the functor on the basis of shared types. Such a situation is illustrated in the following code fragment.

```
signature SYMBOL = sig type symbol ... end

signature LEX =
```

```
    sig
      structure Symbol : SYMBOL
      val next : unit -> Symbol.symbol
      ...
    end

  signature SYMBOLTABLE =
    sig
      structure Symbol : SYMBOL
      type var
      val bind : Symbol.symbol * var -> unit
      ...
    end

  signature PARSE_ARGS =
    sig
      structure Lex : LEX
      structure SymTab : SYMBOLTABLE
      sharing Lex.Symbol = SymTab.Symbol
    end

  functor Parse(A: PARSE_ARGS) =
    struct ... A.SymTab.bind(A.Lex.next(), v) ... end
```

The functor **Parse** essentially takes two structure arguments, **Lex** (implementing a lexical analyzer) and **SymTab** (implementing a symbol table), which are bundled as components of a single parameter structure. The sharing specification in the signature **PARSE_ARGS** requires that the same **Symbol** structure be used in both **Lex** and **SymTab**. This insures that **Lex** and **SymTab** can consistently interact, as in the expression ""**A.Symtab.bind(A.Lex.next(),v)**," which is well typed only if **A.Lex.Symbol.symbol** and **A.Symtab.Symbol.symbol** can be statically determined to denote the same type. In effect, we can add some equational constraints between structures and types that are used by the type checker to establish needed type equivalences.

Strictly speaking, the type checker is only concerned with type equivalences, so we could do without structure sharing constraints and deal only with the component types. For example, in the above example we could replace the given sharing specification with

**sharing type L.Symbol.symbol = SymTab.Symbol.symbol**

and this would satisfy the type checker. However there are a couple of reasons for also allowing sharing constraints between structures. One is that this gives us a way of specifying sharing "wholesale" instead of type by type. The other is that we are often concerned not about the type *per se* but about the type in context, as interpreted by associated operations. An example would be a structure presenting integers as an ordered set, where we would be concerned not only that the type be *int*, but that it be ordered in a given way. Another structure with the same signature might have the same type component, but the ordering operation could be different. So the sharing of structures allows us to statically identify types with interpretations as well as bare types. The generative nature of structure definitions is what makes the static checking of such structure sharing relations possible.

It might be argued that sharing constraints are an awkward way of establishing the desired type coherency between functor parameters, but there are problems with the alternatives. As pointed out in [4], another way to achieve coherency is via nested lambda abstractions. For this approach, we need to be able to parameterize signatures with respect to structures and to define "curried" functors. Then we could rewrite the above example as follows:

```
signature SYMBOL = sig type symbol ... end

signature LEX(Symbol: SYMBOL) =
  sig
    val next : unit -> Symbol.symbol
    ...
  end

signature SYMBOLTABLE(Symbol: SYMBOL) =
  sig
    type var
    val bind : Symbol.symbol * var -> unit
    ...
  end

functor Parse(Symbol: SYMBOL)
              (Lex: LEX(Symbol),
                  SymTab: SYMBOLTABLE(Symbol)) =
  struct ... SymTab.bind(Lex.next(), v) ... end
```

As this example indicates, the functor parameters tend to recapitulate the hierarchical relationships between structures. Since in practice it is not unusual to have a hierarchical depth of 4 or 5 and half a dozen or so top-level parameters, functor parameter specifications can get extremely unwieldy in this approach. These problems were the original motivation for the use of substructures to express hierarchical dependency relations. Sharing specifications actually provides a much more succinct notation for establishing coherency, because we can establish hierarchical relations once and for all in the signatures, and we do not have to express them again in each functor parameter list.

## 7 *Closure Rules*

Free variables are a problem for modularity. The more free variables appearing in a construct, the more complicated and diffuse is its interface with the external environment. This applies in particular to signature and structure definitions. The number of free variables can be reduced in several ways:

1. Bundle free variables together into a structure and refer to them indirectly via the name of the structure.

2. Internalize structures named by free variables in the current structure by including them as a substructure.

3. Lambda abstract over the free name to make it a parameter.

All three methods are supported in the module system to focus and minimize the interfaces between modules.

The original closure rules were that signature expressions could mention only signature names freely, and that structure and functor definitions could mention only signatures, structures, and functors freely. These rules strongly encouraged tight, well-defined interfaces, but they also could be unnaturally constraining, particularly when applied within a structure definition among its component structures. The latest version of the SML of New Jersey compiler has relaxed these restrictions in order to allow a fuller and more natural exploitation of the underlying dependent type system as suggested by the idealized languages in [20, 27]. However, at the top level, and particularly when separate compilation comes into play, the more stringent closure rules are advisable.

## 8 *Functor Signatures*

One major gap in the original design was the omission of functor signatures. However, the implementation, the formal semantics, and the type-theoretic analyses have all demonstrated that there is a natural notion of a functor signature. Furthermore, the ability to define and name a functor signature independently of any particular functor definition is a practical requirement for separate compilation, where one must be able to provide specifications for free functor names that appear in a separately compiled module.

In the type-theoretical analysis, functor signatures are just dependent product types with bound variables ranging over dependent sums. In the operational semantics [15, 33] the model is somewhat more complicated, because one must account for the generative nature of structure and datatype declarations; every time a functor is applied, its body structure is regenerated, resulting in new structures and datatypes. These investigations are leading toward the addition of functor signatures to Standard ML. And this in turn may lead toward other extensions like functors as functor parameters and structure components (i.e., allowing bound variables of dependent types to range over dependent product types as well as dependent sums).

## 9 Conclusion

I have attempted to review the rationale for the design of the Standard ML module system in the light of our recent experience with implementation, semantic specification, and type-theoretic analysis of the system. The design has stood up well under these tests, and we have considerable confidence in its conceptual soundness as well as its practical utility.

However, it is certainly not the last word. The insights that have been derived from the study of this design are already leading to interesting attempts to develop simpler, more refined, and more unified systems. It will be left to some new descendent of Standard ML to reap the full benefits of our current understanding.

### Acknowledgments

My work on the development of the Standard ML module system have benefited enormously from collaboration with Rod Burstall and Robin Milner over the last decade or more. More recently, Mads Tofte, Bob Harper, and John Mitchell have contributed much to my understanding of the type theory and semantics of modules, and Andrew Appel has provided crucial help with the implementation of modules in Standard ML of New Jersey.

### References

[1] Appel, A. and MacQueen, D. "A Standard ML compiler." *Proceedings of the Conference on Functional Programming and Computer Architecture* (Portland, September), G. Kahn, ed., pp. 301–324. Lecture Notes in Computer Science, vol. 274. Springer-Verlag, Berlin, 1987.

[2] Burstall, R., Collins, J., and Popplestone, R. *Programming in POP-2*. Edinburgh University Press, Edinburgh, 1977.

[3] Burstall, R. and Goguen, J. "Putting theories together to make specifications." *Proceedings of the Fifth Joint International Conf. on Artificial Intelligence*. Cambridge, Mass., August 1977, pp. 1045–1058.

[4] Burstall, R. "Programming with modules as typed functional programming." *Proceedings of the International Conference on Fifth Generation Computing Systems*, ICOT, Tokyo.

[5] Burstall, R., MacQueen, D., and Sannella, D. "Hope: An experimental applicative language." *Proceedings of the 1980 LISP Conference*, Stanford, August 1980, pp. 136–143.

[6] Cardelli, L. "A polymorphic lambda calculus with type: type." Report 10, Digital Equipment Corp. Systems Research Center, Palo Alto, Calif.

[7] Cardelli, L. and Wegner, P. "On understanding types, data abstraction, and polymorphism." *Computing Surveys 17*, 4 (December 1985), pp. 471–522.

[8] Constable, R. and Zlatin, D. "The type theory of PL/CV3." *ACM Transactions on Programming Languages and Systems 6*, 1 (January 1984), pp. 94–117.

[9] Coquand, T. and Huet, G. "The calculus of constructions." *Information and Computation 76* (1988), pp. 95–120.

[10] Damas, L. and Milner, R. "Principal type-schemes for functional programs." *Proceedings of the Ninth ACM Symposium on Principles of Programming Languages* (Albuquerque, January), pp. 207–212. ACM, New York, 1982.

[11] Donahue, J. and Demers, A. "Data types are values." *ACM Transactions on Programming Languages and Systems 7*, 3 (July 1985), pp. 426–445.

[12] Girard, J.-Y. "Interpretation fonctionelle et élimination des coupres de l'arithmétique d'order supérieur." Thèse d'État, Université Paris VII, 1972.

[13] Harper, R., MacQueen, D., and Milner, R. "Standard ML." Laboratory for Foundations of Computer Science, Dept. of Computer Science, Univ. of Edinburgh, ECS–LFCS–86–2, 1986.

[14] Harper, R., Milner, R., and Tofte, M. "A type discipline for program modules." *Proceedings of TAPSOFT 87*, pp. 308–319. Lecture Notes in Computer Science, vol. 250. Springer-Verlag, Berlin, 1987.

[15] Harper, R., Milner, R., and Tofte, M. "The semantics of Standard ML, Version I." Laboratory for Foundations of Computer Science, Dept. of Computer Science, Univ. of Edinburgh, ECS–LFCS–87–36, 1986.

[16] Lampson, B. and Burstall, R. "Pebble, a kernel language for modules and abstract data types." *Information and Control 76* (1988), pp. 278–346.

[17] MacQueen, D. "Structure and parameterization in a typed functional language." Symposium on Functional Languages and Computer Architecture, Gothenburg,

Sweden, June 1981, pp. 525–537.

[18] MacQueen, D. "Modules for Standard ML." Laboratory for Foundations of Computer Science, Dept. of Computer Science, Univ. of Edinburgh, ECS–LFCS–86–2, 1986.

[19] MacQueen, D. "Modules for Standard ML." *Proceedings of the 1988 Lisp and Functional Programming Conference* (Snowbird, Utah, July). ACM, New York, 1988. (An earlier version appeared in *Proceedings of the 1984 ACM Symposium on Lisp and Functional Programming* (Austin, August), pp. 198–207.)

[20] MacQueen, D. "Using dependent types to express modular structure." *Proceedings of the Thirteenth ACM Symposium on Principles of Programming Languages* (St. Petersburg Beach, Fla., January), pp. 277–286. ACM, New York, 1986.

[21] MacQueen, D. and Sethi, R. "A higher order polymorphic type system for applicative languages." *Proceedings of the 1982 ACM Symposium on Lisp and Functional Programming* (Pittsburgh, Pa., August). pp. 243–252. ACM, New York, 1982.

[22] MacQueen, D., Plotkin, G., and Sethi, R. "An ideal model for recursive polymorphic types." *Information and Control 71*, 1/2 (October/November 1986), pp. 95–130.

[23] Martin-Löf, P. "Constructive mathematics and computer programming." *Proceedings, Sixth International Congress for Logic, Methodology, and Philosophy of Science*, pp. 153–175. North-Holland, Amsterdam, 1982.

[24] Matthews, D. "An implementation of Standard ML in Poly." Unpublished article, 1987.

[25] Meyer, A. and Reinhold, M. "'Type' is not a type." *Proceedings of the Thirteenth ACM Symposium on Principles of Programming Languages* (St. Petersberg Beach, Fla., January), pp. 287–295. ACM, New York, 1986.

[26] Milner, R. "A theory of type polymorphism in programming." *Journal of Computer and System Sciences 17*, 3 (1978), pp. 348–375.

[27] Mitchell, J. C. and Harper, R. "The essence of ML." *Proceedings of the Fifteenth ACM Symposium on Principles of Programming Languages* (San Diego), pp. 28–46. ACM, New York, 1988.

[28] Mitchell, J. C. and Plotkin, G. "Abstract types have existential types." *Proceedings of the Twelfth ACM Symposium on Principles of Programming Languages* (New Orleans, January), pp. 37–51. ACM, New York, 1985.

[29] Plotkin, G. "A structural approach to operational semantics." Computer Science Dept., Aarhus University, Report DAIMI FN–19, September 1981.

[30] Reynolds, J. C. "Towards a theory of type structure." *Paris Colloquium on Programming*, pp. 408–425. Lecture Notes in Computer Science, vol. 19. Springer-Verlag, Berlin, 1977.

[31] Reynolds, J. C. "Three approaches to type structure." *Mathematical Foundations of Software Development*, pp. 97–138. Lecture Notes in Computer Science, vol. 185. Springer-Verlag, Berlin, 1985.

[32] Tofte, M. "Operational semantics and polymorphic type inference." Ph.D. Dissertation, Dept. of Computer Science, University of Edinburgh, 1987.

[33] Tofte, M. "On functor matching." Unpublished working note, February 1988.

# The Authors

SAMSON ABRAMSKY is a Reader in Computing Science at Imperial College, London. He has an MA in Philosophy and a Diploma in Computer Science from Cambridge and a Ph.D. in Computer Science from London. His research interests include programming language semantics and logics, domain theory, concurrency, abstract interpretation and functional programming. Address: Dr Samson Abramsky, Department of Computer Science, Imperial College, 180 Queen's Gate, London SW7 2BZ, ENGLAND.

JOHN BACKUS was educated at the Hill School and Columbia University. His interest in programming languages led to involvement in the development of Fortran, BNF, Algol, and, more recently, the function-level languages FP and FL. He is currently an IBM Fellow and Manager of Functional Programming at the IBM Almaden Research Center, where he and his colleagues are developing an optimizing compiler for FL that makes use of the algebraic properties of the combining forms of FL. Address: John Backus, 91 Saint Germain Avenue, San Francisco, California 94114.

RICHARD BIRD is a fellow of Lincoln College and member of the Programming Research Group, Oxford University. His main research interest is to develop an effective calculus for deriving programs from specifications and he has published over twenty papers in this field. A related interest is functional programming and its applications, and a text on this subject (in collaboration with Dr. P. Wadler) was published by Prentice-Hall in 1988. Address: Dr Richard S. Bird, Oxford University Programming Research Group, 8-11 Keble Road, Oxford OX1 3QD, ENGLAND.

HANS-JUERGEN BOEHM received his bachelors degree from the University of Washington and his Ph.D. from Cornell University. Dr. Boehm was an associate professor at Rice University before joining Xerox Corporation. He is interested in a broad range of programming-language issues, ranging from programming logics to garbage collection. For his dissertation, he developed a Hoare-style logic for Russell, an expression-oriented language that allows side-effects as well as higher-order functions. His recent work has concentrated on compiler-related issues for languages such as Russell. He has produced a high-quality implementation of Russell. This project has resulted in several significant developments, including an undecidability theorem for automatic type inference in the presence of type parameters. The implementation uses a general-purpose garbage collector that can operate in conjunction with both Russell programs and conventional C or Pascal programs. On the practical side, Hans Boehm has used the Russell implementation to develop a system for programming with exact real arithmetic and has fully integrated the system into the local Fortran programming environment.

PETER BUNEMAN is Associate Professor in the Department of Computer and Information Sciences at the University of Pennsylvania. His main research interests are in the area of databases and programming languages. He holds a Ph.D. from the University of Warwick in England. Address: Dr. Peter Buneman, Department of Computer and Information Science, University of Pennsylvania, 200 South 33rd Street, Philadelphia, PA 19104-6389.

ROBERT "Corky" CARTWRIGHT earned a bachelor's degree (Magna Cum Laude) in Applied Mathematics from Harvard College in 1971 and a doctoral degree in Computer Science from Stanford University in 1977. As a graduate student, he studied program semantics and programming logic under the supervision of David Luckham and John McCarthy. From September 1976 until June 1980, he served as Assistant Professor of Computer Science at Cornell University. In July 1980, he joined the faculty of Rice University as Associate Professor of Computer Science, and in July 1986 he was promoted to the rank of Professor.

He is now chairman of the Department of Computer Science at Rice University. While on leave from Rice University, Professor Cartwright has worked as visiting scientist at Stanford University, Carnegie-Mellon University, and Xerox Palo Alto Research Center. Professor Cartwright's principal research interests include the design and implementation of very high level programming languages, the semantic definition of programming languages, and the specification and testing of programs. Address: Dr. Robert C. Cartwright, Department of Computer Science, Rice University, Houston, Texas 77005.

JOSEPH A. GOGUEN is Professor of Computing Science and Fellow of St. Anne's College at the University of Oxford. Formerly a Senior Staff Scientist in the Computer Science Laboratory at SRI International, and a senior member of the Center for the Study of Language and Information at Stanford University, he has a bachelor degree from Harvard and a doctorate from Berkeley, both in mathematics, and previously he taught Computer Science at Berkeley, Chicago and UCLA, where he was a full Professor. His current research interests include theorem proving, hardware verification, the design and implementation of programming languages based on logical systems, particularly multi-paradigm languages that combine object-oriented programming with functional and logic programming, and the design and implementation of massively parallel architectures to execute such languages efficiently. Dr. Goguen has also done research on semantics, and is particularly well known for his work on abstract data types, initial model semantics, and algebraic specification. Other research interests include linguistics, logic, psychology, and computer security. Address: Dr. Joseph A. Goguen, Oxford University Computing Laboratory, Programming Research Group, 8-11 Keble Road, Oxford OX1 3QD, England (UK).

JOHN HUGHES received his B. A. in Mathematics from Churchill College, Cambridge, and his D. Phil in Computer Science from Oxford University in 1983. He remained a member of the Programming Research Group as a research fellow until Summer 1984, when he became a European Research Fellow at Chalmers University, Gothenburg. In summer 1985 he returned to Oxford as a lecturer, and in 1986 took up a personal chair at the University of Glasgow. John contributed the notion of super-combinators to the functional programming vocabulary. More recently his research has focused on compile-time analysis of functional programs. Address: Professor R. J. M. Hughes, Department of Computer Science, Glasgow University, 14 Lilybank Gardens, Glasgow G12 8QQ, SCOTLAND.

DAVID MACQUEEN was educated at Stanford University and MIT, where he received a Ph.D. in mathematics in 1972. After active duty with the U.S. Air

Force he went to the University of Edinburgh, where he was a research fellow in the Department of Artificial Intelligence from 1975 until 1979. He then spent a year at the USC Information Sciences Institute before joining Bell Laboratories in 1981. His research interests include semantics, type theory, and programming language design and implementation. He has been intimately involved in the development of the languages Hope and Standard ML. Address:Dr. David B. MacQueen, AT&T Bell Laboratories, Room 2C–322, 600 Mountain Avenue, Murray Hill, NJ 07974.

KESHAV PINGALI received the Bachelor of Technology from IIT Kanpur and the ScD from MIT, Cambridge. Since September 1986, he has been an assistant professor at Cornell University, where his research interests include functional and logic languages, dataflow and reduction architectures, and compilation issues for parallel architectures. Address: Dr. Keshav K. Pingali, Cornell University, Department of Computer Science, 4502 Upson Hall, Ithaca, NY 14853.

SIMON THOMPSON has been a lecturer in Computer Science in the Computing Laboratory at the University of Kent since October 1983. Having studied mathematics as an undergraduate at Cambridge, he worked for a D.Phil. at Oxford, in recursion theory — the mathematical study of the foundations of computability. Specifically, he worked on the recursion theory of the higher-order, total, continuous functionals. His interests have swung more towards computing science since then, and he has worked on various aspects of functional programming, including functional programming and rewriting ('laws' in Miranda), implementing functional languages using categorical combinators (with R. D. Lins), and large-scale applications of functional programming. He is also interested in the use of logical techniques for program verification, and in the application of type theory to computing science. Address: Dr. Simon J. Thompson, Computing Laboratory, University of Kent, Canterbury, Kent CT2 7NF, ENGLAND.

DAVID TURNER holds the Chair in Computation at the University of Kent, where he has taught since 1977. From 1972 to 1976 he was a lecturer in Computational Science at the University of St. Andrews. He has a Ph.D. from the University of Oxford. He has been engaged in research into functional programming languages and their implementations since 1972. He is well known for his pioneering work on combinator graph reduction as an implementation technique, and has designed a series of influential functional programming languages— SASL, KRC, and, most recently, Miranda. Address: Professor D. A. Turner, Computing Laboratory, University of Kent, Canterbury, Kent CT2 7NF, ENGLAND.

ED WIMMERS was educated at MIT and the University of Wisconsin, where he received a Ph.D. in mathematical logic in 1982. He has been working at the IBM Almaden Research Center since 1983. He participated in the design of the function-level language FL. He is currently working on the development of an optimizing compiler for FL that takes advantage of the algebraic properties of a functional language such as FL. Address: Dr. Edward L. Wimmers, IBM Almaden Research Center, K53/803, 650 Harry Road, San Jose, CA 95120.

*A*ll six of the Programming Institutes were recorded on videotape, and edited versions of these tapes have been prepared by MPA Productions, Inc., under the auspices of the Computer Sciences Department of The University of Texas at Austin. They are available for purchase in various combinations from individual lectures to the complete set. Tapes can be provided in all formats and standards; for most sessions, photocopies of the speakers' overhead-projector transparencies are also available.

For a complete listing of the tapes, including prices, please write to

Year of Programming (Tapes)
3103 Bee Caves Road, Suite 235
Austin, TX 78746
U.S.A

or call (512) 328–9800.